THE CLASH OF ORTHODOXIES

THE CLASH OF ORTHODOXIES

Law, Religion, and Morality in Crisis

ROBERT P. GEORGE

ISI BOOKS
WILMINGTON, DELAWARE

Cataloging-in-Publication Data:

George, Robert P.
    The clash of orthodoxies : law, religion, and morality in crisis /
Robert P. George. — 1st ed. — Wilmington, Del. : ISI Books, 2001.

    p. ; cm.

    ISBN 1-882926-62-5
    1. Religion and law. 2. Law and ethics. I. Title. II. Law, religion, and morality in crisis.

BL65.L33 .G46 2001   2001-87755
344.096—dc21   CIP

Interior book design by Sam Torode

Published in the United States by:

    ISI Books
    Post Office Box 4431
    Wilmington, DE 19807-0431

Manufactured in the U.S.

This book is dedicated, with fraternal affection, to
Leonard Joseph George, Kent Joseph George, Keith Joseph George,
and Edward Joseph George.

CONTENTS

THE COURTS

THE CHURCH

FOREWORD

Faith, Reason, and Truth

ACADEMIC LEGEND has it that there once was an A+ student in a moral philosophy class whose passionately argued term paper was titled "There Is No Such Thing as Justice." Without penning a single remark on the paper, the professor gave it a failing grade. Stunned, the student went to see the professor. "Professor," the student began, "I worked extremely hard on that paper. I thought it was quite good." "Quite so," the professor interrupted. "In fact," he continued, "it was perhaps the best term paper I have read in thirty years of teaching this class. Your arguments were lucid. Your writing was brilliant. And your withering attack on all legal, moral, and religious orthodoxies concerning justice was profound. In fact, you persuaded me 'There's no such thing as justice,' so don't complain!"

As our student may have learned, trifling with long-established legal, moral, and religious truths can be self-defeating and dangerous. But from the dawn of the Enlightenment down to the present, generation upon generation of well-meaning Western intellectuals and their students have trifled with or trashed virtually every traditional understanding of human nature, human sexuality, and human decency.

Thus have Judeo-Christian orthodoxies honoring human life in all its stages and conditions been thrust into competition with neo-pagan orthodoxies promoting everything from abortion on demand to death for the severely disabled. Thus has the conventional moral case for "traditional" marriage begun to clash with same-sex marriage apologetics. Thus have godly people been made increasingly unwelcome in the public square, even when and where they have entered it only to give witness to their religious faith through civic good works, and even as advocates of almost every conceivable anti-religious orthodoxy and ism have had their say and, increasingly, gotten their way.

Of course, to opponents of traditional ideas about humankind and society, "orthodoxy" is itself a dirty word, one associated in their minds mainly with orthodox religious beliefs which, or so they insist, inevitably beget intolerant ideologies, unscientific beliefs, and all manner of unreasoning legal and moral arguments. Rarely, however, do these critics pluck the beam of true intolerance from their own eyes or ponder how their own worldviews—modern, postmodern, or whatnot—are often wholly unreflective orthodoxies by another name.

A document such as *Fides et Ratio*, written by that rather ortho-dox religious character, Pope John Paul II, gives them little cause. Voltaire himself, however, might have been a bit surprised had he known that at the end of the twentieth century, having confidently relegated Faith to intellectual limbo, his latest disciples would count among their "contested" concepts Truth, leaving the enlightened leader of the Roman Catholic Church to defend Reason.

As Professor Robert P. George suggests in chapter 15 of the masterful work now in your hands, the truly radical religious orthodoxy about humankind and society embedded within the Pope's defense of Reason is rooted in the traditional Catholic understanding of Faith as friend and companion to Reason, and all Truth—philo-sophic, religious, scientific—as ultimately one with God. Or, if I may quote the Catechism: "In defending the ability of human reason to know God, the Church is expressing her confidence in the possibility of speaking about him to all men and with all men, and therefore of dialogue with other religions, with philosophy and science, as well as with unbelievers and atheists."

The Clash of Orthodoxies will upset many readers, especially orthodox secularists who are not used to having their often facile attacks on traditional legal, moral, and religious understandings balanced or rebutted by so unfailingly logical, learned, and lucid a mind as that of Princeton's Professor George.

A distinguishing mark of Professor George's scholarship is how scrupulous he is in dealing with the ideas and arguments of all, including those with whom his disagreements could hardly be wider or go deeper. In fact, I recall one accomplished senior scholar expressing acute discomfort at having been on the receiving end of a George review of his work, but conceding that George had, in fact, "rendered his argument for slaughter" better than he himself had "rendered it for feast." How George can be so temperate yet so powerful, passionate, and persuasive remains a mystery—and a joy—to me.

Not, mind you, that Professor George, either in the present volume or in previous works, is at all wishy-washy about puncturing myths that need no-frills puncturing. For example, in the book's opening chapter, he lets the stale air out of the orthodox secularists' myth that "there is only one basis for disbelieving its tenets: namely, the claim that God has revealed propositions contrary to these tenets." He likewise unmasks orthodox secularism's pseudo-intellectual pretensions to scientific probity and political moderation in all things. Orthodox secularism, he bluntly argues, "stands for the strict and absolute separation of not only church and state, but also faith and public life: no prayer, not even an opportunity for silent prayer, in public schools; no aid to parochial schools; no display of religious symbols in the public square; no legislation based on the religiously informed moral convictions of legislators or voters."

Agree or disagree with Professor George, it is impossible not to be intellectually awed and rewarded by the essays in this volume. I close with a word to readers of opposite orthodoxies who will almost certainly disagree with nearly all that he argues: Suspend disbelief just enough to consider whether Faith has its central place in a well-ordered and just society, whether Truth is in fact not all relative, and whether Reason has not long since taken tradition's side in these debates. As we of Professor George's orthodoxy say, "Be not afraid."

JOHN J. DIIULIO, JR.

PREFACE

THE CLASH OF ORTHODOXIES in contemporary American social and political life manifests itself above all in conflicts over "life issues," such as abortion, infanticide, physician-assisted suicide, and euthanasia, as well as issues pertaining to sex, marriage, and family life. Underlying these disputes are profound differences regarding the source and nature of morality and the proper relationship of moral judgment to law and public policy.

This clash of worldviews characteristically pits morally conservative Jews, Christians, and other believers against secular liberals and those who, though remaining within religious denominations, have adopted liberal ideas about personal and political morality. Orthodox Jews, conservative and evangelical Protestants, faithful Catholics, and eastern Orthodox Christians today find themselves allied with one another in defending, say, the sanctity of human life or the traditional conception of marriage against their liberal co-religionists who have joined forces with secularists of various stripes to support such things as legal and publicly funded abortion, physician-assisted suicide, no-fault divorce, and the social acceptance of homosexual and other forms of nonmarital sexual conduct.

Does the predominance of orthodox Christians and Jews on one side of these conflicts, and of secular liberals on the other, indicate that the battle is between the forces of "faith" and those of "reason"? Secularists frequently depict the struggle in these terms, and occasionally their opponents appear to acquiesce in this depiction. In the chapters that follow I seek to persuade readers to understand the conflict differently. For those on the conservative side in what is sometimes called the "culture war" should not, and in a great many cases do not, understand faith and reason as separated in the way that many secularists and some believers hold them to be. Faith and reason are, rather, mutually supportive, the "two wings on which the human spirit rises to contemplation of truth," in the words of Pope John Paul II. I want to show that Christians and other believers are right to defend their positions on key moral issues as *rationally* superior to the alternatives proposed by secular liberals and those within the religious denominations who have abandoned traditional moral principles in favor of secularist morality. My criticism of secular liberal views is not that they are contrary to faith; it is that they fail the test of reason.

In proposing reasonableness as the criterion of moral validity, I do not pretend to write from a position of neutrality. I am a Christian. At the same time, my arguments for the soundness of what I take to be the Christian position (which is also, of course, very often the Jewish position) will not presuppose propositions that can be asserted only on the basis of religious faith. Inasmuch as my claim is that the positions I defend are superior *rationally* to the secularist alternatives, it is incumbent upon me to make the case for my positions without appealing to the *authority* of religion. Otherwise, I would be begging the question.

Because the essays collected in this volume are meant to be accessible to non-specialist readers, I have tried to avoid presenting technical philosophical arguments. As a result, specialists who do me the honor of reading the book will desire to have more thorough argumentation on various points. To that end, I regularly refer readers in notes to writings published in scholarly books and professional journals in which I (or scholars with whom I collaborate) defend in greater detail key propositions asserted here.

Some chapters repeat points made or examples used in other chapters. For this I beg the reader's indulgence. My goal has been to retain each chapter's capacity to function as a free-standing essay.

It is my pleasure to acknowledge the help of many friends. William L. Saunders deserves recognition as co-author of chapters 7, 12, and 14. I owe a similar debt of gratitude to Dennis Teti for his work on chapter 9. If anything in this book is worthwhile, it is due, no doubt, to what I have learned in discussions with these friends, as well as Hadley Arkes, Stephen Balch, Jeffrey Bell, Joseph M. Boyle Jr., Gerard V. Bradley, James Burtchaell, C.S.S.C., Frank Cannon, Charles Colson, Midge Decter, Christopher DeMuth, John DiIulio, Jean Bethke Elshtain, John Finnis, Kevin L. Flannery, S.J., Jorge Garcia, Rabbi Marc Gellman, Peter Gellman, Elizabeth Fox-Genovese, Mary Ann Glendon, Germain Grisez, Russell Hittinger, Robert Jenson, Leon Kass, John Keown, James Kurth, Patrick Lee, Gilbert Meilaender, Douglas Minson, Anne Morse, Walter F. Murphy, Fr. Richard John Neuhaus, Rabbi David Novak, Michael Novak, Ramesh Ponnuru, William C. Porth, Dermot Quinn, Roberto Rivera, Daniel N. Robinson, Seana Sugrue, Herbert W. Vaughan, George Weigel, Robert Wilken, Bradford Wilson, and Christopher Wolfe.

I am also grateful to friends on the other side of the moral and political divide with whom I have "clashed" in public and private debate. In particular, I thank Josh Dever and James Fleming for their kind permission to reprint the texts of our vigorous exchanges on important questions of law and morality.

Though for this book they have been revised in various ways, many of these pieces originally appeared in other places, including *American Journal of Jurisprudence*, *Arizona State Law Review*, *Catholic University Law Review*, *Crisis*, *Fellowship of Catholic Scholars Quarterly*, *First Things*, *Fordham Law Review*, *Loyola Law Review*, *Notre Dame Law Review*, *Touchstone*, and *The Wall Street Journal*. I thank these periodicals, as well as Catholic University of America Press, Eerdmans Publishing, Georgetown University Press, the Linacre Center, St. Augustine's Press, Spence Publishing, and Villanova University Press, for permission to reprint them here.

Finally, I thank the Earhart Foundation for its unfailing moral and material support.

THE PUBLIC SQUARE

I

THE CLASH OF ORTHODOXIES

(Including an exchange with Josh Dever)

A FEW YEARS AGO, the eminent Harvard political scientist Samuel Huntington published in *Foreign Affairs* a widely noted article called "The Clash of Civilizations."[1] Looking at contemporary international relations from a geopolitical vantage point, he predicted a clash of the world's major civilizations: the West, the Islamic world, and the Confucian East. Huntington's article provoked a response from one of his own most brilliant former students—Swarthmore's James Kurth. In an article in the *National Interest* entitled "The Real Clash,"[2] Kurth argued persuasively that the clash that is coming—and that has, indeed, already begun—is not so much among the world's great civilizations as it is within the civilization of the West, between those who claim the Judeo-Christian worldview and those who have abandoned that worldview in favor of the "isms" of contemporary American life—feminism, multiculturalism, gay liberationism, lifestyle liberalism—what I here lump together as a family called "the secularist orthodoxy."

This clash of worldviews is sometimes depicted (though not by Professor Kurth) as a battle between the forces of "faith" and those of "reason." I propose to challenge this depiction in a particular and fundamental way. I shall argue that the Christian moral view is rationally defensible. Indeed, my claim is that Christian moral teaching can be shown to be rationally superior to orthodox secular moral beliefs.

In defending the rational strength of Christian morality, I do not mean either to denigrate faith or to deny the importance—indeed, the centrality—of God's revealed Word in the Bible, or of sacred Christian tradition. My aim is to offer a philosophical defense of Christian morality; and to put forward a challenge to the secularist worldview that has established itself as an orthodoxy in the academy and other elite sectors of Western culture.

FIRST, let's get clear what is at stake in the conflict between Christian (and Jewish and to a large extent Islamic) morality and the secularist orthodoxy. The issues immediately in play have mainly, though not exclusively, to do with sexuality, the transmitting and taking of human life, and the place of religion and religiously informed moral judgment in public life.

According to the secularist orthodoxy, a child prior to birth—or some other marker event sometime before or soon after birth, such as the emergence of detectable brain-wave function or the acquisition of self-awareness—has no right not to be killed at the direction of its mother, no right, at least, that the law may legitimately recognize and protect. At the other edge of life, orthodox secularists believe that every individual has a right to commit suicide and to be assisted in committing suicide, should that person, for whatever reasons, prefer death to life.

In short, secularism rejects the proposition central to the Judeo-Christian tradition of thought about issues of life and death: that human life is intrinsically, and not merely instrumentally, good and therefore morally inviolable. It rejects traditional morality's condemnation of abortion, suicide, infanticide of so-called defective children, and certain other life-taking acts.

The secularist orthodoxy also rejects the Judeo-Christian understanding of marriage as a bodily, emotional, and spiritual union of one man and one woman, ordered to the generating, nurturing, and educating of children, marked by exclusivity and permanence, and consummated and actualized by acts that are reproductive in type, even if not, in every case, in fact. Marriage, for secularists, is a legal convention whose goal is to support a merely emotional union— which may or may not, depending upon the subjective preferences of the partners, be marked by commitments of exclusivity and permanence, which may or may not be open to children depending on whether partners want children, and in which sexual acts of any type mutually agreeable to the partners are perfectly acceptable.

As any type of mutually agreeable consensual sexual act is considered as good as any other, secularist orthodoxy rejects the idea, common not only to Judaism and Christianity but to the world's other great cultures and religious traditions, that marriage is an inherently heterosexual institution. According to secularist orthodoxy, same-sex "marriages" are no less truly marriages than those between partners of opposite sexes who happen to be infertile.

And orthodox secularism, consistent with its view of what marriage is, declines to view marriage as the principle of rectitude in sexual conduct. So orthodox secularists reject as utterly benighted the notion that sex outside of marriage is morally wrong. For them, what distinguishes morally good from bad sex is not whether it is marital, but, rather, whether it is consensual. The consent of the parties involved (or, as in the case of adultery, other parties with a legitimate interest) is the touchstone of sexual morality. So long as there is no coercion or deception involved, orthodox secularism proposes no ground of moral principle for rejecting premarital sex, promiscuity, "open" marriage, etc.

It is not that all secularists believe that sexual passions should be completely unrestrained; it is rather that they conceive constraints on sexual activity other than the principle of consent as merely prudential in nature rather than moral. For example, secularists may counsel against promiscuity, but will do so not on the moral ground that it damages the integrity of people who engage in it, but rather on the prudential ground that it courts disease, unwanted pregnancy, and general unhappiness—which of course it does. To the extent, however, that "safe-sex" techniques can reduce the risk of these and other bad consequences of promiscuity, orthodox secularism proposes no ground for avoiding it.

ON the question of the place of religion and religiously informed moral judgment in public life, orthodox secularism stands for the strict and absolute separation of not only church and state, but also faith and public life: no prayer, not even an opportunity for silent prayer, in public schools; no aid to parochial schools; no displays of religious symbols in the public square; no legislation based on the religiously informed moral convictions of legislators or voters.

Here secularism goes far beyond the views shared by most Americans: namely, that everyone should enjoy the right to be free from coercion in matters of religious belief, expression, and worship; that people should not suffer discrimination or disabilities under civil law based on their religious beliefs and affiliations; and that government should be evenhanded in its treatment of religious groups. Secularism aims to privatize religion altogether, to render religiously informed moral judgment irrelevant to public affairs and public life, and to establish itself, secularist ideology, as the nation's public philosophy.

Orthodox secularism promotes the myth that there is only one basis for disbelieving its tenets: namely, the claim that God has specially revealed propositions contrary to these tenets. Most orthodox secularists would have us believe that their positions are fully and decisively vindicated by reason and therefore can be judged to have been displaced only on the basis of irrational or, at least, nonrational faith.[3] They assert that they have the reasonable position; any claims to the contrary must be based on unreasoned faith. Secularists are in favor of a "religious freedom" that allows everyone to believe as he wishes, but claims based on this "private faith" must not be the grounds of public policy. Policy must be based on what secularists have lately come to call "public reason."

INTERESTINGLY, there have been two different lines of response by religious people to this myth promoted by orthodox secularism. Some concede that religious and even moral judgments depend on faith that cannot be rationally grounded, but they argue that secularism itself is based on a nonrational faith, that secularism must, in the end, also rest on metaphysical and moral claims that cannot be proved. In that way, they suggest, secularism is just like religion, and is not entitled to any special standing that would qualify it as the nation's public philosophy. In fact, its standing would be less than that of the Judeo-Christian tradition, since it is not the tradition upon which the country was founded. On this account, secularism itself is a sectarian doctrine and, as such, is incapable of fulfilling its own demands of being accessible to "public reason."

A second response by people of faith to the myth promoted by orthodox secularism is to affirm the demand for public reasons for public policies and offer to do battle with secularism on the field of rational debate. Those who take this view tend to agree that secularism is itself a sectarian doctrine, but they claim that religious faith, and especially religiously informed moral judgment, can be based upon and defended by appeal to publicly accessible reasons. Indeed, they argue that sound religious faith and moral theology will be informed, in part, by insight into the authentic and fully public reasons provided by principles of natural law and natural justice.

These principles are available for rational affirmation by people of good will and sound judgment, even apart from their revelation by God in the Scriptures and in the life, death, and resurrection of Christ. Based on this view, it is possible for Christians to join forces with believing Jews, Muslims, and people from other religious traditions who share a commitment to the sanctity of human life and to other moral principles.

These two distinct lines of response to orthodox secularism are not entirely incompatible. They agree that secularism itself is a sectarian doctrine with its own metaphysical and moral presuppositions and foundations, with its own myths, and, one might even argue, its own rituals. It is a pseudo-religion. Christians can also agree that orthodox secularism is caught in a dilemma. By defining "public reason" stringently enough to exclude appeals to natural law principles, secularism will make it impossible for its own proponents to meet its demand for public reasons. If, on the other hand, it loosens the definition of public reasons sufficiently to pass its own test, it will not be able to rule out principles of natural law, natural rights, or natural justice,[4] as in "We hold these truths to be self-evident, that all men are created equal, that they are endowed by their Creator with certain inalienable rights, and that among these are life, liberty, and the pursuit of happiness"—appeals to "the laws of nature and nature's God."

Both religious responses I have outlined deny that reason vindicates secularist morality. The first, however, denies that reason can identify moral truths, content with the claim that secularism is no more rational than, say, Christian belief. The second, by contrast, accepts the proposition that reason can and should be used to identify moral truths, including truths of political morality, but claims that Judeo-Christian morality is rationally superior to the morality of orthodox secularism. As already noted, this is my own position.

LET'S take the central issues of life and death. If we lay aside all the rhetorical grandstanding and obviously fallacious arguments, questions of abortion, infanticide, suicide, and euthanasia turn on the question of whether bodily life is intrinsically good, as Judaism and Christianity teach, or merely instrumentally good, as orthodox secularists believe.

If the former, then even the life of an early embryo or a severely retarded child or a comatose person has value and dignity. Their value and dignity are not to be judged by what they can do, how they feel, how they make us feel, or what we judge their "quality" of life to be. Their value and dignity transcend the instrumental purposes to which their lives can be put. They enjoy a moral inviolability that will be respected and protected in any fully just regime of law.

If bodily life is, as orthodox secularists believe, merely a means to other ends and not an end in itself, then a person who no longer gets what he wants out of life may legitimately make a final exit by suicide. If he is unable to commit suicide under his own power, he is entitled to assistance. If he is not lucid enough to make the decision for himself, then judgment must be substituted for him by the family or by a court to make the "right to die" effectively available to him.

Secularists would have us believe that, apart from special revelation, we have no reason to affirm the intrinsic goodness and moral inviolability of human life. That simply isn't true. In fact, the secularist proposition that bodily life is merely instrumentally good entails a metaphysical dualism of the person and the body that is rationally untenable.[5]

Implicit in the view that human life is merely instrumentally and not intrinsically valuable is a particular understanding of the human person as an essentially non-bodily being who inhabits a nonpersonal body. According to this understanding—which contrasts with the Judeo-Christian view of the human person as a dynamic unity of body, mind, and spirit—the "person" is the conscious and desiring "self" as distinct from the body which may exist (as in the case of pre- and post-conscious human beings) as a merely "biological," and, thus, sub-personal, reality.[6] But the dualistic view of the human person makes nonsense of the experience all of us have in our activities of being dynamically unified actors—of being, that is, embodied persons and not persons who merely "inhabit" our bodies and direct them as extrinsic instruments under our control, like automobiles. We don't sit in the physical body and direct it as an instrument, the way we sit in a car and make it go left or right.

THIS experience of unity of body, mind, and spirit is itself no mere illusion. Philosophical arguments have undermined any theory that purports to demonstrate that the human being is, in fact, two distinct realities, namely, a "person" and a (sub-personal) body. Any such theory will, unavoidably, contradict its own starting point, since reflection necessarily begins from one's own conscious awareness of oneself as a unitary actor. So the defender of dualism, in the end, will never be able to identify the "I" who undertakes the project of reflection. He will simply be unable to settle whether the "I" is the conscious and desiring aspect of the "self," or the "mere living body." If he seeks to identify the "I" with the former, then he separates himself inexplicably from the living human organism that is recognized by others (and, indeed, by himself) as the reality whose behavior (thinking, questioning, asserting, etc.) constitutes the philosophical enterprise in question. And if, instead, he identifies the "I" with that "mere living body," then he leaves no role for the conscious and desiring aspect of the "self" which, on the dualistic account, is truly the "person." As a recent treatment of the subject sums up the matter, "person" (as understood in dualistic theories) and "mere living body" are "constructs neither of which refers to the unified self who had set out to explain his or her own reality; both of them purport to refer to realities other than that unified self but somehow, inexplicably, related to it." In short, "person/body dualisms" purport to be theories of something, but cannot, in the end, identify something of which to be the theory.

From these arguments one rationally concludes that the body, far from being a nonpersonal and indeed sub-personal instrument at the direction and disposal of the conscious and desiring "self," is irreducibly part of the personal reality of the human being. It is properly understood, therefore, as fully sharing in the dignity—the intrinsic worth—of the person and deserving the respect due to persons precisely as such.

A comatose human being is a comatose person. The early embryo is a human being and, precisely as such, a person—the same person who will be an infant, a toddler, an adolescent, an adult. The genetically complete, distinct, dynamically unified, self-integrating human organism that we currently identify as, say, the sixty-three-year-old Father Richard John Neuhaus is the same organism, the same human being—the same person—who was once a twenty-eight-year-old civil rights and anti-war activist, a precocious sixteen-year-old high school student, a mischievous adolescent, a toddler, an infant, a fetus, an embryo. Although he has grown and changed in many ways, no change of nature (or "substance") occurred as he matured—with his completeness, distinctness, unity, and identity fully intact—from the embryonic through the fetal, infant, child, and adolescent stages of his development, and finally into adulthood. He was a human being—a whole, living member of the species Homo sapiens—from the start. He did not become a human being sometime after he came to be; nor will he cease being a human being prior to his ceasing to be (i.e., his dying). In view of these facts, it is evident that the central ground of the secularist defense of abortion, infanticide, suicide, and euthanasia is decisively undercut. And it is undercut, not by appeal to revelation, as important as revealed truth is to the life of faith, but by engagement directly with the best arguments that secularists make on the very plane in which they make them.

MUCH the same is true in the area of sexual morality. Secularists would have us believe that marriage is a social and legal convention that in a variety of possible ways serves a purely emotional bond between two persons. (And if it is a purely emotional bond, some ask, why only two?) They believe that, apart from revealed religious doctrine (which other people may, in the exercise of their religious freedom, happen not to share), no one has reasons for believing marriage to be anything more. Again, this is untrue.[7]

Marriage is a basic human good. By that I mean it is an intrinsic good that provides noninstrumental reasons for choice and action, reasons that are knowable and understandable even apart from divine revelation. Rational reflection on marriage as it is participated in by men and women makes it clear: since men and women are essentially embodied (and not simply inhabitors of a suit of flesh), the biological union of spouses in reproductive-type acts consummates and actualizes their marriage, making the spouses truly, and not merely metaphorically, "two in one flesh." The sexual union of spouses—far from being something extrinsic to marriage or merely instrumental to procreation, pleasure, the expression of tender feelings, or anything else—is an essential aspect of marriage as an intrinsic human good. Marital acts are the biological matrix of the multi-level (bodily, emotional, dispositional, spiritual) sharing of life and commitment that marriage is.

But, one might ask, is a true bodily or "biological" union of persons possible? Indeed it is. Consider that for most human functions or activities, say, digestion or locomotion, the organism performing the function or act is the individual human being. In respect of the act of reproduction, however, things are different. Reproduction is a single act or function, yet it is performed by a male and female as a mated pair. For purposes of reproduction, the male and female partners become a single organism, they form a single reproductive principle. This organic unity is achieved precisely in the reproductive behavior characteristic of the species—even in cases (such as those of infertile couples) in which the nonbehavioral conditions of reproduction do not obtain.

Properly understood in light of a non-dualistic account of the human person, the goodness of marriage and marital intercourse simply cannot be reduced to the status of a mere means to pleasure, feelings of closeness, or any other extrinsic goal. Indeed, it cannot legitimately be treated (as some Christians have, admittedly, sought to treat it) as a mere means to procreation, though children are among the central purposes of marriage and help to specify its meaning as a moral reality even for married couples who cannot have children.

So marital acts realize the unity of marriage, which includes the coming to be of children. In consensual nonmarital sex acts, then, people damage this unity, the integrity of the marriage, inasmuch as the body is part of the personal reality of the human being and no mere sub-personal instrument to be used and disposed of to satisfy the subjective wants of the conscious and desiring part of the "self."

THE psychosomatic integrity of the person is another of the basic or intrinsic goods of the human person. This integrity is disrupted in any sexual act that lacks the common good of marriage as its central specifying point. Where sex is sought purely for pleasure, or as a means of inducing feelings of emotional closeness, or for some other extrinsic end, the body is treated as a sub-personal, purely instrumental, reality. This existential separation of the body and the conscious and desiring part of the self serves literally to dis-integrate the person. It takes the person apart, disrupting the good of acting as the dynamically unified being one truly is.[8]

Did our Christian forebears invent this idea of integrity? Did they dream up the notion that sexual immorality damages integrity by dis-integrating the person? No. Christianity has had, to be sure, a very important role in promoting and enhancing our understanding of sexual morality. But in the dialogues of Plato and the teachings of Aristotle, in the writings of Plutarch and the great Roman stoic Musonius Rufus, and, of course, in Jewish tradition, one can find the core of this central, important teaching about the way sex is so central to integrity, and therefore so central not only to us as individuals but to us as a community.[9] Dis-integrated, individual human beings cannot form an integrated community.

Secularist orthodoxy—unlike not only Christianity and Judaism but also the classical philosophical tradition—both misidentifies the good to be realized in marriage (imagining that the value of marriage and marital sexual intercourse is purely instrumental to other goods, rather than something good in itself) and overlooks the harm—the dis-integration of persons and the communities they form—which grounds the Christian, Jewish, and classical condemnations of nonmarital sex.

Of course, there are various possible objections to the arguments I have been advancing.[10] Secularists cannot honestly say, however, that these arguments appeal to religious dogmas or fail to state public reasons for, say, forbidding abortion and euthanasia, or preserving the institution of marriage as traditionally understood. The reasons I have identified are central among the reasons why the Christian tradition has rejected abortion and euthanasia and supported the institution of marriage. This is not to deny that Christians, like our Jewish "elder brothers" in faith (to quote the words of Pope John Paul II), seek the illumination and full understanding of moral principles in the light of Scripture and sacred tradition. But Christians and other believers need not—and typically do not—suggest that abortion, for example, is wrong (or that we know it to be wrong) because God whispered it into our ear, or the ear of a pope or another religious leader, or even into the ear of a sacred writer.

The wrongness of abortion follows from the truth—fully accessible even to unaided reason—that the life of a human being is intrinsically, and not merely instrumentally, good. As a Christian, I believe that each human life is a precious gift from God. But even if one doesn't share that belief, reason nevertheless grasps the truth that human life is intrinsically, and not merely instrumentally, valuable. Reason detects the falsity of the dualistic presuppositions of secularism's belief that human life is merely instrumentally valuable. It identifies the unreasonableness of denying that every innocent human being—irrespective of age, size, stage of development, or condition of dependency—has an inviolable moral right to life.

Reason affirms that if any of us have a right to life, then all of us have it; if we have it at one stage of life, we have it at every stage of life; if we have it in the middle of life, we have it at both edges. There is no rational argument that anybody has been able to come up with—and the best and the brightest in the academy have struggled for more than twenty-five years to do so—that shows that a healthy thirteen-year-old or forty-two-year-old has a right to life, but a comatose eighty-year-old or an unborn child has no right to life. There is no rational basis for distinguishing a class of human beings who have a right to life (and other fundamental human rights) and a class of human beings who do not. This is the moral core of the great "self-evident truth" upon which our nation was founded: the proposition that all human beings are "created equal."

Knowledge of this truth does not presuppose Christian faith, although biblical revelation profoundly enriches our understanding of it, and often enough leads to religious conversion. There are many examples of this. A notable recent case is that of Bernard Nathanson, a founder of the organization now known as the National Abortion and Reproductive Rights Action League. He was an atheist and a practicing abortionist who had taken the lives of many unborn children, including one of his own. But he gradually came to see that the deliberate killing of unborn human beings is a violation of the most basic principle of morality and natural justice. So he abandoned the practice of abortion and relinquished his important role in the advocacy of abortion as a political matter. Soon, he joined the pro-life movement and began working to roll back the abortion license. A few years later, he abandoned atheism and entered into Christian faith—which to him made sense of, grounded, and profoundly enriched the basic moral understanding that he had initially achieved by way of rational, self-critical reflection.

ORTHODOX secularist moral belief portrays personal morality as being essentially concerned with extrinsic constraints upon appetite or passion. It presupposes that the ultimate motives for whatever we do are grounded in our desires; reason's role is purely instrumental. The eighteenth-century philosopher David Hume, a founding father of modern secularism, summed up the position: "Reason is and ought only to be the slave of the passions, and may never pretend to any office other than to serve and obey them."[11] Reason's role, in other words, is not to identify what is rational, what people should want, but merely to devise means of obtaining goals that people happen to want.

Ultimately, this view of reason makes it impossible to vindicate any fundamental moral principles, including any fundamental human rights. If reason is purely instrumental and can't tell us what to want but only how to get to what we want, how can we say that people have a fundamental right to freedom of speech? Freedom of the press? Freedom of religion? Privacy? Where do those fundamental rights come from? What is their basis? Why respect someone else's rights?

By contrast, the Christian understanding of morality starts from an appreciation of the basic human goods that provide more than merely instrumental reasons for action. In morally good actions, people choose for the sake of these goods in ways that are compatible with a will toward the integral fulfillment and well-being of individuals and communities. Moral norms govern free choices by excluding possible actions that are incompatible with such a will. Emotion or passion, when rightly ordered, supports what reason commends and helps us to accomplish the morally good ends that we have basic reasons to pursue.[12]

Here again the Christian view lines up in important ways with that of the pre-Christian Greek philosophers—Plato and Aristotle, in particular—in understanding reason to be the master of passion in what the ancient thinkers unhesitatingly referred to as the "rightly ordered soul."

Of course, Christianity, like classical philosophy, understands perfectly well that the soul can be wrongly ordered, that emotion or passion can overcome reason and reduce it to the status of a slave that produces rationalizations for morally wrongful behavior. That is what Christians call sin. Yes, it happens, but our goal should be to order our souls rightly so that reason controls passion, and not the other way around. When passion is in control, reason is reduced to a mere instrument, becoming its own worst enemy as it cooks up rationalizations for actions that we know to be morally wrong.

Christians can and should challenge at the most fundamental level secularism's instrumentalist view of reason and morality. Secularism's account of the relationship between reason and desire, far from being brutally rigorous in eschewing unprovable metaphysical hypotheses, rests upon and entails metaphysical propositions that not only are controversial, but in the end (say, in the case of person/body dualism) are demonstrably false.

CHIEF among secularism's philosophical vulnerabilities is its implicit denial of free choice or free will. People can make free choices just to the extent that they are capable of understanding and acting upon reasons that are not reducible to desire or emotion. In denying the possibility of rationally motivated action, secularism denies the possibility of free choice since it claims that we don't, in any fundamental sense, cause our own actions. What are they caused by? Either by the force of external pressures (whether one knows it or not), or by internal factors (such as desires). In the secularist worldview, "hard" and "soft" forms of determinism constitute the universe of possible accounts of all human behavior. Free choice is written off as an illusion.

Christian philosophers such as Germain Grisez, Joseph M. Boyle, Jr., and Olaf Tollefsen have rigorously shown, however, that the denial of free choice is rationally untenable, because it is a self-referentially contradictory claim, a self-defeating proposition.[13] No one can rationally deny free choice, or claim as illusory our ordinary experience of freely choosing, without presupposing the possibility of free choice. To deny free choice is to claim that it is more rational to believe that there is no free choice than to believe that there is. But this, in turn, presupposes that one can identify norms of rationality and freely choose to conform one's beliefs to those norms. It presupposes that we are free to affirm the truth or falsity of a proposition, our desires or emotions or preferences to the contrary notwithstanding. Otherwise, the assertion of no free choice is pointless. The person who says people can't freely choose presupposes that there are reasons for accepting his claim, otherwise his act of asserting it would be pointless. But our ability to understand and act upon such reasons is incompatible with the idea that one is caused by his desires or by outside forces to accept or not accept such claims. So someone who denies free choice implicitly contradicts his own claim.

Here again, orthodox secularists are stuck, not because they have been beaten over the head with the Bible, but on the plane where they have made the argument—the plane of rationality. No position can be reasonable if it is self-referentially inconsistent, if it presupposes the opposite of the very claim it asserts. But if the "no free choice" claim is self-defeating, then we have an additional reason for affirming the existence of basic, intelligible, understandable reasons for action—reasons that are not reducible to desires or emotions or merely instrumental to the satisfaction of desires. And we have an additional reason for rejecting secularism's conception of morality as basically concerned with extrinsic restraints on appetite, rather than the integral directiveness of the basic human goods that provide such reasons for action.

ORTHODOX secularists typically say that we should respect the rights of others, even as we go about the business of satisfying our own desires. Ultimately, however, secularism cannot provide any plausible account of where rights come from or why we should respect others' rights. Of course, most secularists emphatically believe that people have rights. Indeed, they frequently accuse Christians and other religious believers of supporting policies that violate people's rights. We are all familiar with the rhetoric: You religious people shouldn't be imposing your values on other people. You are violating their rights! If it is between consenting adults, stay out of it! Any two (or more?) people have the right to define "marriage" for themselves. Women have a right to abortion. People have a right to take their own lives. Who are you to say otherwise?

But on the presuppositions of the secularist worldview, why should anybody respect anybody else's rights? What is the reason for respecting rights? Any answer must state a moral proposition, but what, on orthodox secularist premises, could provide the ground of its moral truth?

You may ask, Why doesn't the secularist cheerfully affirm moral subjectivism or moral relativism? Indeed, isn't some sort of moral relativism at the heart of secularism?

While one still hears subjectivism or relativism invoked at cocktail parties and in undergraduate classrooms—and even occasionally in faculty lounges—it seems that the heyday of moral relativism is over, even among doctrinaire secularists. Most sophisticated secularists have concluded that relativism is ultimately inconsistent with many of their own cherished moral claims, particularly those having to do with claims about rights—the right to abortion, the right to sexual freedom, the right to die. As the distinguished liberal political philosopher Joel Feinberg has warned: "Liberals must beware of relativism—or, at least, of a sweeping relativism—lest they be hoist on their own petard."[14]

If relativism is true, then it is not wrong in principle to have an abortion, but neither is it wrong for people who happen to abhor abortion to attempt to legislate against it or to interfere with someone else's having an abortion by, say, blockading clinics or even shooting abortionists. Claims of a right to abortion are manifestly moral claims. Claims that it is wrong to shoot abortionists are moral claims. They could possibly be true only if moral relativism and subjectivism are false. So the mainstream of orthodox secularism at the end of the twentieth century has become self-consciously moralistic and nonrelativistic.

This is not to say that secularism is no longer, in significant respects, a relativist doctrine. It is merely to say that secularism is no longer a thoroughgoing and self-consciously relativist doctrine. Insofar as it remains relativistic, it has a massive philosophical problem. Secularism, at least in its liberal manifestations, makes the rights of others the principle of moral constraints upon action, relativizing allegedly self-regarding actions. But it generates a critical question it has no way of answering: Why should anyone respect the rights of others? Merely prudential answers—such as, people should respect the rights of others so that others will respect their rights, or people should respect the rights of others to avoid being punished—simply won't do. The fact is that people can often get away with violating others' rights. And they know it. And many do it.

If people shouldn't violate the rights of others, it must be because doing so is morally wrong, but on the secularist account, why is it morally wrong? What is the source of its moral wrongness? The eminent philosopher and Christian convert Alasdair MacIntyre observes that traditions of thought about morality go into crisis when they generate questions they lack the resources to answer.[15] By this standard, orthodox secularism is a tradition in crisis. It generates the question, Why should I respect the rights of others? Yet it possesses no adequate resources for answering it.

BY contrast, Christian thought understands that human rights are rooted in intelligible and basic human goods. It, therefore, has no logical difficulty explaining why each of us has an obligation to respect the rights of others, as well as to act in conformity with other moral principles. And recent Christian teaching, including the teaching of popes and Protestant bodies, speaks unhesitatingly of universal human rights, without fear of collapsing into relativism or individualism of the sort that is characteristic of orthodox secularism.

It is true that church teaching about human rights often overlaps with liberal secularist ideology. For example, Christian conservatives and liberal secularists agree on certain questions pertaining to religious freedom and have sometimes—as in the case of political advocacy in support of persecuted Christians and animists in the Sudan—joined together in political coalitions.

When church teaching and secularist ideology overlap, particularly on the question of rights, Christian thought has proved itself capable of giving a far superior account of these rights and why each of us has an obligation to respect the rights of others. From this I conclude that Christian teaching is rationally superior to secularism, not only when these worldviews disagree, as over abortion, euthanasia, marriage, and family, but even when they agree.

At the end of the day, whatever is to be said for and against secularism, there can be no legitimate claim for secularism to be a "neutral" doctrine that deserves privileged status as the national public philosophy. As MacIntyre has argued, secularism (which he calls liberalism) is far from being a "tradition-independent" view that merely represents a neutral playing field on which Judaism, Christianity, Marxism, and other traditions can wage a fair fight for the allegiance of the people. Instead, it is itself a tradition of thought about personal and political morality that competes with others.[16]

Secularism rests upon and represents a distinct and controversial set of metaphysical and moral propositions having to do with the relationship of consciousness to bodiliness and of reason to desire, the possibility of free choice, and the source and nature of human dignity and human rights. Secularist doctrine contains very controversial views about what constitutes a person—views every bit as controversial as the Jewish and Christian views. Secularism is a philosophical doctrine that stands or falls depending on whether its propositions can withstand arguments advanced against them by representatives of other traditions. I have tried to show that secularist orthodoxy cannot withstand the critique to be advanced against it by the tradition of Christian philosophy.

AN EXCHANGE WITH JOSH DEVER

Josh Dever

AS AN ATHEIST, a liberal, and a philosopher, I suppose I'm as likely as anyone to qualify as a proponent of Robert P. George's "secular orthodoxy." As such, I'd like to say a few words in defense of that orthodoxy. I want to raise three categories of objection to Professor George's comments: first, that his characterization of that orthodoxy is highly tendentious; second, that the philosophical failings of that orthodoxy are not nearly so numerous as Prof. George takes them to be; and third, that the corresponding philosophical triumphs of the "Judeo-Christian" worldview are not so triumphant as he represents them.

Prof. George feels that committed members of the secular orthodoxy hold a number of unpalatable views. We are supposed to reject the "condemnation of...infanticide of so-called defective children," and to believe that "marriage...is a legal convention whose goal is to support a merely emotional union"; that there should be "not even an opportunity for silent prayer in public schools"; that there should be "no legislation based on the religiously informed moral convictions of legislators or voters"; that a person desiring but unable to commit suicide is "entitled to assistance"; that if such a person "is not lucid enough to make the decision for himself, then judgment must be substituted for him by the family or court"; that reason is purely instrumental; and that persons lack free will (to pick a few of the ascriptions that struck me as most objectionable).

I suppose Prof. George is free to define his target category of "secular orthodoxy" in any way he sees fit, but if he wants his "orthodoxy" to be in any real sense an orthodoxy, I'm afraid he has set up a straw man. While I suppose I could hunt down individuals holding each of the views listed above, I think it's clear that all of the above views (with the regrettable exception of the view that reason is slave to the passions, and even there I think recent work on externalism in practical reason is beginning to turn the tide) are extreme minority views. Were they not, Peter Singer's notoriety would be hard to understand. If Prof. George is genuinely out to compare the prospects of secularism and Judeo-Christianity as philosophical foundations of morality, both charity and good academic practice would seem to require focusing on the best that secularism has to offer, rather than on its extremists.

THE characterization of the so-called secular orthodoxy (I'll suggest below that there's good reason to doubt that there is such a thing) is, however, the least of my three complaints. Let's now consider more substantive issues, beginning with the particular philosophical charges that Prof. George raises against secular orthodoxy. According to him, those of us doing our moral reasoning within this tradition are guilty of the following crimes: endorsing a mind/body dualism, rejecting (in a self-contradictory manner) free will, eliminating any intrinsic reason for pursuit of the moral good, and embracing relativism. All of these charges are, I think, wholly false.

Prof. George claims that secularists who believe that bodily life is not intrinsically valuable are committed to mind/body dualism. The secularist view in question here holds that the mere fact that an organism is alive and of the human species is not enough to endow it with (full) moral worth—other qualities, such as consciousness, phenomenology, or future-directedness, are needed also. Since, however, mind/body dualism is almost entirely a dead philosophical position these days, secularists who have thought through their position carefully also believe that whether an organism has these further characteristics is entirely a function of the physical structure of that organism (as well as, perhaps, the causal embedding of that organism in some larger environment). Believing that these structural features are important to moral worth no more commits one to mind/body dualism than does believing that the structural features that come with life morally differentiate a person from a corpse. Views on when morally protected personhood begins and ends can vary greatly—at conception, at birth, after birth, before death, at death, after death—without in any way endorsing a metaphysical separation between person and body.

Deciding that not all living organisms of the human species are persons is dangerous territory, of course, and we must be guided by the terrible misdeeds of the past that have frequently come under the banner of denying full personhood to various groups. But the line must be drawn somewhere by everyone, so mere accusations of line-drawing can carry no weight. And just as there is a price to pay for drawing the line too narrowly, there is also a price to pay for drawing the line too widely, since the moral duties owed toward persons can place a heavy burden on others. Thus there is reason to try to find the right place to draw the line, and not to fence about the law too broadly.

Furthermore, while secularists may deny the intrinsic value of bodily life by way of denying that all human life enjoys the full moral protection of personhood, they are not thereby committed to denying that persons have intrinsic value. This leads to the broader point of whether secularists must lose entirely the concept of intrinsic value. Prof. George seems to feel that they must, but I admit I see no reason why this is the case. It is true that British Empiricism left philosophy with a legacy whose twin denial of the motivational power of reason and of epistemic access to objective normative facts made it hard to find conceptual room for intrinsic values (although these difficulties hardly stopped people from trying). However, under the corrective influence of philosophers such as W. V. O. Quine, Wilfrid Sellars, and Donald Davidson, strict empiricism has largely been abandoned as a philosophical position, and (while the philosophical problems certainly have not been fully resolved) a more full-blooded epistemology, which allows for real knowledge of moral facts, has been widely adopted. Similarly, Bernard Williams's work has led to a revival of interest in the broadly Socratic idea that reason can be intrinsically motivating.

THUS it is not all true to say that secular orthodoxy possesses no resources for answering the question "Why should I respect the rights of others?" We can offer both the "internal" reason that I should do so because it would be wrong to do otherwise, and at least the beginnings of an external reason based on considerations about the nature of agency. The latter reason is far from complete as of yet, but if one considers the corresponding questions about theoretical reason—"why should I obey the rules of logic in my thought?"—and looks at work arguing that it is in the nature of being a holder of beliefs (as opposed to wishes, desires, etc.) that one is committed to certain norms governing beliefs, the outlines of its future directions may become clear. That we don't yet have all the answers is, I take it, not a very serious charge against secular orthodoxy (especially since, as I'll suggest below, the same is true of the Judeo-Christian philosophical foundation).

Prof. George's charge that secular orthodoxy is committed to relativism I find particularly baffling, both because he gives no reason to think that this is the case, and because it runs so counter to my experience as a professional philosopher. Anyone who has spent time teaching in the philosophy classroom can tell you how much effort is devoted to trying to convince students that it's not acceptable to talk blithely about what's "true for you" and "true for me."

Prof. George's further charge that secular orthodoxy is committed to the denial of free will I also find baffling, since the view that there is no free will is an extreme minority position in philosophy. As I read Prof. George, we secularists are supposed to reject free will because it comes into conflict with "hard" or "soft" determinism. However, the dominant (although hardly universal) view among philosophers these days is that there is no genuine conflict between determinism and free will. Donald Davidson, for example, has said that arguments for that supposed conflict are no more than "superficially plausible." Far from being "written off as an illusion," free will is alive and well under the secularist orthodoxy.

The argument that the denial of free will is "rationally untenable," by the way, is fallacious. While it may well be the case that, if there were no free will, there would be no point in announcing that there is no free will, or even that the nature of our subjective experience is such that none of us can seriously doubt the existence of free will, this does nothing to show that there is free will. Those few who become philosophically convinced that there is no free will might be correct in what they announce, even if there's no point in telling us and even if, like Hume, they immediately slip back into their pre-philosophical endorsement of free will.

I fail to see, then, that Prof. George has provided any evidence that secular orthodoxy suffers from philosophical bankruptcy. As I have said, the philosophical foundations of morality are a work in progress, and we certainly don't claim to have all the answers yet, or even universal agreement about the right directions to go in, but I don't see any reason to think that we're obviously on the wrong track.

LET'S look now at some of the supposed philosophical successes of the Judeo-Christian orthodoxy: its account of free will, its defense of the rights of others, its explanation of the intrinsic value of bodily life, and its account of the intrinsic value of marriage. I don't mean in any case to claim that the Judeo-Christian framework is a failure on these issues, but I do want to try to show that that framework is subject to the same difficulties as the secular framework.

Prof. George chastises secular orthodoxy for its (supposed) abandonment of free will in the face of determinism, but he gives no indication of how the Judeo-Christian framework will escape any threat that determinism poses to free will (if there is no threat, of course, there's no problem for secular orthodoxy either). Will he deny determinism? This is a hard row to hoe in light of what we now know about the connections between brain states and mental life, and (as many philosophers have argued) it doesn't seem to help with the underlying issues anyway. Will he appeal to "rationally motivated action"? Then he needs a theory of reason to back up this possibility, and an explanation of why deterministic control of which reasons we act on doesn't threaten our freedom. None of these things appear (or are even alluded to) in the article.

Prof. George also suggests that Judeo-Christian moral foundations enjoy an explanatory advantage over the secular orthodoxy in that they are able to explain why one ought to respect the rights of others—by showing that these rights are "rooted in intelligible and basic human goods." However, rooting the rights in basic human goods does nothing to solve the problem if there is not some further reason why we ought to pursue the good. If Judeo-Christian philosophy provides such a reason, Prof. George has made no mention of it. If it provides no such reason, then it is unclear why basic goods are any better than basic rights as a foundation that must be respected.

Prof. George also holds that Judeo-Christian philosophy, through its rejection of mind/body dualism, upholds the intrinsic value of bodily life. As I have argued above, there is no intimate connection between one's views on mind/body dualism and the intrinsic value (or lack thereof) of the body. To show that bodily life is intrinsically valuable, one must give some explanation of the source of its intrinsic value; merely saying that there is no person separate from the body does nothing to provide such an explanation. Judeo-Christian philosophy, as I understand it, traditionally finds the roots of the intrinsic moral value of the human person in the scriptural assertion that humanity is created in God's image, but until it is specified in what way we are in God's image, conclusions about what aspects of our existence give rise to our intrinsic value are premature.

FINALLY, Prof. George holds that Judeo-Christian philosophy can provide an explanation of the intrinsic value of marriage. Details of this explanation are sketchy in his article, but it would seem that the explanation derives from the biological fact that we come in two sexes who interact sexually. This fact, however, would seem to leave us very far from the desired conclusion. Some explanation of why this particular feature of our biology is normative (and normative only when sexuality manifests itself in the heterosexual variety) must be added, as well as a demonstration that the purported normativity of the biological facts requires the institution of monogamous and indissoluble marriage.

My own inclination would be to locate the intrinsic value, and non-conventionality, of marriage in (or at least in part in) the objective obligations incurred through the marital vows, but this is clearly common secular territory, and does little to capture specifically heterosexual or monogamous marriage.

Again, it is not my intention to claim that the secular orthodoxy is free of philosophical difficulties or that Judeo-Christian philosophical foundations are hopelessly flawed. My impression, rather, is that both philosophies are faced with many serious questions to which they lack complete answers, but few (if any) issues that threaten a complete overturn of the program. Indeed, I find it revealing that, for the most part, the very same questions hound both programs.

I want to close by commenting briefly on whether there is such a thing as "secular orthodoxy," and on whether such a thing could provide neutral territory for the pursuit of public debate. In my view, what is orthodox, and common ground for all, are the rules of right reason that situate the various philosophical tensions in conceptual space and provide the rules for navigating among those tensions. Provided one rejects (as I think one should) the pseudo-Kierkegaardian idea that religious faith is a rationally unwarranted leap into the dark, this orthodoxy is open to secularists and nonsecularists alike, because our reason is both universal and prior to our particular convictions as Christians, Jews, atheists, etc.

An orthodoxy based on rationality provides us a common arena in which to do battle, but I think it is an error to believe that any one view will emerge victorious from that arena. That's just not the way reason works. As Peter van Inwagen so eloquently observes, reason, outside of special fields like mathematics and logic, rarely delivers unequivocal responses. The typical situation is that many views will be rationally permissible, not that one will be rationally compelling. How to construct public policy when we cannot expect our best reasons to convince all good-willed rational agents is a problem to which I don't have a solution, but one that our sadly limited epistemic status seems to force on to us.

Robert P. George

I AM GRATEFUL to Josh Dever for his thoughtful challenge to my essay.

Professor Dever states candidly his religious views and moral-political commitments: he is an atheist and a liberal. He begins by proposing to defend the secularist orthodoxy, though later he suggests that no such orthodoxy exists. With a single exception—which, interestingly, Prof. Dever himself considers to be "regrettable"—he claims that the positions I have attributed to secularist liberalism are, in truth, "extreme minority views." The most he is prepared to concede is that one could probably "hunt down individuals holding each of [these] views."

I'm afraid I cannot yield to Prof. Dever's claim. Perhaps things are different at the University of Texas, where Prof. Dever teaches, but even on a rainy day when most people stay indoors I could "hunt down" dozens of people who hold these views simply by taking a stroll across the Princeton campus.

Let's consider some of the specific positions I attributed to the secularist orthodoxy. I said that orthodox secularists "reject traditional morality's condemnation of abortion, suicide, infanticide of so-called defective children, and certain other life-taking acts." That the overwhelming majority of Prof. Dever's fellow atheists and liberals support abortion and suicide is hardly a disputable proposition. Indeed, Prof. Dever himself doesn't dispute it. He complains about my claim that orthodox secularists reject the "condemnation of... infanticide of so-called defective children." Readers will take note of what is omitted in the ellipsis.

What about infanticide? Is the "letting die" (as the more squeamish insist on describing it) of mentally retarded or severely physically handicapped babies an "extreme minority view" among orthodox secularists, as Prof. Dever maintains? It must be, he suggests, for otherwise "Peter Singer's notoriety would be hard to understand." It is true, of course, that Singer has been a particularly vocal (and notably non-squeamish) defender of infanticide. Nevertheless, Prof. Dever could not have chosen a worse piece of evidence for an alleged consensus among orthodox secularists against the killing of handicapped newborns. Opposition to Singer's appointment as DeCamp Professor of Bioethics at Princeton has come *entirely* from outside the University faculty, mostly from outside the University community, and mainly from believing Jews and Christians. Among orthodox secularists at Princeton and elsewhere, Singer's appointment is uncontroversial. With the single exception of John DiIulio—the eminent social scientist (and devout Christian) who has, alas, since resigned from the Princeton faculty to accept a new chair in faith and public policy at the University of Pennsylvania—I know of no member of the Princeton faculty who has publicly spoken out against Singer for his defense of infanticide.

I have no doubt that there are secularists who have qualms about killing handicapped newborns. (Prof. Dever himself suggests that infanticide is not part of "the best that secularism has to offer.") Some—perhaps many—secularists believe that Singer's defense of infanticide goes too far and would permit the practice in too many cases. But there are two points worth making.

First, even those secularists who oppose infanticide generally admit, in defending abortion, that it is difficult on their own premises to identify a mistake in Singer's argument that newborns—particularly severely handicapped newborns—do not suddenly become "persons" merely by emerging from the womb. Second, the secularist orthodoxy—like any orthodoxy—consists not only of those views which all members of the group share, but also of those views which are considered within the group to be reasonable and accept-able to hold, even if not everybody in the group happens to share them. (For example, Catholic orthodoxy holds that the Virgin Mary was, at the end of her life on earth, assumed bodily into heaven. Although most orthodox Catholics believe that Mary's assumption occurred after her death, it is a mark of Catholic orthodoxy to con-sider it reasonable and acceptable to believe, as others do, that Mary was assumed into heaven without dying.) No one can doubt that, among orthodox secularists, Singer's willingness to defend infanti-cide in the case of severely handicapped newborns is considered rea-sonable and acceptable in a way that it is not among observant Jews and Christians.

Another position that Prof. Dever insists is held only by "an extreme minority" of orthodox secularists is opposition to "even an opportunity for silent prayer in public schools." On this point, I must say, I am astonished by Prof. Dever's claim. The Supreme Court's anti–school prayer decisions, beginning with *Engel v. Vitale* in 1962, and including its 1985 ruling in *Wallace v. Jaffree* striking down even a minute of silence for "meditation or voluntary prayer" in public schools, have been joined by every liberal justice on the Court and applauded by liberals of every stripe. Neither Prof. Dever nor I would have the slightest difficulty "hunting down" secularist liberal pun-dits, constitutional scholars, political theorists, and others who en-thusiastically support *Jaffree* and the other school prayer decisions. Indeed, the true challenge would be finding a few secularists who actually oppose them. Theirs would be an altogether *un*orthodox secularism.

Yet another issue Prof. Dever raises is assisted suicide and "sub-stituted judgment" for mentally incapacitated people who are not able to make the decision whether to end their suffering by suicide. As with infanticide, I have no doubt that there are dissenters among secularist liberals on this issue; but the consensus is plainly in favor of assisted suicide and substituted judgment. Prof. Dever's field is philosophy. He is certainly aware of the celebrated amicus curiae brief filed by Ronald Dworkin, John Rawls, Robert Nozick, Thomas Nagel, Tim Scanlon, and Judith Jarvis Thomson—arguably the six most influential liberal moral philosophers in the United States—asking the Supreme Court to invalidate laws prohibiting assisted suicide and to establish a right to assistance in dying. Dworkin is the author of a much-admired book defending euthanasia and substituted judgment. No one I know thinks that Dworkin's advocacy of a "right to die" places him on the extreme fringes of the liberal camp. I doubt that Prof. Dever actually thinks that.

I could make similar points about the issues of marriage and legislation based on religiously informed moral judgments, but at this point let me go straight to some of the big philosophical issues to which Prof. Dever devotes most of his space.

He concedes that most secularists subscribe to the "subjectivist" or "noncognitivist" view of practical reason as purely instrumental—the "slave of the passions," in Hume's famous characterization—though he himself happens to deviate from the secularist orthodoxy on this particular question. Indeed, he regrets the continuing dominance of the instrumental view of practical reason and hopes that the tide will soon turn against it. (This is the "regrettable exception" I made reference to at the beginning of these remarks.)

However, Prof. Dever thinks that I am wrong to ascribe to secularist liberals the belief that people lack what he calls free will (and what I call free choice). But if, as he concedes, the instrumental view of practical reason remains dominant among secularists, then what grounds could those who hold to it possibly have for believing in free choice? The problem is that free choice is impossible if practical reason is purely instrumental. One chooses freely if, and only if, one has, is aware of, and chooses for the sake of more-than-merely-instrumental reasons for action. If reason *is* merely passion's ingenious servant—if *rationally motivated action* is impossible because our ultimate ends are necessarily provided by feeling, emotion, or other subrational motivating factors—then even externally uncoerced action cannot be truly freely chosen. Rather, our actions are the products of—are determined by—such factors.

Of course, people often cling to beliefs that are incompatible with other beliefs that they hold, but among those philosophers, social scientists, and people in other fields who subscribe to the instrumental view of practical reason, I perceive little evidence for Prof. Dever's claim that "free will is alive and well under the secularist orthodoxy."

Indeed, that claim is all the more remarkable in view of Prof. Dever's admission that secularist liberals, including himself, are in fact determinists. His method of squaring this particular philosophical circle is by endorsing what he says is now the "dominant (although hardly universal) view among philosophers these days...that there is no genuine conflict between determinism and free will." According to this view, our actions can be *both* determined and freely chosen. Determinism must be true, he suggests, in light of "what we now know about the connections between brain states and mental life."

But on both counts Prof. Dever is mistaken. An action is truly freely chosen if and only if two things are the case: (1) the choice to do it is between (or among) alternatives considered in deliberation, and (2) both (or all) of those alternatives are really possible in the sense that only the choosing itself settles which alternative will be realized. And nothing "we now know" about brain states, mental life, and their connections compels the conclusion that our actions are determined rather than freely chosen in light of reasons that provide motivation but do not compel a decision one way or another.

PROF. Dever bluntly claims that the self-referential argument I sketched to establish the rational untenability of the denial of free choice is "fallacious." He supposes (mistakenly) that my claim is merely that it is pointless for people who deny that there is free will *to announce their denial,* since "if there were no free will, there would be no point in announcing that there is no free will." He then replies: "Those few who become philosophically convinced that there is no free will might be correct in what they announce." But my argument had nothing to do with "announcements." Its focus is the activity that Prof. Dever misleadingly puts into the passive "becom[ing] philosophically convinced."

Philosophical reflection is a matter not simply of passively receiving the truth about, for example, free will. It is an activity in which one has every opportunity of falling into error unless one is willing to pursue truth with an energy and care that only devotion to truth can sufficiently motivate. In this activity, anyone motivated by concern for truth will be guided not only by the requirements of logic but also by the less formal norms of rationality that enable us to distinguish sound from unsound investigative procedures in science, history, philosophy, etc. These norms direct sound thinking, but they can be violated, and are violated, in all shoddy investigations and inquiries in any and every field of intellectual endeavor.

The question whether people can make free choices is not a question settled by formal logic alone; rather, the investigation of it is addressed also by norms of rationality. Everyone who engages in this reflective investigation has the opportunity of violating those norms in the interest of reaching answers that his prejudices favor, or of taking shortcuts for other motives. Everyone is confronted, right here, with the opportunity of choosing to respect, or not to respect, rationality's norms.

Those who deny that people can make truly free choices cannot claim that the truth of their position is established by bare formal logic. They must contend that those who assert the possibility of free choices are failing to attend with sufficient care to the evidence (regarding, e.g., brain states, mental life, and their connections), and ought to think the issues through more carefully, listen to reason, etc. By that *ought* they concede the very claim they are concerned to deny: the claim that one can *choose* between, say, lazy reaffirmation of one's prejudices or wishes and authentic philosophical reflection and pursuit of truth. Thus their concern that they and we should get to the truth of the matter about (not simply "announce") freedom of choice refutes their own denial that free choices can be made, and sometimes are made.

PROF. Dever is also critical of my claim that the secularist denial of the intrinsic, and not merely instrumental, value of human bodily life entails a rationally untenable dualism of "person" and "body." "Mind/body dualism," he says, "is almost entirely a dead philosophical position these days." It is true that most philosophers have concluded that certain positions falling under the label "dualism" (including some, such as Cartesianism, that were once widely entertained) are untenable. But there is a particular form of person/body dualism that is far from uncommon today. It reduces the person to the intermittently conscious (genderless) subject, which regards its (male or female) body as a possession or instrument that unlike other property or tools is untransferable, though discardable by suicide. My claim is that the denial of the intrinsic value of bodily life which underwrites the secularist defense of abortion, infanticide, euthanasia, and other forms of homicide entails precisely this form of dualism.

Either the body is a part of the personal reality of the human being, in which case the human person, properly speaking, is a dynamic unity of body, mind, and spirit, *or* the body is a subpersonal dimension of the human being that functions as an instrument at the service of the conscious and desiring aspect of the self—the "person," strictly speaking, who controls and uses the body. The secularist position on issues such as abortion, infanticide, and euthanasia straightforwardly treats the body as a subpersonal reality: a living human body is not a person, or, at least, is not a person until it comes to be associated (somehow) with a mind or other center of conscious self-awareness; and a living human body ceases to be a person not necessarily by dying, but at any point at which it loses this association, which may be long before death. The body, as such, according to secularists, lacks the dignity of personhood—that is why they believe it isn't necessarily wrong to kill "pre-personal" or "post-personal" human beings (fetuses, handicapped infants, the irreversibly demented, or other human "nonpersons").

Prof. Dever seems to suggest that the secularist position avoids dualism because its understanding of human beings and their attributes and capacities is purely materialist or physicalist. But that is, if I may borrow a term from Prof. Dever, fallacious. He says that "whether an organism has these further characteristics" that give it (full) moral standing and a right not to be killed (e.g., "consciousness, phenomenology, future-directedness") "is entirely a function of the physical structure of that organism (as well as, perhaps, the causal embedding of that organism in some larger environment)." Note well: "a function of." Of course, Prof. Dever wants to avoid the claim that the "physical structure" as such gives the organism moral standing. Rather, it is *something else,* albeit something that on Prof. Dever's account is "a function of" the organism's physical structure, that works the magic of converting what would otherwise be a *mere* physical organism with no right to life (e.g., a fetus, a severely demented person, etc.) into a "person" with a dignity so profound that it is morally wrong to kill it (e.g., a healthy infant, a normal adult).

THE dualism of orthodox secularism is not erased by the materialist insistence that the attributes of personhood are "entirely a function" of the physical structure of the human organism. For secularist liberals, it is the conscious, desiring, self-aware, and future-directed part of the human being that is truly the "person"; it is the psychological attributes of consciousness, self-awareness, etc. that confer "moral standing." By contrast, the living body, as such, is not part of the *personal* reality of the human being. And it is the status of the body as *subpersonal* that accounts for the willingness of secularists to authorize the killing of human beings before they become "persons" (fetuses and even infants) and after they cease being "persons" (the demented, the permanently comatose, etc.). The dualism of orthodox secularism consists in treating the "person" and the "mere living body" as really separable. "Persons" have dignity and rights; (their) "mere" living bodies do not.

Prof. Dever concedes that we enter "dangerous territory" when deciding that not all living organisms of the human species are persons. (Note, once again, the fruit of the dualistic presuppositions: there are "persons" and then there are "living organisms of the human species"—e.g., unborn and some newborn human beings, the demented, those in permanent comas—who are human beings but, according to orthodox secularists, not persons.) But, he insists, "the line must be drawn somewhere by everyone, so mere accusations of line-drawing can carry no weight." The fact, however, is that we needn't and shouldn't draw this line. The reasonable standard—the one that follows from a proper rejection of person/body dualism—is that living members of the species Homo sapiens are persons whose dignity is incompatible with a license to kill them.

Prof. Dever—believing that it is necessary to draw a line between "persons" and certain living human beings who are nonpersons—warns that "just as there is a price to pay for drawing the line too narrowly, there is also a price to pay for drawing the line too widely, since the moral duties owed toward persons can place a heavy burden on others." I'm worried, on the other hand, about our natural human desire to be free of the moral duties we owe to others—particularly the weak, the infirm, and the dependent—a desire that tempts us to credit the idea of a distinction between "persons" and human nonpersons. The supposition that such a distinction can rationally be drawn does not merely place us in "dangerous territory"; it perforce implicates us in a form of injustice against the most vulnerable of our fellow human beings.

Prof. Dever professes bafflement at what he takes to be my charge that secular orthodoxy is committed to relativism. As a professional philosopher, he reports, he is at pains to talk his students out of the mindless relativism they bring to the classroom. On this point, however, he seems not to have understood my claim. Indeed, I went so far as to say that "the mainstream of orthodox secularism at the end of the twentieth century has become self-consciously moralistic and *nonrelativistic.*" The defense of relativism, I said, is today largely confined to "cocktail parties and undergraduate classrooms." (On this score, at least, it sounds as though things don't vary much between Austin and Princeton.) At the same time, I asserted that secularism remains *in significant respects* a relativistic doctrine. And how could it be otherwise, if, as Prof. Dever freely concedes, the mainstream of secularist thought clings to the Humean subjectivist account of practical reason and morality?

One area in which this subjectivism makes itself felt is by relativizing allegedly self-regarding conduct. The familiar idea here is that what goes on between consenting adults simply isn't subject to critical moral evaluation. A moral issue arises only where the "rights of others" are violated or placed in jeopardy. Why, though, on a secularist understanding, should people restrain themselves—and even bear the sometimes heavy burden of moral duties—out of regard for the rights of others? On purely atheistic and materialistic premises, how can it be rational for someone to bear heavy burdens and suffer great cost—perhaps even death—to honor other people's rights? No satisfactory answer is forthcoming. None, I submit, is possible.

Prof. Dever suggests that when Judeo-Christian philosophy confronts the same question, it relies for an answer on the bare "scriptural assertion that humanity is created in God's image." But here, as elsewhere, Jewish and Christian thinkers find in revelation the confirmation, but not the root, of their philosophical affirmation of the nature and value of the human person—an affirmation found clearly (though not unmixed with error) in the philosophies of Plato and Aristotle, as well as in the thought of the greatest Roman jurists. Christian philosophers in particular hold that there are sound philosophical reasons—having to do with the contingency and intelligibility of the universe—to judge that God is personal in nature, that is, able to envisage and choose between intelligible options.

IN concluding, let me return to that point about the nature of practical reasoning on which even Prof. Dever regrets the established orthodoxy of secular liberalism. He is part of a "moral realist" movement in contemporary analytic philosophy that seeks to dislodge the "twin denial of the motivational power of reason and of epistemic access to objective normative facts" that is a central "legacy" of British Empiricism. As Prof. Dever himself recognizes, this makes him something of an unorthodox secularist. Fine. I wholeheartedly approve his heresy. But until this movement gains the upper hand, it remains the case that secularist orthodoxy, on its own terms, "possesses no resources for answering the question 'Why should I respect the rights of others?'" And, should it succeed in overcoming the Humean hegemony, it will be interesting to see whether the logic of moral realism begins to undermine the practical atheism, materialism, and, with them, the moral-political liberalism that are the defining features of contemporary secularism.

For my part, I am hopeful that people who come to see that the Humean tradition has been wrong, and that the Judeo-Christian tradition has been right all along, about the possibilities of free choice, rationally motivated action, and objective moral truth, will soon come to the realization that these possibilities point beyond themselves to a more-than-merely-human source of meaning and value, a divine ground of human intelligence and free will who freely discloses Himself to us when we are prepared to open our minds—and hearts—to Him.

2

LIBERAL POLITICAL THEORY AND THE CULTURE OF DEATH

CONTEMPORARY liberal political theory abets the culture of death. My point in so bluntly saying so is not to be polemical or even provocative; rather, it is to be soberly descriptive. Self-described liberal political theorists in the United States and elsewhere have, over the past two decades or so, quite explicitly set for themselves the task of justifying and defending the regime of abortion, euthanasia, and, increasingly, infanticide that constitutes the culture of death in the contemporary developed world. Indeed, six of the most prominent liberal theorists in the United States—John Rawls, Ronald Dworkin, Thomas Nagel, Robert Nozick, Tim Scanlon, and Judith Jarvis Thomson—have taken their attack on traditional sanctity of life principles out of the common room and the classroom and into the courts, filing with the Supreme Court of the United States in 1997 a much acclaimed amicus curiae brief urging the justices (unsuccessfully, as it turned out) to declare a federal constitutional right to physician-assisted suicide.[1]

Now, I am not maintaining (nor do I wish to be thought to maintain) that liberal political theorists who abet the culture of death are moral monsters. They are not Nazis or hatemongers. They are our colleagues and very often our friends. Many of them are doing their level best to think through the moral issues at the heart of our cultural struggle and arrive at conclusions that are right and just. They view themselves as partisans of a culture of freedom. In most cases, they carefully and honestly *argue* for those *choices for death* whose moral worthiness they proclaim and whose legal permission and constitutional protection they defend. As a matter of reciprocity, it is, in my view, incumbent upon us, as their opponents, to engage them in debate, to answer their arguments, to say why they are wrong.[2] While we must oppose them with resolution and, indeed, determination to win, we cannot content ourselves merely to denounce them, as we would rightly denounce the moral monsters who created a different culture of death on the European continent in the 1930s and 1940s.

In the previous paragraph, I stated that contemporary liberal political theorists defend "choices for death." The phrase is not my own, nor have I foisted it upon liberal theorists. It is Ronald Dworkin's description of abortion and euthanasia in the opening sentence of his book *Life's Dominion*—a book devoted in its entirety to defending abortion and euthanasia and their immunization from legal prohibition. "Abortion," Dworkin says "which means killing a human embryo, and euthanasia, which means killing a person out of kindness, are both choices for death."[3]

Of course, when Dworkin and other liberal theorists talk this way, they place the accent on the idea of "choice." They understand and present their view not as the political theory of the culture of death, but rather as the political theory of "the republic of choice," or, if you will, "the culture of freedom." The subtitle of Dworkin's book clearly signals the author's ideological bent, to wit, "an Argument about Abortion, Euthanasia, and Individual Freedom." And the sentence immediately following his candid acknowledgment of the death-dealing nature of the choices he proposes to defend is already in ideological spin mode: "Abortion," he declares, "chooses death before life *in earnest* has begun; euthanasia chooses death after it has ended."[4] Well, as that master of sentence parsing—and of spin—Bill Clinton might say, it all depends on what the meaning of "in earnest" is. Those two little words foreshadow Dworkin's vast argumentative effort to show that the lives of very young and very old or infirm human beings are not valuable in a way that makes it wrong to kill them or makes it right for the law to protect them against being killed.

That effort in its details needn't long detain us here. Its political theoretical apparatus was plainly gotten up for the occasion and has been thoroughly explored and decisively rebutted in, among other places, the submission made by the Linacre Centre (Britain's influential Catholic think tank) to the House of Lords Select Committee on Medical Ethics, which considered the introduction of euthanasia in Britain and, in 1994, unanimously rejected it. Dworkin's central claim that liberals and those whom he dubs "conservatives"—that is, people who oppose abortion and euthanasia—actually *share* a belief in the intrinsic and, indeed, "sacred" value of human life, and disagree merely over the *interpretation* of this shared value, is utterly fallacious. Dworkin's proposal was that law rightly treats human life as a central, protected value, but must maintain strict neutrality as between the views of those who "interpret" life's value as existing in merely "biological life"—i.e., the life of an unborn child or comatose or demented person—and those who see life's intrinsic and sacred value as consisting in "exercisable abilities, especially for rational control of one's life, in virtue of which people can give the shape and significance they wish to their lives." Dworkin's talk about the "shared" ideal of the sanctity of life is, as the Linacre Centre's submission observed, "practically empty." The differences Dworkin describes as differences of *interpretation* of an allegedly shared fundamental value are, in truth, themselves fundamental, precisely in the sense of being basic. Neutrality between them is literally impossible. Law must come down on one side or the other, and what is at stake is not freedom versus authority, but the basic principle of the equality-in-dignity of all human beings—without regard to age, size, stage of development, or condition of dependency—a principle at the heart of our laws against homicide, and which the Select Committee expressly declined to abandon.

Its abandonment would have required a decision, at least implicitly, to embrace an essentially dualistic understanding of the human being as a non-bodily person (that is, the self-aware, conscious, and desiring "self") who inhabits and uses as a mere instrument a non-personal body. Indeed, Dworkin himself more or less explicitly adopts this dualistic view in defending euthanasia. But it is simply untenable philosophically, for the very reason identified in the Linacre Centre's submission:

> It renders inexplicable the unity in complexity which one experiences in everything one consciously does. It speaks as if there were...a non-bodily person and a non-personal living body. But neither of these can one recognize as oneself. One's living body is intrinsic, not merely instrumental to one's personal life. Each of us has a human life (not a vegetable life plus an animal life plus a human life); when it is flourishing that life includes all one's vital functions including speech, deliberation, and choice; when gravely impaired it lacks some of those functions without ceasing to be the life of the person so impaired.[5]

Traditional ethics is on solid ground then in refusing to distinguish between, on the one hand, a class of human beings who are to count as "persons," and, on the other, "pre-" or "post-personal" human beings who are relegated to the status of "merely biologically human nonpersons." And the tradition of our homicide laws is on equally firm footing in treating the lives of all human beings—all persons—as equal in worth and dignity. Dworkin's argument—gotten up, as I say, specifically to justify abortion and euthanasia—casts no real doubt on the sanctity of life principles of traditional Western law and ethics or the prohibitions of deliberate feticide and other forms of homicide which they ground.

But there is a more general liberal strategy—a strategy of theorizing that is general precisely in the sense that it is not gotten up to justify (or, at least, merely to justify) the liberal position on life issues—though, in the end, it purports to do that—but to respond to a more general problem or set of social conditions. This strategy does not *directly* attack traditional sanctity of life principles or understandings or cast doubt on their reasonableness of truth. What it does, rather, is to rule out as illegitimate for public-policy making these and other principles, their reasonableness and even their truth notwithstanding. It leaves them in place as quite possibly good reasons for certain forms of *private* action and restraint (such as not having an abortion or taking one's own life), but it excludes them from the class of "public reasons"—that is, reasons justifying the restriction of liberty in certain contexts.

Moral Pluralism

I said that this strategy responds to a general problem or set of social conditions. This is the problem of moral pluralism. Liberal political theory's preoccupation with the problem of pluralism reflects an important social fact about Great Britain, the United States, and other Western nations: People no longer disagree merely about the proper or most effective means of protecting public goods and combating public evils. People today disagree—reasonably or otherwise—about what is a public good and what is a public evil. And this disagreement is not merely about what is to count as a *public*, as opposed to a purely *private*, good or evil; it is about what is morally good or evil in itself.

Consider, for example, the question of homosexuality. No longer are people divided merely over the question whether the criminalization of sodomy is a proper or effective means of discouraging homosexual conduct. Their disagreement goes beyond the question whether such conduct implicates a legitimate *public* interest justifying legal restriction or is merely a *private* vice that the state has a duty to tolerate. The old consensus about the immorality of homosexual conduct and relationships integrated around such conduct has broken down. Although many people, particularly those who cling to traditional Catholic, Protestant, or Jewish religious faith, continue to believe that homosexual acts and relationships are morally bad, many other people, notably including a great many journalists, intellectuals, and other opinion-shaping elites, have adopted the belief that homosexual conduct is no vice at all. "Gay is good," they say. So the debate has shifted from whether or not the state is justified in prohibiting sodomy to the question whether it is justified in refusing to honor homosexual relationships by, for example, declining to issue marriage licenses to same-sex couples.

And, of course, fundamental disagreement also characterizes the issue of abortion. In the United States, polling consistently reveals that a majority of citizens continue to believe that, except in certain rare and exceptional cases (i.e., where pregnancy threatens the life of the mother or would cause her severe and irreparable physical harm, or where it is the result of rape), abortion is morally evil. And something approaching a majority of Americans believe that abortion is a moral evil indistinguishable from infanticide and other forms of homicide. At the same time, a substantial number of Americans support legal abortion and even its public funding for indigent women, not merely on the ground that abortion is a "private" immorality that as such, the state has a duty to tolerate, but in the belief that abortion is, or can be, a morally good choice.

A similar moral pluralism obtains when it comes to physician-assisted suicide and euthanasia, the recreational use of drugs, and a host of other issues. Some disputed moral issues—particularly, I think, the issue of abortion—bring to mind the moral disagreement over slavery in the United States in the middle third of the nineteenth century. By then, supporters of slavery were no longer content to argue, as they had been in the late-eighteenth century, that the "peculiar institution" was a "necessary evil" whose toleration was required under circumstances in which abolition would produce disastrous, and therefore morally unacceptable, social and economic consequences. Instead, they argued that slavery was morally good and right, and that the position of their abolitionist opponents represented not a practically unattainable—albeit noble—moral ideal, but, rather, a morally repulsive religious fanaticism. Despite repeated efforts at political compromise, the moral disagreement over slavery proved, in the end, incompatible with peace and social stability. The issue had to be resolved finally by civil war which cost something approaching three-quarters of a million lives.

Reflection on the carnage of the American Civil War inclines me to think that contemporary political theory is right to take seriously the problem of moral pluralism. I am, however, skeptical about the mainstream of, if you will, liberal political theory whose ambitions are to identify basic principles of "political" justice which can be agreed upon by all reasonable people and which promise to provide social stability by constraining the grounds of political advocacy and action when it comes to fundamental moral issues (such as abortion and euthanasia) upon which people today disagree. The most notable—and ambitious—example of philosophical work of this type is the "political liberalism" of John Rawls. In the remainder of this chapter, I shall describe Rawls's effort to identify basic principles of justice which, as the fruit of an "overlapping consensus" among people who otherwise differ over fundamental moral and religious issues, promise to make possible social stability for morally good reasons. Then I shall give my reasons for rejecting Rawls's political liberalism. In particular, I shall argue that Rawls's conception of "public reason(s)," that is, reasons which may legitimately be introduced in political advocacy and acted upon legislatively, is unreasonably narrow and restrictive.

Public Reason and Liberal Legitimacy

IN his influential 1971 book *A Theory of Justice*, Rawls defended a liberal conception of justice, which he called "justice as fairness," whose basic principles for a well-ordered society were identified as those that would be chosen by free and equal persons in what he called "the original position." Parties in "the original position" select principles of justice in a state of ignorance regarding their personal moral and religious convictions, social and economic status, and related factors that will distinguish them from many of their fellow citizens when they emerge from behind "the veil of ignorance" to live in a society governed in accordance with the principles they had selected.

In 1993, Rawls published a new book, *Political Liberalism*, which amends certain features of the theory of justice he had advanced in 1971. Most importantly, he now says that the argument for "justice as fairness" as adumbrated in *A Theory of Justice* relied on a premise that was inconsistent with the theory itself, namely, the belief that "in the well-ordered society of justice as fairness, citizens hold the same comprehensive doctrine, and this includes aspects of Kant's comprehensive liberalism, to which the principles of justice as fairness might belong."[6] The problem with this belief is that neither liberalism, considered as what he calls a "comprehensive" (as opposed to a merely "political") doctrine, nor any other comprehensive view (e.g., Catholicism, Judaism, Platonism, Aristotelianism, communism), is held by citizens generally in contemporary pluralistic societies. And a plurality of comprehensive views is, Rawls suggests, natural and unavoidable in the circumstances of political freedom that characterize constitutional democratic regimes. Political theorizing that accepts the legitimacy of such regimes must begin, therefore, by acknowledging what Rawls calls "the fact of reasonable pluralism."

Recognition of "the fact of reasonable pluralism," according to Rawls, rules out the possibility of legitimately defending principles of justice for constitutional democratic regimes by appealing to comprehensive doctrines—including comprehensive forms of liberalism. Some alternative must, therefore, be found. Otherwise, the social stability of such regimes would be in constant jeopardy. Everything would depend on the capacity and willingness of people with fundamentally different moral views—including radically different conceptions of justice and human rights—to reach and preserve a modus vivendi. The alternative Rawls proposes is "political liberalism." Its ideal is that "citizens are to conduct their public political discussions of constitutional essentials and matters of basic justice within the framework of what each sincerely regards as a reasonable political conception of justice, a conception that expresses political values that others as free and equal also might reasonably be expected to endorse."[7]

In such a framework, "deeply opposed though reasonable comprehensive doctrines may live together and all affirm the political conception of a constitutional regime."[8] Where constitutional essentials and matters of basic justice are at issue, public discussion and debate must be conducted—for moral reasons and not as a mere modus vivendi—in terms of a "strictly political conception of justice,"[9] and not in terms of moral doctrines of justice associated with the various comprehensive views about which reasonable people disagree. The common affirmation of a "political conception" by adherents of competing comprehensive views enables them to participate in what Rawls refers to as "an overlapping consensus" on basic principles of justice. It is this consensus which makes social stability in the face of moral pluralism not only possible, but possible "for the right reasons."[10]

The core of "political liberalism" is the idea that whenever constitutional essentials and matters of basic justice are at stake political actors, including citizens as voters and insofar as they engage in public advocacy of candidates and causes, must refrain from acting on the basis of principles drawn from their comprehensive views (as Kantians, Catholics, communists, or whatever) except to the extent that "public reasons, given by a reasonable political conception, are presented sufficient to support whatever the comprehensive doctrines are introduced to support."[11] Thus, citizens are constrained from appealing to and acting upon beliefs drawn from their most fundamental moral understandings and commitments precisely at the most fundamental political level, namely, the level of constitutional essentials and matters of basic justice. And they are so constrained on grounds entirely separate from the putative falsity, unreasonableness, or unsoundness of those understandings and commitments or the beliefs drawn therefrom.[12]

Rawls insists that "political liberalism is not a form of Enlightenment liberalism, that is, a comprehensive liberal and often secular doctrine founded on reason and suitable for the modern age now that the religious authority of Christian ages is said to be no longer dominant."[13] It is, rather,

> a political conception of political justice for a constitutional democratic regime that a plurality of reasonable doctrines, both religious and nonreligious, liberal and nonliberal, may freely endorse, and so freely live by and come to understand its virtues. Emphatically, it does not aim to replace comprehensive doctrines, religious or nonreligious, but intends to be equally distinct from both and, it hopes, acceptable to both.[14]

"Political liberalism" aspires, then, to be impartial with respect to the viewpoints represented by the various reasonable doctrines which compete for the allegiance of citizens. It "does not attack or criticize any reasonable [comprehensive] view."[15] Rawls says that "rather than confronting religious and nonliberal doctrines with a comprehensive liberal philosophical doctrine, the thought is to formulate a liberal political conception that those nonliberal doctrines might be able to endorse."[16] Hence, the crucial idea of an "overlapping consensus" among comprehensive views which, inasmuch as they accept the fundaments of constitutional democracy, are "reasonable."

So "political liberalism" is a doctrine that is not just for liberals. If Rawls is correct, not only proponents of Kant's or Mill's liberalism, but also faithful Catholics, evangelical Protestants, and observant Jews—assuming the reasonableness of Catholicism, Protestantism, and Judaism (something Rawls suggests he is willing to assume)—ought to be able to join the "overlapping consensus" by reasonably embracing "political liberalism" without compromising their basic religious and moral convictions.[17]

Although Rawls observes that a mere political compromise or

modus vivendi might, under propitious circumstances, develop into an "overlapping consensus," he carefully distinguishes an "overlapping consensus" from a mere modus vivendi. Unlike a modus vivendi, an "overlapping consensus" is constituted by a certain level of *moral agreement* about what constitute fair terms of social cooperation among people who, being reasonable, view each other as free and equal citizens. So, although Rawls presents the liberal "political conception" of justice as standing independent of any particular comprehensive doctrine (in that sense it is, he says, a "freestanding" conception), it is nevertheless a *moral* conception, containing "its own intrinsic normative and moral ideal."[18]

Rawls maintains that terms of cooperation offered by citizens to their fellow citizens are fair only insofar as "citizens offering them...reasonably think that those citizens to whom such terms are offered might also reasonably accept them."[19] This "criterion of reciprocity" is the core of what Rawls labels "the liberal principle of legitimacy," namely, that "our exercise of political power is fully proper only when it is exercised in accordance with a constitution the essentials of which all citizens as free and equal may be expected to endorse in the light of principles and ideals acceptable to their common human reason."[20] When, and only when, political power is exercised in accordance with such a constitution do political actors— including voters—maintain fidelity to the ideal of "public reason."

The Challenge of Natural Law Theory

THE "liberal principle of legitimacy" and ideal of "public reason" exclude as illegitimate in political discourse and in the exercise of public authority, at least insofar as basic matters of justice—including constitutional rights—are concerned, appeal to principles and propositions drawn from comprehensive doctrines even though they are, or may well be, *true.* It would be one thing to argue that in certain circumstances prudence requires such an exclusion, at least temporarily, as part of a modus vivendi. It is quite another thing, however, to claim, as Rawls does, that such an exclusion is *morally* required by virtue of "the fact of reasonable pluralism" even in circumstances in which people are not restrained by prudence from acting on principles they reasonably believe to be true, and which are not ruled out as reasons for political action by their reasonable comprehensive doctrines of justice and political morality. So, we must examine the justification Rawls offers for this exclusion. To that end, let us consider what Rawls has in mind in demanding, as a matter of reciprocity, that citizens offer to their fellow citizens with whom they disagree about basic moral, metaphysical, and religious matters terms of social cooperation that they reasonably think their fellow citizens may reasonably accept.

If Rawls's "criterion of reciprocity" and "liberal principle of legitimacy" are interpreted narrowly, then citizens offering terms of cooperation to their fellow citizens who happen to disagree with them about a matter in dispute must merely think that they are presenting to their fellow citizens sound reasons, accessible to them as reasonable people of goodwill, for changing their minds. The scope of "public reason" under this narrow interpretation of reciprocity and legitimacy would be wide. It would, to be sure, rule out as illegitimate claims based on the allegedly "secret knowledge" of a gnostic elite or the putative truths revealed only to a select few and not accessible to reasonable persons as such, but it would not exclude any principle or proposition, however controversial, that is put forward for acceptance on the basis of rational argumentation.

Now, even on this narrow interpretation, some religious believers would object that their views would be unfairly excluded from public political discourse. Others, however, would have no objection to a principle of reciprocity that demands only that they offer "public reasons" in this very wide sense. They would have no interest in restraining the liberty of their fellow citizens, or in disfavoring them or their preferred ways of life or modes of behavior, on the basis of claims they could not defend by rational argumentation. They would accept the claim that to do so would be unfair. It seems clear, however, that Rawls himself cannot accept the narrow interpretation of reciprocity and the correspondingly very wide conception of public reason. His goal, after all, is to limit the range of morally acceptable doctrines of political morality in circumstances of moral pluralism to a single doctrine: "political liberalism." The very wide conception of public reason simply will not accomplish that goal. It will not, for example, rule out appeals to principles and propositions drawn from comprehensive forms of liberalism. More importantly, it will not exclude appeals to principles and propositions drawn from nonliberal comprehensive doctrines which content themselves with appeals to "our common human reason."

Notable among such doctrines is the broad tradition of natural law thinking about morality, justice, and human rights. This tradition poses an especially interesting problem for Rawls's theory of public reason because of its integration into Roman Catholic teaching. So it is, at once, a nonliberal comprehensive philosophical doctrine *and* part of a larger religious tradition which, in effect, proposes its own principle of public reason, namely, that questions of law and policy (including what Rawls has in mind when he refers to "constitutional essentials and matters of basic justice") ought to be decided in accordance with natural law, natural right, natural rights, and/or natural justice (where, as in Aquinas's natural law theory, something is good or right or just "by nature" insofar as it is *reasonable*).[21]

If Rawls is to successfully defend a conception of "public reason" narrow enough to exclude appeals to natural law theory, he must show that there is something unfair about such appeals. And he must, of course, demonstrate this unfairness without appeal to comprehensive liberalism or any other comprehensive conception of justice that competes with the natural law conception. In other words, he must avoid smuggling into the defense of his claim that "*only* a political conception of justice...can serve as a basis of public reason and justification"[22] principles or propositions that are themselves in dispute among adherents to reasonable comprehensive doctrines (including, of course, Catholicism and natural law theory). This, it seems to me, he has not done and, I believe, cannot do.

Rawls does not explicitly address the claims of natural law theorists—Catholic or otherwise. He seems, however, to have something like their beliefs in mind in his critique of what he calls "rationalist believers who contend that [their] beliefs are open to and can be fully established by reason."[23] Rawls's argument against the so-called rationalist believers rests entirely on the claim that they unreasonably deny "the fact of reasonable pluralism." But do they? I am myself something of a "rationalist believer," at least according to Rawls's definition, and I certainly do not deny the fact that people in our culture, including reasonable people, disagree about fundamental moral questions, including questions pertaining to euthanasia, abortion, homosexuality, and the recreational use of drugs. Nor do I deny that some measure of moral disagreement—though not necessarily moral disagreement on the scale of what we find today in the United States or Great Britain, for example—is inevitable under circumstances of political and religious liberty. So I do not see how Rawls can justify his claim that "rationalist believers" deny "the fact of reasonable pluralism."

Rawls own methodological and moral commitments require him to avoid denying the soundness, reasonableness, or truth of the reasonable, if controversial, moral, metaphysical, and religious claims that his "political" conception of justice would exclude from political discourse and as grounds for political action. So he cannot rule out the views of natural law theorists or "rationalist believers" on issues such as homosexuality, abortion, euthanasia, and drugs on the grounds that their views are unsound, unreasonable, or false. If he is reduced to arguing for the unsoundness, unreasonableness, or falsity of these views, then his "*political* liberalism" will have collapsed into "*comprehensive* liberalism." And we are left with the conflict of comprehensive views to which "political liberalism" is meant to provide an alternative.

Understandably, then, Rawls seeks to avoid engaging the specific claims and arguments of the "rationalist believers." He limits himself to a simple denial that their claims "can be publicly and fully established by reason."[24] But how can this denial be sustained independently of some engagement "on the merits" with the specific arguments they advance in their public political advocacy— arguments that Rawls's idea of "public reason" is meant to exclude in advance without the need to address their soundness and reasonableness or the truth or falsity of the principles and propositions in support of which they are offered?

It will not do for Rawls to claim that he is not denying the truth of "rationalist believers'" claims but merely their assertion that these claims can be publicly and fully established by reason. What makes a "rationalist believer" a "rationalist" is precisely his belief that his principles can be justified by *rational argument* and his willingness to provide just such *rational argumentation*. The arguments he offers by way of justifying his principles and their applications to specific political issues will be either sound or unsound. If they are sound, then Rawls can give no reason for excluding the principles they vindicate on the ground that they are illegitimate reasons for political action; if they are unsound, then they ought to be rejected precisely on that basis, and not because the principles in support of which they are offered are, in Rawls's sense, "nonpublic."

Let us return, though, to Rawls's claim that "rationalist believers" deny "the fact of reasonable pluralism." He states that "[i]t is unrealistic—or worse, it arouses mutual suspicion and hostility—to suppose that all our differences are rooted in ignorance and perversity, or else in the rivalries for power, status, and economic gain."[25] Natural law theorists and (other?) "rationalist believers" do not deny this. Indeed, they recognize that differences of opinion and commitment often arise from factors that reason does not control—matters of taste and sentiment, for example. Moreover, matters can sometimes be rationally underdetermined even where reason guides reflection by excluding as unreasonable certain possibilities, but leaving more than one possibility open and, in that sense, rationally available. On some issues, there is a variety of unreasonable opinions, but no uniquely reasonable or correct one.

Natural law theorists (and others) maintain, however, that on certain other issues, including certain fundamental moral and political issues, there are uniquely correct answers. The question whether there is a human right against being enslaved, for example, or being punished for one's religious beliefs, admits of a uniquely correct answer which is available in principle to every rational person. Pro-life advocates assert that there is similarly a human right against deliberate feticide and other forms of direct killing of innocent persons. Differences over such issues as slavery, religious freedom, abortion, and euthanasia may be "reasonable" in the sense that reasonable persons can err in their judgments and arrive at morally incorrect positions. But, assuming there is a truth of these matters—something Rawls cannot deny and, one would think, has no desire to deny—errors of reason must be responsible for anyone's failure to arrive at the morally correct positions. There are many possible roots of such errors, not all of which involve culpability or subjective guilt on the part of the individuals who make them. Ignorance of, or inattention to, certain relevant facts or values may be the source of a particular error. Prejudice or other subrational influences—which may be pervasive in a culture or subculture making it difficult for any of its individual members to reason well about certain issues—may block insights that are critical to sound moral judgments. And, of course, logical failures or other errors in the reasoning process can deflect judgment in the moral field as they can in all other fields of inquiry. Nothing in the position of natural law theorists (or "rationalist believers") entails the proposition that we can always easily arrive at correct moral positions or that we will not sometimes (perhaps often) get things wrong.

Is anything in their view *unreasonable*? Rawls certainly cannot declare their view unreasonable because they maintain that on certain morally charged and highly disputed political questions—including questions of human rights—there are uniquely morally correct answers. The fact that "reasonable people" can be found on competing sides of such questions in no way implies that the competing views are equally reasonable. Reasonable people can be wrong—as Rawls himself implicitly acknowledges in his claims against the "rationalist believers" who are, after all, reasonable people even if their claim that their beliefs can be fully and publicly justified by reason is unreasonable. There is simply no unreasonableness in maintaining that otherwise reasonable people can be less than fully reasonable (sometimes culpably, other times not) in their judgments of particular issues.[26]

In *A Theory of Justice,* Rawls identified the two basic principles of "justice as fairness" by the method of "political constructivism" which asked what substantive principles would be chosen by parties in the "original position" behind the "veil of ignorance" which hides from them (among other things) what Rawls now calls their "comprehensive views." In a key passage of *Political Liberalism,* he says that the "liberal principle of legitimacy" and the ideal of "public reason" have "the same basis as the substantive principles of justice."[27] It seems to me, however, that this basis was, and remains, insecure. Over more than twenty-five years, Rawls and his followers have failed to provide any reason to suppose that "perfectionist" principles—principles of justice or political morality more generally drawn from "comprehensive views" about what is humanly valuable and morally upright—which would not be selected under conditions of artificial ignorance by the unnaturally risk-averse parties in the "original position" are *unjust* (or cannot be valid principles of justice). Rawlsians seem to suppose that from the proposition that principles that would be selected *by such parties under such conditions* are just (i.e., involve no injustice), it follows that perfectionist principles—which might very well be chosen by reasonable and well-informed persons outside the original position—are unjust. *Non sequitur.*

Conclusion

CONTEMPORARY liberalism, the liberalism of Dworkin, Rawls, and Thomson, cannot withstand intellectual scrutiny. Its efforts to identify sound reasons to exclude sanctity of life ideals as illegitimate reason for political action by Catholics and others to protect the basic right to life of every human being—every person—

not to be directly killed, and to the equal protection of the laws against killing, utterly and manifestly fails. Its failure is identifiable by rational critical inquiry and dialectical argumentation. The effective critique of liberalism as the political theory of the culture of death in no way relies on esoteric information, private revelation, or any other non-public reasons.

There is, however, another liberalism. And, as I shall argue in chapter 12, this old-fashioned liberalism is a liberalism that is not only consistent with Catholic faith and the culture of life, but demanded by it.[28] This is not the liberalism of abortion, euthanasia, and the sexual revolution. It is the liberalism, rather, of the rule of law, democratic self-government, subsidiarity, social solidarity, private property, limited government, equal protection, and basic human freedoms, such as those of speech, press, assembly, and, above all, religion. This, as I say, is a decidedly old-fashioned liberalism—if you will, a "conservative liberalism." It is the liberalism of Lincoln and the American founders, of Newman and Chesterton, of the Second Vatican Council and John Paul II: A liberalism of life.

Appendix: Abortion and Public Reason

ALTHOUGH the defense of political liberalism requires John Rawls to resist the very wide view of public reason which could be endorsed by so-called rationalist believers, he is nevertheless eager to show that the scope of his doctrine of public reason is not excessively narrow. For example, his "political liberalism" allows people to have resort to beliefs drawn from their comprehensive doctrines in a variety of areas that do not touch upon constitutional essentials and matters of basic justice.[29] And even in areas that do touch upon such matters it allows appeals to comprehensive doctrines subject to the proviso that citizens making such appeals "in due course" show that their position can be justified in terms of public reason(s).[30] In *Political Liberalism*, Rawls offers the following explanation of the demands of public reason:

What public reason asks is that citizens be able to explain their vote to one another in terms of a reasonable balance of public values, it being understood by everyone that of course the plurality of reasonable comprehensive doctrines held by citizens is thought by them to provide further and often transcendent backing for those values. In each case, which doctrine is affirmed is a matter of conscience for the individual citizen. It is true that the balance of political values a citizens holds must be reasonable, and one that can be seen to be reasonable by other citizens; but not all reasonable balances are the same. The only comprehensive doctrines that run afoul of public reason are those that cannot support a reasonable balance of political values.[31]

Precisely at this point, Rawls inserts a footnote (32) that, "as an illustration," takes up what he describes as "the troubled question of abortion." After stipulating that "we are dealing with the normal case of mature adult women," he asks the reader to "consider the question in terms of three important political values: the due respect for human life, the ordered reproduction of political society over time, including the family, in some form, and finally the equality of women as equal citizens." After acknowledging, parenthetically, that these are not the only important political values, he declares flatly that "any reasonable balance of these three values will give a woman a duly qualified right to decide whether or not to end her pregnancy during the first trimester."[32]

How, one may ask, could this bold conclusion be justified without appeal to moral or metaphysical views widely in dispute about the status of embryonic and fetal human beings and the justice or injustice of choices to bring about their deaths, or to perform acts that include among their foreseeable side effects the bringing about of their deaths?

Here is Rawls's entire account of himself: "at this early stage of pregnancy the political value of the equality of women is overriding, and this right is required to give it substance and force." Why does the value of women's equality override the value of fetal life? Rawls does not say. The absence of argument for this claim is especially remarkable in view of the fact that opponents of abortion contend that the right to life, which, in their view, the unborn share with all other human beings, is fundamental and inviolable and, as such, cannot be "balanced" against other considerations. Rawls goes on to comment that he doesn't think that the introduction of other political values into the calculation would alter his conclusion, and, indeed, that a reasonable balance of political values might allow a right to abortion even beyond the first trimester, "at least in certain circumstances." He explicitly declines to argue the point further, however, stating that his purpose in raising the question of a right to abortion at all is simply "to illustrate the point of the text by saying that any comprehensive doctrine that leads to a balance of political values excluding that duly qualified right in the first trimester is to that extent unreasonable."[33]

Needless to say, Rawls's footnote has elicited vigorous criticism.[34] As an argument for a right to abortion, it does worse than beg centrally important questions—it ignores them altogether. Moreover, it seems plainly, if silently, to import into the analysis of the question a range of undefended beliefs of precisely the sort that "political liberalism" is supposed to exclude. This smuggling in of controversial moral and metaphysical beliefs is especially egregious in view of the fact that abortion is often put forward as a question that simply cannot be resolved, one way or the other, without introducing such beliefs into the deliberations.[35] As such, it presents a particular challenge to Rawls's central argument that constitutional essentials and matters of basic justice (assuming, as Rawls does, that we treat abortion as falling within these categories) ought to be resolved by appeal to a purely "political" conception of justice, rather than to general doctrines of justice as parts of reasonable comprehensive views.

In a footnote to the introduction to the paperback edition of *Political Liberalism*,[36] Rawls acknowledges the force of some of these criticisms and offers a brief reply:

Some have quite naturally read the [original] footnote as an argument for the right to abortion in the first trimester. I do not intend it to be one. (It does express my opinion, but an opinion is not an argument.) I was in error in leaving it in doubt that the aim of the footnote was only to illustrate and confirm the following statement in the text to which the footnote is attached: "The only comprehensive doctrines that run afoul of public reason are those that cannot support a reasonable balance [or ordering] of political values [on the issue]." To try to explain what I meant, I used three political values (of course, there are more) for the troubled issue of the right to abortion, to which it might seem improbable that political values could apply at all. I believe a more detailed interpretation of those values may, when properly developed as public reason, yield a reasonable argument. I don't say the most reasonable or decisive argument; I don't know what that would be, or even if it exists.

At this point Rawls cites with approval—noting only that he would add several (unspecified) "addenda" to it—Judith Jarvis Thomson's argument for a right to abortion in her then recent article "Abortion: Whose Right?"[37] Here is Thomson's summation of her argument:

First, restrictive regulation [of abortion] severely constrains women's liberty. Second, severe constraints on liberty may not be imposed in the name of considerations that the constrained are not unreasonable in rejecting. And third, the many women who reject the claim that the fetus has a right to life from the moment of conception are not unreasonable in doing so.[38]

The affinities of Thomson's approach with Rawlsian political liberalism are, I trust, obvious. The central pro-life claims are that (a) human beings in the embryonic and fetal stages, like innocent human beings at all other stages of life, have a right not to be directly (or otherwise unjustly) killed, and (b) they, like all other human beings, are entitled to the equal protection of the laws against homicide. Thomson defends the right to abortion not by claiming that the central pro-life claims are false, but, rather, by arguing that their truth or falsity are irrelevant to the political resolution of the question of abortion. What matters is that people are "not unreasonable" in judging the central pro-life claims to be false. Therefore, even those who judge them to be true should refrain from taking political action which would restrict women's freedom based on their judgment. They should join those who consider the central pro-life claims to be false in a sort of Rawlsian overlapping consensus which recognizes a woman's right to abortion.

Here, I submit, we have fully on display all the equivocations, ambiguities, and weaknesses of the Rawlsian criterion of reciprocity, liberal principle of legitimacy, and doctrine of public reason. Immediately after offering the summary of her argument I quoted a moment ago, Thomson, evidently struggling to be generous, says that "[t]here is of course room for those who accept Catholic doctrine on abortion to declare it in the public forum."[39] But, she adds, "those who accept the doctrine ought not say that reason requires us to accept it, for that assertion is false."[40] What is Thomson claiming here? Is it that the central pro-life claims should be rejected because they are untrue or, even if true, somehow unreasonable? To establish that, she would have to engage pro-life arguments on the merits and refute them. This, however, she makes no serious effort to do. To have done so would, in any event, have shifted the ground of the argument for a right to abortion from the sphere of Rawlsian public reason to unrestricted debate of a sort that would engage, in violation of Rawlsian scruples, principles connected with competing comprehensive doctrines.[41]

What Thomson seems to mean is that not all "reasonable people" accept pro-life claims or that the rejection of pro-life claims does not mark a person as "unreasonable." There are, as I suggested earlier, important senses in which assertions like these are true. But, contrary to what Thomson supposes, from the senses in which they are true nothing follows for the question whether women have a right to abortion or the unborn have a right not to be aborted. If, in truth, the latter right obtains—if, that is to say, it is true that the unborn have a right not to be aborted and, thus, that the pro-life position is more reasonable than its alternative—then the fact that reasonable people, perhaps without culpability, hold the contrary view in no way vitiates the human right of the unborn not to be killed, or confers upon women a moral right to the more or less unrestricted legal freedom to bring about their deaths. What matters, from the moral point of view, is that basic human rights be identified where they obtain and, to the extent possible, protected.

In the end, Thomson's argument that people are "not unreasonable" in rejecting the pro-life position boils down to an assertion that the argument over the moral status of the human conceptus and early embryo ends in a sort of stalemate: "While I know of no conclusive reason for denying that fertilized eggs have a right to life, I also know of no conclusive reason for asserting that they do have a right to life."[42] But one is entitled to this conclusion about the moral status of newly conceived human beings (Thomson's "fertilized eggs") only if one can make an argument sufficient to support it. And such an argument would have to rebut the arguments put forward to show that the unborn have a right to life even in the earliest stages of their existence. There is all the difference in the world between rebutting these arguments and ruling them out in advance on the ground that they implicate deep moral and metaphysical questions in dispute among reasonable people subscribing to competing comprehensive doctrines.

3

GOD'S REASONS

APPEALS TO RELIGIOUS AUTHORITY have their place. That place is plainly not, however, in philosophical debates, including philosophical debates about public policy. Do such appeals have a legitimate place in political advocacy? I think they do, but, at the same time, I have some sympathy with John Rawls's proposition that such appeals are legitimate only where they are offered to buttress and motivate people to act on positions that are defensible without such appeals. Like Rawls, I believe that public policy should be based on "public reasons." And while I believe that Rawls's own particular conception of what qualifies as a "public reason" is unreasonably narrow—its narrowness in effect stacking the deck in favor of legal abortion, "same-sex marriage," and other positions held by liberals in contemporary debates over morally charged issues of public policy—the idea that public policy ought to be based on public reasons strikes me as, well, reasonable.[1]

It is not, however, unproblematic. Anyone who believes that God has revealed that the public policy of a certain polity must be settled in a certain way has, so far as he can tell, an absolute, indefeasible reason for supporting that way of settling public policy irrespective of whether there are any grounds apart from revelation for the policy. My scruples, or Rawls's, would—and should—simply cut no ice for a person in this position. And if I happen to be the person in that position, or if Rawls happens to be that person, then I, or he, would be irrational in declining to lay aside our scruples. I suppose that when push comes to shove, those of us who hold these scruples believe that it just isn't the case that God sometimes reveals that public policy ought to be settled in a certain way irrespective of whether there are any grounds apart from revelation for settling policy in this way. Such people either don't believe in God, or (and this is my view) don't believe that God operates this way (at least we don't believe that He operates this way anymore). It seems to me, then, that our differences with those who don't hold these scruples implicate in this way certain theological judgments.

People who do not hold these scruples may believe either that God (at least sometimes) has no reason for the public policies He commands or (at least sometimes) has no reason He chooses to make available to human understanding. As they see it, God's reasons, if He has any, are (at least sometimes) opaque to us. "Ours is not to question why, ours is but to do or die." But, of course, this understanding of how God operates is one possible theological understanding among others. Many, perhaps most, serious religious believers in our society have a different understanding. To be sure, they believe—we believe—that God is a God of *justice,* who cares what the public policy of our society is on morally significant questions— for example, abortion, euthanasia, and marriage and sexuality, not to mention capital punishment, civil and human rights, military policy, economic justice, etc. And a great many believers, though not all, believe, as I do, that God wills that the unborn, handicapped, and frail elderly be protected by law, and that the institution of marriage as a permanent and exclusive union of one man and one woman be preserved against what we believe are the corrupting influences of sexual immorality. But we also believe not only that there are reasons (apart from revelation) for these policy positions, but also that these reasons are (or, at least, are among) God's reasons for willing what He wills. Indeed, it is our view that often the identification of these reasons by philosophical inquiry and analysis, supplemented sometimes by knowledge derived from the natural and/or social sciences, is critical to an accurate understanding of the content of revelation in, say, the Bible or Jewish or Christian tradition.

Perhaps the best example is in the area of marriage and sexual morality. Philosophical inquiry is indispensable to the project of fully understanding the meaning and implications of the proposition revealed in chapter two of Genesis and in the Gospels that marriage is a "one-flesh union" of a man and a woman.[2]

Another example is that of abortion, where both philosophical analysis and knowledge obtainable only by scientific inquiry were essential to settling, and continue to be essential to understanding the precise content of, the authoritative teaching of the magisterium of the Catholic Church declaring direct abortion to be intrinsically immoral and a violation of human rights.[3]

In short, many religious people—most informed Catholics and many Protestants and observant Jews—understand reason not only as a truth-attaining power, but as a power by and through which God directs us as individuals and communities in the way of just and upright living. In his formal account of natural law as a participation in what he called the "eternal law," Aquinas says that although God directs brute animals to their proper ends by instinct, God directs man—made in God's image and likeness and thus possessing reason and freedom—to his proper ends by practical reason through which men grasp the intelligible point of certain possible actions for the sake of ends (goods, values, purposes) which, *qua* intelligible, provide reasons for choice and action.[4] Where these reasons have their intelligibility not, or not merely, by virtue of their utility in enabling us to realize our other valuable or desirable ends, but also by virtue of their intrinsic value and choice-worthiness, they constitute the referents of the most fundamental principles of practical reason and precepts of natural law.[5] Aquinas gives an expressly non-exhaustive list of examples: human life itself, marriage and the transmission of life to new human beings, and knowledge, particularly of religious truth.[6] The integral directiveness of these principles, when specified, constitutes the body of moral norms available to guide human choosing *reasonably,* namely, in conformity with a good will—a will toward integral human fulfillment.[7]

IN his contributions to the February 1996 issue of *First Things* magazine—contributions in which what he has to say (particularly in his critique of liberalism) is far more often right than wrong—Stanley Fish of Duke University cites the dispute over abortion as an example of a case in which "incompatible first assumptions [or] articles of opposing faiths"—make the resolution of the dispute (other than by sheer political power) impossible. Here is how Fish presented the pro-life and pro-choice positions and the shape of the dispute between their respective defenders:

> A pro-life advocate sees abortion as a sin against God who infuses life at the moment of conception; a pro-choice advocate sees abortion as a decision to be made in accordance with the best scientific opinion as to when the beginning of life, as we know it, occurs. No conversation between them can ever get started because each of them starts from a different place and they could never agree as to what they were conversing *about.* A pro-lifer starts from a belief in the direct agency of a personal God, and this belief, this religious conviction, is not incidental to his position; it is his position, and determines its features in all their detail. The "content of a belief" is a *function* of its source, and the critiques of one will always be the critique of the other.[8]

It is certainly true that the overwhelming majority of pro-life Americans are religious believers and that a great many pro-choice Americans are either unbelievers or less observant or less traditional in their beliefs and practice than their fellow citizens. Indeed, although most Americans believe in God, polling data consistently show that Protestants, Catholics, and Jews who do not regularly attend church or synagogue are less likely than their more observant co-religionists to oppose abortion.[9] And religion is plainly salient politically when it comes to the issue of abortion. The more secularized a community, the more likely that community is to elect pro-choice politicians to legislative and executive offices.

Still, I don't think that Fish's presentation of the pro-life and pro-choice positions, or of the shape of the dispute over abortion, is accurate. True, inasmuch as most pro-life advocates are traditional religious believers who, as such, see gravely unjust or otherwise immoral acts as sins—and understand sins precisely as offenses against God—"a pro-life advocate sees abortion as a sin against God." But most pro-life advocates see abortion as a sin against God *precisely because it is the unjust taking of innocent human life.* That is their reason for opposing abortion; and that is God's reason, as they see it, for opposing abortion and requiring that human communities protect their unborn members against it. And, they believe, as I do, that this reason can be identified and acted on even independently of God's revealing it. Indeed, they typically believe, as I do, that the precise content of what God reveals on the subject ("in thy mother's womb I formed thee") cannot be known without the application of human intelligence, by way of philosophical and scientific inquiry, to the question.

Fish is mistaken, then, in *contrasting* the pro-life advocate with the pro-choice advocate by depicting (only) the latter as viewing abortion as "a decision to be made in accordance with the best scientific opinion as to when the beginning of life...occurs." First of all, supporters of the pro-choice position are increasingly willing to sanction the practice of abortion even where they concede that it constitutes the taking of innocent human life. Pro-choice writers from Naomi Wolfe to Judith Jarvis Thomson have advanced theories of abortion as "justifiable homicide."[10] But, more to the point, people on the pro-life side *insist* that the central issue in the debate is the question "as to when the beginning of life occurs." And they insist with equal vigor that this question is not a "religious" or even "metaphysical" one: it is rather, as Fish says, "scientific." In response to this insistence, it is pro-choice advocates who typically want to transform the question into a "metaphysical" or "religious" one. It was Justice Harry Blackmun who claimed in his opinion for the Court legalizing abortion in *Roe v. Wade* (1973) that "at this point in man's knowledge" the scientific evidence was inconclusive and therefore cold not determine the outcome of the case. And twenty years later, the influential pro-choice writer Ronald Dworkin went on record claiming that the question of abortion is inherently "religious."[11] It is pro-choice advocates, such as Dworkin, who want to distinguish between when a human being comes into existence "in the biological sense" and when a human being comes into existence "in the moral sense." It is they who want to distinguish a class of human beings "with rights" from pre- (or post-) conscious human beings who "don't have rights." And the reason for this, I submit, is that, short of defending abortion as "justifiable homicide," the pro-choice position collapses if the issue is to be settled purely on the basis of scientific inquiry into the question of when a new member of Homo sapiens comes into existence as a self-integrating organism whose unity, distinctiveness, and identity remain intact as it develops without substantial change from the point of its beginning through the various stages of its development and into adulthood.[12]

All this was, I believe, made wonderfully clear at a debate at the 1997 meeting of the American Political Science Association between Jeffrey Reiman of American University, defending the pro-choice position, and John Finnis of Oxford and Notre Dame, defending the pro-life view. That debate was remarkable for the skill, intellectual honesty, and candor of the interlocutors. What is most relevant to our deliberations, however, is the fact that it truly was a debate. Reiman and Finnis did not talk past each other. They did not proceed from "incompatible first assumptions." They *did* manage to agree as to what they were talking *about*—and it was not about whether or when life was infused by God. It was precisely about the *rational* (i.e., scientific and philosophical) grounds, if any, available for distinguishing a class of human beings "in the moral sense" (with rights) from a class of human beings "in the (merely) biological sense" (without rights). Finnis did not claim any special revelation to the effect that no such grounds existed. Nor did Reiman claim that Finnis's arguments against his view appealed implicitly (and illicitly) to some such putative revelation. Although Finnis is a Christian and, as such, believes that the new human life that begins at conception is in each and every case created by God in His image and likeness, his argument never invoked, much less did it "start from a belief in the direct agency of a personal God." It proceeded, rather, by way of point-by-point philosophical challenge to Reiman's philosophical arguments. Finnis marshaled the scientific facts of embryogenesis and intrauterine human development and defied Reiman to identify grounds, compatible with those facts, for denying a right to life to human beings in the embryonic and fetal stages of development.[13]

Interestingly, Reiman began his remarks with a statement that would seem to support what Fish said in *First Things*. While allowing that debates over abortion were useful in clarifying people's thinking about the issue, Reiman remarked that they "never actually cause people to change their minds." It is true, I suppose, that people who are deeply committed emotionally to one side or the other are unlikely to have a road-to-Damascus type conversion after listening to a formal philosophical debate. Still, any open-minded person who sincerely wishes to settle his mind on the question of abortion—and there continue to be many such people, I believe—would find debates such as the one between Reiman and Finnis to be extremely helpful toward that end. Anyone willing to consider the *reasons* for and against abortion and its legal prohibition or permission would benefit from reading or hearing the accounts of these reasons proposed by capable and honest thinkers on both sides. Of course, when it comes to an issue like abortion, people can have powerful motives for clinging to a particular position even if they are presented with conclusive reasons for changing their minds. But that doesn't mean that such reasons do not exist.

I believe that the pro-life position is superior to the pro-choice position precisely because the scientific evidence, considered honestly and dispassionately, fully supports it.[14] A human being is

conceived when a human sperm containing twenty-three chromosomes fuses with a human egg also containing twenty-three chromosomes (albeit of a different kind) producing a single-cell human
zygote containing, in the normal case, forty-six chromosomes that
are mixed differently from the forty-six chromosomes as found in
the mother or father. Unlike the gametes (that is, the sperm and
egg), the zygote is genetically unique and distinct from its parents.
Biologically, it is a separate organism. It produces, as the gametes do
not, specifically human enzymes and proteins. It possesses, as they
do not, the active capacity or potency to develop itself into a human
embryo, fetus, infant, child, adolescent, and adult.

Assuming that it is not conceived *in vitro,* the zygote is, of course,
in a state of dependence on its mother. But independence should
not be confused with distinctness. From the beginning, the newly
conceived human being, not its mother, directs its integral organic
functioning. It takes in nourishment and converts it to energy. Given
a hospitable environment, it will, as Dianne Nutwell Irving says,
"develop continuously without any biological interruptions, or gaps,
throughout the embryonic, fetal, neo-natal, childhood and adulthood stages—until the death of the organism."[15]

SOME claim to find the logical implication of these facts—that
is, that life begins at conception—to be "virtually unintelligible." A
leading exponent of that point of view in the legal academy is Jed
Rubenfeld of Yale Law School, author of an influential article entitled "On the Legal Status of the Proposition that 'Life Begins at
Conception.'"[16] Rubenfeld argues that, like the zygote, *every* cell in
the human body is "genetically complete"; yet nobody supposes that
every human cell is a distinct human being with a right to life.
However, Rubenfeld misses the point that there comes into being at
conception, not a mere clump of human cells, but a distinct, unified,
self-integrating organism, which develops itself, truly himself or
herself, in accord with its own genetic "blueprint." The significance
of genetic completeness for the status of newly conceived human
beings is that no outside genetic material is required to enable the

zygote to mature into an embryo, the embryo into a fetus, the fetus into an infant, the infant into a child, the child into an adolescent, the adolescent into an adult. What the zygote needs to function as a distinct self-integrating human organism, a human being, it already possesses.

At no point in embryogenesis, therefore, does the distinct organism that came into being when it was conceived undergo what is technically called "substantial change" (or a change of natures). It is human and will remain human. This is the point of Justice Byron White's remark in his dissenting opinion in *Thornburgh v. American College of Obstetricians & Gynecologists* that "there is no non-arbitrary line separating a fetus from a child."[17] Rubenfeld attacks White's point, which he calls "[t]he argument based on the gradualness of gestation," by pointing out that, "[n]o non-arbitrary line separates the hues of green and red. Shall we conclude that green is red?"[18]

White's point, however, was *not* that fetal development is "gradual," but that it is *continuous* and is the (continuous) development of a single lasting (fully human) being. The human zygote that actively develops itself is, as I have pointed out, a genetically complete organism directing its own integral organic functioning. As it matures, *in utero* and *ex utero*, it does not "become" a human being, for it is a human being *already*, albeit an immature human being, just as a newborn infant is an immature human being who will undergo quite dramatic growth and development over time.[19]

These considerations undermine the familiar argument, recited by Rubenfeld, that "the potential" of an *unfertilized* ovum to develop into a whole human being does not make it into "a person." The fact is, though, that an ovum is not a whole human being. It is, rather, a part of another human being (the woman whose ovum it is) with merely the potential to give rise to, in interaction with a part of yet another human being (a man's sperm cell), a new and whole human being. Unlike the zygote, it lacks both genetic distinctness and completeness, as well as the active capacity to develop itself into an adult member of the human species. It is living human cellular material, but, left to itself, it will never become a human being, however hospitable its environment may be. It will "die" as a human ovum, just as countless skin cells "die" daily as nothing more than skin cells. If successfully fertilized by a human sperm, which, like the ovum (but dramatically unlike the zygote), lacks the active potential to develop into an adult member of the human species, then *substantial* change (that is, a change of *natures*) will occur. There will no longer be merely an egg, which was part of the mother, sharing her genetic composition, and a sperm, which was part of the father, sharing his genetic composition; instead, there will be a genetically complete, distinct, unified, self-integrating human organism whose nature differs from that of the gametes—not mere human material, but a human being.

These considerations also make clear that it is incorrect to argue (as some pro-choice advocates have argued) that, just as "I" was never a week-old sperm or ovum, "I" was likewise never a week-old embryo. It truly makes no sense to say that "I" was once a sperm (or an unfertilized egg) that matured into an adult. Conception was the occasion of substantial change (that is, change from one complete individual entity to another) that brought into being a distinct self-integrating organism with a specifically human nature. By contrast, it makes every bit as much sense to say that I was once a week-old embryo as to say that I was once a week-old infant or a ten-year-old child. It was the new organism created at conception that, without itself undergoing any change of substance, matured into a week-old embryo, a fetus, an infant, a child, an adolescent, and, finally, an adult.

But Rubenfeld has another argument: "Cloning processes give to non-zygotic cells the potential for development into distinct, self-integrating human beings; thus to recognize the zygote as a human being is to recognize all human cells as human beings, which is absurd."[20]

It is true that a distinct, self-integrating human organism that came into being by a process of cloning would be, like a human organism that comes into being as a monozygotic twin, a human being. That being, no less than human beings conceived by the union of sperm and egg, would possess a human nature and the active potential to mature as a human being. However, even assuming the possibility of cloning human beings from non-zygotic human cells, the non-zygotic cell must be activated by a process that effects substantial change and not mere development or maturation. Left to itself, apart from an activation process capable of effecting a change of substance or natures, the cell will mature and die as a human cell, not as a human being.

THE scientific evidence establishes the fact that each of us was, from conception, a human being. Science, not religion, vindicates this crucial premise of the pro-life claim. From it, there is no avoiding the conclusion that deliberate feticide is a form of homicide. The only real questions remaining are moral and political, not scientific: Although I will not go into the matter here, I do not see how direct abortion can ever be considered a matter of "justified homicide."[21] It is important to recognize, however, as traditional moralists always have recognized, that not all procedures that foreseeably result in fetal death are, properly speaking, abortions. Although any procedure whose precise objective is the destruction of fetal life is certainly an abortion, and cannot be justified, some procedures result in fetal death as an unintended, albeit foreseen and accepted, side effect. Where procedures of the latter sort are done for very grave reasons, they may be justifiable.[22] For example, traditional morality recognizes that a surgical operation to remove a life-threateningly cancerous uterus, even in a woman whose pregnancy is not far enough along to enable the child to be removed from her womb and sustained by a life support system, is ordinarily morally permissible.[23] Of course, there are in this area of moral reflection, as in others, "borderline" cases that are difficult to classify and evaluate. Mercifully, modern medical technology has made such cases exceptionally rare in real life. Only in the most extraordinary circumstances today do women and their families and physicians find it necessary to consider a procedure that will result in fetal death as the only way of preserving maternal life. In any event, the political debate about abortion is not, in reality, about cases of this sort; it is about "elective" or "social indication" abortions, viz., the deliberate destruction of unborn human life for non-therapeutic reasons.

A final point: In my own experience, conversion from the pro-choice to the pro-life cause is often (though certainly not always) a partial cause of religious conversion rather than an effect. Frequently, people who are not religious, or who are only weakly so, begin to have doubts about the moral defensibility of deliberate feticide. Although most of their friends are pro-choice, they find that position increasingly difficult to defend or live with. They perceive practical inconsistencies in their, and their friends', attitudes toward the unborn depending on whether the child is "wanted" or not. Perhaps they find themselves arrested by sonographic (or other even more sophisticated) images of the child's life in the womb. So the doubts begin creeping in. For the first time, they are really prepared to listen to the pro-life argument (often despite their negative attitude toward people—or "the kind of people"—who are pro-life); and somehow, it sounds more compelling than it did before. Gradually, as they become firmly pro-life, they find themselves questioning the whole philosophy of life—in a word, the secularism—associated with their former view. They begin to understand the reasons that led them out of the pro-choice and into the pro-life camp as God's reasons, too.

4

"SAME-SEX MARRIAGE" AND "MORAL NEUTRALITY"

FREQUENTLY I HEAR students (and others) say: "I believe that marriage is a union of one man and one woman. But I think that it is wrong for the state to base its law of marriage on a controversial moral judgment, even if I happen to believe (on religious grounds, perhaps) that judgment to be true. Therefore, I support proposals to revise our law to authorize same-sex 'marriages.'" The thought here is that the state ought to be neutral as between competing understandings of the nature and value of marriage.

Of course, the claim that the law ought to be morally neutral about marriage or anything else is itself a moral claim. As such, *it* is not morally neutral, nor can it rest on an appeal to moral neutrality. People who believe that the law of marriage (and/or other areas of the law) ought to be morally neutral do not assert, nor does their position presuppose, that the law ought to be neutral as between the view that the law ought to be neutral and competing moral views. It is obvious that neutrality between neutrality and non-neutrality is logically impossible. Sophisticated proponents of moral neutrality therefore acknowledge that theirs is a controversial moral position whose truth, soundness, correctness, or, at least, reasonableness, they are prepared to defend against competing moral positions. They assert, in other words, that the best understanding of political morality, at least for societies such as ours, is one that includes a requirement that the law be morally neutral with respect to marriage. Alternative understandings of political morality, insofar as they fail to recognize the principle of moral neutrality, are, they say, mistaken and ought, as such, to be rejected.

Now, to recognize that any justification offered for the requirement of moral neutrality cannot itself be morally neutral is by no means to establish the falsity of the alleged requirement of moral neutrality. My purpose in calling attention to it is not to propose an argument purporting to identify self-referential inconsistency in arguments for moral neutrality. Although I shall argue that the moral neutrality of marriage law to embrace same-sex relationships is neither desirable nor, strictly speaking, possible, I do not propose to show that there is a logical or performative inconsistency in saying that "the law (of marriage) ought to be neutral as between competing moral ideas." It is not like saying "No statement is true." Nor is it like singing "I am not singing." At the same time, the putative requirement of moral neutrality is neither self-evident nor self-justifying. If it is to be vindicated as a true (correct, sound, etc.) proposition of political morality, it needs to be shown to be true (etc.) by a valid argument.

It is certainly the case that implicit in our matrimonial law is a (now controversial) moral judgment: namely, the judgment that marriage is inherently heterosexual—a union of one man and one woman. (In a moment, I'll discuss the deeper grounds of that judgment.) Of course, this is not the only possible moral judgment. In some cultures, polygyny or (far less frequently) polyandry is legally sanctioned. Some historians claim that "marriages" (or their equivalent) between two men or two women have been recognized by certain cultures in the past.[1] However that may be, influential voices in our own culture today demand the revision of matrimonial law to authorize such "marriages."

There are two ways to argue for the proposition that it is unjust for government to refuse to authorize same-sex (and, for that matter, polygamous) "marriages." The first is to deny the reasonableness, soundness, or truth of the moral judgment implicit in the proposition that marriage is a union of one man and one woman. The second is to argue that this moral judgment cannot justly serve as the basis for the public law of matrimony irrespective of its reasonableness, soundness, or even its truth.

In this chapter, I shall mainly be concerned with the second of these ways of arguing. The task I have set for myself is to persuade you that the moral neutrality to which this way of arguing appeals is, and cannot but be, illusory. To that end, however, it will be necessary for me to explain the philosophical grounds of the moral judgment that marriage is inherently heterosexual and monogamous—a union of one man and one woman—and to discuss the arguments advanced by certain critics of traditional matrimonial law in their efforts to undermine this judgment.

HERE is the core of the traditional understanding: Marriage is a two-in-one-flesh communion of persons that is consummated and actualized by acts that are reproductive in type, whether or not they are reproductive in effect (or are motivated, even in part, by a desire to reproduce). The bodily union of spouses in marital acts is the biological matrix of their marriage as a multi-level relationship: that is, a relationship that unites persons at the bodily, emotional, dispositional, and spiritual levels of their being. Marriage, precisely as such a relationship, is naturally ordered to the good of procreation (and to the nurturing and education of children) as well as to the good of spousal unity, and these goods are tightly bound together. The distinctive unity of spouses is possible *because* human (like other mammalian) males and females, by mating, unite organically—they become a single reproductive principle. Although reproduction is a single act, in humans (and other mammals) the reproductive act is performed not by individual members of the species, but by a mated pair as an organic unit. The point has been explained by Germain Grisez:

> Though a male and a female are complete individuals with respect
> to other functions—for example, nutrition, sensation, and loco-
> motion—with respect to reproduction they are only potential parts
> of a mated pair, which is the complete organism capable of repro-
> ducing sexually. Even if the mated pair is sterile, intercourse, pro-
> vided it is the reproductive behavior characteristic of the species,
> makes the copulating male and female one organism.[2]

Although not all reproductive-type acts are marital,[3] there can be no
marital act that is not reproductive in type. Masturbatory, sodomitical, or other sexual acts that are not reproductive in type cannot
unite persons organically: that is, as a single reproductive principle.[4]
Therefore, such acts cannot be intelligibly engaged in for the sake of
marital (i.e., one-flesh, bodily) unity as such. They cannot be marital
acts. Rather, persons who perform such acts must be doing so for
the sake of ends or goals that are extrinsic to themselves as bodily
persons: Sexual satisfaction, or (perhaps) mutual sexual satisfaction,
is sought as a means of releasing tension, or obtaining (and, sometimes, sharing) pleasure, either as an end in itself, or as a means to
some other end, such as expressing affection, esteem, friendliness,
etc. In any case, where one-flesh union cannot (or cannot rightly) be
sought as an end-in-itself, sexual activity necessarily involves the
instrumentalization of the bodies of those participating in such activity to extrinsic ends.

In marital acts, by contrast, the bodies of persons who unite
biologically are not reduced to the status of mere instruments. Rather,
the end, goal, and intelligible point of sexual union is the good of
marriage itself. On this understanding, such union is not a merely
instrumental good, i.e., a reason for action whose intelligibility as a
reason depends on other ends to which it is a means, but is, rather,
an intrinsic good, i.e., a reason for action whose intelligibility as a
reason depends on no such other end. The central and justifying
point of sex is not pleasure (or even the sharing of pleasure) *per se,*
however much sexual pleasure is sought—rightly sought—as an aspect of the perfection of marital union; the point of sex, rather, is

marriage itself, considered as a bodily ("one-flesh") union of persons consummated and actualized by acts that are reproductive in type. Because in marital acts sex is not instrumentalized,[5] such acts are free of the self-alienating and dis-integrating qualities of masturbatory and sodomitical sex. Unlike these and other nonmarital sex acts, marital acts effect no practical dualism which volitionally and, thus, existentially (though, of course, not metaphysically) separates the body from the conscious and desiring aspect of the self which is understood and treated by the acting person as the true self which inhabits and uses the body as its instrument.[6] As John Finnis has observed, marital acts are truly unitive, and in no way self-alienating, because the bodily or biological aspect of human beings is "part of, and not merely an instrument of, their *personal* reality."[7]

But, one may ask, what about procreation? On the traditional view, isn't the sexual union of spouses instrumentalized to the goal of having children? It is true that St. Augustine was an influential proponent of something like this view, and there has always been a certain following for it among Christians. The strict Augustinian position was rejected, however, by the mainstream of philosophical and theological reflection from the late Middle Ages forward, and the understanding of sex and marriage that came to be embodied in both the canon law of the Roman Catholic Church and the civil law of matrimony does not treat marriage as a merely instrumental good. Matrimonial law has traditionally understood marriage as consummated by, and only by, the reproductive-type acts of spouses; by contrast, the sterility of spouses—so long as they are capable of consummating their marriage by a reproductive-type act (and, thus, of achieving bodily, organic unity)—has *never* been treated as an impediment to marriage, even where sterility is certain and even certain to be permanent (as in the case of the marriage of a woman who has been through menopause or has undergone a hysterectomy).[8]

According to the traditional understanding of marriage, then, it is the nature of marital acts as reproductive in type that makes it possible for such acts to be unitive in the distinctively marital way. And this type of unity has intrinsic, and not merely instrumental, value. Thus, the unitive good of marriage provides a noninstrumental (and thus sufficient) reason for spouses to perform sexual acts of a type that consummates and actualizes their marriage. In performing marital acts, the spouses do not reduce themselves as bodily persons (or their marriage) to the status of means or instruments.

At the same time, where marriage is understood as a one-flesh union of persons, children who may be conceived in marital acts are understood not as ends which are extrinsic to marriage (either in the strict Augustinian sense, or the modern liberal one), but, rather, as gifts which supervene on acts whose central justifying point is precisely the marital unity of the spouses.[9] Such acts have unique meaning, value, and significance, as I have already suggested, because they belong to the class of acts by which children come into being—what I have called "reproductive-type acts." More precisely, these acts have their unique meaning, value, and significance because they belong to the *only* class of acts by which children can come into being, not as "products" which their parents choose to "make," but, rather, as perfective participants in the organic community (i.e., the family) that is established by their parents' marriage. It is thus that children are properly understood and treated—even in their conception—not as means to their parents' ends, but as ends-in-themselves; not as *objects* of the desire or will of their parents,[10] but as *subjects* of justice (and inviolable human rights); not as *property,* but as *persons.* It goes without saying that not all cultures have fully grasped these truths about the moral status of children. What is less frequently noticed is that our culture's grasp of these truths is connected to a basic understanding of sex and marriage which is not only fast eroding, but is now under severe assault from people who have no conscious desire to reduce children to the status of mere means, or objects, or property.

IT is sometimes thought that defenders of traditional marriage law deny the possibility of something whose possibility critics of the law affirm. "Love," these critics say, "makes a family." And it is committed love that justifies homosexual sex as much as it justifies heterosexual sex. If marriage is the proper, or best, context for sexual love, the argument goes, then marriage should be made available to loving, committed same-sex as well as opposite-sex partners on terms of strict equality. To think otherwise is to suppose that same-sex partners cannot really love each other, or love each other in a committed way, or that the orgasmic "sexual expression" of their love is somehow inferior to the orgasmic "sexual expression" of couples who "arrange the plumbing differently."

In fact, however, at the bottom of the debate is a possibility that defenders of traditional marriage law affirm and its critics deny, namely, the possibility of marriage as a one-flesh communion of persons. The denial of this possibility is central to any argument designed to show that the moral judgment at the heart of the traditional understanding of marriage as inherently heterosexual is unreasonable, unsound, or untrue. If reproductive-type acts in fact unite spouses interpersonally, as traditional sexual morality and marriage law suppose, then such acts differ fundamentally in meaning, value, and significance from the only types of sexual acts that can be performed by same-sex partners.

Liberal sexual morality which denies that marriage is inherently heterosexual necessarily supposes that the value of sex must be instrumental *either* to procreation *or* to pleasure, considered, in turn, as an end-in-itself or as a means of expressing affection, tender feelings, etc. Thus, proponents of the liberal view suppose that homosexual sex acts are indistinguishable from heterosexual acts whenever the motivation for such acts is something other than procreation. The sexual acts of homosexual partners, that is to say, are indistinguishable in motivation, meaning, value, and significance from the marital acts of spouses who know that at least one spouse is temporarily or permanently infertile. Thus, the liberal argument goes, traditional matrimonial law is guilty of unfairness in treating sterile heterosexuals as capable of marrying while treating homosexual partners as ineligible to marry.

Stephen Macedo has accused the traditional view and its defenders of precisely this alleged "double standard." He asks:

> What is the point of sex in an infertile marriage? Not procreation: the partners (let us assume) know that they are infertile. If they have sex, it is for pleasure and to express their love, or friendship, or some other shared good. It will be for precisely the same reason that committed, loving gay couples have sex.[11]

But Macedo's criticism fails to tell against the traditional view because it presupposes as true precisely what the traditional view denies, namely, that the value (and, thus, the point) of sex in marriage can only be instrumental. On the contrary, it is a central tenet of the traditional view that the value (and point) of sex is the *intrinsic* good of marriage itself which is actualized in sexual acts which unite spouses biologically and, thus, interpersonally. The traditional view rejects the instrumentalization of sex (and, thus, of the bodies of sexual partners) to any extrinsic end. This does not mean that procreation and pleasure are not rightly sought in marital acts; it means merely that they are rightly sought when they are integrated with the basic good and justifying point of marital sex, namely, the one-flesh union of marriage itself.

It is necessary, therefore, for critics of traditional matrimonial law to argue that the apparent one-flesh unity that distinguishes marital acts from sodomitical acts is illusory, and, thus, that the apparent bodily communion of spouses in reproductive-type acts—which, according to the traditional view, form the biological matrix of their marital relationship—is not really possible.

And so Richard Posner declares that Finnis's claim that "the union of reproductive organs of husband and wife unites them biologically" is unclear in its meaning and moral relevance, and cannot "distinguish...sterile marriage, at least when the couple *knows* that it is incapable of reproducing, from homosexual coupling."[12] Turning to my own claim that "intercourse, so long as it is the reproductive behavior characteristic of the species, unites the copulating male and female as a single organism," Posner asserts that "[i]ntercourse known by the participants to be sterile is not 'reproductive behavior,' and even reproductive intercourse does not unite the participants 'as a single organism.'"[13]

On the question of "reproductive behavior" or, better, the idea of "reproductive-type" acts, it is important to see that identical behavior can cause conception or not depending entirely on whether the nonbehavioral conditions of reproduction obtain. And the intrinsic, and not merely instrumental, good of marital communion gives spouses reason to fulfill the behavioral conditions of procreation even in circumstances in which they know the nonbehavioral conditions do not obtain. This is true just in case the fulfillment of the behavioral conditions of reproduction is, in truth, unitive. So the question is whether Posner is right to deny what Finnis, Grisez, and I affirm: namely, that reproductive-type acts unite a male and female as a single organism, viz., make them "two-in-one-flesh."

It is, it seems to me, a plain biological fact that, as Grisez says, reproduction is a single function, yet it is carried out not by an individual male or female human being, but by a male and female as a mated pair. So, in respect of reproduction, albeit not in other respects (again, like locomotion or digestion), the mated pair is a single organism, the partners form a single reproductive principle, they become "one flesh." So, I would ask Judge Posner, what is there not to understand?[14] The issue is not one of translating medieval Latin; it is a matter of simple biology. Of course, the question remains, is there any particular value to the biological (organic) union of spouses. And one will judge the matter one way or another depending, for example, on whether one understands the biological reality of human beings, as Finnis says, as part of, rather than a mere instrument of, their personal reality. But as to the fact of biological unity, there is no room for doubt. As to its moral implications, I suspect that Posner's difficulty is simply a specific instance of his general skepticism regarding the possibility of noninstrumental practical reasons and reasoning. If pressed to deal with the question, Posner would no doubt deny that the biological reality of human beings is anything more than an instrument of ends which are themselves given by feelings, emotions, desire, or other subrational motivating factors. As I have elsewhere sought to show, the implicit operating premise of

Posner's treatment of sex, and other moral questions, is the Humean noncognitivist understanding of practical reason as the "slave of the passions."[15] Marital communion cannot be a noninstrumental reason so far as Posner is concerned, because, on this account, there are no noninstrumental reasons.

Steven Macedo, by contrast, is no Humean. He rejects Posner's instrumentalist understanding of practical reason. Still, Macedo claims that "the 'one-flesh communion' of sterile couples would appear...to be more a matter of appearance than reality." Because of their sterility such couples cannot really unite biologically: "their bodies, like those of homosexuals, can form no 'single reproductive principle,' no real unity."[16] Indeed, Macedo argues that even fertile couples who conceive children in acts of sexual intercourse do not truly unite biologically, because, he asserts, "penises and vaginas do not unite biologically, sperm and eggs do."[17]

John Finnis has aptly replied that

> in this reductivist, word-legislating mood, one might declare that sperm and egg unite only physically and only their pronuclei are biologically united. But it would be more realistic to acknowledge that the whole process of copulation, involving as it does the brains of the man and woman, their nerves, blood, vaginal and other secretions, and coordinated activity is biological through and through.[18]

Moreover, as Finnis points out,

> the organic unity which is instantiated in an act of the reproductive kind is not, as Macedo...reductively imagine[s], the unity of penis and vagina. It is the unity of the persons in the intentional, consensual *act* of seminal emission/reception in the woman's reproductive tract.[19]

The unity to which Finnis refers—unity of body, sense, emotion, reason, and will—is, in my view, central to our understanding of humanness itself. Yet it is a unity of which Macedo and others who deny the possibility of true marital communion can give no account. For this denial presupposes a dualism of "person" (as conscious and desiring self), on the one hand, and "body" (as instrument of the conscious and desiring self), on the other, which is flatly incompatible with this unity. Dualism is implicit in the idea, central to Macedo's denial of the possibility of one-flesh marital union, that sodomitical acts differ from what I have described as acts of the reproductive type only as a matter of the arrangement of the "plumbing." According to this idea, the genital organs of an infertile woman (and, of course, all women are infertile most of the time) or of an infertile man are not really "reproductive organs"—any more than, say, mouths, rectums, tongues, or fingers are reproductive organs. Thus, the intercourse of a man and a woman where at least one partner is temporarily or permanently sterile cannot really be an act of the reproductive type.

But the plain fact is that the genitals of men and women are reproductive organs all of the time—even during periods of sterility. *And acts that fulfill the behavioral conditions of reproduction are acts of the reproductive-type even where the nonbehavioral conditions of reproduction do not happen to obtain.* Insofar as the point or object of sexual intercourse is marital union, the partners achieve the desired unity (i.e., become "two-in-one-flesh") precisely insofar as they mate, that is, fulfill the behavioral conditions of reproduction, or, if you will, perform the type of act—the only type of act—upon which the gift of a child may supervene.[20]

The dualistic presuppositions of the liberal position are fully on display in the frequent references by Macedo and other proponents of the position to sexual organs as "equipment." Neither sperm nor eggs, neither penises nor vaginas, are properly conceived in such impersonal terms. Nor are they "used" by persons considered as somehow standing over and apart from these and other aspects of their biological reality. The biological reality of persons is, rather, part of their personal reality. (Hence, where a person treats his body as a subpersonal object, the practical dualism he thereby effects brings with it a certain self-alienation, a damaging of the intrinsic good of personal self-integration.) In any event, the biological union of persons—which is effected in reproductive type acts but not in sodomitical ones—really is an interpersonal ("one-flesh") communion.

Now, Macedo considers the possibility that defenders of the traditional understanding are right about all this: that marriage truly is a "one-flesh union" consummated and actualized by marital acts; that sodomitical and other intrinsically nonmarital sexual acts really are self-alienating and, as such, immoral; that the true conception of marriage is one according to which it is an intrinsically heterosexual (and, one might here add, monogamous) relationship. But even if the traditional understanding of marriage is the morally correct one—even if it is true—he argues, the state cannot justly recognize it as such. For, if disagreements about the nature of marriage "lie in...difficult philosophical quarrels, about which reasonable people have long disagreed, then our differences lie in precisely the territory that John Rawls rightly marks off as inappropriate to the fashioning of our basic rights and liberties."[21] And from this it follows that government must remain neutral as between conceptions of marriage as intrinsically heterosexual (and monogamous) and conceptions according to which "marriages" may be contracted not only between a man and a woman, but also between two men or two women (and, presumably, a man or a woman and multiple male and/or female "spouses"). Otherwise, according to Macedo, the state would "inappropriately" be "deny[ing] people fundamental aspects of equality based on reasons and arguments whose force can only be appreciated by those who accept difficult to assess [metaphysical and moral] claims."[22]

It seems to me, however, that something very much like the contrary is true. Because the true meaning, value, and significance of marriage are fairly easily grasped (even if people sometimes have difficulty living up to its moral demands) where a culture—including, critically, a legal culture—promotes and supports a sound understanding of marriage, both formally and informally, and because ideologies and practices which are hostile to a sound understanding and practice of marriage in a culture tend to undermine the institution of marriage in that culture, thus making it difficult for large numbers of people to grasp the true meaning, value, and significance of marriage, it is extremely important that government eschew attempts to be "neutral" with regard to competing conceptions of marriage and try hard to embody in its law and policy the soundest, most nearly correct conception. Moreover, any effort to achieve neutrality will inevitably prove to be self-defeating. For the law is a teacher. And it will teach *either* that marriage is a reality that people can choose to participate in, but whose contours people cannot make and remake at will (e.g., a one-flesh communion of persons consummated and actualized by acts which are reproductive in type and perfected, where all goes well, in the generation, education, and nurturing of children in a context—the family—which is uniquely suitable to their well-being), *or* the law will teach that marriage is a mere convention which is malleable in such a way that individuals, couples, or, indeed, groups, can choose to make it whatever suits their desires, interests, subjective goals, etc. The result, given the biases of human sexual psychology, will be the development of practices and ideologies which truly do tend to undermine the sound understanding and practice of marriage, together with the pathologies that tend to reinforce the very practices and ideologies that cause them.

Joseph Raz, though himself a liberal who does not share my views regarding homosexuality or sexual morality generally, is rightly critical of forms of liberalism, including Rawlsianism, which suppose that law and government can and should be neutral with respect to competing conceptions of morality. In this regard, he has noted that "monogamy, assuming that it is the only valuable form of marriage, cannot be practiced by an individual. It requires a culture which recognizes it, and which supports it through the public's attitude and through its formal institutions."[23] Now, Raz does not suppose that, in a culture whose law and public morality do not support monogamy, someone who happens to believe in it somehow will be unable to restrict himself to having one wife or will be required to take additional wives. His point, rather, is that even if monogamy is a key element of a sound understanding of marriage, large numbers of people will fail to understand that or why that is the case—and will therefore fail to grasp the value of monogamy and the intelligible point of practicing it—unless they are assisted by a culture that supports, formally and informally, monogamous marriage. And what is true of monogamy is equally true of the other marks or aspects of a morally sound understanding of marriage. In other words, marriage is the type of good that can be participated in, or fully participated in, only by people who properly understand it and choose it with a proper understanding in mind; yet people's ability properly to understand it, and thus to choose it, depends upon institutions and cultural understandings that transcend individual choice.

But what about Macedo's claim that when matrimonial law deviates from neutrality by embodying the moral judgment that marriage is inherently heterosexual it denies same-sex partners who wish to marry "fundamental aspects of equality?" Does a due regard for equality require moral neutrality? Well, I think that the appeal to neutrality actually does not work here. If the moral judgment that marriage is inherently heterosexual is false, then the reason for recognizing same-sex marriages is that such unions are as a matter of moral fact indistinguishable from marriages of the traditional type. If, however, the moral judgment that marriage is inherently heterosexual is true, then Macedo's claim that the recognition of this truth by government "denies fundamental aspects of equality" simply cannot be sustained. If, in other words, the marital acts of spouses consummate and actualize marriage as a one-flesh communion, and serve thereby as the biological matrix of the relationship of marriage at all its levels, then the embodiment in law and policy of an understanding of marriage as inherently heterosexual denies no one fundamental aspects of equality.

True, persons who are exclusively homosexually oriented lack a psychological prerequisite to enter into marital relationships. But this is no fault of the law. Indeed, the law would embody a lie (and a damaging one insofar as it truly would contribute to the undermining of the sound understanding and practice of marriage in a culture) if it were to pretend that a marital relationship could be formed on the basis of, and integrated around, sodomitical or other intrinsically nonmarital (and, as such, self-alienating) sex acts.

It is certainly unjust arbitrarily to deny legal marriage to persons who are capable of performing marital acts and entering into the marital relationship. So, for example, laws forbidding interracial marriages truly were violations of equality. Contrary to the published claims of Andrew Sullivan, Andrew Koppelman, and others, however, laws that embody the judgment that marriage is intrinsically heterosexual are in no way analogous to laws against miscegenation. Laws forbidding whites to marry blacks were unjust, not because they embodied a particular moral view and thus violated the alleged requirement of moral neutrality; rather, they were unjust because they embodied an unsound (indeed a grotesquely false) moral view—one that was racist and, as such, immoral.

A sound law of marriage is not one that aspires to moral neutrality; it is one that is in line with moral truth.

5

THE CONCEPT OF PUBLIC MORALITY

PUBLIC MORALITY, like public health and safety, is a concern that goes beyond considerations of law and public policy. Public morals are affected, for good or ill, by the activities of private (in the sense of "nongovernmental") parties, and such parties have obligations in respect to them. The acts of private parties—indeed, sometimes even the apparently private acts of private parties—can and do have public consequences. And choices to do things that one knows will bring about these consequences, whether directly or indirectly (in any of the relevant senses of "directly" and "indirectly") are governed by moral norms, including, above all, norms of justice. Such norms will often constitute conclusive reasons for private parties to refrain from actions that produce harmful public consequences.

Let us for just a moment lay aside the issue of public morality and focus instead on matters of public health and safety. Even apart from laws prohibiting the creation of fire hazards, for example, individuals have an obligation to avoid placing persons and property in jeopardy of fire. Similarly, even apart from legal liability in tort for unreasonably subjecting people to toxic pollutants, companies are under an obligation in justice to avoid freely spewing forth, say, carcinogenic smoke from their factories. Concerns for public health and safety are, to be sure, justificatory grounds of criminal and civil laws; but they also ground moral obligations that obtain even apart from laws or in their absence.

What is true of public health and safety is equally true of public morals. Take, as an example, the problem of pornography. Material designed to appeal to the prurient interest in sex by arousing carnal desire unintegrated with the procreative and unitive goods of marriage, where it flourishes, damages a community's moral ecology in ways analogous to those in which carcinogenic smoke spewing from a factory's stacks damages the community's physical ecology.

The central harm of pornography is not, as some people—especially some American judges—seem to suppose, that it shocks and offends people, any more than the central harm of carcinogenic smoke is that it smells bad. Rather, the central harm of pornography is moral harm—harm to character, and thus to the human goods and institutions, such as the good and institution of marriage, that are preserved and advanced by the disposition to act uprightly, and damaged and defiled by a contrary disposition, in respect to them. So the analogy is with the harmful impact of carcinogenic pollutants on the physical health of people subjected to them. And just as companies have an obligation in justice quite apart from considerations of legal liability to avoid damaging people's health by polluting the air, so, too, people have an obligation in justice even apart from legal prohibition to avoid harming people's character (and the goods and institutions that depend on widespread good character) by producing and disseminating pornographic materials.

Of course, an objection will immediately be raised. Pornography, it will be said, is unlike toxic environmental pollutants, even if it is true that pornography is morally bad in the way I have asserted. The difference is that members of a community *cannot* avoid breathing carcinogens that are spewed forth by a factory's smokestacks (except by leaving town); but they *can* avoid the morally harmful effects of pornography simply by declining to purchase and look at it. So, the argument goes, environmental polluters *really* do an injustice in spewing carcinogenic and other toxic pollutants into the air; pornographers, however, do no injustice to those who, after all, freely choose to subject themselves to their offerings. (This counterargument is ordinarily raised in connection with the question whether *laws* against pornography are justified, but let us consider it here simply on its own merits and, for the moment, apart from questions of legal regulation.)

This counterargument does not succeed. First of all, it can be, and often is, unjust to subject people to powerful temptations to do things that are harmful to them, morally or otherwise, and whether or not they are cognizant of the harm. It seems to me mere liberal superstition to hold otherwise. Second, and even more importantly, the accumulation of private decisions to use pornography affects— sometimes profoundly—the community as a whole. For example, where pornography flourishes, as it does in our own culture, it erodes important shared public understandings of sexuality and sexual morality on which the health of the institutions of marriage and family life in any culture vitally depend. This is a classic case in which the accumulation of apparently private choices of private parties has big public consequences.

So, the pornographer, though a private party, fails in respect of his duties in justice to public morality, just as the environmental polluter—ordinarily motivated by the same consideration, that is, money—fails in respect of his duties to public health. And pornographers are not alone among the private parties whose unjust actions damage public morality: people who write and pose for pornographic publications and films, people who distribute pornography and make it available in newsstands, bookstores, theaters, and video shops, and, notably, people who purchase pornography (thus sustaining the industries that produce and disseminate it), and even those who in noncommercial contexts circulate it to friends, fellow workers, and other acquaintances.

THERE is much more to be said about pornography and public morality, and later in this chapter I will say a little in relation to a

particular species of liberal argument against public morals legislation. I have introduced the subject here only for purposes of illus-
trating the first point I wanted to make: namely, that public morality is not simply an issue about what laws we should have. Nor is it a
concern that has no bearing on the moral deliberations and obligations of private parties, as opposed to public officials. The common
good of public morality, that is, the good of a healthy moral ecology,
generates obligations in justice for all of us, just as do the common
goods of public health and safety.

Now let me make a second point, namely, that law and government play a secondary (or "subsidiary") role in upholding public
morality. The primary role is played by families, religious communities, organizations such as the Boy Scouts, and other institutions
that, by working closely with individuals, inculcate an understanding of morality and promote virtue. Even though public morality is a
public good, its maintenance depends far more on contributions of
private institutions than on those of law and government. Where
families, churches, and other institutions of civil society fail (or are
unable) to play their parts, laws will hardly suffice to preserve public
morals. Ordinarily, at least, law's role is to *support* families, churches,
and the like. And, of course, law goes wrong when it displaces these
institutions and usurps their authority. At the same time, the role of
law in upholding public morality is undermined by families, churches,
and other institutions who abdicate their responsibilities or, even
worse, promote false and morally destructive practices.

Consider the current turmoil over marriage. If, as I believe, the
good of marriage and its institutional integrity in our society depend on a firm understanding of, and public commitment to, marriage as a sexual union of one man and one woman, then a threat to
marriage can come either from bad public policy or the misguided
actions of key nongovernmental associations (or both). On the one
hand, law and public policy, in the name of a false neutrality, could
undermine marriage by authorizing as marriages or their equivalent
intrinsically nonmarital (e.g., same-sex or polygamous) sexual relationships. In so doing, law and policy would make it immeasurably

more difficult for families, churches, and other institutions of civil society to fulfill their primary role in upholding public morals in respect to marriage. On the other hand, even where the law maintains a sound doctrine of marriage, the institutional integrity of marriage could be gravely damaged by, for example, churches that, in the name of whatever moral or theological principle, bless same-sex or polygamous unions, or companies that treat employees' nonmarital sexual partners as "spouses."

Of course, the validity of what I am saying about marriage per se entirely depends on whether I am right about its true nature. However, my point about public morality holds even if I am wrong about marriage. Suppose I *am* wrong. Suppose that the true understanding of marriage extends to a range of possibilities including same-sex and polygamous relationships, and that it is mere bigotry that stands in the way of my perceiving this truth. In that case, public morals regarding marriage can be damaged either by laws unreasonably restricting marriage (as did anti-miscegenation laws that both reflected and reinforced racism in an earlier day) or by churches whose theologies and disciplines pertaining to marriage embody and promote bigotry.

What I have written so far is the sum and substance of what I have to say here about the obligations in justice of private parties to avoid damaging public morality and the primary role and responsibility of nongovernmental institutions in inculcating virtue and, thus, upholding public morals. I hope that the preceding helps to elucidate the concept of public morality by detaching it from the question of law's part in protecting it. Now, however, let's turn to that much-debated question.[1]

As traditionally conceived, the "police powers" of governments of general jurisdiction extend to the protection and advancement of public health, safety, *and morals*. Particularly in the American setting, where, as a constitutional matter, power is shared between state governments of general jurisdiction and a national government of delegated and enumerated powers, it is important to bear in mind the distinction between the two. Governments of the former sort exercise police powers, including the police power to protect and promote public morals; governments of the latter sort do not, except to the extent that such governments are constitutionally empowered to act in a certain domain to combat particular threats to public health, safety, and morals.

What is meant by governments of "general jurisdiction"? Such governments are constitutionally empowered to act by way of legislation, regulation, and the like to preserve and advance the common good of the polities they serve, subject only to limitations constitutionally imposed on the scope of their power. (Of course, such empowerment and limitations are in some cases expressly set forth in written constitutions. In other cases, however, they are either implied by written constitutions or take the form of unwritten constitutional principles.)

In the United States, the governments of the states are, in form, at least, governments of general jurisdiction. They exercise police powers legally subject only to state or federal constitutional limitations on the scope of their authority. So, for example, in Massachusetts and other states whose constitutions include "Blaine Amendments," state governments are disempowered from using public funds to support religiously affiliated primary and secondary schools. In addition to such state constitutional limits on the powers of state governments, the Constitution of the United States imposes certain limits: for example, Article 1, Section 10 forbids states from entering into treaties, granting letters of marque and reprisal, coining money, granting titles of nobility, passing bills of attainder, ex post facto laws, and laws impairing the obligation of contracts. In addition to these express limitations, the Supreme Court of the United States claims to have discovered in the federal Constitution implied limitations of the police powers of states that forbid them from, for example, prohibiting or significantly restricting abortion, limiting what a candidate can spend from his own resources on a political campaign, and making it an offense to desecrate the American flag. Whatever one thinks of the validity of these rulings, it is plain that in the absence of express or implied constitutional limitations, any state, as a government of general jurisdiction, would be legally empowered to support religious schools, release people from contractual obligations, grant titles of nobility, limit campaign spending, restrict abortion, and prohibit flag desecration.

In this respect, the governments of the states differ markedly—again, in form, at least—from the government of the United States. The latter government is not a government of general jurisdiction; it is not constitutionally authorized to exercise police powers. On the contrary, it is a government of delegated and enumerated powers. Where the states are *generally* authorized to act for the sake of the common good, enjoying the authority to act *except* to the extent that their jurisdiction is constitutionally limited, the federal government may, as a constitutional matter, act *only where it has been constitutionally delegated the power to act.* Again, this delegation can be express or implied. Article 1, Section 8 of the Constitution of the United States expressly delegates to the Congress power to coin money, to establish a Post Office, to declare war, to create armies and a navy, and do various other things. The same section authorizes Congress to "make all Laws necessary and proper for carrying into Execution the foregoing Powers...." So, the Supreme Court long ago held that the chartering by Congress of a national bank, though nowhere mentioned among the enumerated powers of the national government, was "necessary and proper" to the execution of certain powers expressly delegated to that government by the Constitution. So, too, we must suppose, the power to create and maintain a welfare system and a system of social security. Again, for our purposes it does not matter whether one agrees with the Court's rather expansive interpretation of the implied powers of the government of the United States. The point is that, as a government of delegated powers, the United States may lawfully do *only* those things it is—expressly or impliedly—constitutionally empowered to do.

Since the Constitution originally contained no authorization of federal income taxation without apportionment among the several states, proponents of the income tax found it necessary to amend the Constitution, as they succeeded in doing in 1913, to confer this power on the national government. However desirable its proponents judged the income tax to be as a means of preserving or enhancing the welfare of the nation, they could not simply put an income tax bill through Congress. It was necessary for them first to bring into being by amendment a constitutional delegation of the power to impose the tax. Likewise the prohibition of intoxicating liquors. Prior to the ratification of the Eighteenth Amendment to the Constitution in 1919, the federal government, lacking police powers, had no authority to regulate or prohibit the sale of alcoholic beverages. One year after ratification, according to the terms of the amendment, "the manufacture, sale, or transportation of intoxicating liquors within, the importation thereof into, or the exportation thereof from the United States" was constitutionally prohibited, and Congress was empowered to legislate concurrently with the states to enforce this constitutional prohibition. There the matter rested until a thirsty America effected repeal of the Eighteenth Amendment by the Twenty-First in 1933. Repeal, in turn, restored public policy decisions regarding regulation of alcoholic beverages to the states, which, as governments of general jurisdiction, were free to exercise their police powers as they saw fit to regulate (and even prohibit) alcohol in the interests of public health, safety, and morals.

Of course, the century just concluded witnessed a massive expansion of the power of the national government, largely at the expense of the states. Formal constitutional amendment, as with the income tax, is one way this happened. More often, however, the courts (after some initial resistance in the New Deal era) and the American people as a whole simply acquiesced in the federal government's claims to be exercising implied delegated powers (as, for example, with the federal welfare and Social Security systems). As we enter the new century, the delegated powers doctrine, as a limitation on the jurisdiction of the national government, seems as false in practice as it is true in theory. For all *practical* purposes, the government of the United States functions as a government of *general* jurisdiction, more or less freely exercising what can only be termed police powers. Of course, the formalities associated with the delegated powers doctrine continue to be observed: Whenever, and for whatever reason, Congress acts, it purports to do so under some power granted to it by the Constitution—ordinarily the power to regulate commerce among the several states. True, the Supreme Court has found an occasion or two in the last decade to invalidate acts of Congress as overstepping the delegated powers of the national government; by and large, however, the federal government acts as a government of general jurisdiction constrained only by those limitations expressly or impliedly set forth in the Constitution, such as provisions forbidding the government from establishing religious tests for public office, prohibiting the free exercise of religion, abridging the freedom of speech, conducting unreasonable searches and seizures, and imposing excessive fines.

The federal government's effective exercise of police powers is evident in a variety of areas of public health and safety. Federal environmental laws, occupational safety and health regulations, and so forth preempt state legislation across a vast swath of terrain and, for better or worse, affect all of us every day. Even in areas of public morality the federal government has taken on a role. The classic instance was the Mann Act prohibiting the transportation of women across state lines for immoral purposes (that is, prostitution). Similarly, Congress has prohibited the use of the mails for the distribution of obscene materials, including child pornography, and is attempting, albeit so far unsuccessfully in the face of judicial resistance, to restrict children's access to indecent material on the Internet. And there are other examples.

Whether it is the federal or state governments exercising the police power to protect public morality, what is the nature of the power? As an abstract matter of political morality, what is its justification? Putting aside the specifics of contemporary interpretation, what is its scope and what are its limits?

LET'S return to the question I began to explore earlier: What is public morality? One way of understanding it is simply as morality—the moral uprightness of individual people and the associations they form—considered insofar as it is a public good. But morality of what sort? Political morality, that is, the principles and norms of right and wrong as they pertain to the establishment of a system of government and to the government's actions, is, in an obvious sense, a public good. It is certainly for the common good—indeed, it is a strict requirement of the common good of political society—that a just system of government be established and maintained and that the government act justly. But political morality is not what the government upholds—it is not the public good for whose sake a government of general jurisdiction acts—when it successfully exercises its police power to protect public morality. Public morals legislation does not regulate the government or governmental actors, as such. Rather, it regulates the behavior of individuals—citizens and those residing permanently or temporarily within the government's jurisdiction. It limits *their* choices and behaviors. But, insofar as these are private (that is to say, nongovernmental) actors, in what sense do these regulations protect a public good?

As we have seen, public morals laws, like health and safety regulations, regulate private conduct insofar as it harms, or threatens to harm, the public interest. Now, here it is important to avoid confusion. Sometimes, the term "private," when used to describe or classify conduct, is meant to refer to conduct that does not bear on the public interest, or that is not legitimately subject to government prohibition or restriction even if it does affect the public interest. The term thus figures in accounts of, or arguments about, political morality. Typically, it is invoked as part of a claim about the alleged injustice of certain acts of government that, say, violate the right of the individual against certain forms of regulation—including morals laws. Such laws, it is commonly asserted, violate citizens' "constitutional liberty," or "right to privacy," or "right to moral independence." Obviously, this is not how I am here using the term. Rather, I use it to refer to conduct by individuals or groups acting as private parties, as opposed to those exercising the power of the state.

Now this is not to suggest that the actions of governments cannot harm public morality. Nothing could be further from the truth. And I have in mind here not merely the failure of government prudently to act where it can to protect public morality against the damaging acts of private parties. That is certainly one thing. Another thing, however, is government action that itself positively undermines public morals by, for example, encouraging and facilitating immoral acts by private citizens. If prostitution, for example, is, as I believe it to be, a wicked practice, then the governments of some municipalities in the Netherlands undermine public morality by (assuming, as I do with the greatest caution, that the *New York Times* is to be believed) providing free prostitutes to physically disabled (though evidently not too physically disabled) men (and, I have no doubt, women) who request them. But, of course, no government is going to legislate against its own bad moral judgments. However bizarre the Dutch policy, it would be even more peculiar to find the Dutch governments concerned enacting morals legislation to prohibit themselves from providing prostitutes (though there wouldn't be anything odd about the people of the Netherlands, were they so inclined, constitutionally prohibiting their governments from getting up to such shenanigans). If the Dutch governments saw the thing rightly from the moral point of view, there would be no need for legislation; they would simply discontinue the policy of providing prostitutes.

Staying with the example of prostitution—a classic subject of morals laws—let us think further about what public good is damaged, what public harm is done, by the provision of prostitutes, whether by governments in the grip of sexual-liberationist ideology or by private businessmen motivated by greed.

Assuming, again, that prostitution is indeed immoral, then the availability of prostitutes is going to facilitate immoral acts by individuals—prostitutes and their customers. Of course, the commercial sex acts will likely take place in "private," that is, behind closed doors, and it could be the case that there is no highly visible publicizing of the prostitutes' availability (though unless there is some way of getting the word out publicly, there won't be much work for the prostitutes). Still, *public* interests are damaged. The public has an interest in men not engaging prostitutes: for when they do, they damage their own characters; they render themselves less solid and reliable as husbands and fathers; they weaken their marriages and their ability to enter into good marriages and authentically model for others (including their children) the virtue of chastity on which the integrity of marriages and of marriage as an institution in any given society depends; they set bad examples for others. In short, they damage what I have referred to as the community's "moral ecology"—an ecology as vital to the community's well-being, and, as such, as integral to the public interest, as the physical ecology which is protected by environmental laws enacted pursuant to the police powers to protect public health.

Now, the question arises as to the scope of the police power to protect public morality. Much of what I've said about the harm of prostitution applies equally to fornication and adultery. And, to be sure, public morals legislation has traditionally forbidden these vices, just as it has forbidden prostitution. However, some people argue that while the legal prohibition of prostitution is legitimately within the scope of the police powers, the prohibition of fornication and adultery is not. The latter vices, however wicked and destructive of important public interests, are truly private, at least insofar as they are engaged in by consenting adults. Apparently, the view is that it is the commercial aspect of prostitution that makes the immoral acts of consenting adults in this case an issue of *public,* as opposed to purely *private,* morality.

It is, of course, true that prostitutes and their pimps are inviting and doing business with "the public" in a way that ordinary fornicators and adulterers are not. And I can certainly see how this distinction could be relevant to the prudential reasoning of legislators considering enactment or repeal of legal prohibitions of noncommercial sexual vice. What I cannot see, however, is the ground for claiming *that a strict principle of justice* excludes the criminal prohibition of noncommercial sexual vice. The reasons for prohibition—namely, the protection a community's moral ecology against the corrosive effects on marriage and family life of vices such as fornication and adultery—may be defeated by competing prudential considerations; but where they are not defeated by such considerations, no principle of justice of which I am aware provides a trumping reason.

Needless to say, a great many people believe the contrary. Some doubt that there is anything morally wrong with any type of sex act between consenting adults. Where there is no coercion or, perhaps, dishonesty involved, they find nothing morally objectionable against prostitution, much less adultery and fornication. If such acts tend to undermine the institutions of marriage and the family, as these institutions are traditionally understood, then so much the worse for these institutions. These institutions are, in any event, in need of transformation, partisans of sexual liberation insist, in light of a new, "uninhibited," more "enlightened" and "inclusive" morality. Well, perhaps you will excuse my ignoring people who see things this way for present purposes. If they are correct, then traditional public morals legislation, at least insofar as it pertains to what has been considered sexual vice, is misguided at its root. And the reason for not enforcing by law traditional concepts of sexual morality is that these concepts are themselves unsound. Of course, I think people who suppose that prostitution, adultery, fornication, and the like are morally innocent are profoundly mistaken, and I have set forth my reasons for so thinking at great length in various publications.[2] I shall not repeat my arguments here.

The more interesting moral criticisms of the criminal prohibition of vices like adultery and fornication come from people who agree, or are, at least, willing to grant for the sake of argument, that these are in fact vices. The most familiar form of argument along these lines appeals to the idea of a basic individual moral right to "autonomy," "privacy," or "moral independence." Why is it allegedly wrong to criminalize fornication? Because, it is asserted, people have a right to fornicate—a "moral right to do wrong." Perhaps this is because fornication is a "private" matter. The trouble here, though, is that fornication is one of those vices that, when widely practiced, tolerated, and, inevitably, accepted, has very big and very public consequences—consequences that provide a perfectly intelligible reason for legal proscription, or, short of that, non-coercive public efforts to discourage it.

To his credit, Ronald Dworkin candidly acknowledges that apparently private vices—including vices, such as pornography, to which he believes people have a moral right—can and do damage the public interest. And Dworkin does not propose to derive rights to such vices from a general right to liberty or autonomy. He doesn't believe in any such general right. Government restricts liberty and autonomy all the time without touching upon, much less violating, anybody's rights. For Dworkin, it is a basic right to equality—a right of individuals to be treated by government with equal concern and respect—that grounds a right of moral independence that provides the principled, moral reason for government to refrain from criminalizing pornography (or, a Dworkinian might easily argue, adultery, fornication, and even prostitution), despite its harm to the public interest.[3]

Dworkin maintains that government violates the basic right to equal concern and respect when it restricts liberty on the ground that one citizen's conception of what makes for or detracts from a valuable and morally worthy way of life is superior to another citizen's conception. For example, in forbidding pornography, the government limits Larry Flynt's liberty—unjustly, by hypothesis—on the ground that Billy Graham's view of whether pornography is wicked or harmless is the correct one. Of course, Dworkin does not claim that the government's error is in supposing that there *is* a right answer to the moral question of pornography, or even that it is Graham, rather than Flynt, who has the right answer. Indeed, he candidly—and rightly—concedes that pornography, where it is permitted to flourish, makes the community worse off in very concrete moral respects, namely, it

> sharply limit[s] the ability of individuals consciously and reflectively to influence the conditions of their own and their children's development. It limit[s] their ability to bring about the cultural structure that they think best, a structure in which sexual experience in general has dignity and beauty, without which their own and their families' experience are likely to have these qualities in less degree.[4]

As I say, Dworkin is right to concede what he concedes about the way in which pornography (and we might add other forms of sexual vice) damages the community's moral ecology—and thus the public interest. The trouble is that, having made these concessions, his argument from the principle of equality falls apart. The basic problem is that legislators and other officials who act on the proposition that pornography, for example, is damaging to the community in the way Dworkin concedes it is, are not judging between Larry Flynt and Billy Graham, or even the moral convictions of Larry Flynt and Billy Graham, *inasmuch as they are Flynt's and Graham's.* They are acting, assuming (as Dworkin does) that they are responsible, conscientious officials, on *their* best judgment as to whether and how pornography is bad. They are not banning pornography because *Flynt is for it* or *Graham is against it.* Nor does Dworkin imagine that that is *why* they are banning it. As he is perfectly aware, the fact that the judgment that pornography is morally bad and destructive of the common good is Graham's (or Dworkin's or mine) is of *no particular relevance* to the officials' deliberations. They are interested in reasons and arguments—not individuals. In judging the anti-pornography view to be sound and the pro-pornography view to be unsound, they are, to be sure, treating *positions* differently (and inasmuch as these positions are held by people, one might say, at some small risk of misleading, that they are treating *different people's positions* "unequally"). But insofar as it is the *positions* as such being judged, they are in no way treating *people—including the people holding the positions*—unequally. So, although I agree with Dworkin that government has an obligation in justice to treat those under its authority with equal concern and respect, I find no violation of this principle in laws against pornography, prostitution, adultery, fornication, and the like.

IN his recent work, John Finnis has proposed a principled moral limit to the authority of the state to enforce morality.[5] Finnis's argument is far less sweeping in its scope than Dworkin's, and he eschews the anti-perfectionism that Dworkin's thought shares with other orthodox liberal approaches to the question. It does not appeal to alleged rights to privacy, autonomy, liberty, or moral independence, as grounds for limitation on governmental authority to criminalize immoral behavior; and only in the most highly attenuated and strictly limited sense can it be said to license a moral right to do moral wrong, that is, a right to be free of governmental interference with the strictly private immoral acts of consenting adults. Nothing in Finnis's argument implies or entails the "expressive individualism," and accompanying elements of relativism, characteristic of liberal political theories.

The premise of Finnis's argument is that the common good of the political community is, fundamentally, an instrumental, rather than an intrinsic, constitutive, and, as such, basic, human good. This is not to suggest that the political common good is unimportant or dispensable. On the contrary, Finnis recognizes that care of the political common good is profoundly important to the well-being of human persons and the associations they form—including associations, such as the family and church, whose common good is itself intrinsic and *not* merely instrumental. Moreover, the political common good is "great and godlike," to quote Aristotle, in its profoundly ambitious range, which is, Finnis says, "to secure the whole ensemble of...conditions to favour, facilitate, and foster the realization by each individual of his or her personal development."[6] Thus, political authority legitimately extends even to the regulation, within limits, "of friendships, marriage, families, and religious associations, as well as all the many organizations and associations which, like the state itself, have only an instrumental common good."[7]

Still, inasmuch as the political common good *is* an instrumental good, Finnis argues, political authority is limited by the inherent limits of its general justifying aim: viz., to secure the social conditions of the well-being of individuals and their communities. So, he quotes from the teaching of the Second Vatican Council, which, in its Declaration on Religious Freedom (*Dignitatis Humanae*), clearly affirms the instrumental quality of the political common good. Speaking of restrictions on religious liberty, the declaration proposes that such restrictions are justified where required "for [1] the effective protection of the rights of all citizens and of their peaceful coexistence, [2] a sufficient care for the authentic public peace of an ordered common life in true justice, and [3] a proper upholding of public morality."

Now, as Finnis says, the council's idea of public morality is precisely the preservation of a social environment conducive to virtue and inhospitable to at least the grosser forms of vice. This is not to say, however, that government may legitimately promote virtue and repress vice, *as such,* that is, *just for their own sakes,* at least via coercive means. Finnis does not claim that the council expressly rules this sort of legal moralism and paternalism out of bounds; his claim is merely that "government is precisely not presented here as dedicated to the coercive promotion of virtue and the repression of vice, as such."[8] I'm not sure whether the term "precisely" in Finnis's remark is doing any real work. Perhaps it is meant to suggest that the council really did face the issue more or less squarely and come down the way Finnis thinks we should come down once we've taken on board the implications for the scope of political authority of the fact that the common good of political society is an instrumental, rather than intrinsic, good. In any event, the key point is that Finnis thinks that, having taken on board this fact, we should see that law and the state exceed their just authority—thus violating a principle of justice—when they go beyond the protection of the public moral environment and criminalize "even secret and truly consensual adult acts of vice."[9]

I disagree. Perhaps I'm blinded by what Joseph Boyle once described—in jest, I hope—as my "incorrigibly authoritarian impulses." Or perhaps I've caught John Finnis, in his great generosity of spirit, straining to find a kernel of wisdom in the liberal account of freedom and public morality. However it may be, let me note that the difference between Finnis and me, as a practical matter, is quite small. First of all, even in the absence of a principled limit to the authority of the state to enforce true moral obligations along the lines of the one Finnis proposes, it seems to me that there are often compelling prudential reasons for law to tolerate vices, lest efforts to eradicate them produce worse evils still. (This is Aquinas's position in *Summa Theologiae* I–II, q. 96, a. 1, and one that I have endorsed in all of my writings on the subject.) Second, Finnis's position is hardly a liberal, much less a strictly libertarian, one. Unlike, say, Dworkin and other mainstream liberal political theorists, Finnis goes so far as to say that "the political community's rationale requires that its public managing structure, the state, should deliberately and publicly identify, encourage, facilitate, and support the truly worthwhile (including moral virtue), should deliberately and publicly identify, discourage and hinder the harmful and evil, and should by its criminal prohibitions and sanctions (as well as its other laws and policies) assist people with parental responsibilities to educate children and young people in virtue and to discourage their vices."[10] Moreover, virtually the entire range of traditional morals legislation can and would be justified on grounds that fit well within Finnis's conception of the scope of the police power to uphold public morals. Laws against intrinsic evils such as prostitution, pornography, drug abuse, and the like, as well as those regulating gambling and alcohol are justified, in part, by a concern to protect the public environment in ways that Finnis's approach to the question does not exclude in principle.

On the subject of moral paternalism, on which we disagree, I suspect that the difference between Finnis's position and mine is narrow. He would exclude *in principle,* and I would not, laws against "private" (e.g., noncommercial) fornication, adultery, and sodomy. But where he would permit regulation, as in prohibiting prostitution, shutting down bathhouses, and criminalizing the sale of illicit drugs, I suspect he would see any good paternalistic side effects of such state action as welcome. In other words, if I'm right, Finnis would not see paternalism as a valid justification for criminalization of a vice; but where criminalization is justified for other reasons, he would welcome good paternalistic consequences and would believe the state to be acting within its rightful authority in structuring its laws and activities to produce such consequences where possible. (What I have in mind here is analogous to the way in which some non-retributive goals of punishment systems—such as deterrence and rehabilitation—are welcome, and may rightly be sought, though, by themselves, they do not justify punishment, nor are they its central purpose.)

Why, then, do I resist Finnis's argument on the basic point? Two reasons: First, it does not follow, or so it seems to me, from the instrumental nature of the political common good that moral paternalism, where it can be effective, is beyond the scope of that good. Second, I think that the concept of truly secret vices is, when it comes to laws such as those pertaining to fornication, adultery, and sodomy, a very slippery and unsatisfactory one. "Secret" vices have a way of not staying secret. There may be good prudential reasons not to attack them with the full force of the law—and even where the law is employed, authorities should be careful not to employ excessive zeal in enforcing it—but that is not to say that, *as a matter of principle,* the law may not forbid them.

6

MAKING CHILDREN MORAL

Pornography, Parents, and
the Public Interest

O
N TWO OCCASIONS in October of 1965, Sam
Ginsberg, proprietor of Sam's Stationery and Luncheon-
ette in Bellmore, New York, sold magazines containing
photographs of nude women to a sixteen-year-old boy. Ginsberg was
tried in state court and convicted of violating Section 484-h of the
New York Penal Law, which prohibited the sale of pornographic
materials to minors (defined by the statute as persons under seven-
teen years of age). His conviction was upheld by the relevant department of the Appellate Term of the New York Supreme Court, after
which he was denied leave to appeal to the New York Court of Appeals.
The Supreme Court of the United States heard the case on appeal and
in April of 1968 affirmed Ginsberg's conviction in an opinion by
Justice William Brennan.[1] Justice John Marshall Harlan concurred in
the judgment and joined the opinion of the Court. Justice Potter
Stewart concurred in the result. Justice William O. Douglas, joined by
Justice Hugo Black, dissented. Justice Abe Fortas also dissented.

Ginsberg argued that the New York law violated the First
Amendment's guarantee of freedom of expression. He did not challenge the authority of the state to ban obscene publications. (The

Supreme Court has always held that obscenity—like defamation and certain other types of harmful and valueless expression—is outside the First Amendment's protections of freedom of speech and the press.) Rather, he claimed that the New York law was unconstitutional on its face because it banned the sale (to minors) of *non-obscene* publications.

Justice Brennan conceded that the pornographic magazines Ginsberg sold were not legally obscene for adults.[2] Thus, according to the prevailing doctrine, New York could not forbid Ginsberg or others from stocking them and selling them to adults. The Court ruled, however, that New York was constitutionally permitted to adopt "*variable* concepts of obscenity," according to which the magazines sold by Ginsberg were, nevertheless, legally obscene *for minors.*[3] The justices rejected Ginsberg's argument that "the scope of the constitutional freedom of expression secured to a citizen to read or see material concerned with sex cannot be made to depend upon whether the citizen is an adult or a minor."[4]

Brennan identified two interests that, he said, justified the state, acting pursuant to its police powers to protect public health, safety, and morals, in placing limitations on the availability of material to minors that it could not constitutionally prohibit to adults.[5] First, he said, is the state's interest in assisting parents in fulfilling their child-rearing responsibilities. Quoting from *Prince v. Massachusetts,* Brennan wrote that "[i]t is cardinal with us that the custody, care and nurture of the child reside first in the parents, whose primary function and freedom include preparation for obligations the state can neither supply nor hinder."[6] But, he continued, "[t]he legislature could properly conclude that parents and others, teachers, for example, who have this primary responsibility for children's well-being are entitled to the support of laws designed to aid discharge of that responsibility."[7]

The second interest justifying special limitations on children's access to pornographic material, according to Brennan, is the state's "independent interest in the well-being of its youth."[8] In defense of this interest, he quoted with approval the concurring opinion of Judge Fuld of the New York Court of Appeals in *People v. Kahan:*

While the supervision of children's reading may best be left to their parents, the knowledge that parental control or guidance cannot always be provided and society's transcendent interest in protecting the welfare of children justify reasonable regulation of the sale of material to them. It is therefore, altogether fitting and proper for a state to include in a statute designed to regulate the sale of pornography to children special standards, broader than those embodied in legislation aimed at controlling dissemination of such materials to adults.[9]

Then, quoting again from *Prince v. Massachusetts,* Brennan observed that the Supreme Court had itself recognized the state's independent interest in children's welfare and the need for them to be "'safeguarded from abuses' which might prevent their 'growth into free and independent well-developed men and citizens.'"[10] The sole question before the Court, he concluded, was "whether the New York Legislature might rationally conclude, as it has, that exposure to the materials proscribed by section 484-h constitutes such an 'abuse.'"[11] His conclusion, and that of a majority of the justices, was that the New York Legislature might rationally conclude that exposing minors to pornographic materials, even of a sort not considered to be obscene for adults, constitutes an abuse that, as he put it, might impair "the ethical and moral development of youth."[12]

There are a great many people today who would disagree with Justice Brennan's conclusion. Indeed, it is altogether likely that Justice Brennan himself would today disavow his conclusion. I, however, think it was right. In fact, Brennan quite correctly identified both the harm of exposing young people (but, I shall argue, not just young people) to pornography and the interests justifying governmental efforts to protect them (and, I think, the rest of us) from that harm.

It is often supposed—particularly by judges who would invalidate anti-pornography laws—that the "harm" of pornography is offense to the sensibilities of those—like themselves, the judges are often quick to add—who find it distasteful.[13] Pornography, they say, may shock and offend many people; but putting up with being shocked and offended is the price we must pay for the great blessing of freedom of expression. Those who *are* shocked and offended can simply avert their eyes. Justice Douglas, in his dissent in *Ginsberg*, informed his readers that he personally finds the pornographic material that comes to the Court for review "exceedingly dull and boring."[14] Still, he allowed that some people "can and do become very excited and alarmed and think that something should be done to stop the flow [of pornography]."[15] And, indeed, those who wish to do something about it—Douglas made particular mention of parents and religious organizations—can act in their private capacities, albeit in ways Douglas did not specify, to combat it; they may not, however, implicate the state as a censor. "As I read the First Amendment," Douglas declared, "it was designed to keep the state and the hands of all state officials off the printing presses of America and off the distribution systems for all printed literature."[16]

I think that this is a very dubious account of what the First Amendment was "designed" to do. If we are really going to let our constitutional jurisprudence be governed by what the provisions of the Constitution, including the First Amendment, "were designed to do," then very little that is pornographic will be given any protection at all—which would be fine with me.[17] The point I wish to make here, though, is that the harm of pornography about which legislators have traditionally (and, in my view, rightly) been concerned, as Brennan seemed to understand perfectly well, but Douglas grasped (or, perhaps, credited) not at all, is not its capacity to shock and offend, but, rather, its tendency to corrupt and deprave. (Indeed, its capacity to shock and offend is, I think, more or less derivative of the judgment that it tends to corrupt and deprave.) Here, I think, the dissenting members of the President's Commission on Obscenity and Pornography, which issued its Report in 1970, were right on the mark: "The government interest in regulating pornography has always related primarily to the prevention of moral corruption and *not* to...the protection of persons from being shocked and/or offended."[18]

But, it will be objected, in this day and age, when we (whoever "we" are) are enlightened about sex and have rightly relegated Comstockery to the ash heap of history, who could credit the idea that pornography is a source of moral corruption? Sure, there are still folk—parents and religious organizations—who get themselves worked up ("excited and alarmed," in Douglas's dismissive characterization) about the prevalence of pornography in our culture and call for its censorship, but, is it not the case, as Justice Douglas was pleased to observe in *Ginsberg*, that "[c]ensors are, of course, propelled by their own neuroses?"[19] Well, if so, permit me to put some of my neuroses on display.

HARRY CLOR, in his new book *Public Morality and Liberal Society,* reports on a content analysis he conducted of "a typical general circulation magazine called *Swank.*"[20] Clor describes *Swank* as "somewhat less crudely salacious than *Hustler* magazine and somewhat more so than *Playboy* or *Penthouse.*"[21] Perusing *Swank,* he says, "is, in some sense, like entering a world unto itself; one gets an introduction to the world of pornography."

First of all, we encounter a number of what the trade calls "spreader" or "beaver" pictorials: close-up shots of nude women with their legs spread wide apart and sexual organs prominently displayed. A series of page-size photographs portrays a man and a woman, both completely naked, simulating intercourse; in some scenes oral sex is simulated by both partners. One set of pictures depicts group sex.[22]

Now, it seems to me that images such as those offered to readers of *Swank* tend to corrupt and deprave by doing precisely what they are designed to do, namely, arousing sexual desire that is utterly unintegrated with the procreative and unitive goods that give the sexual congress of men and women, as husbands and wives, its value, meaning, and significance. Such images tend to induce (and/or reinforce) in persons (particularly, I think, in men, who, in any event, tend to be more attracted to and tempted by pornography than women tend to be) a certain disposition—a more-than-merely-temporary state of the imagination and emotions—which makes it difficult for people to understand, intend, and experience sexual relations as other than a kind of self-gratification involving, as part of its end, the "using" and, in some sense, "possessing" of another.

Even, to take the best possible case for pornography, when spouses employ pornographic materials as means of stimulating their sexual desire for each other or "spicing up" their sex lives, as morally liberated sex experts frequently advise couples to do, they accomplish their goal by means that unavoidably de-personalize themselves and their relationship. What pornography arouses in, say, Mr. Smith is the desire for a woman (perhaps a desire for a certain sort of woman—a woman with large breasts, for example), not a desire for the bodily actualization and expression of his unique relationship of marital union with Mrs. Smith as such. Mrs. Smith may be willing to go along with this, since Mr. Smith might be otherwise uninterested in her, but she ought not to be. Mrs. Smith is, after all, a unique person who is uniquely related to Smith as his wife; it is dehumanizing for her to be taken by him (and dehumanizing for him to take her) as "a mere convenient, available instance of [a] 'desirable woman' whose presence in the man's aroused imagination impels him towards her until the moment when his biological tension is released, the appealing figure fades in his imagination, and his failure to integrate his insistent words and actions to a common life of friendship becomes obvious even to him."[23]

This dehumanization—this reduction of persons to the status of things—in and by pornography is highlighted by Harry Clor in his characterization of the contents of *Swank*, which, you will recall, is by no means the most salacious of the pornographic magazines available for sale in a typical newsstand.

> First, this is an area of wholly loveless, affectionless sex. The sexuality it portrays and invites is thoroughly depersonalized; the passion it appeals to is the desire for the possession of someone's body without any interest in the personality to which, in ordinary life, a body belongs. . . . Second, there is an invasion of privacy; physical intimacies and reactions normally protected from public

observation are placed conspicuously on display. This "invasion," this aggressive intrusion upon the intimately private, is by no means incidental to *Swank*'s pornographic intent and effect; it is an integral element in the experience that *Swank* is designed to give us, and it is one of the features that make the magazine recognizable as pornography. Third, the magazine presents a pervasive "objectification" of the erotic experience and the female in particular. The erotic activity is reduced, in graphic detail, to its physical components, and the participants are viewed as instruments for the production of pleasurable sensations.[24]

If Clor's characterization is accurate, however, why would anybody be interested in pornography? Why does it have any appeal to people? Why is there a market for it—indeed, according to a recent cover story on the pornography industry in *U.S. News and World Report*, an $8 billion market in the United States alone?[25] The answers, I think, have to do with the complexities of human sexual psychology. As John Finnis has observed, "sexuality is a powerful force which only with some difficulty, and always precariously, can be integrated with other aspects of human personality and well-being—so that it enhances rather than destroys friendship and the care of children, for example. . . . [Moreover,] human sexual psychology has a bias towards regarding other persons as bodily objects of desire and potential sexual release and gratification, and as mere items in an erotically flavoured classification (e.g., "women"), rather than as full persons with personal and individual sensitivities, restraints, and life plans."[26] Pornography, precisely by arousing sexual desires unintegrated with the human goods to which sexuality is morally ordered, induces in its consumers states of emotion, imagination, and sentiment that dispose them to understand and regard themselves and their bodies, and others and their bodies, as, in essence, instruments of sexual gratification—sex objects. Pornography corrupts by appealing to and heightening the tendency toward selfishness, which, even in the most virtuous among us, represents a danger to our integrity and to the precious relationships (husband-wife,

parent-child, friendships) which depend, in part, on the proper integration of our sexuality into our lives.

ANYONE who has the temerity to question the tenets of liberal sexual ideology exposes himself to the risk of being misunder-
stood and misrepresented. So, as a matter of caution, let me here
make explicit what I am *not* saying (and do not believe). I am *not*
saying (nor do I believe) that sex is bad, or, in itself, sinful, or only for
procreation (though I think its procreative significance is always a
part of what makes sex humanly valuable, even when it is not, and
perhaps isn't even intended to be, procreative); nor am I saying that
we should be ashamed of our bodies, or of our sexuality, or that we
should dress the nude figures painted by Michelangelo on the ceil-
ing of the Sistine Chapel, or cover up the table legs, or excise the
Song of Songs from the Bible. In fact, I think that sex, when it is
humanly valuable, is *intrinsically,* and not merely instrumentally, valuable.[27] And I think that part of why we should be concerned about
sexual immorality generally, and the tendency of pornography to
corrupt and deprave in particular, is that it damages people's capacities properly to channel sexual desire so that they can realize in their
marriages the intrinsic value of sexual union. This capacity is, I think,
utterly dependent on the understandings and self-understandings
practically and effectively available to us only to the extent of our
self-integration, self-possession, and self-control in matters pertaining to our sexuality.[28]

Of course, the judgment that pornography is bad in the ways I
claim it is depends on the validity of my more general claims about
sexuality and sexual morality.[29] And to many people today my understanding of sexuality and sexual morality is an antiquated and
unliberated one. It is denounced by David Richards, for example,
who celebrates pornography "as the unique medium of a vision of
sexuality, a 'pornotopia'—a view of sensual delight in the erotic celebration of the body, a concept of easy freedom without consequences,
a fantasy of timelessly repetitive indulgence."[30] Well, this like other
aspects of sexual liberationism, is a fantasy all right. In matters of

sexuality, there simply is no "easy freedom without consequences," nor should we want there to be. The dignity, beauty, and value of our sexuality depends on the fact that it does have consequences, even when the coming to be of new human persons happens to be not among those consequences.

In fact, "sexual *liberationism*" is a sort of self-contradiction. Freedom lies not in sexual self-indulgence or self-gratification, but rather in sexual self-integration, self-possession, and self-control. Justice Brennan was onto this, I think, in *Ginsberg* when, quoting Judge Fuld, he concluded that the New York Legislature could quite reasonably conclude that exposing young people to pornography was an "abuse" that threatened their growth into "free and independent well-developed men and citizens." The freedom pornography imperils is freedom from a sexuality that is unintegrated, selfish, impulsive, depersonalized, disordered, out of control.

But vulnerability to the risk of anarchic sexuality is by no means confined to the young. Nor is the harm of such sexuality limited to individuals as opposed to communities. Nor can the young, or anyone else, be protected from the threats posed by pornography to their interests by efforts to keep pornography out of their hands unless those efforts are part of a larger project to restrict its availability. Again, those who dissented from the 1970 Report of the President's Commission on Obscenity and Pornography rightly observed that "pornography has an eroding effect on society, on public morality, on respect for human worth, on attitudes toward family love, on culture."[31] Even in defending an alleged "right to pornography," Ronald Dworkin conceded this most crucial of all points in the debate about pornography and censorship: Legal recognition of such a right, he observed,

> would sharply limit the ability of individuals consciously and reflectively to influence the conditions of their own and their children's development. It would limit their ability to bring about the cultural structure they think best, a structure in which sexual experience generally has dignity and beauty, without which their

own and their families' sexual experiences are likely to have these
qualities in less degree.[32]

So, I think, the very considerations that justify the paternalistic
concern to limit the rights of minors to obtain pornographic materials—even the "soft-core" stuff whose sale to a minor landed Ginsberg
in the dock—justify, and indeed demand, a broader concern to protect from the corroding and corrupting effects of pornography the
social milieu in which people lead their lives and rear their children.
The very interests identified by Justice Brennan as justifying the
prohibition of sales of pornography to minors equally, I think, justify a more sweeping prohibition of pornography—a broader definition of "obscenity" if we are to stick with the idea, which the Court
seemed eager to stick with in *Ginsberg,* that whatever lewd material
the state is justified in banning gets classified as "obscene."

I should say a word here about the feminist argument for repress-
ing pornography. As the reader will have surmised by now, I am a
traditionalist, as opposed to a feminist. If I understand feminist
opponents of pornography, such as Susan Brownmiller and Catharine
MacKinnon, they are eager to distance themselves from the "moralistic" arguments made by people like me. I am less interested, I think,
in distancing myself from arguments made by people like them—
arguments equally moralistic, and none the worse for that. I think
that pornography is degrading and dehumanizing for everyone, but
I have no doubt that women and girls get the worst of it in a society
in which pornography flourishes. Even when pornography depicts
women in dominant and powerful, as opposed to subordinate and
humiliating, roles (which, according to Clor and others, is not that
often), the understandings and self-understandings, the dispositions and feelings, the sentiments and sensibilities it promotes conduce to a "cultural structure," as Dworkin says, in which sexuality
lacks "dignity and beauty."[33] In the context of such a cultural structure in the real world of male and female sexual psychology and
relationships, women and girls are bound to suffer even more than
men and boys. Women, for example, are more likely to be abandoned

and left unsupported by their sexual partners. They are overwhelmingly more likely to be "traded in" for younger and sleeker models, even by "respectable" husbands. It would be very surprising if they were not more likely to suffer domination, exploitation, and abuse.

Now, legal prohibition of anything works well only when supported by a widespread recognition of the evil of the thing prohibited. This is not only because effective enforcement requires public support for the law; it is also because law is only effective where most people recognize moral reasons (and thus have motives other than respect for law as such or fear of punishment) for refraining from the activity prohibited by the law. There is a core of truth in the idea that laws work best when they are needed least. Or, to state things the other way around, laws are likely to be least effective when they are needed most. So, it seems, the damage to the moral ecology (Dworkin's "cultural structure") of modern societies already done by the traffic in pornography (and other desiderata of the sexual revolution) limits the social payoff of strengthening the legal attack on the pornography industry. Still, I believe that it is worth doing.

At the same time, public and private institutions, including schools, libraries, museums, and the like, should do their part by observing the maxim: First do no harm. Such institutions should not abet the pornography trade by catering in any way to the desire for pornography. *Anyone* who makes the stuff available—from street vendors to libraries—does an injustice to decent people, particularly decent men, by putting what will in many cases be a powerful temptation in their way, and to everybody, and particularly to women (and children), since everybody has a stake in the moral ecology of the community that pornography degrades. Where these injustices are perpetrated by public institutions whose very reason for existence is to serve the public good, it is a special outrage and scandal.

NOW, even if I am right in thinking that pornography damages the moral environment (and, thus, the public interest) of communities in which it flourishes, and that those communities are therefore entitled to enact and enforce laws restricting and even prohibiting it,

difficult questions remain. Even non-pornographic artistic and liter-
ary evocations of sexual love—the Song of Songs, for example—can be
used as stimuli or occasions for the indulgence of unintegrated sexual
desire of the sort deliberately aroused by pornography. And there are
certainly borderline cases in which it is difficult to distinguish the
pornographic from the non-pornographic. What is to be done?

Here, I think, there is no hope of identifying strict rules. A certain
sort of practical or prudential judgment is required, and democratic
deliberation must take place in every community. Although I know
that it is supposed to be especially unenlightened to consider concerns about the pornographic use of non-pornographic materials to
be in any way legitimate, these concerns do strike me as worth taking
seriously, particularly when it comes to young people. So I think that
public (and private) institutions ought to do what they can, in
Brennan's words, to "support" parents in "the discharge of their
responsibilities." So, warnings, ratings systems, restricted access, requirements that children be accompanied by adults, all have their
place where the access of minors to sexually oriented material is
concerned. Free speech considerations are relevant here, but should
not be treated as trumps. Instituting such policies should not, however, be permitted to become a pretext for expanding the offering of
pornographic materials in the public media. This, according to George
Will, was an effect of the movie rating system; he fears, as I do, that it
could be a consequence of the television rating system and the v-chip.

Nudity in anything like a sexual context should, I think, be kept
off television precisely because easy access by young people makes
the already difficult task of parents even more difficult. I don't know
enough about the technology of the Internet to have any real idea of
whether or how the presentation of questionable material there could
be controlled, but certainly any conceivable ways of supporting parents ought to be explored and considered. I recognize that where
legitimate material with sexual content is concerned, there is a trade-
off. Protecting the young means making access to some such material more difficult for adults. Balances can be struck in different
ways, and I see no reason in principle why different communities

(and, indeed, different institutions) ought not to be able to strike them differently. My real point is that absolutism (or, dare I call it, "fundamentalism") ought to be eschewed by everybody: Parents have no absolute right to raise their children in an antiseptic environment entirely free from materials that, though legitimate, can constitute for young people what, in the old language, was called "an occasion of sin." At the same time, adults have no absolute right to easy access even to non-pornographic materials where the interests of young people may be adversely affected.

When it comes to the borderline cases of legitimacy, it seems to me that here, too, prudential judgment, exercised in light of local and contingent circumstances, is required. I am not sufficiently impressed by John Stuart Mill's argument in *On Liberty* to agree with his judgment that in civilized societies we can always count on "the salutary permanent effects of freedom."[34] Rather, different circumstances and conditions call for different policies. Different societies differ even as to the degree of personal autonomy that is consistent with the maintenance of a minimally decent moral environment. And while it is true that in some societies a puritanical spirit threatens genuine progress in the arts and literature, in others, licentiousness, abetted, as always, by a false vision of freedom, imperils the interest of all in a morally decent cultural milieu. In *any* society, careful deliberation by citizens committed to the common good and informed by both sound moral judgment and prudent practical understanding, needs to be brought to bear in the effort to, at the same time, preserve honorable liberties *and* protect public morality.

THE COURTS

7

THE TYRANT STATE

AMERICA'S DEMOCRATIC EXPERIMENT has been remarkably successful. Constitutional democracy in the United States has survived a civil war, a great depression, and two world wars. Our nation has assimilated into the mainstream of American life generations of immigrants—many fleeing poverty and oppression in their native lands. We have made tremendous strides toward overcoming a tragic legacy of slavery and racial segregation. We have secured safer conditions for working people and a meaningful social safety net for the most disadvantaged among us. We have demonstrated that citizens of different religious faiths can live and work together in peace and mutual respect. America's economic prosperity has made our nation the envy of the world. Oppressed peoples around the globe look to our Declaration of Independence for inspiration and our Constitution as a model of free government. In the great ideological struggles of the twentieth century, American ideals of personal, political, and economic freedom have triumphed over fascist and communist tyranny. Two cheers for American democracy!

Why not three?

In his encyclical *Evangelium Vitae* (1995), Pope John Paul II reminds us that "fundamentally democracy is a 'system' and as such is a means and not an end. Its 'moral value' is not automatic, but depends on conformity to the moral law to which it, like every other form of human behavior, must be subject." This doctrine of the necessary conformity of civil law to moral truth long predates the rise of modern democracy. It is present in both Plato and Aristotle, and was given careful, systematic expression by St. Thomas Aquinas. It has been a central feature of the tradition of papal social teaching.

As applied to modern democracy, the idea is that the moral legitimacy of a law or public policy cannot be established merely by showing that it was put into place through the workings of democratic institutions. It is true, as the Pope affirms, that democracy is uniquely valuable because it embodies more fully than any alternative system the principle of the fundamental moral equality of citizens. For this reason, the Pope says that the "almost universal consensus with regard to the value of democracy...is to be considered a positive 'sign of the times,' as the Church's magisterium has frequently noted." Nevertheless, even a democratic regime may compromise its legitimacy and forfeit its right to the allegiance of its citizens.

This happens when the institutions of a democracy are manipulated so that "'right' ceases to be such, because it is no longer firmly founded on the inviolable dignity of the person.... In this way, democracy, contradicting its own principles, effectively moves towards a form of totalitarianism." In such an event, democratic institutions become mechanisms of injustice and oppression, thus defying the moral law to which they, like all human institutions and actions, are subject. As Pope John XXIII wrote in his encyclical *Pacem in Terris* (1963), "*Any* government which refused to recognize human rights, or acted in violation of them, would not only fail in its duty; its decrees would be wholly lacking in binding force."

These are no mere sectarian teachings. Belief that laws and the regimes that make and enforce them must be evaluated by reference to universal standards of justice is shared by people of different faiths and of no particular faith. It is the premise of any serious conception of human rights. And few people who are serious about human rights are naive enough to believe that democratic institutions can never be used to violate human rights. Indeed, a central justification for judicial review of legislation is to provide a check against the possibility that more democratically responsive institutions of government will disregard constitutional guarantees and tread upon people's fundamental rights.

One of the saddest lessons of American history, however, is that courts exercising the power to invalidate legislation as unconstitutional can themselves trample upon fundamental rights, and, indeed, can do so precisely in the name of protecting such rights. This happened, for example, when the Supreme Court of the United States, in a ruling that helped to precipitate the Civil War, held in *Dred Scott v. Sandford* that blacks were noncitizens—and, for all practical purposes, nonpersons—possessed of no rights that white people must respect. In our own time, the Supreme Court, in *Roe v. Wade,* struck down the abortion laws of all fifty states, effectively wiping out all legal protection of unborn human beings against being killed upon the request of their mothers. Most recently, federal courts of appeal for the Second and Ninth Circuits—the latter court relying explicitly on the abortion jurisprudence of *Roe* and its progeny—have invalidated laws prohibiting physician-assisted suicide in New York and California. In this case, fortunately, they were reversed by the Supreme Court.

A familiar and important argument against the "judicial activism" on display in these cases is that such decisions constitute the judicial usurpation of legislative authority. This argument highlights the anti-democratic character of the decisions. It prescinds, however, from the substance of the moral questions involved—the rightness or wrongness of slavery or legalized abortion and euthanasia as a matter of public policy. Justice Antonin Scalia, perhaps the leading exponent of this criticism, emphasizes the purely procedural quality of the argument by declaring abortion, for example, to be a matter entirely outside the purview of constitutional law and, therefore, beyond the jurisdiction of courts.

In criticizing *Roe,* Scalia argues that the Constitution, properly interpreted, leaves the people of the states free to legislate against abortion. In a noteworthy address at the Pontifical Gregorian University in Rome, however, he recently declared that by the same token, "if the people want abortion, the state should permit abortion in a democracy." While the justice made clear his own preference for pro-life public policies, he argued that in itself democracy is neutral as between competing positions on issues such as abortion and euthanasia. "I do not know how you can argue on the basis of democratic theory," he said, "that the government has a moral obligation to do something that is opposed by the people." Responding to a questioner who raised the issue of the rights of minorities, Scalia declared that "the whole theory of democracy, my dear fellow, is that the majority rules; that is the whole theory of it. You protect minorities only because the majority determines that there are certain minority positions that deserve protection."

The Pope's argument in *Evangelium Vitae,* by contrast, highlights the sense in which the abandonment of the unborn to abortion and the infirm to euthanasia betrays the substantive principle of equal worth and dignity that is the moral linchpin of democracy. Any regime, including a democratic one, degenerates into what the Pope calls a "tyrant state" when its law exposes the weakest and most vulnerable members of the community—those most in need of the law's protection—to private lethal violence or other forms of oppression. The dark irony of American constitutional democracy is that our judges—whose special responsibility it is to preserve the core democratic principle of equality before the law—are the ones whose edicts have betrayed this principle. When considered in light of the substantive moral basis of democratic governance, *Roe v. Wade* and similar decisions stand out as "undemocratic" in a far more radical sense than the one Justice Scalia has in mind.

If the moral law is anything like what Christians and Jews have long supposed it to be, then there are profoundly important respects in which the institutions of American democracy—particularly the courts—have made themselves its enemy. Mary Ann Glendon has observed that the abortion license manufactured in *Roe* and upheld in *Planned Parenthood v. Casey* is more sweeping than that of any other democratic nation on the face of the earth. "No other democracy," she remarks, "is so careless of the value of human life." Predictably, the legalization of abortion is paving the way to assisted suicide and euthanasia. The decisions of the Second and Ninth Circuit Courts will give the Supreme Court an opportunity to declare that the right "to define one's own concept of existence, of meaning, the universe, and the mystery of human life," to which it appealed in upholding the abortion license in *Casey,* includes the right to kill yourself, to a physician's assistance in killing yourself, and to someone else's "substituted judgment" that you should be killed when you are too infirm to decide for yourself.

What are serious Jews, Christians, and other pro-life citizens to say about such laws and the institutions that bring them into being? In *Evangelium Vitae,* John Paul II teaches that "laws which authorize and promote abortion and euthanasia are radically opposed not only to the good of the individual but also to the common good; as such they are completely lacking in juridical validity." The Pope is not here making a claim about the technical status of such laws within the legal systems of the countries that have them. He is, rather, concerned with their moral force, that is to say, their capacity objectively to bind the conscience of citizens. "A civil law authorizing abortion or euthanasia," he declares, "ceases by that very fact to be a true, morally binding law.... Abortion and euthanasia are crimes which no human law can claim to legitimize. There is no obligation in conscience to obey such laws; instead there is a grave and clear obligation *to oppose them by conscientious objection.*"

Plainly, the Pope's teaching is a firm rebuke to those who claim to be "personally opposed" to abortion and euthanasia but who act to advance these evils in the public sphere. "In the case of an intrinsically unjust law, such as a law permitting abortion or euthanasia," the Pope says, "it is...never licit to obey it, or to take part in a propaganda campaign in favor of such a law, or vote for it." But the Pope's call for disobedience and conscientious objection goes beyond even the condemnation of the craven "personally opposed, but pro-choice," position. His teaching is directed not merely to those who would join the ranks of Mario Cuomo, Bill Clinton, and Father Robert Drinan, but to all of us. We are, the Pope says, in the midst of a great conflict between "the culture of life" and "the culture of death": "We are all involved and we all share in it, with the inescapable responsibility of *choosing to be unconditionally pro-life.*"

When *Evangelium Vitae* was issued, the Pope's warning that ours is becoming a "culture of death" grabbed the headlines—and rightly so. An equally important aspect of his teaching, however, received less publicity. This was the Pope's call for all of us to "live the Gospel of Life." The Pope emphasizes again and again that this is a call to action. All of us must give witness to the sanctity of human life, not merely by personally refraining from abortion and euthanasia, but by working in various spheres—including the political sphere—to overcome these "crimes against life" and create a new "culture of life."

For some, this will mean making financial sacrifices to support the pro-life cause in its various dimensions. For others, it will mean volunteering to assist in the critical work of pro-life pregnancy centers and hospices. For still others, it will mean working in the educational, legal, and political realms to reverse the judicial decisions and legislative and executive acts that have ushered in the "culture of death." For all who believe in a God of love, justice, and mercy, it will mean constant prayer not only for the victims of the "culture of death," but also for those who are joined in the great struggle on their behalf, and, indeed, for those misguided souls who, by political action or by personal involvement in the killing of the unborn or infirm, have made themselves their oppressors.

To all who work in shaping public policy, the Pope directs a special plea to make a concern for the health of the family "the basis and driving force of all social policies." In this vein, he says, it is essential to resist "the trivialization of sexuality," which is "among the principal factors which has led to contempt for new life." Moreover, the Pope calls for greater support for adoption as a true pro-life alternative to abortion. Here, one is reminded of the profound witness of Mother Teresa at the National Prayer Breakfast in February of 1994: "Please do not kill the child. I want the child. Please give me the child. I am willing to accept any child who would be aborted." Those of us who would resist the culture of death must join our voices with hers. For us, and the society we must strive to create, there can be no such thing as an "unwanted" child.

Does the Pope not, however, call for even more? How are we to understand his teaching that resistance to the "culture of death" demands "disobedience" and even "conscientious objection" to unjust laws? Laws that authorize the killing of the unborn or infirm are permissive in form. They license and sometimes encourage private killing, but do not positively command it. (This is what enables supporters of abortion to describe themselves as "pro-choice." Of course, by this logic, so were supporters of antebellum laws that permitted slavery, yet required no one to own slaves or to demand return of fugitive slaves.) Therefore, disobedience and conscientious objection to such laws must, in most cases, be indirect. A good example is that of physicians in United States military hospitals abroad who announced their refusal to perform elective abortions when President Clinton issued an executive order lifting the ban on these abortions in such hospitals. Another example is that of citizens of states that pay for abortions with public funds who refuse, as a matter of conscience, to remit to state government a portion of their taxes corresponding to the percentage of the state budget that goes to abortion funding. Yet another example is that of nonviolent protestors at abortion clinics who defy unjust restrictions of their freedom of speech in order to plead the case for the unborn to women contemplating abortion.

In upholding the abortion license in the *Casey* decision, a plurality opinion of Justices Souter, O'Connor, and Kennedy called upon pro-life Americans to stop their resistance to legalized abortion and accept "a common mandate rooted in the Constitution." For reasons the Pope makes clear, this is a proposition that Catholics and other pro-life Americans cannot accept. The doctrine of the necessary conformity of civil law to moral truth imposes on conscientious citizens of a regime that authorizes the killing of the unborn and infirm a clear obligation of resistance. It is not merely that the claim of these justices to have found a pro-abortion "mandate" in the Constitution is manifestly ludicrous. The value of constitutional democracy lies ultimately in its capacity to serve and secure the common good, which demands, above all, the protection of fundamental human rights. If the Constitution really did abandon the vulnerable to private acts of lethal violence, and, indeed, positively disempowered citizens from working through the democratic process to correct these injustices, then it would utterly lack the capacity to bind the consciences of citizens. Our duty would not be to "accept a common mandate," but to resist.

Has the regime of American democracy forfeited its legitimacy? One way of avoiding an affirmative answer to this question is to observe that the judicial decisions at issue are gross misinterpretations of the Constitution. They are examples of what Justice Byron White, dissenting in *Roe v. Wade,* called the "exercise of raw judicial power." At the same time, however, these decisions have consistently been acquiesced in by the legislative and executive branches of government. Congress has not defied the Supreme Court, as it ultimately did in *Dred Scott.* And, although not every president has actively abetted the culture of death—as President Clinton did, for example, in issuing a series of pro-abortion executive orders and vetoing the congressional ban on partial-birth abortions—no recent president has worked steadily to ensure, by judicial appointments and other actions, that anti-life judicial decisions are reversed.

To say that the worst abuses of human rights have come from the least democratic branch of government—the judiciary—is true, but of increasingly questionable relevance to the crisis of democratic legitimacy brought on by judicial action in the cause of abortion and euthanasia. In practice, the American scheme of constitutional democracy invests the courts with ultimate authority to decide what the Constitution is to mean. Judicial action and appointments can, and sometimes do, become major issues in national elections. The refusal of the courts for almost thirty years to reverse *Roe v. Wade* must, then, be accounted a failure of American democracy.

The judicial movement toward euthanasia makes it plain that the hour is late. The "culture of death" is well advanced in our nation. As the Pope says, "given such a grave situation, we need now more than ever to have the courage to look the truth in the eye and to *call things by their proper names,* without yielding to convenient compromises or to the temptation of self-deception." Let us, therefore, speak plainly: The courts, sometimes abetted by federal and state executives and legislators, have imposed upon the nation immoral policies that pro-life Americans cannot, in conscience, accept. Since the legitimacy of institutions of governance—be they democratic or otherwise—depends ultimately on their capacity and willingness to preserve and promote the common good by, above all, protecting fundamental human rights, the failure of the institutions of American democracy to fulfill their responsibilities has created what is truly a crisis. People of goodwill—of whatever religious faith—who are prepared to consider seriously the Pope's teaching in *Evangelium Vitae* cannot now avoid asking themselves, soberly and unblinkingly, whether our regime is becoming the democratic "tyrant state" about which he warns.[1]

8

JUSTICE, LEGITIMACY, AND ALLEGIANCE

"The End of Democracy"
Symposium Revisited

I N ITS NOVEMBER 1996 ISSUE, *First Things* magazine published a symposium titled "The End of Democracy? The Judicial
Usurpation of Politics." It provoked an enormous controversy,
particularly among conservative scholars and commentators. Some
praised the editors and contributors for boldly challenging judicial
abuses of power. Others condemned them for allegedly questioning
the legitimacy of the government of the United States. Three distinguished conservative scholars resigned their association with the
magazine.

My contribution to the symposium—reprinted here as chapter 7—
was a commentary on the encyclical letter *Evangelium Vitae* ("The Gospel
of Life") by Pope John Paul II. That letter, which had been issued a year
and a half earlier, forcefully reasserted the Catholic Church's firm and
constant teaching regarding the value and inviolability of human life.[1]
Thus, it condemned abortion and euthanasia as "crimes which no
human law can claim to legitimize."[2] Moreover, the encyclical argued
against use of the death penalty, stating that criminal punishment
"ought not go to the extreme of executing the offender except in cases

of absolute necessity: in other words, when it would not be possible otherwise to defend society."[3] The print and broadcast media duly recorded the Pope's vigorous reaffirmation of the Church's teachings on the moral wrongfulness of abortion and euthanasia and took particular note of what Joseph Cardinal Ratzinger, prefect of the Congregation for the Doctrine of the Faith, described as the Pope's development of the Church's doctrine in opposition to capital punishment.[4] What received scant attention, however, was the Pope's philosophical analysis of legally sanctioned injustice and its implications for the authority of laws and the legitimacy of political regimes.[5]

The principal purpose of this chapter is to further highlight the Pope's analysis and consider its relevance to the concrete circumstances of the United States, where the abortion license, among other evils, has been imposed on the nation by judicial fiat and where, at the time of the *First Things* symposium, the Supreme Court was considering whether to uphold decisions by lower federal courts establishing a constitutional right to physician-assisted suicide.[6] Although the Pope did not consider the question of judicial authority in relation to the authority of legislators and other elected officials, much less address the scope and limits of constitutional judicial review in the United States (or anywhere else), the editors of *First Things* commissioned my essay for the symposium precisely because *Evangelium Vitae* addressed so directly, and with such a high degree of philosophical sophistication, the issues of legal authority and political legitimacy in modern constitutional democracies. The editors believed, as I believe, that the Pope's teaching on these issues is highly pertinent to circumstances in which a judiciary, charged to interpret and apply the fundamental law of a democratic republic, has, under the pretext of performing that function, usurped the authority of the people to act through the institutions of representative democracy to protect the unborn and other potential victims of injustice and to secure the overall common good.

THE first thing to notice about the Pope's teaching is that it is pro-democratic.[7] Perhaps it goes without saying that not every pope has been an admirer of democracy. Critics of democracy, including some popes, have worried that belief in the superiority of democratic institutions in some sense presupposes or entails the denial of objective moral truth. Even some who sympathize with democracy as an ideal have been concerned that, in practice, democratic institutions subtly inculcate in the people living under them the spirit of moral relativism or subjectivism. Certain critics of the subjectivist or relativist spirit of our age suggest that the sources of society's pathology are precisely in the democratic institutions bequeathed to the public by the nation's founders.[8] Throughout his pontificate, however, John Paul II has robustly defended the principles and institutions of democratic governance.[9] And his defense of these principles and institutions has been neither halfhearted nor merely pragmatic. John Paul II enthusiastically promotes democracy not as some sort of "lesser evil," but as a system that more perfectly than any other embodies the great moral truth of the fundamental dignity of each human person.[10] It is for this reason, the Pope says in *Evangelium Vitae,* that the "almost universal consensus with regard to the value of democracy...is to be considered a positive 'sign of the times.'"[11]

At the same time—and this is the second thing to notice about the teaching of *Evangelium Vitae*—the Pope warns against making a fetish of democracy, or "idoliz[ing] [it] to the point of making it a substitute for morality or a panacea for immorality."[12] After all, democratic institutions are *procedures* for making political decisions; they cannot guarantee substantive justice. As the Pope reminds us:

> Fundamentally, democracy is a "system" and as such is a means and not an end. Its "moral" value is not automatic, but depends on conformity to the moral law to which it, like every other form of human behaviour, must be subject: in other words, its morality depends on the morality of the ends which it pursues and of the means which it employs.[13]

What is interesting about human positive law, from the moral point of view, is not merely that laws enforce obligations that already exist as a matter of moral law, but that laws sometimes create moral obligations that would otherwise not exist.[14] The moral obligation to obey the law is, however, conditional and, as such, defeasible.[15] The injustice of a law or a system of laws can destroy its power to bind the consciences of those ostensibly subject to it. This is the central core of truth in the oft-misunderstood statement *lex iniusta non est lex* ("an unjust law is not law")—a proposition taught not only by St. Augustine and St. Thomas Aquinas, but also in substance by Plato, Aristotle, and Cicero.[16] And, as the Pope affirms, the democratic provenance of a law does not render its obligation-imposing power indefeasible.[17] Even a law enacted by impeccably democratic procedures can be unjust, and insofar as it is unjust it can fail to create an obligation to obey.[18]

Indeed, certain sorts of unjust laws may not licitly be obeyed. For example, it is morally wrong to comply with laws requiring people to perform actions that are themselves unjust or otherwise immoral. From the moral point of view, people subject to such laws do not have the option of obeying them. The fulfillment of their moral responsibilities requires people to disobey the laws. So, for example, a conscientious physician would simply refuse to comply with a law requiring him to administer a lethal injection to any patient whom he diagnoses as carrying HIV. Not only is there no moral obligation to obey such a law, there is a strict moral obligation not to obey it. It matters not whether the law in question was put into place by a military junta, a judicial oligarchy, or a democratically elected legislature.

But what of laws, such as those permitting abortion and euthanasia, which do not require anybody to do anything, but are, rather, *permissive* of gravely unjust actions? The Pope says that such laws are "radically opposed not only to the good of the individual but also to the common good; as such they are completely lacking in authentic juridical validity."[19] The wholesale legal permission of evils such as abortion and euthanasia constitutes a failure of government to fulfill its primary responsibility, which is to protect the weak and vulnerable against unjust physical assaults. Moreover, such a permission is gravely unjust inasmuch as it denies the unborn, the handicapped, the frail elderly, and other vulnerable persons their rights to the equal protection of the laws. Where such a denial of equality is worked by democratic means, as with the abortion license in most European countries for example, it damages the integrity of democracy itself— for, as the Pope has so clearly seen, the principle of equality is itself central to the democracy's moral justification.[20] By the same token, where the denial of equal protection is worked by oligarchic judicial action, as in the United States, it constitutes not only a usurpation of democratic authority, but an assault on democracy's core principle.

Certain critics of the *First Things* symposium have alleged that the symposium was driven not by a concern about judicial usurpation as such, but by opposition to abortion and euthanasia. Writing in *Commentary* magazine's "On the Future of Conservatism: A Symposium," Peter Berger argued that the concern of the editors of *First Things* and most of the contributors to its symposium on judicial usurpation "has been not so much the power the courts have improperly assumed but rather what they have done with this power. And at the center of this concern is the issue of abortion."[21] To illustrate what he referred to as "the problem here," Berger proposed a thought experiment:

> Imagine that abortion in the United States had achieved its present legal status through an act of Congress rather than a Supreme Court decision. Imagine further that the Supreme Court had then ruled this action to be unconstitutional. I doubt very much that most of the *First Things* contributors would have viewed the latter action as a serious usurpation of power....[22]

Berger is correct that I and, I suspect, others involved in the *First Things* symposium (with the possible exception of Robert Bork, despite his firm pro-life convictions)[23] would have applauded a decision by the Supreme Court invalidating an act of Congress or, to make Berger's point more sharply than he did, acts of state legislatures to deprive the unborn of legal protection against abortion. But, if we attend to the Pope's analysis of democracy and its moral presuppositions in *Evangelium Vitae,* we can see that this is not the "problem" for the *First Things* symposiasts that Berger thinks it is.

I had occasion in my contribution to the symposium to contrast the Pope's analysis of the moral presuppositions of democracy with extracurial remarks by Justice Antonin Scalia.[24] Scalia, of course, is a passionate and relentless critic of *Roe v. Wade* who has long argued that the Court's invalidation of state laws restricting abortion was a gross usurpation by the judicial branch of democratic legislative authority.[25] He is also firmly committed to the pro-life cause.[26] Yet, Scalia's view is that the Constitution commits the nation to neither pro-life nor "pro-choice" principles; rather, he maintains, abortion is a "political" and not a constitutional issue.[27] And the Constitution leaves such issues entirely to democratic resolution by Congress or the state legislatures. So, Scalia declared to an apparently scandalized audience at the Pontifical Gregorian University in Rome, "if the people want abortion, the state should permit abortion in a democracy."[28]

But if, as I think, and as the Pope teaches, and as Justice Scalia agrees, abortion is the unjust killing of innocent human beings who, as a matter of right, are entitled to the equal protection of the laws, then there *is* a problem for a democracy in permitting abortion. (Of course, whether it is a problem that judges in any particular democratic society are empowered to do anything about is another question.) Since it is the principle of equality which provides the moral justification for democratic rule in the first place, the denial of equality, even if effected by democratic means, is inconsistent with democratic principles. In this sense, democracy is not a morally "neutral" mechanism for deciding disputed questions. Its own moral presuppositions exclude certain outcomes—even where these outcomes represent the preferences (or, for that matter, the considered, but gravely mistaken moral judgments) of a majority.

As I suggested a moment ago, to understand the moral basis of democracy in this way is not, by itself, to decide in every or any particular case that judges should invalidate legislation (including permissive abortion legislation) that conflicts with their views—however sound—of what equality requires. The existence and scope of judicial power to invalidate democratically enacted laws, including laws whose injustice compromises the principles of democracy itself, is settled not by natural law (i.e., the moral law), but by the positive constitutional law of a given democratic polity.[29] On this important point, Justice Scalia is plainly correct. But to adopt this understanding is to begin to see the dubiousness of the simple symmetry presupposed by Berger's criticism of the *First Things* symposium. And we can go much farther toward undermining belief in this alleged symmetry if we consider the commitment to the principle of equality concretely embodied in the Constitution of the United States.

The Fourteenth Amendment expressly forbids the states from denying to any person within their jurisdiction the equal protection of the laws.[30] So, a court exercising judicial review of abortion laws must decide the following two questions: (1) are the unborn "persons" within the meaning of that term as it is used in the Fourteenth Amendment, and, if so, (2) does the abortion law under review deny to unborn persons the "equal protection of the laws"?

Justice Harry Blackmun, in his opinion for the Court in *Roe v. Wade*,[31] purported to deal with the question of whether the unborn are persons within the meaning of the Fourteenth Amendment, noting that if the unborn are persons then their right not to be killed is specifically protected by the Fourteenth Amendment.[32] Thus, the Court's duty would be to strike down permissive abortion laws as violative of the constitutional rights of unborn persons.[33] In the end, however, Blackmun effectively dismissed the question by observing that in places in the Constitution outside the Fourteenth Amendment where the term "person" is used (as, for example, in the provision that says that "persons" must have attained the age of thirty-five in order to serve as president of the United States)[34] it applies only postnatally.[35] He also argued, famously, that the Court could not, and, therefore, need not, "resolve the difficult question when life begins" given that the matter is "at this point in the development of man's knowledge" disputed by scientists, philosophers, theologians, and other experts.[36] Of course, Blackmun went on implicitly to resolve *precisely* this question *quite against* the proposition that "life begins" anytime prior to birth. Yet this is absurd from the scientific viewpoint, and indefensible philosophically.[37] And it set Blackmun up for precisely the criticism he received, namely, that *Roe* was an utterly unprincipled decision, an exercise, as Justice Byron White said in dissent, of "raw judicial power" in which the Court merely substituted its own policy preferences for the contrary judgment of the elected representatives of the people.[38]

Could the matter have been decided otherwise? Can a principled argument for the outcome in *Roe* be constructed? Blackmun's manifest failure to identify a principled ground for the decision has sparked a massive industry, now in its twenty-eighth year, of "rewriting *Roe*" to put it on an intellectually secure constitutional footing. Many of the best and brightest in the legal academy have joined in this effort—all to no avail. It is not merely that there is no specifically enumerated constitutional right to abortion. It is that there simply is no principle in the Constitution by whose affirmation the American people have committed themselves to a regime of abortion-on-demand. The matter is not even close. The best that plausibly can be said for the cause of abortion as a constitutional matter is what Justice Scalia says, namely that, though the Constitution does not forbid the States to restrict abortion, it does not require them to do so.[39]

By contrast, a far stronger case—a genuinely principled argument—can be made that the American people have, by ratifying the Fourteenth Amendment's guarantee of equal protection, committed themselves to a proposition that is inconsistent with the regime of abortion-on-demand. One way of stating the argument is to observe that "person," in ordinary language, connotes what logicians call a "substance sortal," that is to say, an essential property, which implies that whatever has it *has it necessarily* and never exists without it. Human beings come to be and become persons at the same time; they do not become persons at some point after coming to be (nor do they cease being persons without ceasing to be).[40] The forty-two-year-old person who is now, say, John J. DiIulio, is the same being (or, in philosophical terms, the "substance") who was at earlier stages of his life a thirty-two-year-old Princeton professor, a twenty-two-year-old Harvard graduate student, a twelve-year-old adolescent, a six-year-old child, a one-year-old infant, a five-month-old fetus, a four-week-old embryo, and a newly conceived human being. Professor DiIulio progressed from his conception through the embryonic, fetal, infant, and adolescent stages of his life into his adult stage as a distinct, unified, self-integrating organism without undergoing substantial change, that is without ceasing to be one kind of being or substance (possessing one kind of nature) and becoming a different sort of being.[41] Of course, there was a time when he did not exist. He was never a sperm cell or an ovum, much less a twinkle in his father's eye. But when he came into existence, he came into existence as a person. There was no stage in his life at which he existed but was not yet a person. Just as *he* was once an adolescent and before that an infant, the very same *he* was once a fetus and before that an embryo.

John Finnis summed up the matter nicely in his critique of John Rawls's argument that restrictions on abortion violate the liberal principle of public reason which, according to Rawls, ought to govern legislative decision making on questions of constitutional essentials and matters of basic justice.[42] Any justification for denying unborn human beings the right to the equal protection of the laws, Finnis argues,

> will have to have abandoned the one real basis of human equality and equality rights, namely the fact that each living human being possesses, *actually and not merely potentially,* the radical capacity to reason, laugh, love, repent, and choose *as this unique, personal individual,* a capacity which is not some abstract characteristic of the species but rather consists in the unique, individual, organic functioning of the organism which comes into existence as a new substance at the conception of that new human being and subsists until his or her death whether ninety minutes, ninety days, or ninety years later—a capacity, individuality and personhood which subsists as real and precious even while its operations come and go with many changing factors such as immaturity, injury, sleep, and senility.[43]

But someone may object: Is it not possible that the framers and ratifiers meant something very different by "person" when they used that term in the Fourteenth Amendment? Indeed, it is possible. Whether the framers really did have something very different in mind is certainly relevant to whether a court would now be justified in striking down a legislatively enacted regime of abortion-on-demand as a violation of the equal-protection rights of the unborn. Important questions of the proper understanding and role of "original understanding," for example, would immediately be put into play. As yet, however, the argument has not been made. Although the ratifiers of the Fourteenth Amendment did not have the question of abortion in mind—what they were concerned about, rather, was racial bias against the recently freed slaves—they very deliberately framed the Equal Protection (and Due Process) Clause(s) in general terms to forbid the denial of equal protection (and due process) to *any* person or class of persons, and all the evidence from the ratification debates is consistent with the proposition that by "persons" the framers and ratifiers meant (and meant to protect) all human beings, all living members of Homo sapiens.

In any event, I am not here arguing that Justice Scalia is certainly wrong to suggest that courts could not be justified in striking down liberal abortion laws. To make that argument, I would have to address the panoply of reasons militating in favor of judicial restraint when it comes to an issue such as abortion.[44] I am here interested merely in showing that, unlike the Court's decision in *Roe,* a decision outlawing or substantially restricting abortion could be supported by a plausible and truly principled constitutional argument. Thus, the symmetry presupposed by Berger's criticism of the *First Things* symposium does not in fact exist.

The conception of democracy, and the understanding of America's democratic institutions, that the symposiasts had in mind when expressing their concerns about the possible "end of democracy" and offering their criticisms of "the judicial usurpation of politics," were not conceptions according to which democracy is (as Justice Scalia supposes) a simple, morally neutral mechanism of majority rule, whereby fifty-one percent of the people do as they please. Rather, it is a conception of democracy that, as the Pope's analysis in *Evangelium Vitae* brings to light, is shaped by its own justifying moral principle of the equality-in-dignity of all human beings—a conception that, I and others connected with *First Things* believe, was operative in the central proposition of the Declaration of Independence ("all men are created equal") and enshrined in our Constitution (particularly, though not exclusively, in the Equal Protection Clause of the Fourteenth Amendment). Under our conception of democracy, the function of democratic institutions is to serve as the mechanisms by which the people act to fulfill their moral-political responsibilities to protect the weak and innocent, preserve and promote public health, safety, and morals, and secure the overall common good.

IN engaging the question of the legitimacy of the regime of judicial rule, a point that I and other participants in the *First Things* symposium should have made more explicitly is that apart from the most tyrannical regimes (which conscientious citizens may rightly—and where possible should—work to subvert), the question of legitimacy is a matter of degree, rather than an either-or proposition. Consider the case of non-tyrannical authoritarian regimes. Because democracy, as the Pope teaches, embodies the principle of human equality, a regime that fails to adopt, or move in the direction of, democratic rule will necessarily implicate itself in a measure of injustice. And insofar as a regime implicates itself in injustice, it weakens the citizens' reasons for giving their loyalty or allegiance to the regime. In a word, it *weakens*, even if it does not destroy, a regime's *legitimacy*. However, no regime this side of God's sovereign rule in the kingdom of heaven is perfectly just, utterly free of injustice. But that certainly does not mean that every regime is simply illegitimate and may rightly be subverted. Even non-democratic regimes can deserve the allegiance of their citizens. Citizens of non-democratic regimes are certainly justified in working by peaceful means toward the goal of democratic rule; if their government is not a tyrannical one, they even now have reasons for obeying the laws enacted by their rulers, serving in the military, and treating the official acts of government as politically authoritative. In short, they have reasons for giving the regime their allegiance.

So, even if we are correct in arguing that the regime of judicial rule in the United States is doubly unjust—first, in its usurpation of democratic authority and, second and not unrelatedly, in the wicked ends it has sometimes, as in *Roe,* served—that does not mean that we should support revolutionary action against the government of the United States. While these injustices weaken the legitimacy of the regime they do not render our whole government simply illegitimate. The unjust and unconstitutional acts of the judiciary should be resisted; loyal citizens of the United States should work to restore those aspects of constitutional self-government which have been undermined by usurping judges. But, the means used to resist judicial usurpation and restore democratic rule must themselves be constitutionally and morally pure. The identification and use of such means will itself require careful democratic deliberation—what Mary Ann Glendon, writing in response to the *First Things* symposium, called "the hard work of citizenship."[45]

But the courts, and the Supreme Court in particular, should recognize the profound dilemma in which their usurpations have placed conscientious and loyal American citizens. It would be bad enough for citizens who recognize the equality-in-dignity of unborn human beings to find themselves on the losing side of a democratic debate over the question of abortion. (This is the position in which pro-life citizens of the United Kingdom or Sweden find themselves.) It is even worse, however, when citizens are deprived of any right to work through normal democratic processes to preserve or restore legal protection for the unborn. It is not merely that the judicial manufacture of a constitutional right to abortion-on-demand makes the political task of protecting the unborn especially difficult, but that the institution claiming the ultimate authority to specify the meaning of the nation's fundamental moral-political commitments, namely the Supreme Court, tells the nation that the Constitution to which citizens are asked to give their allegiance includes so grave an injustice as the unlimited abortion license. Thus, citizens are asked to be loyal to a constitution that not only fails to protect the basic right to equality of the unborn, but also one that denies them any democratic means to effect the protection of that basic right short of amending the Constitution.

Even prior to the *Dred Scott* decision in 1857,[46] the legitimacy of the regime of government in America was weakened by the grave injustice of slavery. Still, conscientious citizens such as Abraham Lincoln, who opposed that monstrous evil, could, he and many others believed (and I believe), honestly swear to uphold the Constitution because, whatever its inadequacies, it did not contain a strict right to own slaves. True, it failed to secure the moral right of every human being not to be enslaved, but it did not remove the authority of democratic institutions to abolish slavery and secure the moral right against it. The people in their states retained the authority to act through democratic means to effect abolition within their jurisdictions, and the people of the northern states chose to exercise this authority. Congress, in its exercise of general jurisdiction in the federal territories, had (or so it was thought) the authority to act against slavery, albeit in a limited way, and did so act. Of course, inasmuch as the southern states permitted slavery, they were guilty of grave injustice, and insofar as the United States Constitution permitted slavery in states that chose to retain "the peculiar institution," and even facilitated it in certain ways, it failed to protect the right of those enslaved to the equal protection of the laws.[47] But as bad as this situation was, no citizen was asked to pledge allegiance to a regime whose basic constitutional principles included something so unjust as a right of some human beings to buy, sell, use, and use up other human beings.

Then came *Dred Scott*.[48] According to the understanding of the Constitution by which Roger Brooke Taney and those justices joining him sent Dred Scott back into slavery, the American people, acting through the constitutionally established institutions of democracy at the federal level, had no authority to interfere with the right of slaveholding, even where, as in the territories, general jurisdiction was in the hands of the federal government.[49] This was, in effect, to manufacture a constitutional right to slaveholding.[50] Indeed, it is difficult to see how the practical import of this decision was not to deprive even the free states of their effective power to prohibit slavery within their borders. So not only was *Dred Scott*'s central holding unjust, but it was also a gross usurpation of the people's authority to act through their democratic institutions to prohibit, or, at least, contain slavery. And, in these respects, *Dred Scott* resembles nothing so much as *Roe v. Wade*,[51] creating for morally conscientious citizens of the antebellum era precisely the dilemma that *Roe* creates for such citizens today.

When it comes to cases such as *Dred Scott* and *Roe,* there seem to be but two options available to citizens who recognize the profound injustices these decisions work: either citizens are to treat the legitimacy of the Constitution as gravely weakened, or they are to deny that the Court has the authority to settle definitively the meaning of the Constitution—in other words, either the Constitution is illegitimate or the Court is behaving illegitimately. In reaction to the *Dred Scott* case, a not insignificant number of abolitionists chose the former option—some going so far as to denounce the Constitution as a "covenant with death and agreement with hell"[52] and even to burn copies of it. Lincoln, however, chose the latter option. While recognizing the authority of the Court to resolve the particular case (despite the incorrectness and injustice of its ruling), he refused to concede to the justices the right to lay down a rule permanently binding the other branches of government to recognize a constitutional right of slaveholding.[53] Plainly referring to the decision in *Dred Scott,* Lincoln stated:

> I do not forget the position assumed by some that constitutional questions are to be decided by the Supreme Court, nor do I deny that such decisions must be binding in any case upon the parties to a suit as to the object of that suit, while they are also entitled to very high respect and consideration in all parallel cases by all other departments of the Government. And while it is obviously possible that such decision may be erroneous in any given case, still

the evil effect following it, being limited to that particular case, with the chance that it may be overruled and never become a precedent for other cases, can better be borne than could the evils of a different practice. At the same time, the candid citizen must confess that if the policy of the government, upon vital questions affecting the whole people is to be irrevocably fixed by decisions of the Supreme Court, the instant they are made in ordinary litigation between parties in personal actions, the people will have ceased to be their own rulers, having to that extent practically resigned their government into the hands of that eminent tribunal.[54]

I would suggest that the proper response of pro-life citizens to the call by Supreme Court Justices Sandra Day O'Connor, Anthony Kennedy, and David Souter in *Casey* to end the debate over abortion and "[accept] a common [pro-abortion] mandate rooted in the Constitution"[55] is to reassert Lincoln's argument in response to judicial usurpation and injustice in *Dred Scott*. We should say, in effect, that while we could not in conscience give our unfettered allegiance to a regime committed in its very constitution to abortion-on-demand, any more than we could give wholehearted allegiance to a regime constitutionally committed to chattel slavery, we do not accept the authority of judges to read into the Constitution a right to abortion. On the contrary, we reject the justices' claim to have their ruling treated as a legitimate and authoritative interpretation of the Constitution. And we will resist their usurpation of our authority, as a people, to act through the institutions of representative democracy to protect the rights of the unborn. In other words, our response to judicial usurpation and injustice in our own time should not be to denounce the Constitution or to withdraw our allegiance to the United States, but rather to reassert the true principles of the Constitution, and to reaffirm our allegiance to this nation, under God,[56] in its aspiration to secure true liberty and justice for all.

9

NATURAL LAW AND CIVIL RIGHTS

*From Jefferson's "Letter to Henry Lee"
to Martin Luther King's "Letter from
Birmingham Jail"*

EVER SINCE Jeremy Bentham scorned the idea of natural or
moral rights as no ordinary nonsense, but "nonsense upon
stilts,"[1] a certain stream of thought about rights has held them
to be merely conventional and historically contingent. According to
the conventionalist or historicist view, moral rights cannot come as a
divine gift because there is no divine giver; nor can they derive from
human nature because there is no determinate human nature. Moral
rights, according to conventionalists and historicists, exist only in
the sense that certain people, or peoples, happen to believe—as a
contingent matter of fact, that is, subjectively—that rights exist and
are willing to honor them. Where people, or peoples, do not happen
to believe in their existence, rights simply do not exist.

Now historicists and conventionalists do not doubt the existence of *legal* rights. For legal or "positive" rights can easily be accom-
modated and accounted for in historicist and conventionalist terms.
What they deny, and what theorists of natural law and natural rights
affirm, is that legal rights can embody or express moral rights that
are not merely contingent and conventional. In other words, the

issue dividing historicists and conventionalists, on the one side, and partisans of natural law and natural rights, on the other, is whether positive law can be designed to embody, or can validly be criticized for failing to embody, objective or true principles of justice. Such principles are principles that people, or peoples, have sound reasons to hold and honor whether or not they happen to hold and honor them in fact.

Any serious student of civil rights must inquire into the moral ground and epistemic status of civil rights. Is the mode of existence of civil rights *simply* historically contingent and conventional? That is, do civil rights come into being merely at some specific time and place, and then possibly disappear as "history" or experience unfolds?

To be sure, our civil rights, as the rights of citizens of this nation, considered as legal rights—i.e., as rights that are posited legislatively and enforceable in court—are certainly historically contingent. Laws, including laws that create rights, are human artifacts. They come into force by authoritative enactment, and they can, by authoritative act, be repealed. They may exist as legal fact at one historical moment and not at another. Their existence or nonexistence in a positive code depends on human acts of positing and enforcing them. Thus, they can and do change.

Abraham Lincoln expressed the relation between the *time-bound historicity* and the *timeless rationality* of the principle of equal rights in his 1857 speech on the *Dred Scott v. Sandford* decision.[2] He said of those who had written the Declaration of Independence that

> [t]hey defined with tolerable distinctness, in what respects they did consider all men created equal—equal in "certain inalienable rights, among which are life, liberty, and the pursuit of happiness." This they said, and this they meant. They did not mean to assert the obvious untruth, that all were then actually enjoying that equality, nor yet, that they were about to confer it immediately upon them. In fact they had no power to confer such a boon. They meant simply to declare the *right*, so that the *enforcement* of it might follow as fast as circumstances should permit. They meant

to set up a standard maxim for free society, which should be familiar to all, and revered by all; constantly looked to, constantly labored for, and even though never perfectly attained, constantly approximated, and thereby constantly spreading and deepening its influence, and augmenting the happiness and value of life to all people of all colors everywhere.[3]

If there are objective or true principles of justice (such as the principle of equality) that constitute a higher standard, then legislative action may be rationally guided and criticized in the light of those principles; and legal rights, or the absence of certain legal rights, can be judged morally good or bad. Authoritative actors in a legal system may fail to secure or enforce a right that, morally speaking, ought to be secured and enforced; or they may posit and enforce a right that ought not to be posited and enforced. For example, the law might unjustly fail to give a certain class of human beings a legal right not to be enslaved or arbitrarily killed; that is, it might unjustly confer upon another class a legal right to enslave or kill them. The justice or injustice of such acts of positive law is measured by reference to standards of the higher law—the moral (or "natural") law— that are objective or true eternally and universally.

Two weeks before Justice Thurgood Marshall resigned from the Supreme Court, I sat in my office in Princeton chatting with then-Judge Clarence Thomas who was in town to address a judicial education seminar. I was, at the time, putting together the volume of essays that appeared under the title *Natural Law Theory*,[4] and our discussion turned to the question of natural law and civil rights. However much Judge Thomas's confirmation hearings left the public confused about his ideas of natural law and natural rights, he made his position on the issue crystal clear to me: "Those who deny natural law," he said, "cannot get me out of slavery."[5] Of course, Justice Thomas was not suggesting that contemporary historicists or conventionalists—"those who deny natural law"—believe in slavery, and he well knows that some nineteenth-century believers in natural law argued for a natural right to own slaves. His point was

that the moral relativism that informs historicist and conventionalist accounts of rights precludes the proponents of such accounts
from offering a rational moral argument against slavery. All they can
say is that once upon a time in this country white people had the
legal right to own black people, and now black people (and, indeed,
all people) have the legal right not to be enslaved. For the latter
proposition they can cite the Thirteenth Amendment of the United
States Constitution. Their historicism and conventionalism preclude
them, however, from saying that the Thirteenth Amendment embodies or gives legal force to a moral or natural right not to be
enslaved. Under their account, no one would have had objective moral
reasons (though some could have had economic or other instrumental or nonmoral reasons) to support the abolition of slavery. Of
course, people may have believed (and acted upon their belief) in a
natural right not to be enslaved, which provided a moral reason for
them to support abolition, but this subjective belief, under the historicist and conventionalist account, lacked a rational ground. That
is to say, it was in no sense *rationally* superior to the belief of other
people that no such right existed or, indeed, that they had a right to
own slaves. It also follows that neither history nor convention could
provide an adequate rational defense against the return in the future
of some form of slavery.

Like Justice Thomas, I reject historicism and conventionalism in
favor of the natural law and natural rights position. It is probably
true, however, that in this respect we are in the minority in today's
legal and academic communities. We can, however, take comfort at
finding ourselves in agreement with America's greatest statesmen,
from Thomas Jefferson to Lincoln to Martin Luther King Jr. They—
and the central philosophic tradition of which they were, in turn,
our nation's principal bearers—argued that the basis of civil rights
and liberties was natural law and the natural rights that derive from
the natural law.

Let me pay what is due to the natural law skeptics of our day: the
central tradition was by no means clear and united on the meaning
or content of the natural law. But the proponents of natural law in

all its varieties—from Aristotle to St. Thomas Aquinas, from Enlightenment philosophers such as Locke to Jefferson, Lincoln, and, not least, King—would probably all have been appalled to hear that natural law thinking is irrelevant or dangerous, which was the conventional view expressed again and again during round one of Justice Thomas's confirmation hearings.

IF *the* official act of foundation of the American regime was the publication of the Declaration of Independence—as our Founders themselves plainly believed—then at the basis of American republicanism is the explicit recognition of "the Laws of Nature and Nature's God."[6] In justifying the act of independence, the Declaration says that we Americans "hold these truths to be self-evident, that all men are created equal, that they are endowed by their Creator with certain unalienable Rights, among these are Life, Liberty and the pursuit of Happiness."[7] Thomas Jefferson, the author of these immortal lines, acknowledged that there was nothing new about the natural law and natural rights philosophy of the Declaration. Years later, he wrote to Henry Lee that it was

> [n]ot to find out new principles or new arguments never before thought of, nor merely to say things which had never been said before, but to place before mankind the common sense of the subject.... [I]t was intended to be an expression of the American mind, and to give to that expression the proper tone and spirit called for by the occasion. All its authority rests then on the harmonizing sentiments of the day, whether expressed in conversation, in letters, printed essays, or in the elementary books of public right, as Aristotle, Cicero, Locke, Sidney, etc.[8]

Notice that according to Jefferson, these writers—two ancients and two moderns—described ideas of natural law in their "books of public right." That there were significant differences among these thinkers about the content of natural law was less important than their shared confidence that there is such a moral-political reality that is accessible to reason and that supplies theoretical justification for "public right." Jefferson was certain that the idea of natural law is "common sense"—that is, something ordinary citizens can and do understand—and that this common sense rests on certain "harmonizing sentiments of the day"—some core set of beliefs about which citizens, whatever their disagreements, could come to agreement.

Despite all the differences among the greatest minds that ever applied themselves to the fields of ethics and politics, there is one proposition on which those within the natural law tradition agree, namely, that human nature is, in significant respects, determinate, unchanging, and structured. This does not mean that human nature is a closed nature;[9] for practical knowledge—knowledge of what is morally right and good for man—is not knowledge of what is (already) the case, but, rather, knowledge of what is to be (and ought to be) done, that is, knowledge of possible human fulfillment through rationally motivated action.[10] Because human beings as practically rational agents can understand and act upon *reasons* provided by the basic goods of human nature, they, unlike beings whose natures are closed, possess the capacity for free choice. Thus, human beings are capable of understanding a moral law, a law of practical reasonableness, constituted by principles of right reason in practical affairs.[11]

The standard historicist and conventionalist argument against natural law and natural rights appeals to the brute fact of moral diversity in the world.[12] Different people, and peoples, hold or have held, different and conflicting beliefs about issues such as slavery, racial segregation, and abortion. From this observable fact, historicists and conventionalists conclude that there is no moral truth, no natural law. But this inference is unwarranted. The existence of moral truth is logically compatible with any range of moral diversity. As Leo Strauss observed,

> [K]nowledge of the indefinitely large variety of notions of right and wrong is so far from being incompatible with the idea of natural right that it is the essential condition for the emergence of

that idea: realization of the variety of notions of right is *the* incentive for the quest for natural right.[13]

A different objection to the idea of natural law and natural rights is its alleged incompatibility with a legitimate range of human freedom, ways of life, and diversity of choices.[14] But this argument fares no better. In the first place, it appears to be self-referentially inconsistent inasmuch as it presupposes a moral obligation to respect freedom and diversity as a matter not of mere convention, but of natural justice or natural rights. It is, in short, a palpably moralistic critique of moral objectivity. Second, the argument misses its target; because the belief that some choices and ways of life are objectively morally wicked does not entail the proposition that there is always a single correct choice or way of life. Natural law theorists recognize a legitimate variety of choices and ways of life that reflect the spectrum of human goods as well as the diverse opportunities and legitimate ways that people can realize and instantiate these goods. Natural law theory has never demanded uniformity or celebrated conformism.[15]

Now historicism and conventionalism are, so to speak, polite expressions of skepticism. They are, however, unstable. This politeness is not principled, but reflects the habits of civility or the mild temperament of intellectuals who happen to hold these positions. But others may be found, of stronger will and greater ambition, who reject natural law. They are not constrained by politesse from drawing the truly radical conclusions that flow from the proposition that there are no objective standards of justice and right. They correctly reason that if man is radically free—free from any standards of practical reasonableness, which is to say, morality—then, as Nietzsche put it, "all things are permitted."[16] This suggests that men are free to pursue their desires and interests, whatever they happen to be; they are, that is to say, morally free, whether or not they are legally free, to deny freedom to others, to manipulate, exploit, even enslave them. Where reason has no sway in practical affairs, the sole question is who has the power. And the powerful have *no reason* to spare the

weak. The radical or nihilist critique of moral objectivity understandably, on its own terms, denounces natural law thinking as a "slave
morality."[17]

The instability of historicism and conventionalism leads to a
conclusion worth pondering, namely, that the choice for us is not
between natural law and freedom, as Clarence Thomas's liberal critics suggested; the choice is between natural law (and a morally
ordered freedom based on natural law) and nihilism.

Prior to the revolution in, or as some say, the invention of, philosophy by Socrates, law (*nomos*) meant the conventional, and nature
(*physis*) was regarded as its opposite. We hear tentative beginnings of
natural law argumentation in Plato, who put the opposed terms
"nature" and "law" together only twice, I believe, in his corpus—
neither time suggesting a nonconventional rule of equity. The Pla-
tonic Socrates did not speak of natural law—for Plato a paradox—but
of that which is "right by nature," or "natural right."[18]

Yet in the dialogue *Minos,* or *On Law,* Socrates did suggest that
there is some unwritten transcendent standard of "worthiness" and
"wickedness" that disqualifies bad laws (*nomoi*) from being considered truly law.[19] Moreover, in Xenophon's *Memorabilia,* Socrates mentioned an unwritten law against incest that is enforced by the natural penalty of having ill-begotten offspring.[20]

Plato's more confident successor, Aristotle, developed the system of ethics from which the tradition of natural law theorizing
emerged. Like Socrates and Plato, Aristotle did not speak of "natural
law," yet he wrote of an unchanging "law based on nature."[21] Practical reason, in Aristotle's ethical writings, is concerned with discovering this law by rational inquiry and putting it into effect in human
affairs.

A self-conscious commitment to the idea of natural law is more
fully evidenced, however, in the writings of Cicero, who mentioned it
repeatedly. He said, for example, that

> "law...is the highest reason implanted in nature, which prescribes
> those things which ought to be done, and forbids the contrary."

And when this same reason is confirmed and established in men's minds, it is then law.

[The Romans] therefore conceive that prudence is a law, whose operation is to urge us to good actions, and restrain us from evil ones.[22]

Now remember that these early natural law philosophers were ignorant of the revealed teachings of Sacred Scripture. Therefore, we may put to rest the oft-expressed objection that belief in natural law is a sectarian religious doctrine. To the contrary, on its own terms, whether advanced by pagans, Christians, or Jews,[23] natural law philosophy seeks to vindicate principles accessible to, and thus binding upon, every reasonable person. If natural law is based upon "faith," it is a faith in reason, and in the possibility of practical reason in particular. It is as much the opponent of religious doctrines that deny the power of practical reason and make all ethical principles nothing but matters of divine command as it is the enemy of the nihilist doctrine that replaces the quest for rationality in ethics with the pure will to power.

It is precisely because the natural law is held to be accessible to reason and thus binding on all rational persons irrespective of religious faith or its absence that St. Paul could say in his *Letter to the Romans* that

it is not the hearers of the law who are righteous before God, but the doers of the law who will be justified. When the Gentiles who have not the law do by nature what the law requires, they are a law to themselves, even though they do not have the law. They show that what the law requires is written on their hearts, while their conscience also bears witness....[24]

Of course, once the revealed teachings began to challenge paganism, the tradition of classical philosophy could not avoid its impact, and the natural law tradition became integrated into (and enriched by) Christian thought in the writings of St. Augustine, for example, and especially St. Thomas Aquinas. In the most comprehensive expression of the premodern teaching on natural law, Aquinas said in his *Summa Theologiae:* "[The human being] has a share of the Eternal Reason, whereby it has a natural inclination to its proper act and end: and this participation of the eternal law in the rational creature is called the natural law."[25]

Since many people today think of natural law thinking as a distinctively Catholic phenomenon, it is worth observing that the Anglican divine Richard Hooker adopted Aquinas's teaching on the subject with very little change.[26] And, despite his distrust of rationalism, Martin Luther was careful not to dismiss "[t]he noble gem called natural law and reason [which] is a rare thing among the children of men."[27] Even John Calvin acknowledged "that internal law, which...is in a manner written and stamped on every heart,"[28] though, to be sure, Calvin was Calvinist enough to insist that it had been grossly distorted and obscured by sin.

I would not deny that there is a fundamental division in moral and political thought between the ancient and medieval philosophers, on the one side, and the moderns, on the other. What is of interest here, however, is not the profound points of divergence, but, rather, the common belief in a natural law of personal and political morality that enabled Jefferson to speak of ancient and modern authors together as responsible for the "elementary books of public right"[29] whose teachings informed his Declaration.

If St. Thomas Aquinas is the classic premodern natural law thinker, the modern *par excellence* is John Locke. Echoing the dispassionate rhetoric of "the judicious Hooker," Locke wrote that "[t]he *State of Nature* has a Law of Nature to govern it, which obliges every one: And Reason, which is that Law, teaches all Mankind, who will but consult it, that being all equal and independent, no one ought to harm another in his Life, Health, Liberty, or Possessions."[30] Unfortunately, few men are "studiers" of the natural law, yet "every *Man hath a Right to punish the Offender, and be Executioner of the Law of Nature.*"[31] Thus, there is an urgent need to escape the uncertainties of the state of nature and institute governments that will secure life, liberty, and property rights in part by creating a governmental monopoly of the executive power. Like Locke, Algernon Sidney wrote partly in response to the arguments for tyranny in Robert Filmer's book *Patriarcha*.[32] Both Sidney and Locke maintained that a sound account of natural law provides the most persuasive bulwark against oppression. Sidney wrote:

> [N]othing but the plain and certain dictates of reason can be generally applicable to all men as the law of their nature; and they who, according to the best of their understanding, provide for the good of themselves and their posterity, do all equally observe it. He that enquires more exactly into the matter may find, that reason enjoins every man not to arrogate to himself more than he allows to others, nor to retain that liberty which will prove hurtful to him; or to expect that others will suffer themselves to be restrain'd, whilst he, to their prejudice, remains in the exercise of that freedom which nature allows. He who would be exempted from this common rule, must shew for what reason he should be raised above his brethren; and if he do it not, he is an enemy to them. This is not popularity, but tyranny; and tyrants are said...to throw off the nature of men, because they do unjustly and unreasonably assume to themselves that which agrees not with the frailty of human nature, and set up an interest in themselves contrary to that of their equals, which they ought to defend as their own.[33]

Tyrannicide is a legitimate remedy, according to Sidney, when violations of natural rights by leaders chosen to secure those rights become systematic and intolerable. "The tree of liberty," wrote Thomas Jefferson, Sidney's disciple in the White House, "must be refreshed from time to time with the blood of patriots and tyrants."[34] Notice that Sidney's defense of liberty, like any plausible defense of liberty, is a natural law defense. His critique of tyranny, like any plausible critique of tyranny, is openly moralistic. What is wrong with tyranny is not that it is unpopular or economically inefficient or contrary to tradition; what is wrong with tyranny is that it is unjust and, as such, morally wrong.

AS I have conceded, there are different and conflicting accounts or theories of natural law and natural rights. There are particularly profound differences on crucial points between the ancient and medieval thinkers and the moderns. For what it is worth, I agree with the ancients and medievals on some of these points, particularly their perfectionist concern with the inculcation of virtue, and with the moderns on others, such as the importance of civil and, particularly, religious liberty.[35]

Nevertheless, virtually all the philosophers of the central tradition that fed the American Founding shared with the authors of "the books of public right" a belief in an order of natural law and justice (which the moderns refer to aptly in terms of natural rights) that is what it is because human nature, and therefore the human good, is what *it* is, and that this moral order is constituted by principles accessible to reason that transcend tastes, preferences, or subjective will.

When Jefferson claimed that the Declaration of Independence was based on the common sense of the ancients and moderns that provided a harmonizing sentiment, it is clear that natural law philosophy is at the very core of this common sense.

When Madison pleaded for New York to ratify the proposed Constitution, he returned in the forty-third *Federalist* paper "to the great principle of self-preservation; to the transcendent law of nature and of nature's God, which declares that the safety and happiness of society are the objects at which all political institutions aim, and to which all such institutions must be sacrificed."[36] The foundation of America's regime of freedom and equality, the world's first liberal democracy, would be incomprehensible in terms that reject the idea of natural law and natural rights.

The idea of "civil rights" currently enjoys a great deal of prestige in our culture. Reverend King's prophecy from the Birmingham jail is already being fulfilled:

One day the South will know that when these disinherited children of God sat down at lunch counters, they were in reality standing up for what is best in the American dream and for the most sacred values in our Judaeo-Christian heritage, thereby bringing our nation back to those great wells of democracy which were dug deep by the founding fathers in their formulation of the Constitution and the Declaration of Independence.[37]

Unlike earlier generations, no one would be afraid today to be described as a "civil rights leader," or even a "civil rights commissioner." In large measure, we owe the fulfillment of Reverend King's prophecy to his own words and actions. But it is important to keep in mind in reflecting on the nature of civil rights and the future of the cause of civil rights that King himself was careful to anchor the defense of civil rights, and of his own actions in their behalf, in the idea of natural law and natural rights. The supreme expression of his view is his "Letter from Birmingham Jail," the Pauline echo of which could hardly be accidental in the thought of a Protestant minister. The entire letter, in my view, is a meditation on natural law and civil rights. Reverend King reminded his fellow clergymen that in the tradition to which they, as Protestants, Catholics, and Jews, all in one way or another participate,

> there are two types of laws: just and unjust. I would be the first to advocate obeying just laws. One has not only a legal but a moral responsibility to obey just laws. Conversely, one has a moral responsibility to disobey unjust laws. I would agree with St. Augustine that "an unjust law is no law at all."[38]

King slightly exaggerated his case here. We are not always morally obligated to disobey unjust laws and it is sometimes the case that we are morally obligated to obey them, their injustice notwithstanding. This is, however, a quibble. Seriously unjust laws never bind in conscience, and laws that require people to *do* that which is unjust may never rightly be obeyed.[39] Civil disobedience in the face of seriously unjust laws is often permissible and is sometimes required. And that, I take it, is Reverend King's point.

He continued,

> Now, what is the difference between the two?.... To put it in the
> terms of St. Thomas Aquinas: An unjust law is a human law that is
> not rooted in eternal law and natural law. Any law that uplifts
> human personality is just. Any law that degrades human personal-
> ity is unjust. All segregation statutes are unjust because segrega-
> tion distorts the soul and damages the personality. It gives the
> segregator a false sense of superiority and the segregated a false
> sense of inferiority.... Hence segregation is not only politically,
> economically and sociologically unsound, it is morally wrong and
> sinful.... I can urge [disobedience to] segregation ordinances, for
> they are morally wrong.[40]

Note that the violation of natural law, according to Reverend King, has its worst effects by distorting the character of human beings. It is the harm done to properly human powers in their proper development that makes for the moral wrong of segregation. The harm would be in no way ameliorated if, as a matter of false consciousness, the strong had persuaded the weak of the "justice" of segregation and made them content with their condition. A happy slave is no less degraded in his nature by his condition of servitude than is a rebellious one. The goods of human nature are, as I have maintained, determinate. Human nature lacks the plasticity and malleability to which the nihilist appeals in defense of the will to power.

King then articulated the principle of justice whose violation in segregation laws accounts for their injustice:

> An unjust law is a code that a numerical or power majority group
> compels a minority group to obey but does not make binding on
> itself.... By the same token, a just law is a code that a majority
> compels a minority to follow and that it is willing to follow itself.[41]

Now, as we have seen, Reverend King perceived that natural law enjoins human beings to obey just laws and just authority. And even in the defiance of unjust laws, he rejects the Nietzschean maxim that "everything is permitted":

> In no sense do I advocate evading or defying the law, as would the rabid segregationist. That would lead to anarchy. One who breaks an unjust law must do so openly, lovingly, and with a willingness to accept the penalty. I submit that an individual who breaks a law that conscience tells him is unjust, and who willingly accepts the penalty of imprisonment in order to arouse the conscience of the community over its injustice, is in reality expressing the highest respect for law.[42]

King saw, as no political or civil rights leader before or after him has seen, that securing the civil rights of the descendants of those unjustly enslaved under the "peculiar institution" of slavery was implicit in the natural law principles to which America aspired but which, from the beginning, she had failed to live up to.

Although his struggle was not easy and ultimately cost him his life, it is unsurprising that Reverend King so accurately predicted the success of the civil rights struggle that he embodied and has come to symbolize. When the proponents of civil rights occupy the high ground of natural law, and reject the nihilism that reduces everything to power, there is no moral space left for the enemies of civil rights to occupy.

After King's martyrdom, however, many in the civil rights movement lost the moral compass that King's philosophy of natural law and natural rights provided. As traditional liberalism collapsed under the radical critique that has produced such phenomena as postmodernism, deconstructionism, radical feminism, and the like, many veterans of the civil rights struggle bought into the moral radicalism of what former Vice President Quayle accurately labeled a "cultural elite." For this elite, "natural law" is a mere euphemism for legitimizing the status quo, thus reinforcing structures of domination and power. At the same time, elite opinion rejects as, at best, benighted the idea of objective moral truth. Thus, no truly rational critique of racism and other forms of unjust discrimination is possible. There is, quite simply, the brute struggle for power. And the noble cause of civil rights, to the extent that its advocates and spokesmen accept this nihilistic outlook, is reduced to the status of a mere interest group. Moreover, the eclipse of natural law thinking among those who speak for the civil rights movement makes it difficult to say anything very compelling about the problems of irresponsibility, drug abuse, promiscuity, crime, and collapsing family structures in many impoverished communities. In the absence of a natural law philosophy of civil rights, the politics of victimhood becomes understandable and perhaps even inevitable. But it is an altogether inadequate philosophy to guide those who would complete the task Reverend King so notably advanced.

Unlike the politics of victimhood, natural law philosophy implies rights *and responsibilities.* It is evenhanded in its condemnation of prejudice, irrationality, and injustice, whether of the Right or the Left. Its principles are universal. A right is a right, whether the holder of the right is white, black, or yellow; a wrong is a wrong, whether the perpetrator of that wrong is male or female, rich, poor, or middle class.

Some people today say that the civil rights revolution has stalled. Some call for a new philosophy of civil rights. What is needed, however, is not a new philosophy but an old one, albeit an old one refreshed and revivified. As we suffer the relativism and nihilism that have become orthodoxy in sophisticated political and academic circles (but whose consequences bear hardest on the poor, the powerless, and the most vulnerable of our people), we await the next Jefferson, Lincoln, or Reverend King to recall us to the higher law that each of them so eloquently invoked in the cause of ordered liberty and civil rights.

10

NATURAL LAW, THE CONSTITUTION, AND THE THEORY AND PRACTICE OF JUDICIAL REVIEW

(Including an exchange with James Fleming)

THE CONCEPT of "natural law" is central to the Western tradition of thought about morality, politics, and law. Although the Western tradition is not united around a single *theoretical account* of natural law, its principal architects and leading spokesmen—from Aristotle and Thomas Aquinas to Abraham Lincoln and Martin Luther King Jr.—have shared a fundamental belief that humanly created "positive" law is morally good or bad—just or unjust—depending on its conformity to the standards of a "natural," (viz., moral) law that is no mere human creation. The natural law is, thus, a "higher" law, albeit a law that is in principle accessible to human reason and not dependent on (though entirely compatible with and, indeed, illumined by) divine revelation.[1] Saint Paul, for example, refers to a law "written on [the] heart" which informs the consciences of even the Gentiles who do not have the revealed law of Moses to guide them.[2] Many centuries later, Thomas Jefferson appeals to "the Laws of Nature and of Nature's God" in justifying the American Revolution.[3]

Most modern commentators agree that the American founders were firm believers in natural law and sought to craft a constitution that would conform to its requirements, as they understood them, and embody its basic principles for the design of a just political order. The framers of the Constitution sought to create institutions and procedures that would afford respect and protection to those basic rights ("natural rights") which people possess, not as privileges or opportunities granted by the state, but as principles of natural law which it is the moral duty of the state to respect and protect. Throughout the twentieth century, however, a lively debate has existed regarding the question of whether the Constitution incorporates natural law in such a way as to make it a source of judicially enforceable, albeit unwritten, constitutional rights and other guarantees.[4] In this chapter, I will discuss two significant "moments" in this debate: (1) the exchange between majority and dissenting justices in the 1965 Supreme Court case of *Griswold v. Connecticut*;[5] and (2) an important effort by a distinguished constitutional law scholar, the late Edward S. Corwin of Princeton University, to specify, and draw out the implications of, the rootedness of American constitutional law in natural law concepts.

The Griswold Problem

IN 1965, the Supreme Court of the United States, by a vote of seven to two, invalidated a Connecticut anti-contraception law on the ground that it violated a fundamental right of marital privacy that, though nowhere mentioned or plainly implied in the text of the Constitution, was to be found in "penumbras formed by emanations"[6] from various "specific guarantees in the Bill of Rights."[7] Writing in dissent, Justice Hugo Black accused the majority of indulging in "the natural law due process philosophy"[8] of judging. Although critics would later heap ridicule on the majority's metaphysics of "penumbras formed by emanations," Black was content on this score to merely record his view that we "get nowhere in this case by talk about a constitutional 'right of privacy' as an emanation from one or more constitutional provisions."[9] His focus, rather, was on unmasking what he judged to be an implicit revival by the majority of the long discredited "natural law" doctrine.

As far as Black was concerned, bringing to light the "natural law" basis of the *Griswold* decision was sufficient to establish the incorrectness of the ruling and the unsoundness of the reasoning set forth in Justice William O. Douglas's opinion for the Court. Black assumed that Douglas would not dare to defend the proposition that judges are somehow authorized to enforce an unwritten "natural law," or invalidate legislation that allegedly violated unwritten "natural rights" or substantive due process.[10] He was correct in this assumption. Douglas emphatically denied that the majority was resurrecting the jurisprudential doctrine under which the Court had earlier in the century struck down worker protection laws and other forms of economic regulation and social welfare legislation as violations of unwritten natural rights (above all the right to freedom of contract) allegedly protected by the due process clauses of the Fifth and Fourteenth Amendments.[11] Indeed, Douglas did not even mention due process in his long catalogue of explicit Bill of Rights guarantees whose penumbral emanations supposedly created a right of married couples to purchase and use contraceptives.[12]

Both Black (in 1937) and Douglas (in 1939) had been appointed by Franklin D. Roosevelt whose manifest intent was to put onto the Supreme Court jurists who could be counted on to oppose the judicial philosophy that had impeded the progressive legislative agenda since at least 1905. The most celebrated cases involved freedom of contract and other economic issues,[13] although a small number of cases invalidated restrictions on non-economic liberties, such as the right of parents to choose private, religiously affiliated schools, rather than public education, for their children,[14] or of teachers to teach foreign languages.[15] Roosevelt and other critics had excoriated the Court for its rulings in cases involving economic regulation and social welfare legislation, suggesting that the justices were, without the slightest constitutional warrant, substituting their

personal political and economic opinions for the contrary judgments of the elected representatives of the people.[16] Under the pretext of giving effect to implied constitutional protections, the critics
alleged, the "nine old men" were reading the social and economic
policies they favored into the Constitution as a means of imposing
them on the public.[17] Even twenty years after Roosevelt's death, no
self-respecting Roosevelt appointee to the Supreme Court would
want to be caught indulging in the practice he had condemned.

In those twenty years, however, much had changed in American
social life, and new issues were before the Court. One of these was
contraception.[18] The development of the anovulent birth control
pill in the early 1960s energized pro-contraception groups, such as
Planned Parenthood, and catapulted the issue into the mainstream
of public discussion. The practice of contraception, which even fifty
years earlier had been condemned not only by the Catholic Church
but across the denominational spectrum (and by such esteemed organs of the American social-political establishment as the *Washington Post*), became increasingly respectable among opinion-shaping
elites and middle- and upper-class Americans generally. Protestant
and Jewish leaders came almost unanimously to endorse the use of
contraceptives by married couples to limit the size of their families,
and more than a few people predicted—wrongly, as it turned out[19]—
that the Vatican would soon revise Catholic teaching to permit contraception for married couples who had legitimate reasons to post-
pone or avoid pregnancy. People of a liberal social and political persuasion, together with more than a few conservatives, came to view
effective contraception as a great boon both for individuals and society alike. The availability of contraceptives would, they supposed,
strengthen marriages by relieving the pressures created by couples
having more children than they desired or could comfortably afford
to take care of. It would, moreover, enable sexually active unmarried
girls to avoid the ignominy and other burdens of illegitimate pregnancy. Above all, perhaps, it would alleviate welfare costs by reducing
out-of-wedlock births to impoverished women.[20]

Many supporters of contraception neither anticipated nor

desired a "revolution" in sexual morality. At the same time, most considered the old moral objections to contraception, not to mention legal prohibitions such as the Connecticut statute, to be relics of an unenlightened—even sexually repressive—age.[21] There is every reason to suppose that all nine of the *Griswold* justices shared this view. Black, who was joined in dissent by Potter Stewart, opened his opinion by remarking that Connecticut's law was "every bit as offensive to me as it is to my Brethren."[22] Stewart's opinion began with a denunciation of the statute as "uncommonly silly."[23] What distinguished Black and Stewart from their brother justices was not any difference of opinion over the morality of contraception or the undesirability of laws against it; rather, it was their unwillingness to declare that anti-contraception laws, however "offensive" or even "silly," violated the Constitution.

Black and Stewart reminded their brethren that the judicial invalidation of legislation in the name of rights that lack any foundation in the constitutional text or its historical understanding was precisely what critics had condemned an earlier Court for doing in the cause of conservative economic and social policy. Doing it in the cause of a particular view of sexual morality—even an "enlightened" view—was, they maintained, no more justifiable. They argued that because the Constitution provided no textual or historical basis for a right to contraception (or "marital privacy"), the only ground on which such a right could be declared is the very ground on which the discredited right to freedom of contract had been declared, namely, the idea of natural law—a law superior to the statutory law to which judges may appeal in striking down a statute even where the constitutional text provides no warrant for doing so. In their view, the majority could not escape the problem merely by declining explicitly to invoke the "natural law due process philosophy" and appealing instead to "penumbras formed by emanations."[24] "Natural law" jurisprudence by any other name remains natural law jurisprudence; and "natural law" jurisprudence is, Black insisted, in principle illegitimate.[25]

But, someone may ask, is it not true that the framers and ratifiers of the Constitution were firm, indeed fervent, believers in natural law and natural rights? Did they not found the United States precisely on the proposition that the institutions of government are justified by the moral imperative that natural rights be protected by civil authority? Did they not design institutions of government with a view to ensuring that civil authority would conform itself to the requirements of natural law and not degenerate into tyranny by violating the very rights government is instituted to protect? But, if so, how could Black and Stewart condemn a jurisprudence of natural rights? And why would Douglas and those joining his majority opinion in *Griswold* go out of their way to deny, rather implausibly, that theirs was such a jurisprudence?

Corwin on Natural Law and American Constitutionalism

IN 1949, more than a decade after the effective demise of *Lochner,* and a decade and a half before the Court's decision in *Griswold,* Edward S. Corwin—Woodrow Wilson's successor as McCormick Professor of Jurisprudence at Princeton and perhaps the nation's preeminent constitutional scholar—delivered an address at the Third Annual Natural Law Institute of the College of Law at the University of Notre Dame. There, Corwin sought to show "how very large a part of its content American Constitutional Law has always owed, and still owes, to its Natural Law genesis."[26] He argued that the positive law of the "documentary Constitution is still, in important measure, [n]atural [l]aw under the skin."[27]

Corwin's analysis was largely historical. His aim was to show that the legal tradition that shaped the understanding of the framers of the American Constitution and the early practitioners of American constitutional law was deeply informed by two central natural law concepts (or "juristic connotations of the concept [of Natural Law]"): "first, that Natural Law is entitled by its intrinsic excellence to prevail over any law which rests solely on human authority; second, that

Natural Law may be appealed to by human beings against injustices sanctioned by human authority."[28]

Central to Corwin's account is the idea that the English common law emerged historically as a sort of positive embodiment of the natural law, that is, as a body of law that is the fruit of (juristic) *reason* and enjoys its status as law precisely as such. It differs from statutory law inasmuch as its legal status does not derive, as does, say, an act of Parliament, from the sheer *will* of a lawmaking authority. Thus, Corwin concludes, "the Common Law becomes higher law, without at all losing its quality as positive law."[29]

From the philosophical viewpoint, however, Corwin's distinction is highly questionable. Common law judges *were* lawmaking authorities. They, no less than legislators, faced choices between options as to what rules to lay down; like legislators, their stipulations conferred upon the rules they selected the status of binding law. In "developing" the law of contract, tort, crime, and so forth, they made decisions based in significant measure on judgments as to how the common good of their communities would best be served. True, the theory of judging associated with the common law places a particular premium on choosing rules that best "fit" with pre-existing patterns of the law. But precisely inasmuch as a new rule is needed, judges must exercise choice and judgment. Sound judgment, to be sure, requires careful reasoning. But this does not mean that the rule selected by a common law judge enjoyed its status as law simply by virtue of its reasonableness. On the contrary, from the intrasystemic viewpoint, its status as law depended entirely on the judge's *authority* ("jurisdiction") to make the choice between (or among) competing possible rules, and (unless reversed by a higher court) its status of law obtained even when the judge made what was, from the point of view of reason, or even justice, a (or the) incorrect choice. In an important sense, then, it was, and was understood to be, the judge's will—that is, the fact that the choice was *his*—that was crucial, though his obligation was certainly to choose as reasonably as possible.

Now, a legislator's choosing is in significant respects less restricted than the choosing of a conscientious common law judge.

But the legislator's (and the legislature's) obligation, no less than the judge's, is precisely to *make the choice as reasonably as possible*—"reasonable" here includes the concepts of morality and justice, such that immoral and, particularly, unjust choices are in principle unreasonable. To be sure, the status of a legislative enactment as law depends on the jurisdictional authority of the legislature, and in this way it is, indeed, a matter of *will*. But, as we have seen, this does not distinguish in principle the (common law) judicial from the legislative office, as Corwin seemed to suppose. It is true that natural law thinkers held (and hold) that the constitutive power of humanly posited law to create (or reinforce existing) moral obligations depends on the substantive justice ("reasonableness") of the law, and not *merely* on the jurisdictional authority of the person or institution purporting to promulgate it. But, again, this is true whether that person or institution in question is a judge (or court) or a legislature. Either way, valid law is the fruit (or, as traditional natural law theorists would put it, "an act") *of both reason and will*.[30]

Corwin suggests that an important strand of the English legal tradition conceives the common law as enjoying a certain superiority to acts of Parliament. He gives significant weight to the "famous 'dictum,' so-called [of Lord Coke] in *Dr. Bonham's Case*[31] which reads: 'And it appears in our books, that in many cases, the common law will controul Acts of Parliament, and sometimes adjudge them to be utterly void: for when an Act of Parliament is against common right and reason, or repugnant, or impossible to be performed, the common law will controul it and adjudge such Act to be void....'" In this "dictum," according to Corwin, we have a jursiprudential notion that, when allied later (as it would be) with John Locke's conception of substantive ("inherent and inalienable") rights of the individual, provides the foundation for American-style judicial review.[32] He notes that "the dictum had won repeated recognition in various legal abridgements and digests before the outbreak of the American Revolution," and cites various invocations of the substance of the dictum by American lawyers and political figures in the years leading up to the Revolution.[33]

A central feature of Corwin's account is his claim that *"judicial review initially had nothing to do with a written constitution."*[34] He asserts that the idea of judicial review appeared in America some twenty years before the first written constitution, and that judicial review was practiced "in a relationship of semi-independence of the written constitution on the basis of 'common right and reason,' Natural Law, natural rights, and kindred postulates throughout the first third of the Nineteenth Century."[35] He argues that the "competing conception of judicial review as something anchored to the *written constitution* had been in the process of formulation in answer to Blackstone's doctrine that in every [s]tate there is a *supreme, absolute power,* and that this power is vested in the *legislature.*"[36] It was one thing, according to Corwin, for Blackstone to reject the idea of judicial review, as he did, in the context of a system in which the supreme will was embodied in the legislature; it was another thing altogether, however, where the supreme will is understood to be that of *the people themselves as expressed in their constitution.* In the latter case, as American authorities such as Alexander Hamilton[37] and John Marshall[38] recognized, the duty of courts facing a conflict between legislation (considered as the act of mere agents of the people) and the constitution (considered as the act of the people themselves) was plainly to give effect to the constitution.

Corwin viewed these competing conceptions of judicial review as clashing near the beginning of our national history in the case of *Calder v. Bull.*[39] There, in a dispute involving the question whether the Constitution's prohibition of ex post facto laws applies only to the criminal legislation, Justice Samuel Chase asserted the authority of the Court to invalidate legislative acts on the basis of "certain *vital* principles in our *free Republican governments,* which will determine and over-rule an *apparent and flagrant* abuse of *legislative* power."[40] In reply, Justice James Iredell, though agreeing with Chase that the constitutional prohibition of ex post facto laws did not extend beyond the criminal law, denied the power of courts to act on the basis of the proposition, advanced by "some speculative jurists...that a legislative act against natural justice must, in itself, be void."[41]

Who had the better view? Characteristically, Corwin appeals to the authority of history, asserting that while Iredell's view prevailed as a matter of official doctrine, his victory was "more in *appearance* than in *reality.*"[42] "[I]n the very process of discarding the doctrine of natural rights and adherent doctrines as the basis of judicial review," Corwin insists, "the courts have contrived to throw about those rights which originally owed their protection to these doctrines the folds of the documentary [C]onstitution."[43]

Natural Law and the Griswold Problem

DOES Corwin's analysis provide what is needed to vindicate the "natural law" jurisprudence Justice Black complained about in *Griswold*?

It is possible to read Corwin as supposing that belief in natural law entails the authority of judges to enforce it when they judge it to be in conflict with positive law, at least in those jurisdictions which authorize courts to exercise judicial review of legislation, and, in particular, where the framers and ratifiers of a written constitution evidently sought to protect natural rights and ensure the conformity of governmental acts to the requirements of natural law. But if this was, in fact, Corwin's view, and his essentially historical approach to the subject leaves the matter a bit unclear, then I do not believe he was correct. It is certainly true that believers in natural law consider positive law to be legitimate and binding in conscience only where it conforms to natural law and, as such, respects the natural rights of people subject to it. But natural law itself does not settle the question of whether it falls ultimately to the legislature or the judiciary in any particular polity to ensure that the positive law conforms to natural law and respects natural rights.[44] And nothing in the record suggests that the American founders believed otherwise. To be sure, there were debates at the margins, such as the debate between Chase and Iredell. But the questions at issue in such debates involved nothing like the *Griswold* problem. Rather, they dealt with whether the judiciary could, in effect, refuse to enforce laws that were incapable of being complied with, for example. Or whether courts could overrule legislative acts that plainly violated "vital principles" that, though not expressly stated, were presupposed by the very institutions of "free republican government."

If we see that natural law does not dictate an answer to the question of its own enforcement, it is clear that authority to enforce the natural law may reasonably be vested primarily, or even virtually exclusively, with the legislature; or, alternatively, a significant measure of such authority may be granted to the judiciary as a check on legislative power. The question whether to vest courts with the power of constitutional judicial review at all, and, if so, what the scope of that power should be, is in important ways underdetermined by reason. As such, it is a matter to be resolved prudently by the type of authoritative choice among morally acceptable options, what Aquinas called *determinatio,* and distinguished from matters that can be resolved "by a process akin to deduction" from the natural law itself.[45] It is a mistake, then, to suppose that believers in natural law will, or necessarily should, embrace expansive judicial review or even "natural law" jurisprudence (of the type criticized by Justice Black in *Griswold*). And that is because questions of the existence and content of natural law and natural rights are, as a logical matter, independent of questions of institutional authority to give practical effect to natural law and to protect natural rights.

Let us now return to the *Griswold* case. Imagine that someone, say Justice Black, accepts the proposition that the framers and ratifiers of the Constitution were fundamentally motivated by a concern to conform governmental acts to natural law and protect natural rights. Suppose further that he agrees that people have a natural right to "marital privacy" which includes the right to use contraceptives. He could, nevertheless, without logical inconsistency, come down on the question of the constitutionality of the Connecticut statute exactly as he did in *Griswold.* Moreover, he could come down that way for precisely the reasons he stated in the case. These reasons do not necessarily involve, and certainly do not logically entail, denial of the existence of natural law or natural rights. Rather, they constitute the denial that judges are authorized under the positive law of the Constitution to invalidate legislation based simply on their (as opposed to the Constitution's) understanding of natural law and natural rights.

As Robert Bork, perhaps the leading contemporary critic of "natural law" jurisprudence, explains his position: "I am far from denying that there is a natural law, but I do deny both that we have given judges authority to enforce it and that judges have any greater access to that law than do the rest of us."[46] Of course, Bork's view of the scope of judicial authority under the Constitution might or might not be correct. A proposition may be logically sound yet substantively false. Perhaps the Constitution, properly interpreted, does, in fact, confer upon judges the power to enforce their views of natural law and natural rights, even in the absence of textual or historical warrant for their views. What matters for purposes of the current analysis is that the issue is itself textual and historical. If judges do, as Ronald Dworkin, for example, claims, legitimately enjoy the constitutional authority to invalidate legislation precisely on the ground that it violates abstract constitutional principles understood in light of the judges' own best judgments of natural law (viz., moral truth), then, as Dworkin himself acknowledges, that is because this power is conferred on courts by the positive law of the Constitution, not by the natural law itself.[47] Any argument seeking to establish the authority of courts to invalidate legislation by appeal to natural law and natural rights ungrounded in the constitutional text or history, therefore, will itself have to appeal to the constitutional text and history. This is by no means to suggest that there is anything self-contradictory or necessarily illicit about such arguments. There is no reason in principle why a Constitution cannot, expressly or by more or less clear implication, confer such authority on courts. It is merely to indicate that the question whether a particular constitution in fact confers it is, as I have said, one of positive, not natural, law.

Now, I should observe before concluding that someone who believes that our own Constitution does, in fact, confer upon judges authority to enforce natural law and natural rights need not come down in favor of the decision in *Griswold*. This is because that decision presupposes not only (a) the authority of courts to enforce natural rights, but also (b) the existence of a substantive natural right to contraception, at least for married couples. Someone who believes in (a) may or may not also believe in (b). Stephen Krason, for example, who relies heavily on Corwin's account of the natural law basis of American constitutionalism to argue for the broad judicial enforcement of natural law principles, at the same time sharply condemns some of the leading decisions in which the Court seems most clearly to have been acting on the justices' understanding of natural law and natural rights, for example, the establishment of a right to abortion in *Roe v. Wade*.[48] Responding to arguments by Bork and others that acceptance of judicial authority to enforce natural law will likely result in decisions incorporating into our constitutional law the modern liberal view of morality, Krason insists that the answer is to appoint judges who reject liberalism and would enforce "the true natural law."[49] According to Krason, the problem with *Roe* (and, he would no doubt add, *Griswold*) is not the judicial enforcement of natural law and natural rights, but, rather, the enforcement of a *false* conception of natural law and natural rights. Challenging the views of Bork and other conservative jurists, including, notably, Justice Antonin Scalia,[50] Krason argues that the correct decision in *Roe* would not have been a form of judicial abstention that would have permitted the question to be resolved legislatively (on the ground, adduced by Bork, Scalia, and others that the Constitution is "silent" on the issue of abortion), but, rather, a decision recognizing the right to life of the unborn and "declar[ing] legalized abortion to be unconstitutional."[51]

I agree with Corwin and his followers that the fabric and theory of our Constitution embodies our founders' belief in natural law and natural rights. And while I also share their view that judicial review itself emerged as part of the strategy of the founding generation to ensure governmental conformity with natural law and to protect natural rights, I do not draw from this the conclusion that judges have broad authority to go beyond the text, structure, logic, and original understanding of the Constitution to invalidate legislation that, in the opinion of judges, is contrary to natural justice. On the contrary, Black, Bork, Scalia, and other "textualists" and "originalists" are nearer the mark, in my judgment, in calling for judicial restraint in the absence of a clear constitutional warrant for overturning duly enacted legislation. This is because the Constitution, as I read the document, places primary authority for giving effect to natural law and protecting natural rights to the institutions of democratic self-government, not to the courts, in circumstances in which nothing in the text, its structure, logic, or original understanding dictates an answer to a dispute as to proper public policy. It is primarily for the state legislatures and, where power has been duly delegated under the Constitution, for the Congress to fulfill the task of making law in harmony with the requirements of morality (natural law), including respect for valuable and honorable liberties (natural rights).

Judicial review is, I believe, constitutionally legitimate, and can, if exercised with proper restraint, help to make the natural law ideal of constitutional government a reality. Courts, however, can usurp, and, I believe, often have usurped, legislative authority under the guise of protecting individual rights and liberties from legislative encroachment. And courts can usurp, and have usurped, legislative authority in good as well as bad causes. Whenever they do so, however, even in good causes, they violate the rule of law by seizing power authoritatively allocated by the framers and ratifiers of the Constitution to other branches of government (even if that power could, rightly, have been allocated to them). And respect for the rule of law is itself a requirement of natural justice.[52]

Sometimes courts have no legitimate authority to set right what they perceive (perhaps rightly) to be a wrong; and where this is the case, it is wrong—because usurpative—for them to do so. There is no paradox in this. Fidelity to the rule of law imposes on public officials in a reasonably just regime (that is, a regime that it would be wrong for judges to attempt to subvert) a duty in justice to respect the constitutional limits of their own authority. To fail in this duty, however noble one's ends, is to behave unconstitutionally, lawlessly, unjustly. The American founders were not utopians; they knew that the maintenance of constitutional government and the rule of law would limit the power of officials to do good as well as evil. They also knew, and we must not forget, that to sacrifice constitutional government and compromise the rule of law in the hope of rectifying injustices is to strike a bargain with the devil.

AN EXCHANGE WITH JAMES FLEMING

James Fleming

IT IS AN HONOR and a pleasure to comment on Professor Robert P. George's elegant and provocative paper. For one thing, he is a leading proponent of reviving the natural law tradition in political, legal, and constitutional theory.[53] For another, he was a reader of my Ph.D. dissertation in constitutional theory at Princeton University over a decade ago. I am happy to have the chance to reciprocate by reading a work of his and providing a critique of it. Fortunately, I learned at Princeton that vigorous criticism and disagreement are fully compatible with friendship and respect.

I want to begin by observing a striking anomaly in George's analysis. While reading his paper, I had to do a double take. I had to ask myself, is George, a sophisticated proponent of a natural law constitutional theory, actually embracing Justice Black's legal positivist harangue against natural law in dissent in *Griswold v. Connecticut*? I can certainly understand why a positivist like Robert Bork would revel in Black's trashing of natural law.[54] I never thought, however, I would see the day when an able defender of natural law would embrace Black's dissent which, along with Justice Iredell's opinion in *Calder v. Bull,*[55] is usually understood as a legal positivist argument against the idea that the Constitution incorporates principles of natural law or natural rights.[56]

George contends that "our Constitution embodies...natural law and natural rights," but tries to claim that it "places primary authority for giving effect to natural law and protecting natural rights to the institutions of democratic self-government, not to the courts." This anomaly provides a clue as to what is going on in his essay. George calls his position a determination of prudence. I would call it by a different name, which, like prudence, also begins with "p"—politics.[57] But I am getting ahead of myself.

My comment, like George's paper, has three parts. The first part will point out some problems with George's analysis of what he calls "the *Griswold* problem." The second part discusses his critique of Edward S. Corwin's argument concerning how American constitutional law is indebted to the natural law tradition. Finally, and most importantly, the third part assesses George's claim that the Constitution embodies natural law and natural rights but leaves their enforcement to legislatures, not courts.

The Griswold Problem

AGAIN, it is remarkable that George seems to embrace Justice Black's critique in dissent in *Griswold* of "the natural law due process philosophy." According to Justice Black, it is specious to maintain that the Constitution incorporates natural law. For Black, to call a decision or doctrine the product of natural law reasoning is to condemn and discredit it as beyond the pale. Indeed, in Black's constitutional lexicon, there is no more contemptible epithet to hurl at a position than "natural law"—except perhaps "*Lochner*" and in Black's mind, the two are one and the same.[58]

It is also notable that George evidently endorses Black's characterization of *Lochner* as a product of natural law reasoning. It is notable because, in doing so, he acquiesces in Black's tarring of natural law with the brush of *Lochner,* that dreaded, infamous case. Notwithstanding George, one might expect most natural lawyers to defend the dignity and honor of natural law against Black's critique. I shall mention three possible avenues of defense. One way would be to argue that Black's understanding of natural law and natural rights is embarrassingly crude, and that *Lochner*, rightly understood, does not embody reasoning from natural law or natural rights at all. On this view, *Lochner* may well read a problematic economic or political theory into the Constitution, but not as a matter of natural law or natural rights. Another move would be to argue that, even if *Lochner* does reflect natural law or natural rights reasoning, its reasoning is erroneous. Contra *Lochner*, natural law or natural rights, properly understood, do not embody an anti-paternalistic theory of laissez-faire capitalism or Social Darwinism. Still another way to defend the honor and dignity of natural law or natural rights against Black's critique would be to argue that *Lochner* does indeed reflect natural law or natural rights reasoning, and that the majority in *Lochner* got the content of natural law or natural rights right.[59] On this view, natural law or natural rights, rightly understood, indeed do embody a vigorous conception of liberty of contract and do impose anti-paternalistic limitations upon the police power of the states and the powers of Congress. On all three views, Black is fundamentally wrong in his critique of natural law reasoning in constitutional interpretation.

In contrast, George reports Black's critique of natural law and natural rights and defends a variation on Black's position! To be fair, George refines Black's position. He claims that it is possible to believe that the Constitution does embody natural law or natural rights, and still agree with Black that judges have no authority to enforce natural law or natural rights against legislative encroachment. One may well be able to hold this position, but not without throwing out much of Black's skeptical critique of the very idea that the Constitution embodies natural law or natural rights.[60] Why would George adopt this argument? It appears he has made the prudential, that is, political judgment that it is worth doing in order to damn *Griswold*, *Roe v. Wade*,[61] and *Planned Parenthood v. Casey*[62] as illegitimate instances of *Lochner*-style natural law judging.[63]

I want to make four points about George's analysis of *Griswold* itself. First, George obstinately and proudly goes against the grain of our constitutional practice by continuing to criticize *Griswold* as wrongly decided. Elsewhere, I have argued that *Griswold*, like *Brown v. Board of Education*,[64] has become a "fixed star in our constitutional constellation."[65] *Brown* in the 1950s, and *Griswold* in the 1960s, provoked methodological crises in constitutional law. Yet like *Brown*, *Griswold* today is a case that any nominee to the Supreme Court must say was rightly decided in order to stand a chance of being confirmed. Thus, after the Senate's rejection of Robert Bork, Justices Kennedy, Souter, and Thomas in their confirmation hearings were as scrupulous about saying that they recognized a constitutional right of privacy and accepted *Griswold* as they were about declining to say whether they recognized a right to abortion and accepted *Roe*.[66] More generally, as with *Brown*, so with *Griswold*, any constitutional theory, to be publicly acceptable, has to entail that it was rightly decided. So one might just as well rail against *Brown* as against *Griswold*.

Second, George states, "[i]n the end, Douglas's opinion [in *Griswold*] rests on the essentially undefended assertion that the availability of contraceptives is good for the institution of marriage." This is erroneous. Douglas's opinion instead rests on two fundamental propositions concerning the institution of marriage. First, it would be destructive to the marriage relationship if we allowed "the police to search the sacred precincts of marital bedrooms for telltale signs of the use of contraceptives."[67] As Douglas added, "[t]he very idea is repulsive to the notions of privacy surrounding the marriage relationship."[68] Second, the marriage relationship or association deserves special protection because it is "intimate to the degree of being sacred" and "it is an association for as noble a purpose as any involved in our prior decisions" such as those protecting freedom of association for political, social, legal, and economic purposes.[69] Neither of these propositions, contra George, rests on the truth or falsehood, as an empirical or moral matter, of the assertion that the availability of contraceptives is good for the institution of marriage. Together, though, the two propositions lead to another proposition: it *is* good that the partners of the marital association have the privacy and the freedom to make important decisions about whether or when to have children.[70]

I happen to think, as an empirical and moral matter, that the right of privacy, including the right to use contraceptives, is good for the institution of marriage. I do not believe that marriage would be an institution worth preserving in its present form if no such rights existed. Indeed, in a toast at my own wedding ceremony, I read from the stirring final passages from Douglas's opinion in *Griswold* that I just quoted. In fact, I believe that marriage is such a good thing that it ought to be made available to all, heterosexuals and homosexuals alike.[71]

Third, George also characterizes as a "remarkable proposition" the argument in Douglas's first draft of the *Griswold* opinion, which would have invalidated the Connecticut statute on the ground that it violated the right to freedom of association. This proposition not only is not remarkable, it also is eminently sound. In fact, the Supreme Court subsequently adopted that ground for the right at issue in *Griswold*.[72] Kenneth Karst, elaborating upon the language from Douglas's opinion concerning freedom of association, put forward a famous justification for the right recognized in *Griswold* in terms of "The Freedom of Intimate Association" (an article whose title nicely encapsulates its argument).[73] The Supreme Court essentially adopted Karst's analysis in an important case regarding freedom of association, *Roberts v. Jaycees*.[74] There the Court characterized *Griswold* and related cases protecting personal liberty under the Fourteenth Amendment in terms of "freedom of intimate association,"[75] just as it characterized *NAACP v. Alabama* and related cases under the First Amendment in terms of "freedom of expressive association."[76]

Fourth and finally, I want to point out the irony in George siding with Justice Iredell and against Justice Chase in the *Calder* debate. That exchange is conventionally framed as a debate between the natural law jurisprudence of Chase and the legal positivism of Iredell.[77] Beyond that, it is striking that George says that "the questions at issue [in the *Calder* debate] involved nothing like the *Griswold* problem." He states that *Calder v. Bull* concerned "whether courts could overrule legislative acts which plainly violated 'vital principles' that, though not expressly stated, were presupposed by the very institutions of 'free republican government.'" This is striking for several reasons. First, in *Griswold,* Justice Black and Justice Harlan thought that the debate in *Calder* between Iredell and Chase concerning the vital principles of free republican government was clearly on point— Black played Iredell to Harlan's Chase. Black relied on the words of Iredell to argue that the Constitution does not protect the right of privacy because it is not expressly mentioned in the text,[78] and Harlan quoted from Chase to argue that the right of privacy is a constitutional right even though it is not specifically enumerated in the text.[79] Furthermore, many scholars, including myself, have argued that the right to privacy, conceived as a right to autonomy, is, in Chase's formulation, a vital principle of free republican government.[80]

Corwin on Natural Law and American Constitutionalism

GEORGE'S particular critique of Corwin—that both common law and legislation depend not only on authority but also on reason—is sound. But Corwin's larger argument is sound and withstands George's critique. In our constitutional tradition, judicial review is not limited to interpretation and enforcement of textual provisions understood as if they were sections of a detailed code.[81]

I would press a different, more fundamental argument concerning Corwin's analysis. I am dubious about any argument that treats our historical practices—whether the common law, statutory law, or even constitutional law—as the deposit of natural law or natural rights. I would argue that natural law or natural rights inherently provide a normative standard for criticizing our historical practices, including the common law, statutory law, and constitutional law of our country. The best evidence for the appropriateness of this critical attitude is the course of human history, including that of American history, which is strewn with both atrocities committed against, and appalling neglect for, basic human rights, dignity, and needs. And so, we should be skeptical about any theory that treats our historical practices or laws themselves as the repository of natural law or natural rights.

For this reason, we should also be wary of any attempt—like that of Scalia—to reduce the liberties fundamental to our constitutional traditions to whatever specific rights have long been recognized in our historical practices as expressed in the common law and the statute books.[82] Our historical practices surely have failed to realize and vindicate the fundamental liberties of our constitutional traditions. We should understand our traditions, not as historical practices, but as aspirational principles that are deeply critical of our historical practices.[83] Aspirational principles are principles to which we as a people aspire—and for which we as a people stand—even though we have failed to realize them in our historical practices. Our aspirational principles are more akin to principles of natural law or natural rights than are our historical practices, including our statutory law, common law, and constitutional law.

Natural Law and the "Griswold Problem"

GEORGE contends that "natural law itself does not settle the question of whether it falls ultimately to the legislature or the judiciary in any particular polity to ensure that the positive law conforms to natural law and respects natural rights." His contention is correct. As I would put it, we should distinguish between the following two fundamental interrogatives of constitutional interpretation: *What* is the Constitution? and *Who* may authoritatively interpret it?[84] To elaborate the distinction: The answer to the question *What* does the Constitution include?—for example, text expressing specific rules only or text embodying abstract principles of natural law or natural rights—does not determine the answer to the question *Who*, as between legislatures and courts, may authoritatively interpret and enforce the Constitution, whatever it includes.

The classical, interpretive justification for judicial review, put forward in *The Federalist No. 78*[85] and *Marbury v. Madison*,[86] is a famous answer to the *Who* question. Courts are obligated to interpret the higher law of the Constitution and to preserve and enforce it against encroachments by the ordinary law of legislation. This justification is agnostic as between the following two competing answers to the *What* question. The first is a legal positivist conception advanced by Bork, Scalia, and Black.[87] On this view, the Constitution is basically a code of detailed rules. It excludes abstract moral principles, including abstract principles of natural law or natural rights. The second answer is a moral realist or natural rights conception put forward by Michael Moore and Sotirios A. Barber;[88] I will lump their conception in with Ronald Dworkin's idea of a "moral reading of the Constitution."[89] These theorists believe the Constitution embodies a scheme of abstract moral principles, which, with some simplification, we can say are principles of natural rights.[90] Thus, the important question becomes *What* is the Constitution?, as well as *What* does it include? In particular, which of the two foregoing general answers is superior?

Narrow originalists like Bork and Scalia have asserted a monopoly on the classical, interpretive justification of judicial review and on concern for fidelity in constitutional interpretation.[91] Again, they offer the foregoing legal positivist answer to the question *What* does the Constitution include. They side with Black in *Griswold* and Iredell in *Calder.* The Constitution consists of the text only, which should be understood as a code of detailed rules, and it excludes natural law or natural rights (and, more generally, any conception of a scheme of abstract principles). For them, the classical, interpretive justification of judicial review requires judges to interpret and enforce the Constitution so understood. And for them, fidelity to the Constitution so understood forbids judicial interpretation and enforcement of principles of natural law or natural rights.[92]

Dworkin, Moore, and Barber have challenged the narrow originalists' pretensions to a monopoly on the classical, interpretive justification of judicial review and on concern for fidelity in constitutional interpretation. They have sought to reclaim and reconstruct the classical, interpretive justification with their own conceptions of the Constitution and fidelity.[93] They roughly side with Douglas in *Griswold* and Chase in *Calder*. The Constitution includes the text, but they understand the text as embodying a scheme of abstract moral principles including (for the sake of argument) principles of natural rights. And so, for them, the classical, interpretive justification of judicial review entails that judges should interpret and enforce the Constitution so understood. And fidelity to the Constitution so understood requires judicial interpretation and enforcement of abstract moral principles including natural rights.

George's move is different from that of the narrow originalists. First, he argues, contrary to the narrow originalists, that "the fabric and theory of our Constitution embodies our founders' belief in natural law and natural rights." Second, he apparently wants to invoke the classical, interpretive justification of judicial review. Nonetheless, he wants to conclude, like the narrow originalists, that judges interpreting and enforcing the Constitution should not interpret and enforce principles of natural law or natural rights. As he puts it, "I do not draw from this [conception of the Constitution as embodying our founders' belief in natural law and natural rights] the conclusion that judges have broad authority to go beyond the text, structure, logic, and original understanding of the Constitution to invalidate legislation that, in the opinion of judges, is contrary to natural justice." He also writes, "Black, Bork, Scalia, and other 'textualists' and 'originalists' are nearer the mark, in my judgment, in calling for judicial restraint in the absence of a clear constitutional warrant for overturning duly enacted legislation."

Yet because of George's conception of *What* the Constitution includes, he cannot embrace the narrow originalist conclusion unless he offers a justification for judicial review besides the classical, interpretive justification. George argues from a conception of *What* is the Constitution like Dworkin's (rather than Bork's)—through a justification of judicial review that is agnostic between a conception of *What* like Dworkin's and a conception of *What* like Bork's—to a conclusion or conception of judicial review like Bork's (as distinguished from Dworkin's). But again, he cannot reach that conclusion without a "noninterpretive" justification of judicial review.[94] For the classical, interpretive justification of judicial review offers no justification for judges to refrain from enforcing any provision, part, or aspect of the Constitution. Instead, it says, interpret and enforce the Constitution, whatever it is. And so, if the Constitution embodies principles of natural law and natural rights, that justification entails that judges should interpret and enforce those principles.

To be sure, there are alternative "noninterpretive" justifications for judicial review that might support George's conclusion that principles of natural law and natural rights, although incorporated into the Constitution, should not be judicially enforced. But in this paper at least, he has not put forward any such alternative justification. He does say, "[A]s I read the document, [the Constitution] places primary authority for giving effect to natural law and protecting natural rights to the institutions of democratic self-government, not to the courts." He continues, "[i]t is primarily for the state legislatures and, where power has been duly delegated under the Constitution, for the Congress to fulfill the task of making law in harmony with the requirements of morality (natural law), including respect for valuable and honorable liberties (natural rights)." He merely reports his conclusion and does not argue for it.

In his closing remarks about fidelity to the rule of law and the Constitution, George suggests that proponents of judicial enforcement of principles of natural law or natural rights have forsaken such fidelity and instead have made a "bargain with the devil." But it is important to note, as just intimated, that he turns against his own understanding of fidelity to the Constitution in order to argue against judicial enforcement of such principles. To be sure, he can argue that principles of natural law and natural rights embodied in the Constitution should be interpreted and enforced by legislatures rather than courts. But it will take an argument besides fidelity to get to that conclusion.

Moreover, I dare say that several common arguments are not

available to George, given his general commitments. For example, he surely would not make skeptical arguments: that even if the Constitution incorporates natural law or natural rights, its content is unknowable or so indeterminate that courts should ignore it or leave it to legislatures to interpret and enforce it. He is hardly such a skeptic. And he presumably would not make democratic arguments: that even if the Constitution incorporates natural law or natural rights, and even if judges can determine its content, courts should ignore it or leave it to legislatures because it is in principle a good thing for our constitutional democracy that legislatures give their own content to natural law or natural rights. I doubt that he is such a democrat. For example, I doubt that he would say that it is a good thing for democracy for New York to decide that women have a natural right to decide whether to terminate a pregnancy through having an abortion.

Finally, George might be able to argue, along the lines suggested by the work of Lawrence G. Sager and Cass R. Sunstein, that the Constitution incorporates principles of natural law or natural rights, but these principles are properly understood as "judicially underenforced norms."[95] On these views, the fuller protection and enforcement of such principles is secure with legislatures and executives in "the Constitution outside the Courts."[96] But thus far George has not made such an argument.

Such arguments against judicial interpretation and enforcement of principles of natural law or natural rights might be good arguments, but again, they are not arguments of fidelity that follow from the classical, interpretive justification of judicial review. They are arguments of policy or prudence that compromise, override, or abandon the quest for fidelity in constitutional interpretation. Ronald Dworkin pointed this out long ago in his book, *Taking Rights Seriously*,[97] and recently reiterated it in his essay in the Fordham symposium on the idea of fidelity in constitutional interpretation.[98] I certainly do not deny that George might be able to make "noninterpretive" or "non-fidelity" arguments for his conclusion that courts should not interpret and enforce principles of natural law or natural rights that he himself believes the Constitution embodies.

Rather, I wish to emphasize two points: (1) George has not made such arguments; and (2) I hope to have punctured the pretensions that manifest themselves in his charge that the theorists with whom he disagrees concerning natural law or natural rights have made a "bargain with the devil" in disregard of fidelity to the rule of law and the Constitution.

In closing, I want to point out that charging that one's theoretical disputants have made a "bargain with the devil" is a game that both sides can play. I could argue that fidelity to the Constitution imposes on judges a duty in justice to give full meaning to the Constitution's charter of liberty, rather than giving in to the temptation to abdicate responsibility by recourse to narrow originalism or to deference to state legislatures.[99] I could argue that Bork, Scalia, and George have made a bargain with the devil by succumbing to versions of the latter temptation. My more general point is that no one proposes breaking with fidelity to the Constitution (as they understand it) in order to achieve the results that they desire. Rather, everyone argues that fidelity to the Constitution, rightly understood, requires the results that they believe are constitutionally sound. Thus, we return to the fundamental question, what is the best understanding of *What* is the Constitution?, and what is the best understanding of fidelity in constitutional interpretation.

Robert P. George

I AM GRATEFUL to James Fleming for his comments on my paper.

The terms "natural law" and "legal positivism" have no stable meaning in contemporary legal, political, and philosophical discourse. It is therefore incumbent upon scholars who participate in discussions in which these terms are employed to attend carefully to the different meanings assigned to them by different writers or by a given writer in different contexts. The price of carelessness in this regard is error and confusion.

Unfortunately, Fleming's comment on my paper demonstrates my point. Fleming imagines that there is a striking "anomaly" in my "embrac[ing]" Hugo Black's "harangue" against natural law. "I can certainly understand," Fleming avers, "why a positivist like Robert Bork would revel in Black's trashing of natural law. I never thought, however, I would see the day when an able defender of natural law [that would be me] would embrace Black's dissent [in *Griswold v. Connecticut*]." "Notwithstanding George," he goes on, "one might expect most natural lawyers to defend the dignity and honor of natural law against Black's critique [of it]."

Anyone who pauses, however, to consider what Hugo Black was rejecting when he condemned "the natural law due process philosophy" of judging (or what Robert Bork is affirming when he accepts the label "legal positivist") will see that Fleming is deeply mistaken. The anomaly he thinks he finds in my analysis is an illusion generated by his failure to observe that the "natural law due process philosophy" that Black rejects has no necessary connection to the "natural law" I affirm. Indeed, no proposition central to Black's criticism of the opinion for the Court in *Griswold* contradicts any proposition I hold or have asserted in defending natural law.

In *Natural Law and Natural Rights*—the 1980 book that revived interest in natural law theory among contemporary legal philosophers in the analytic tradition—John Finnis elaborated an argument to show that "[t]here are human goods that can be secured only through the institutions of human law, and requirements of practical reasonableness that only those institutions can satisfy."[100] It is this proposition that I join Finnis and a number of other contemporary natural law theorists in defending against moral skeptics and relativists, as well as those particular "legal positivists," such as Hans Kelsen,[101] who make the rejection of the objectivity of human goods and moral requirements integral to their jurisprudential theories.

Plainly Robert Bork is not a legal positivist of the Kelsenian stripe. His "positivism" is expressly restricted to the claim that under our Constitution courts are entitled to enforce only the positive law of the Constitution and are obligated to defer to legislative judgments where the positive law does not forbid legislative action.[102] It is simply a mistake to imagine him "reveling" in a "trashing" (to use Fleming's deeply pejorative term) of the "natural law" that Finnis and I defend.

What about Hugo Black? "According to Justice Black," Fleming asserts, "it is specious to maintain that the Constitution incorporates natural law." I do not think that Fleming has any basis for drawing this interpretative conclusion. In condemning "the natural law due process philosophy" of judging, Black rejects the idea that judges have been given authority by the Constitution to enforce natural law principles *that have not been incorporated into the constitutional text.* But nowhere in his *Griswold* dissent—the sole authority cited by Fleming for his interpretation of Black in this matter—does Black deny *that the text incorporates natural law principles as the framers and ratifiers understood them.* Nor does he deny that when judges properly enforce certain constitutional guarantees they are enforcing the Constitution's understanding of natural law and natural rights. Nothing in what Black says contradicts my claim that the framers and ratifiers of the Constitution sought to craft a Constitution that would, as I said in my paper, "conform to [natural law's] requirements, as they understood them, and embody its basic principles for the design of a just political order."

I do not know what Hugo Black's views were on fundamental metaethical questions, or whether he ever revealed them. Perhaps he was inclined toward some form of metaethical skepticism. There are certainly notable jurists who have been so inclined—begin the list with Kelsen, or even before Kelsen, with Black's influential predecessor on the Supreme Court of the United States, Oliver Wendell Holmes.[103] Indeed, metaethical skepticism might have been the (misguided) subjective basis of Black's rejection of "the natural law due process philosophy."[104] It is possible to interpret references to "subjective considerations of 'natural justice'" or "any mysterious and uncertain natural law concept" in Black's *Griswold* dissent[105] as suggesting metaethical skepticism, though, read in context, one certainly need not interpret them in that way. In that dissent, Black was concerned with the specific question of the scope of judicial authority to enforce principles of natural law not fairly discoverable in the text. I would be reluctant to try to infer from the limited data provided in that context anything very strong about his more general philosophical opinions.[106]

Whatever Black's views were on metaethical questions, the key point is that one need not be a metaethical skeptic—one need not reject "natural law" in Finnis's sense and mine—to recognize the force of Black's critique of William O. Douglas's claim in *Griswold* to have divined a right to contraception in "penumbras formed by emanations" of constitutional guarantees that have nothing to do with any alleged right to be free from the legal enforcement of traditional norms of sexual morality.[107] Indeed, someone who accepts "natural law" in Finnis's sense and mine can without logical inconsistency reject what Black denounced as "the natural law due process philosophy" of judging—that is, the idea that judges are empowered as a matter of natural law, to invalidate legislation as "unconstitutional" even where that legislation does not violate any norm fairly discoverable in the constitutional text, or, I would add, its structure, logic, or original understanding, on the basis of the judges' personal—and, in that sense, one might say (without suggesting anything about their metaethical status) "subjective"—beliefs about natural law and natural rights.

As I argued in my paper, the issue of the scope and limits of judicial power is not resolved by natural law; it is settled, rather, by the positive law of the Constitution. And, entirely compatibly with the requirements of natural law, it may reasonably be settled differently, by way of different constitutional arrangements, in different societies. There is nothing in principle unjust or otherwise immoral about a constitution that vests a significant measure of lawmaking authority in courts as a check on legislative power; but there is nothing unjust or otherwise immoral about a constitution that does not confer upon courts even a limited power of judicial review. Among the things natural law requires of judges and other officials of a basically just regime is that they respect the limits of their own authority under the Constitution, whatever those limits are, and avoid usurping authority settled by the Constitution on others.

James Fleming is a thoughtful and careful scholar. I am therefore extremely reluctant to attribute to him the simple-minded mistake of supposing that every natural law theorist should have an interest in defending just anything that someone chooses to label "natural law." Perhaps he believes that Black's rejection of "the natural law due process philosophy" necessarily presupposes or entails metaethical skepticism. If in fact this is what Fleming believes, I can't imagine what his reason is for believing it. He does not challenge the fundamental point of my article, namely, that the natural law itself confers no authority on judges to go beyond the text, logic, structure, or original understanding of the Constitution to enforce principles of natural justice as they understand them. If and when judges possess such authority, they possess it, not as a matter of natural law, but, rather, as a power conferred upon them by the Constitution. But that means that the natural law does not itself demand, though neither does it preclude, what Black referred to as "the natural law due process philosophy" of judging. It all depends on whether this or that particular constitution—the Constitution of the United States, for example—in fact empowers judges to enforce their understandings of natural justice, and to displace the contrary understandings of the people's elected representatives in legislatures, *even in the absence of a warrant provided by the constitutional text, its structure, logic, or original understanding.*

Fleming rightly says that I "report" my conclusions about the scope and limits of judicial power under the Constitution of the United States, rather than argue for them. As he knows, that is because my paper is not about that question. It is about the question whether natural law itself licenses freewheeling judicial review of the sort exemplified by *Griswold*. It does not. Does it forbid freewheeling judicial review? Not in principle. Such review violates natural law when (and only when) it constitutes a usurpation under the positive law of a given constitution. Judges, being human (particularly when they are exercising power that is itself not in practice subject to formal review by other officials), will naturally be tempted to engage in usurpative acts for the sake of causes they favor, whether these causes are liberal or conservative, whether they have to do with contraception, abortion, campaign finance, affirmative action, the death penalty, laissez-faire economics, socialist economics, the election of George Bush, or the election of Al Gore. For the sake of the rule of law, a conscientious and responsible judge will resist the temptation. A proper "judicial restraint" consists precisely in such personal judicial self-discipline. In a basically just regime, judicial usurpations of constitutionally established popular or legislative authority, even in what judges take to be good causes, are themselves unjust. The willingness to do injustice—even for the sake of ends one believes, perhaps rightly, to be just—is what I referred to at the end of my paper as a "bargain with the devil."

Fleming says that "no one proposes breaking with fidelity to the Constitution (as they understand it) in order to achieve the results they desire." Yet Fleming's own approach to constitutional interpretation, one he substantially shares with liberal legal theorist Ronald Dworkin, is one that, according to Dworkin himself, "would . . . be *revolutionary* for a judge openly to recognize."[108] Although liberal (and, Dworkin supposes, conservative) judges frequently put into practice what he approvingly calls "the moral reading" of the Constitution (a reading that corresponds roughly to what Black labeled "the natural law due process philosophy"), Dworkin admits that "against all the evidence, they deny its influence and try to explain their decisions in other—embarrassingly unsatisfactory—ways."[109] I certainly agree with Dworkin on this point.

In fact, I do not see how it can honestly be denied that judges have often exercised power that is simply unjustifiable on the terms of their stated theories of constitutional interpretation. In many cases, perhaps most, their motivation is not some raw lust for power; it is, rather, a desire to produce what they are persuaded are the right policy outcomes in the face of what they take to be retrograde, unenlightened, morally obtuse, or prejudiced legislators or voters. Fleming's response, of course, is that two can play at this game. So he tries to play it. In criticizing my position, he asserts that it "reflects political judgments about what institutions are most likely to realize [my] particular conservative conception of natural law." Really? Fleming's accusation that I am the one who is letting "political judgments" color his view of the scope of judicial power under the Constitution is amazing.

Fleming has moral views, and makes political judgments, about contraception, abortion, homosexuality, and other controversial issues. I do too. In notable cases our moral views and political judgments conflict: He is a liberal; I am, as he reports, a conservative. The depth and intensity of his liberal faith are nicely conveyed by his story about choosing to read at his wedding ceremony from William O. Douglas's opinion in the *Griswold* case. He believes that courts should enforce liberal political judgments about contraception, abortion, and the like.[110] I say that the courts should enforce *neither his liberal political judgments nor my conservative ones* in the absence of a warrant rooted in the text, structure, logic, or original understanding of the Constitution. Where no such warrant can be identified—where the American people cannot fairly be said to have incorporated into their fundamental law a principle that either transfers legislative authority over a subject matter to the judiciary or resolves the issue one way or another without the need for a judicial foray into abstract questions of natural justice—our Constitution leaves the matter to the deliberation and judgment of democratically constituted and accountable legislatures at the state or national level. That is not because the Constitution is not concerned with natural law and natural rights; it is because that is part of the strategy of the Constitution's framers and ratifiers for giving effect to the principles of natural law and protecting natural rights. Now, you the reader decide: Which one of us is allowing our view of the Constitution and the legitimate scope of judicial power to be driven by his "political judgments"?

Fleming may still question my motives. There is nothing I can do about that. He may insist that in my heart of hearts the reason for my willingness to let legislators resolve questions of public policy pertaining to a fairly wide range of morally significant issues without being subject to a judicial veto is a judgment on my part that conservative views will more likely prevail with the people's representatives than in the courts. The truth is, however, that I have no idea whether overall and in the long run the licensing of judges to enact into law their personal moral and political judgments under the guise of interpreting the Constitution would conduce to the advantage of Fleming's moral and political views or my own. Even a cursory review of the historical record should make someone reluctant to predict how things will go in the future. It all depends on unforeseeable social and political developments. One historical constant seems to be that judges will generally come to share elite views where salient divisions develop between elite and popular opinion. And, of course, today elite opinion tends to be on the liberal side of moral and cultural issues. (Does anyone doubt that a poll of the Princeton or Fordham faculty on "partial birth abortion" or "same-sex marriage" will produce results rather different from a poll of the first seven hundred names in the Trenton or Pelham telephone book?) But it has not always been thus; nor is there any reason to suppose that it cannot change.

Fleming suggests that I would be scandalized by the thought that "it is a good thing for democracy for New York to decide that women have a natural right to decide whether to terminate a pregnancy through having an abortion." While I think that pro-abortion policies, whether put into place legislatively or by judicial action, are unjust to their unborn victims, I am not in the least troubled by the proposal to settle the question of abortion via the processes of representative democracy, even in states like New York that are likely to resolve the question in what I judge to be the wrong direction. And, just to be clear, I do in fact think that it is proper (and even "good for

democracy") for the people and their elected representatives to deliberate and decide matters of high moral import. It would, in my
opinion, be a mistake to remove all such matters from the domain of
ordinary democratic deliberation. At the same time, I think it is
proper for the people, upon due deliberation, to "constitutionalize"
certain matters, thus removing them from the domain of ordinary
democratic deliberation, by enshrining in the constitutional text
judicially enforceable principles of natural law and natural rights
that are incompatible with what misguided legislative majorities
might wish to do in the future.

As for abortion itself, it is clear to me that no principle to which
the American people have committed themselves in their Constitution is incompatible with the legal protection of human beings *in
utero*. So *Roe v. Wade*[111] strikes me as a constitutionally unjustified
decision. Frankly, it is not so clear to me that the American people
have not, by ratification of the equal protection clause, committed
themselves to a principle that is incompatible with laws that generally
permit the killing of such human beings by abortion. The issue is
complicated and requires reflection on the publicly understood meaning of the principle of equal protection that was ratified in the post–
Civil War period. If the more careful, rigorous, and historically informed reading of the equal protection clause leads to the conclusion
that the American people have, in fact, *not* committed themselves to
a principle incompatible with the general legal permission of abortion, then the matter is properly within the scope of legislative authority and it is the responsibility of the people and their elected representatives to resolve the issues of natural law and natural rights at the
heart of the debate about abortion justly. I do not find anything
scandalous about that. I see no reason to suppose that those of my
fellow citizens who are not Supreme Court justices are less trustwor-
thy on matters of moral import than are my fellow citizens who are.
Certainly nothing in the historical record inclines me to believe that
judges are better at discovering moral truth than non-judges.

In the context of his efforts to depict my views as somehow
alienated from "the classical interpretive justification for judicial

review," Fleming asserts that I argue "from a conception of *What* is the Constitution like Dworkin's (rather than Bork's)—through a justification of judicial review that is agnostic between a conception of *What* like Dworkin's and a conception of *What* like Bork's—to a conclusion or conception of judicial review like Bork's (as distinguished from Dworkin's)." This assertion is inaccurate. I agree that the question *What* is the Constitution is an important one. And, like Dworkin, I believe that the Constitution embodies principles of natural law and natural rights. However, I further believe that the Constitution includes various strategies for giving effect to natural law and protecting natural rights. And unlike Dworkin (but like Bork, as I understand his thought) I do not think that provisions such as the "equal protection" and "due process" clauses are "abstract principles" or "majestic generalities" whose content is to be supplied by the unrestricted practical (moral) reasoning of judges. Where the content or its application in particular circumstances is unclear, these provisions are to be interpreted by reflection on their legal, historical, and textual context, as well as on the purposes they were meant to serve and goals they were designed to achieve. It is their *legal* meaning that is the object of this particular interpretative quest. Often, disputes about the meaning of constitutional provisions in concrete circumstances can be resolved by such reflection, or by consideration of the logical implications of the content of provisions thus interpreted.

Fleming goes on to say, as if I would disagree, that "if the Constitution embodies principles of natural law and natural rights, [the classical, interpretive justification] entails that judges should interpret and enforce those principles." Of course they should. That isn't the question. The question is *Who* has been given authority under the Constitution to decide and enforce principles of natural law and natural rights *in the many cases in which the Constitution leaves them unspecified.* As I read the document, it falls to the institutions of democratic self-government, not to the courts, to resolve them. Not only is our Constitution not one that attempts to settle in the text every matter of high moral import, it is not one that shifts responsibility for every question of natural law and natural rights to the judiciary, leaving to democratic institutions only mundane matters of policy. I repeat: From this it does not follow that our Constitution is not concerned with natural law and the protection of natural rights. The fact is that our Constitution places a considerable measure of responsibility for resolving disputed questions of natural law and natural rights in the hands of the people and their elected representatives. Again, I find nothing scandalous about that; nor should other believers in natural law.[112]

Let me conclude with brief remarks about Professor Fleming's treatment of *Griswold* (not at his wedding, but in his paper).

He argues that I am wrong to say that there was anything "remarkable" about the first draft of Justice Douglas's opinion for the court in the *Griswold* case, which would have struck down the Connecticut statute on the basis of a First Amendment "freedom of association" claim, rather than on a theory of privacy found in "penumbras formed by emanations." He claims that the Supreme Court has, in fact, since adopted an analysis in line with Douglas's original theory in *Roberts v. Jaycees*.[113] The "penumbras formed by emanations" metaphysics is not something that supporters of the *Griswold* decision have been eager to advertise or defend. Yet the Court itself, while citing *Griswold* many times, has not formally proposed an alternative justification for the ruling. *Griswold* has been categorized and treated in different ways by different justices in different opinions. But it is, in my view, worse than a stretch for Fleming to suggest that the opinion for the court in *Roberts* restores the First Amendment "freedom of association" justification that Douglas originally proposed as the ground for invalidating the statute at issue in *Griswold,* and that his fellow justices rejected. The original Douglas opinion has been published.[114] Readers who are curious can easily compare it with what Justice William Brennan says in his opinion for the Court in *Roberts* and judge for themselves whether my view or Fleming's is the superior one.

Fleming claims that I am also in error in saying that "Douglas's opinion in *Griswold* rests on the essentially undefended assertion that the availability of contraceptives is good for the institution of marriage." It does not presuppose any such belief, Fleming insists. Rather, it is based on the conjunction of two different propositions that "lead to another proposition: that it *is* good that the partners of the marital association have the privacy and the freedom to make important decisions about whether or when to have children." Although Fleming does not use the word "contraception" or "contraceptives" in the statement of his conclusion, I take him to be stating that it is good for spouses to have contraception legally available to them. His point against me is that this is a conclusion that Douglas argued in support of, not an undefended assertion, which is what I said it was.

The quick way to begin seeing that the error here is Fleming's, not mine, is simply to ask how *Griswold* would and should have been resolved had Douglas and the other justices in the majority shared the view, adopted by the State of Connecticut in defending its statute, that the availability of contraceptives would be damaging to the institution of marriage. The majority justices, in fact, had to assume that the state's view was wrong in order to reach their conclusion; yet nothing in the Constitution can be taken to imply an answer one way or another to the question of whether the availability of contraceptives is good or bad for the institution of marriage.

But there is more to be said. The two propositions whose conjunction Fleming believes generate his conclusion are the following: (a) that "it would be destructive to the marriage relationship if we allowed 'the police to search the sacred precincts of marital bedrooms for the telltale signs of the use of contraceptives'"; and (b) that "the marriage relationship or association deserves special protection because it is 'intimate to the degree of being sacred' and 'it is an association for as noble a purpose as any involved in our prior decisions.'" Proposition (b) need not detain us. Connecticut defended its law precisely on the basis of its judgments as to the sources of threats to marriage and the means required to protect so noble and important an institution. Douglas's rhetoric about marriage, however, "stirring" Fleming may find it, does not prove that he and those justices who joined his opinion cared more about marriage than Connecticut's legislators did, or that they better understood what threatened the institution and what was needed to protect it. So the real issue is proposition (a). The point that I want to make is that this proposition, if it is to do any work towards generating the conclusion Fleming wants, must itself presuppose the very proposition that he is at pains to insist the ruling in *Griswold* does not presuppose, namely, that the availability of contraceptives is good for the institution of marriage.

The "sacred precincts of the bedroom" (or, for that matter, the living room, bathroom, or den) are protected by the Constitution by the Fourth Amendment's restrictions on searches. These restrictions protect *space* that *may* be used for a wide range of activities, sexual and nonsexual, lawful and unlawful. They protect bedrooms and other rooms against unreasonable searches whether, as it happens, people are using those rooms for price fixing, bomb making, prohibited sexual conduct, or drug use. Now, the Court has never discovered that "penumbras formed by emanations" of the Fourth Amendment and other constitutional guarantees create a "right to privacy" that would entail invalidation of laws against, say, using hallucinogens, despite the fact that people can use them in bedrooms and can be motivated to use them precisely by a desire to heighten sexual experience and even enhance marital intimacy, as they see it. Why not? Indeed, why doesn't *Griswold* stand for such a right? The answer is that even most judges who are willing to practice the freewheeling judicial review on display in *Griswold* have a different attitude toward drug use than they have toward contraception. Most happen not to believe that LSD, for example, is good or good for marriage. Most judges disagree with people who believe otherwise. They agree with state policies prohibiting such drugs. They find them reasonable. And they would likely be altogether unimpressed by an invocation of *Griswold*'s "sacred precincts" language in the case of a couple arrested—even in their bedroom—for possession of LSD.

On top of this, it is worth noting that the *Griswold* decision struck down not only Connecticut's ban on the *use* of contraceptives, but on their *distribution and sale,* as well. Distribution and sale were not occurring in bedrooms. No "sacred precincts" required searching to discover breaches of the law. Fleming's proposition (a) could be fully complied with, even on his own terms, while enforcing key parts of the Connecticut law that the Court invalidated in the name of "marital privacy." The conclusion is unavoidable: It was the majority justices' undefended moral presuppositions about contraception, and not anything they could actually find in the Constitution's protections of bedrooms and other private places, that accounts for their sweeping decision.

FURTHER COMMENT

James Fleming

IN THIS further comment, I shall not undertake a rebuttal of Professor George's many misinterpretations of my positions. For example, George interprets me as suggesting that *Roberts* adopts the first draft of Douglas's opinion in *Griswold.* But I did not claim that Douglas's first draft itself was a full justification for the right recognized in *Griswold* or that the Supreme Court subsequently adopted the precise argument of that draft. Rather, my claim was that the personal liberty protected in *Griswold* can be justified on the basis of freedom of intimate association and that the Court in *Roberts* characterized it in those terms.

A more pressing matter is not my positions, but George's, and a problem that arises from his evident yet unacknowledged attempt to wed natural law with Borkian legal positivism. I cannot see the sense in which George's is a "natural law" reading *of the Constitution.* George avoids claiming that the Constitution embodies simple or natural justice or a just reading of due process, equal protection, and other normative ideas. He says, in the fashion of a Borkian originalist, that

the Constitution embodies, and that judges and legislatures therefore ought to apply, the framers' views of justice, due process, equal
protection, and other constitutional ideas. Since he cannot deny
that the framers' views of these things can be morally wrong, he is
therefore saying that the Constitution embodies these views even if
they are morally wrong—that the meaning of the Constitution does
not turn on what is morally right or wrong. Now, George may want
to claim (I cannot be sure) that morality requires that judges try to
ignore moral questions when interpreting the Constitution and follow original understanding, as discovered essentially by historical
(not moral) inquiry. If so, he is making what could loosely be called a
"natural law" argument for a form of legal positivism. In neither case
is he defending a natural law theory *of the Constitution.*

Robert P. George

IN THE ADDENDUM to his critique of my essay, James Fleming
says that I have misinterpreted him on several points. My essay,
Fleming's critique, and my reply to his critique are now before the
reader. Happily, readers who care to know the truth of the matter can
easily examine these texts and decide the question for themselves.

Fleming claims that I am trying "to wed natural law with Borkian
legal positivism." It is regrettable that he continues casually to toss
around terms like "natural law" and "legal positivism" without clarifying what he means by them. I can here do little more than repeat
my admonition that nothing but error and confusion comes of this.

Apparently, Fleming supposes that someone who believes in natural law and natural rights, and who acknowledges that the framers
and ratifiers of the Constitution were believers in natural law and
natural rights, should also believe that the meaning of constitutional provisions "turns on what is morally right or wrong," and that
judges exercising the power of judicial review have the authority to

enforce in the name of the Constitution their particular moral judgments. This, I'm afraid, is a *non sequitur.*

Further, Fleming suggests that I have a stake or interest in something he is pleased to call a "natural law reading" of the Constitution. In this, too, he is mistaken. I do indeed believe that the framers and ratifiers of the Constitution sought to incorporate into the nation's positive law key principles of natural justice. And I believe that to a remarkable degree they succeeded. What a judge is authorized to give effect to, however, when interpreting the Constitution is *the positive law that they created.* It is not the prerogative of judges to alter or displace the positive law of the Constitution even when they believe that their own view of what natural justice requires is superior to the view embodied in the constitutional text.

II

WHAT IS LAW?

A Century of Arguments

THERE IS A SENSE in which twentieth-century legal philosophy began on January 8, 1897. On that day, Oliver Wendell Holmes, then a justice of the Supreme Judicial Court of Massachusetts, spoke at a ceremony dedicating the new hall of the Boston University School of Law. In his remarks, which were published that spring in the *Harvard Law Review* under the title "The Path of the Law,"[1] Holmes sought to debunk the jurisprudence of the past and to propose a new course for modern jurists and legal scholars. Holmes's themes—the question of law's objectivity and the relationship between law and morality—have preoccupied legal philosophy in the century that was then dawning and has now drawn to a close.

The opening sentence of Holmes's lecture invited his audience—lawyers, law professors, and law students—to consider what it is we study when we study law. We are not, he said, studying a "mystery," but, rather, "a well-known profession."[2] People are willing to pay lawyers to advise and represent them because "in societies like ours the command of the public force is entrusted to the judges in certain cases, and the whole power of the state will be put forth, if necessary, to carry out their judgments and decrees."[3] Now, this is a fearsome power. So people "will want to know under what circumstances and how far they will run the risk of coming against what is so much stronger than themselves, and hence it becomes a business to find out when this danger is to be feared."[4] The object of the study of law, therefore, "is prediction, the prediction of the incidence of the public force through the instrumentality of the courts."[5]

This was the thesis of "The Path of the Law." It was intended, I believe, as a provocation. And so Holmes formulated it in provocative ways:

> A legal duty so called is nothing but a prediction that if a man does or omits certain things he will be made to suffer in this or that way by judgment of the court.... The prophecies of what the courts will do in fact, and nothing more pretentious, are what I mean by the law.... The duty to keep a contract at common law means a prediction that you must pay damages if you do not keep it—and nothing else.[6]

The power of provocation is usually enhanced to the extent one obscures one's intention to provoke. And so Holmes claimed merely to be proposing a "businesslike understanding of the matter."[7] Such an understanding, he insisted, requires us strictly to avoid confusing moral and legal notions. This is difficult, Holmes suggested, because the very language of law—a language of "rights," "duties," "obligations," "malice," "intent," etc.—lays a "trap" for the unwary. "For my own part," he declared in another famously provocative sentence, "I often doubt whether it would not be a gain if every word of moral significance could be banished from the law altogether, and other words adopted which should convey legal ideas uncolored by anything outside the law."[8]

Holmes's implicit denial of law's objectivity is not unconnected to his insistence on the strict separation of moral and legal notions. "One of the many evil effects of the confusion between legal and moral ideas," he stated, "is that theory is apt to get the cart before the horse, and to consider the right or the duty as something existing apart from and independent of the consequences of its breach, to which certain sanctions are added afterward."[9] A corrective, according to Holmes, was to adopt the viewpoint of a "bad man" when trying to understand the law as such:

> If you want to know the law and nothing else, you must look at it as a bad man, who cares only for the material consequences which [legal] knowledge enables him to predict, not as a good one, who finds his reasons for conduct, whether inside the law or outside of it, in the vaguer sanctions of conscience.[10]

And what exactly is being corrected by adopting the bad man's point of view?

> You will find some text writers telling you that [the law] is something different from what is decided by the courts of Massachusetts or England, that it is a system of reason, that it is a deduction from principles of ethics or admitted axioms or whatnot, which may or may not coincide with the decisions. But if we take the view of our friend the bad man we shall find that he does not care two straws for the axioms or deductions, but that he does want to know what the Massachusetts or English courts are likely to do in fact.[11]

"I am," Holmes declared, "much of his mind."[12]

STILL for all his skepticism—legal and moral—Holmes denied that his was "the language of cynicism":[13]

> The law is the witness and external deposit of our moral life. Its history is the history of the moral development of the race. The practice of it, in spite of our popular jests, tends to make good citizens and good men. When I emphasize the difference between

law and morals I do so with reference to a single end, that of learning and understanding the law.[14]

Going still further, Holmes claimed to "venerate the law, and especially our system of law, as one of the vastest products of the human mind."[15] It was not, he assured his readers, disrespect for the law that prompted him to "criticize it so freely,"[16] but rather a devotion to it that expresses itself in a desire for its improvement.[17]

Holmes's aim was merely, he said, to expose some common fallacies about what constitutes the law. For example, some people— Holmes doesn't tell us who they are—hold that "the only force at work in the development of the law is logic."[18] This erroneous way of thinking is, Holmes advised his audience, "entirely natural" for lawyers, given their training in logic with its "processes" of analogy, discrimination, and deduction, but it is erroneous nevertheless. Moreover, "the logical method and form flatter that longing for certainty and for repose which is in every human mind."[19] "But," Holmes went on to say,

> certainty generally is an illusion, and repose is not the destiny of man. Behind the logical form lies a judgment as to the relative worth and importance of competing legislative grounds, often an articulate and unconscious judgment, it is true, and yet the very root and nerve of the whole proceeding.[20]

Now, this is getting interesting. The man who would later utter, in another connection, the famous aphorism that "the life of the law has not been logic, it has been experience," has already told his audience in this lecture that law is a matter of prediction, of prophecies of what courts will do in fact. He has also expressed great skepticism about the role of logic in guiding the decision making of judges whose rulings, one way or the other, will constitute the law. So, how are those decisions to be rationally guided? What is "the law" from the perspective, not of the "bad man," but of the "good judge" who, facing a disputed question of law, will not be comforted by the assurance that "the law" is a prediction of how he will in fact resolve the case? In fact, what he wishes to do is to resolve the case according to the law. That, he supposes, is his job. He wants to rule on the matter favorably to the litigant whose cause is supported by the superior *legal* argument. But what constitutes legal argument? What are the sources of law upon which legal reasoning operates?

Of course, one candidate for inclusion in the list of legal sources is history. And according to Holmes, "The rational study of law is still to a large extent the study of history."[21] Is this good or bad? "History must," Holmes says, "be a part of the study, because without it we cannot know the precise scope of rules which it is our business to know."[22] But then comes the punch line: "It is a part of the rational study, because it is the first step toward an enlightened skepticism, that is, toward a deliberate reconsideration of the worth of those rules."[23]

So, history is not a source in the sense that the legal rules uncovered (and whose meaning is clarified) by historical inquiry are authorities that guide the reasoning of the conscientious judge. On the contrary, such study has its value in exposing such rules to "an enlightened skepticism" regarding their value. But then, by appeal to what standards are such judgments of value to be made? And—most critically—are these standards internal to the law or external? Does the judge discover the proper standards in the legal materials—the statutes, the cases, the learned treatises—or bring them to those materials? If the latter, then what is the discipline from which he derives them?

THESE are questions that would be central to the theoretical reflections of jurists and legal scholars throughout the twentieth century. They would be answered one way by Jerome Frank and his fellow "legal realists" in the first half of the twentieth century, and precisely the opposite way by Ronald Dworkin and his followers in the second half. H. L. A. Hart—the greatest of the English-speaking legal philosophers of the century—would refer to the realists' answer as the "nightmare" that law does not exist, and to Dworkin's answer as the "noble dream" that law as such provides a "right answer"—a single uniquely correct resolution—to every dispute that makes its way into the courtroom.[24]

Holmes's own answer was tantalizingly ambiguous. In "The Path of the Law" he said at one point, "I think...the judges themselves have failed adequately to recognize their duty of weighing considerations of social advantage."[25] At another point he made this remarkable statement:

> I look forward to a time when the part played by history in the explanation of [legal] dogma shall be very small, and instead of ingenious research we shall spend our energy on a study of the ends sought to be attained and the reasons for desiring them. As a step toward that ideal it seems to me that every lawyer ought to seek an understanding of economics.[26]

Three-quarters of a century later, Richard Posner, Frank Easterbrook, Richard Epstein, Guido Calebresi, and other theorists and practitioners of the "economic analysis of law" would take this last piece of advice quite literally. Their books, law review articles, and—in the cases of Posner, Easterbrook, and, most recently, Calebresi—judicial opinions would subject legal rules and social policies to cost-benefit tests and other forms of economic analysis to assess their instrumental rationality and thus, in some cases, their legal validity. What these scholars and jurists do fits pretty well with Holmes's desire for lawyers and judges to "consider the ends which the several rules seek to accomplish, the reasons why those ends are desired, what is given up to gain them, and whether they are worth the price."[27] But, one must ask, would Holmes really approve their doing it?

Although Holmes was, in his politics, "a moderate, liberal reformer,"[28] he was resolutely determined, as a judge, not to "legislate from the bench." Indeed, during a period of unprecedented "judicial activism," he became the symbol of opposition to the judicial usurpation of legislative authority under the guise of interpreting the

Constitution. As a justice of the Supreme Court of the United States, he drew as sharp a line as any jurist of his time between "law" and "politics"—even when the politics in question concerned political economy. In what is perhaps his most celebrated dissent, Holmes castigated the majority in the 1905 case of *Lochner v. New York* for invalidating a state law setting maximum working hours for employees in bakeries on the ground that such a regulation violated the "freedom of contract" that was held to be implicit in the Due Process Clause of the Fourteenth Amendment.[29] Holmes argued that this "substantive due process" doctrine was an invention designed to authorize what was, in fact, the illegitimate judicial imposition of a theory of economic efficiency and a morality of economic relations on the people of the states and the nation.[30] His claim was not that there was anything defective in that theory; on the contrary, its "Social Darwinist" dimensions held considerable appeal to him. Rather, it was that judges had no business substituting their judgments of efficiency and value for those of the people's elected representatives in Congress and the state legislatures. They, he famously said, should be able to go to hell in their own way.

IT is not that any of this is flatly inconsistent with what Holmes asserted in "The Path of the Law." Indeed, at one point in that lecture he seems to suggest that training in economics and a due weighing of considerations of social advantage will have the salutary effect of encouraging judicial restraint. "I cannot but believe," he declared, "that if the training of lawyers led them habitually to consider more definitely and explicitly the social advantage on which the rule they lay down must be justified, they sometimes would hesitate where now they are confident, and see that really they were taking sides upon debatable and often burning questions."[31]

But plainly Holmes, as a judge—and, above all, as a dissenting judge—is supposing that the law is something more than merely a prophecy of what the courts will in fact decide. As a dissenter, he holds that the courts have decided the case incorrectly. Of course, he does not deny that their rulings—even where incorrect—have the binding force of law, at least until they are reversed by higher courts of appeal; but he does suppose that the judges in the majority "got the law wrong." So, apparently, judges in resolving disputes should be guided, in some significant sense, by law. And this presupposes the reality of law, and indeed, the *pre-existence* of law, as something more than a "prophec[y] of what courts will do in fact."[32]

So we must press the question: To what standards of legal correctness should the judge look in reasoning to the resolution of a case? Are the standards internal to the legal materials and discoverable, by some method, in them? Or are they external? Do judges "find" the law? Or do they, necessarily, "create" it? Can lawyers predict or "prophesy" what a good and conscientious judge will do by figuring out what he should do in light of the legal materials that should control his reasoning? If that is all Holmes means by "prediction" and "prophecy," then his debunking exercise is, for all its provocative language, far less skeptical than it appeared.

DRAWING their inspiration from Holmes, however, there soon emerged a group of legal scholars who were prepared, for a while at least, to expose the idea of law to truly radical skepticism. The legal realist movement, which reached the peak of its influence in the 1930s and 1940s, advanced the debunking project well beyond the point at which Holmes had left things in "The Path of the Law." Felix Cohen, Karl Llewellyn, Jerome Frank, and others pressed to an extreme the idea of jurisprudence as an essentially "predictive" enterprise. "Law," according to Llewellyn, was what *"officials do about disputes."*[33] In accounting for their decisions, he insisted, it could only rarely be true to say that they are guided by rules. The trouble is not—or not just—that judges and other officials are willful, and thus willing to lay aside the clear command of legal rules in order to do as they please. It is that legal rules are necessarily vague and susceptible of competing reasonable interpretations and applications. Even the problem of selecting which rule to apply to a given set of facts can only rarely be solved by looking to a clear rule of selection. The result is a measure of indeterminacy that makes nonsense of the idea of legal objectivity. The key to understanding the phenomenon of law—accounting for what judges and other officials do or predicting what they will do about disputes—is not the analysis of legal rules. It must be something else. True, judges and other officials cite the rules in justifying their decisions. But if we are to be realistic about what is going on, according to Llewellyn, we must recognize that this is the mere legal rationalization of decisions reached on other grounds.

Frank's realism was, if anything, still more extreme in its denial of legal objectivity. Going beyond Llewellyn's "rule-skepticism," Frank declared himself to be a "fact-skeptic" as well.[34] Thus he denied law's objectivity even in the rare cases in which a clear rule was clearly applicable. Since rules must be applied to facts in order to generate a legal outcome, everything depends on findings of fact in trial courts and other fact-finding tribunals. And facts are, in most cases, virtually as indeterminate as legal rules. In statements that seem eerily, well, realistic in the aftermath of the O. J. Simpson trial, Frank argued that our perceptions of facts are deeply influenced by conscious and subconscious beliefs, attitudes, and prejudices that vary among groups and individuals. So the key to understanding law—understood in legal realist terms—is understanding people's beliefs, attitudes, and prejudices, and why they hold them. Since law is a sort of epiphenomenon of human psychology, legal scholarship should be directed to scientific (e.g., psychological) and social scientific studies of human motivation. To be realistic, it should abandon the idea that law pre-exists and is available to guide legal decisions.

The legal realists' insistence on the indeterminacy of law would, in our own time, be reasserted by advocates of "critical legal studies," though this time in the service of a "New Left" political agenda and with nothing like the realists' faith in the objectivity and explanatory power of the natural and social sciences. The realists themselves were, like Holmes, political progressives—moderate liberals—eager to bring instrumental rationality to bear to solve social problems. Many were New Dealers. A few became judges, and those who did were, like Holmes, far less radical in practice than their theoretical views would have led one to predict. Although appeals to the alleged findings of social science became an increasingly common feature of judicial opinions as the twentieth century wore on, realists who became judges rarely cited their own subjective views or prejudices or psychological predilections as grounds for their decisions. Rather, they cited legal rules as the ultimate reasons for their decisions and claimed, at least, to lay aside their own preferences in fidelity to the law. (Interestingly, in the aftermath of the revelation of Nazi atrocities in Europe, Frank declared himself, in the preface to the sixth edition of his *Law and the Modern Mind*, to be a follower of the natural law teaching of St. Thomas Aquinas on the basic questions of law and morality. Nothing in his earlier writings, he insisted, was ever meant to suggest otherwise.)[35]

Of course, realism had its appeal precisely because it was, from a certain vantage point, realistic. Trial lawyers take issues of venue and voir dire very seriously because they know—and knew long before the O. J. Simpson case—that who is on the jury can be critical to whether facts are found favorably to their clients. And one of the first questions lawyers at any level of litigation want to know the answer to is who the judge or judges are who will be making determinations of law at the trial or on appeal. Often enough, different jurors or a different judge or judges means different results. Clearly, then, the phenomenon of law includes strong elements of "subjectivity."

But the realists overstated their case. Their argument falters under the same question we put to Holmes a little while ago. From the point of view of conscientious judges, the law is not—for it cannot be—a prediction of their own behavior. Often they, like Holmes, will be faced with what they themselves perceive to be a duty to follow rules whose application generates outcomes that run contrary to their personal preferences. True, a willful judge can simply give effect to his prejudices under the guise of applying the law, at least until reversed by a higher court of appeal (if there is one). But this is no modern discovery. And it is no more a threat to the possibility of law's objectivity than is the fact that people sometimes behave immorally a threat to the objectivity of morals. Just as a conscientious man strives to conform his behavior to what he judges to be the standards of moral rectitude, the conscientious judge strives to rule in conformity with the controlling rules of law. And no account of the phenomenon of law that ignores the self-understanding of such a judge—that is to say, no account that leaves out his point of view—can do justice to the facts.

THIS, I think, was clear to H. L. A. Hart. He above all other English-speaking juridical thinkers in the wake of legal realism recognized that the shortcomings of legal skepticism had mainly to do not with the dangers of its capacity to undermine the public's faith in the rule of law, but rather with realism's inability realistically to account for the phenomenon of law as it functions in human societies. Realist theories failed to fit the facts. And they failed to fit the facts because they approached the phenomenon of law from a purely external viewpoint. The problem, according to Hart, was not that legal realists were bad lawyers; it was that they were bad psychologists and social scientists, even as they looked to psychology and social science to explain the phenomenon of law.

Social phenomena—phenomena created or constituted, at least in part, by human judgment, choice, cooperation, etc.—can never adequately be understood, Hart argued, without adopting what he called the "internal point of view."[36] This is the point of view of those who do not "merely record and predict behavior conforming to rules" or understand legal requirements as mere "signs of possible punishment," but rather "*use* the rules as standards for the appraisal of their own and others' behavior."[37]

On this score, Hart faulted not only the legal realists, but also the leading figures in his own intellectual tradition, the tradition of analytical jurisprudence inspired by Thomas Hobbes and developed by Jeremy Bentham and his disciple John Austin. The problem with their jurisprudential theories, Hart observed, is that they too fail to fit the facts. And they fail to fit the facts because they do not take into account the practical reasoning of people whose choices and actions create and constitute the phenomenon of law—people for whom legal rules function as reasons for decisions and actions.[38]

Hart in no way denied the wide variability of legal rules. Beyond some basic requirements of any legal system—what Hart called the "minimum content of natural law"—there is a great deal of variation from legal system to legal system. But in all societies that have achieved a legal order—that is, moved from a pre-legal order to a regime of law—law exhibits a certain objectivity and autonomy from other phenomena, including other normative systems. And the law of any system is not truly understood by the theorist until he understands the practical point of the law from the perspective of actors within the system who understand themselves to be making laws for reasons and acting on reasons provided by the laws.

In his masterwork, *The Concept of Law,* Hart invited his readers to treat his analysis as "an essay in descriptive sociology."[39] But his was a sociology designed to make possible the understanding of legal systems "from the inside." So what he proposed, and what the tradition of analytical jurisprudence has now more or less fully accepted as Hart's most enduring contribution, is that even "the descriptive theorist (whose purposes are not practical) must proceed...by adopting a practical point of view.... [He must] assess importance or significance in similarities and differences within his subject matter by asking what would be considered important or significant in that field by those whose concerns, decisions, and activities create or constitute the subject matter."[40]

If Hart rejected the externalism of Bentham and Austin—with its understanding of law (in Hobbesian fashion) as constituted by commands of a sovereign ("orders backed by threats") who is habitually obeyed by a populace but who in turn obeys no one—he retained their commitment to "legal positivism." He described this much-misunderstood commitment as the acknowledgment of a "conceptual separation" of law and morals. Although he was yet another moderate liberal in his politics, Hart did not mean by "positivism" the idea that law ought not to embody or enforce moral judgments. True, in his famous debate with Patrick Devlin over the legal enforcement of morals,[41] Hart defended a modified version of J. S. Mill's "harm principle" as the appropriate norm for distinguishing legitimate from illegitimate state enforcement of morality; but he fully recognized that this principle itself was proposed as a norm of political morality to be embodied in, and respected by, the law. Moreover, he understood perfectly well that the content of legal rules reflected nothing so much as the moral judgments prevailing in any society regarding the subject matters regulated by law. So Hart cheerfully acknowledged the many respects in which law and morality were connected, both normatively and descriptively. In what respect, then, did he insist on their "conceptual separation"?

As I read *The Concept of Law,* as well as Hart's later writings, the "conceptual separation" thesis seems rather modest. It has to do above all, I think, with the legitimate aspiration of the descriptive sociologist to keep his descriptions, to the extent possible, free of coloration by his own normative moral views. One can recognize a law, or even a whole legal system, as a law or legal system, irrespective of whether one believes that that law or legal system is just; indeed, even a gravely unjust legal system can be, from a meaningful descriptive viewpoint, a legal system. And what is true of the descriptive sociologist or legal theorist can also be true of the judge who may conclude in a given case that the law—identified by authoritative criteria or standards of legality—provides a rule of decision in the case at hand that is, from the moral point of view, defective. In repudiating what he took—wrongly, in my view—to be the defining proposition of the natural law theorist, Hart denied in an unnecessarily wholesale fashion the proposition *lex iniusta non est lex* (an unjust law is not law).

Although his views in fundamental moral theory are frustratingly elusive, nothing in Hart's positivism commits him in any way to the moral skepticism, subjectivism, or relativism characteristic of the positivism of, say, Hans Kelsen,[42] or that one detects in the extra-judicial writings of Oliver Wendell Holmes. In fact, the student of Hart's who has remained closest to his views in legal theory, Joseph Raz, combines Hartian legal positivism with a robust moral realism.[43] Hart and Raz have both insisted—rightly, in my view—on the necessity of some conceptual separation of law and morality for the sake of preserving the possibility of moral criticism of law. As John Finnis has recently observed, the necessary separation "is effortlessly established [by Aquinas] in the *Summa* [by] taking human positive law as a subject for consideration in its own right (and its own name), a topic readily identifiable and identified *prior* to any question about its relation to morality."[44]

Nevertheless, Hart's positivism generated one of the century's most fruitful jurisprudential debates when it was challenged by Lon L. Fuller in the late 1950s.[45] Fuller—whose careful explication and working out of the diverse elements of the Aristotelian ideal of the "rule of law" constitutes a genuine achievement of twentieth-century legal philosophy—proposed an argument to show that law and morality are, as a matter of brute fact, more tightly connected than Hart's positivism would allow. He sought to show that law necessarily embodies an "internal morality" that defies Hart's "conceptual separation" thesis.[46] He offered to argue the point, not as a normative matter about moral standards that positive law *ought* to meet, but rather on Hart's own terms, as a descriptive proposition about moral standards that law has to embody before even the purely descriptive theorist can recognize it as law.

In *The Morality of Law,* Fuller offered an apparently "value-free" definition of law that any legal positivist ought to be able to accept: "Law is the enterprise of subjecting of human behavior to the governance of norms."[47] Nothing in this definition demands that those who make and enforce the laws be wise, virtuous, benign, or concerned in any way for the common good. Still, some things follow from it. For example, people cannot conform their behavior to rules that have not been promulgated, or that lack at least some measure of clarity, or that apply retrospectively. So promulgation, clarity, and prospectivity are aspects of the rule of law. Where they are absent, no legal system exists or, at most, only a highly defective legal system exists. And there are other requirements, including some significant measure of reliable conformity of official action to stated rules. Taken together, Fuller argued, the rule of law constitutes a *moral* achievement.

While adherence to the rule of law does not guarantee that a legal system will be perfectly just—in fact, all legal systems contain elements of injustice—it does mean that a certain minimum set of moral standards must be met before a legal system actually exists. And, sure enough, or so Fuller supposed, grave injustice is rarely found in systems in which the rulers—whatever their personal vices and bad motives—govern by law. It is in societies in which the rule of law is absent that the most serious injustices occur. Of course, Hart wasn't buying this for a moment. While he admired and for the most part accepted Fuller's brilliant explication of the rule of law, he saw no reason to refer to its content as an internal *morality*. He contended, moreover, that there is no warrant for supposing that a system of law could not be gravely unjust, or that the rule of law provided any very substantial bulwark against grave injustice. Indeed, Raz later argued against Fuller that the rule of law was analogous to a sharp knife—valuable for good purposes, to be sure, but equally useful to rulers in the pursuit of evil objectives.[48]

THE Hart/Fuller debate (like the Hart/Devlin debate) was an illuminating one. I count on it every year for one or two lively meetings of my seminar in philosophy of law at Princeton. My own judgment is that Fuller scored a powerful point in establishing a certain moral value of the rule of law, but that Hart rightly resisted Fuller's somewhat exaggerated moral claims on its behalf. In any event, I do not think that Fuller undermined the central appeal of the "conceptual separation" thesis: the methodological aspiration to avoid confusing "law as it is" with "law as it ought to be."

For Hart, the question of how much law-creating (or "legislative") authority a judge has, if any, or where that authority obtains, is not to be resolved at the level of general jurisprudence. Legal systems differ—indeed, reasonably differ—on the question of how such law-making authority is to be allocated among judges and other actors in the overall political system. To be sure, Hart observes that legal rules are inevitably "open textured" and, thus, in need of authoritative interpretation in their concrete application; and this entails a certain measure of judicial discretion and lawmaking authority as a matter of fact, even in those systems which exclude it in theory. This means that the wall between legal validity and the moral judgment of judges is porous, even in systems (such as the British one) of avowed legislative supremacy. Hart's legal positivism is, in fact, completely compatible with the recognition that judges in some legal systems are invited or even bound under the positive law of the constitution to bring moral judgment to bear in deciding cases at law. Hart's is not a theory designed to show judges how they can resolve cases without making moral judgments, though neither is it a theory offering to justify their doing so. The theory simply isn't addressed to such questions.

What I think Hart *is* to be faulted for is a failure to see and develop fully the implications of his own refutation of Benthamite and Austinian positivism and of his adoption of the internal point of view. (Some of these implications are acknowledged by Raz in his recent work.)[49] The central or focal case of a legal system, to borrow a principle of Aristotle's method in social study, is one in which legal rules and principles function as practical reasons for citizens, as well as judges and other officials, because the citizens appreciate their moral value.

Yet Hart himself, in *The Concept of Law* and elsewhere, declined to distinguish central from peripheral cases of the internal point of view itself. Thus, he treated cases of obedience to law by virtue of "unreflecting inherited attitudes" and even the "mere wish to do as others do" no differently from morally motivated obedience of fidelity to law. These "considerations and attitudes," like those which boil down to mere self-interest or the avoidance of punishment, are, as Finnis says, "diluted or watered-down instances of the practical viewpoint that brings law into being as a significantly differentiated type of social order and maintains it as such. Indeed, they are parasitic upon that viewpoint."[50]

This is in no way to deny any valid sense to the positivist insistence on the "conceptual separation" of law and morality. It is merely to highlight the ambiguity of the assertion of such a separation and the need to distinguish, even more clearly than Hart did, between the respects in which such a separation obtains and those in which it does not. Still less is it to suggest that belief in natural law or other forms of moral realism entails the proposition that law and morality are connected in such a way as to confer upon judges as such a measure of plenary authority to enforce the requirements of natural law or to legally invalidate provisions of positive law they judge to be in conflict with these requirements. Important work by Finnis and others has clearly identified the misguidedness of such a suggestion. The truth of the proposition *lex iniusta non est lex* is a moral truth, namely, that the moral obligation created by authoritative legal enactment—that is to say, by positive law—is conditional rather than absolute; our prima facie obligation to obey the law admits of exceptions.

What about law's objectivity? Does law "exist" prior to legal decision? Can judicial reasoning be guided by standards internal to the legal materials? At the dawn of the twenty-first century we can, I think, affirm a position more subtle than the one Holmes asserted at the end of the nineteenth. Yes, the standards to guide judicial reasoning can be internal to the law of a system that seeks to make them so, though never perfectly. Positive law is a human creation—a cultural artifact—though it is largely created for moral purposes, for the sake of justice and the common good. That is to say, law exists in what Aristotelians would call the order of technique, but it is created in that order precisely for the sake of purposes that obtain in the moral order. So, for moral reasons, we human beings create normative systems of enforceable social rules that enjoy, to a significant extent, a kind of autonomy from morality as such. We deliberately render these rules susceptible to technical application and analysis for purposes of, for example, fairly and finally establishing limits on freedom of conduct, as well as resolving disputes among citizens, or between citizens and governments, or between governments at different levels. And to facilitate this application and analysis we bring into being a legal profession, from which we draw our judges, that is composed of people trained in programs of study that teach not, or not just, moral philosophy, but the specific tools and techniques of research, interpretation, reasoning, and argument relevant to *legal* analysis.[51]

To stress law's objectivity and relative autonomy from morality is by no means to deny the Thomistic proposition that just positive law is derived from the natural law. For Thomas himself did not suppose that positive law was anything other than a cultural artifact, a human creation, albeit a creation of great moral worth brought into being largely for moral purposes. Nor did he suppose that a single form or regime of law was uniquely correct for all times and places. His stress on *determinationes* by which human lawmakers give effect to the requirements of natural law in the shape of positive law for the common good of their community—enjoying, to a considerable extent, the creative freedom Aquinas analogized to that of the architect—reveals his awareness of the legitimate variability of human laws. Whomever Holmes may have had in mind in criticizing those "text writers" who saw law as a set of deductions from a few axioms of reason, the charge does not apply to Aquinas. In this, as in so many other respects, the Angelic Doctor was a man of the twentieth century and—if I may engage in a bit of prediction and prophecy myself—of the twenty-first and beyond.

THE CHURCH

12

RELIGIOUS VALUES
AND POLITICS

I N PREVIOUS CHAPTERS, I have attempted to show why a certain form of liberalism has been so destructive for our civic and legal culture. In this chapter, I want to suggest that there are important respects in which faithful Catholics not only may, but must, be liberals of a different type, or, perhaps more accurately, must hold positions associated with a certain type of liberalism. On certain issues, in other words, the Catholic Church has identified the position associated with this type of liberalism as true and, therefore, to be held definitively by the Catholic faithful. The "conservatism" that opposes this type of liberalism used to be widely held by Churchmen and by faithful Catholics; some Catholics—perhaps even some Churchmen—continue to cling to it. I believe, however, that a sound understanding of the teachings of modern popes—especially the current pontiff—and of the First and Second Vatican Councils requires the abandonment of key positions associated with this type of conservatism. I hope that what I say here will be of interest and relevance to evangelical and other faithful Protestants and to observant Jews.

Of course, in using the terms "liberal" and "conservative," I face, first, the problem of definition. Precisely what does it mean for someone to be a "liberal" as opposed to a "conservative"? I am reminded of the late Justice Potter Stewart's despair of defining "pornography." "I know it," he famously remarked, "when I see it." After a number of failed attempts, I similarly despair of defining the terms "liberal" and "conservative." In one sense of the term, I know a "liberal" when I see one. Teddy Kennedy is a liberal. So is Mario Cuomo. Their "liberalism" is opposed to the "conservatism" of, say, William F. Buckley and Ronald Reagan. "Liberals," in this sense of the term, defend large-scale government-run health, education, and welfare programs. They support redistributive taxation policies. They favor affirmative action programs for women and minorities and call for the revision of civil rights laws to prohibit discrimination based on "sexual orientation." They may support the legal redefinition of marriage to include same-sex relationships. They certainly support legalized abortion and the government funding of abortions for indigent women. They oppose the death penalty.

There is, however, another sense of the term "liberal." In this sense, a "liberal" is someone who believes in religious freedom, political equality, constitutional democracy, the rule of law, limited government, private property, the market economy, and human rights. This is the "liberalism" of the American Founding and of the Constitution of the United States. For convenience, let me refer to this type of liberalism as "old-fashioned liberalism" and the liberalism of Kennedy and Cuomo as "contemporary liberalism." Of course, a contemporary liberal may also be an old-fashioned liberal. But, it is worth contrasting these two senses of liberalism because many people who are liberals in the old-fashioned sense reject key elements of the contemporary liberal agenda. Indeed, many people who are today thought of as "conservatives" or "neo-conservatives"—myself included—are old-fashioned liberals.

Now, contemporary liberals sometimes claim to be simply working out the implications for modern political life of old-fashioned liberalism. They argue that anyone who accepts the principles of religious freedom, limited government, and the like ought to sign onto the contemporary liberal political program. For example, contemporary liberals, such as Cuomo, suggest that a right to abortion, however alien to the thought of the actual framers and ratifiers of the Constitution, is entailed by the very concept of a constitutional democracy in which religious freedom is guaranteed and government is limited by requirements of respect for individual freedom and women's equality. Cuomo famously describes himself as "personally opposed" to abortion, but, nevertheless, holds that principles of democratic pluralism require the legal recognition of a woman's right to abortion.[1] But, of course, many people who reject legalized abortion and other key items on the agenda of contemporary liberalism share a commitment to the defining principles of liberalism in the old-fashioned sense. Indeed, as Richard John Neuhaus has argued,[2] Pope John Paul II—who is certainly not a liberal in the mold of Teddy Kennedy or Mario Cuomo—is an exemplary liberal if, by the term "liberal," we mean a believer in religious freedom, political equality, constitutional democracy, the rule of law, private property, the market economy, and human rights.

The Old-Fashioned Liberalism of John Paul II and the Contemporary Catholic Church

IT probably goes too far to say that the pontificate of John Paul II has authoritatively excluded the possibility that a good Catholic can ever support non-democratic forms of political governance. After all, the conditions of democracy do not obtain at all times and in all places. So, it would hardly be possible for the Church to teach that support for democratic institutions is required by an exceptionless norm of political morality. Indeed, to my knowledge, neither John Paul II nor any of his predecessors has expressly or definitively taught that democratic institutions must always be preferred whenever the conditions for their establishment and maintenance are in place. It is, however, clear that the Holy Father has brought the full moral force and prestige of his office to bear in the cause of democratization around the world. He has declared that the "almost universal consensus with regard to the value of democracy...is to be considered a positive 'sign of the times,' as the Church's Magisterium has frequently noted."[3] He plainly views democracy as the system of government most in keeping with the fundamental Christian belief in the equality in human rights and dignity of every human being.[4] In his 1987 encyclical letter, he taught that the full development of individuals and communities requires a "healthy" political system "as expressed in the free and responsible participation of all citizens in public affairs, in the rule of law, and in respect for the promotion of human rights."[5] This is a powerful moral plea on behalf of democracy.[6]

Adrian Karatnycky, president of the leading human rights group, Freedom House, and editor of *Freedom in the World 1997-98: The Annual Survey of Political Rights and Civil Liberties,* flatly asserts that "over the last 18 years, the Polish Pope has emerged as the world's most important and effective advocate of freedom and democracy."[7] Noting that the Church's political message began to take on a "prodemocratic cast" during the pontificate of Pope John XXIII, Karatnycky argues that this trend "reached an apogee in the work of John Paul II."[8] He explains the current pontiff's staunch democratic commitments by reference to his experience as a priest and bishop in a nation long oppressed by totalitarian enemies. According to Karatnycky, "ministering to an oppressed nation eager for democracy and liberation from Russian domination...awakened within him a profound attachment to democratic values."[9] Perhaps it goes without saying that not every pope or important Church leader has favored democracy. Even today, certain Catholic conservatives—the sort of conservatives who are decidedly not what I am calling old-fashioned liberals—remain suspicious of democratic institutions and harbor doubts as to whether democratic political principles are compatible with Catholic faith. The current occupant of the Chair of St. Peter—however sharply his moral teachings contrast to the views of contemporary liberals—is no friend of what might be called "old-fashioned" conservatives. His teachings are firmly pro-democratic.[10]

Moreover, the Pope has frequently and forcefully reaffirmed the teachings of the Second Vatican Council on religious liberty.[11] Here, too, John Paul II charts a course fully in line with the "liberalism" of the American Founding and constitutional tradition. For a long time prior to the council, most Churchmen and many other Catholics were deeply suspicious of, and sometimes even hostile to, the idea of religious freedom. They associated the idea with various forms of moral and religious subjectivism, relativism, and indifferentism. They tended to understand the idea of religious freedom as it was manifested in French Revolutionary ideology, with its anti-clericalism, demands for liberation from traditional moral constraints, and belief in the subordination of the Church to the state.[12] Rarely did they advert to the very different conception of religious freedom developed largely by British and American thinkers and manifested in the words and deeds of the American founders. At the Second Vatican Council, however, Karol Woytila (the future John Paul II), as a young bishop, was among those bishops who were instrumental in shaping and winning approval for *Dignitatis Humanae,* the council's *Declaration on Religious Freedom.* This document decisively and, in my view, irrevocably placed the Church behind the proposition that people have a right against coercion by the state in matters of religious belief and worship and in the propagating of religious ideas.[13] Furthermore, the *Declaration* makes clear that the right to religious freedom is enjoyed fully by non-Catholics as well as by Catholics and, subject to the just requirements of public order, extends to non-Catholic as well as to Catholic belief, worship, and religious witness.[14]

Dignitatis Humanae was easily the most controversial document of a highly controversial ecumenical council. "Old-fashioned conservatives" argued that it contradicted authoritative, and even unchangeable, teachings of nineteenth-century popes. Some quietly (and a few not-so-quietly) denied that the new teaching commanded the religious assent of faithful Catholics. "Error," they proclaimed, "*still* has no rights." John Paul II, however, has consistently, and even emphatically, reaffirmed the council's teaching. If there was ever doubt about its authoritative status and the obligation of Catholics to give it their wholehearted assent, his pontificate erases that doubt.[15] On the question of religious freedom, to be a good Catholic one must be a kind of old-fashioned liberal. To deny the moral right to freedom from coercion in religious matters is to place oneself in opposition to an important principle of Catholic faith.[16]

Contemporary libertarians sometimes refer to themselves as "classical liberals" because of their belief in a largely unregulated market economy—what is sometimes called "laissez-faire economics." One need not take so extreme a view to recognize that belief in private property and free (though not necessarily unregulated) markets are central principles of the tradition of what I have been calling "old-fashioned liberalism." We need not be detained either by the extremism of libertarians or by the tendency of many contemporary liberals—who tend, rather, in the direction of socialist thinking about matters of political economy—to reject this aspect of the liberal tradition. It has often enough been noted that the individualism, and even libertarianism, of contemporary liberals in matters of personal morality (or "lifestyle") tends to be accompanied by corporatist and collectivist views when it comes to economics. Why this is the case, and how it came to be the case, are interesting questions, but there is no need to try to answer them here.[17] The important thing for our purposes is to note that the tradition of Catholic social thought, particularly as it has been interpreted and developed by John Paul II, shares important elements of the old-fashioned liberal position on matters of social and economic justice. In particular, the 100 year tradition of papal teaching, extending from Leo XIII's *Rerum Novarum* (1891)[18] to John Paul II's *Centesimus Annus* (1991), affirms both the importance of the private ownership of property and the principle of free exchange.[19]

To be sure, Catholic social thought rejects the libertarian demand for unregulated markets.[20] But, the libertarian conception of the liberal ideal of a market economy is just that—*one* conception. Within the liberal tradition, people have held a range of views about the proper terms and scope of governmental regulation of economic activity. Catholic teaching in this area is decidedly non-absolutist. It rejects the belief that there is a single, uniquely correct scheme of regulation that ought to govern economic activity at all times and in all places. Rather, it acknowledges that different circumstances demand different policies; more or less regulation, or regulation of some sorts rather than those of others, will be appropriate and desirable, depending on the circumstances prevailing in a particular society at a particular time.[21]

Of course, this does not mean that the Church adopts a posture of moral relativism with respect to questions of social and economic justice.[22] On the contrary, the magisterium has repeatedly and forcefully asserted the obligation of policy makers and others involved in economic decision making to bring to bear specific moral principles—such as subsidiarity, solidarity,[23] and the preferential option for the poor[24]—in their decisions.[25] Often enough, the sound application of these principles will exclude some possible courses of action and dictate others. Still, these principles cannot be applied in such a way as to exclude the need for knowledge of contingent local and historical circumstances and for the sound exercise of prudential judgment. They do not, in the absence of such knowledge and judgment, settle, for example, whether there ought to be a national income or sales tax; whether marginal income tax rates should be capped at 28 percent, or something higher or lower; or whether there should be a government-owned airline, a telephone service monopoly, or publicly funded election campaigns.

The Church teaches, however, that the relevant moral principles militate profoundly against the abolition or severe restriction of private property[26] and the concentration of wealth and economic power in the hands of the government.[27] Such principles entail a view of economic freedom as a true and valuable aspect of human liberty.[28] In particular, the principle of subsidiarity strictly demands that government recede in economic and other areas in which the common good is capably served by the initiative of individuals, families, and private enterprises.[29] The displacement of the initiative and authority of the family in particular—if only by excessively burdensome taxation[30]—is a grave offense against this central principle of social and economic justice.[31] Government intervention should be limited to those areas in which private initiative cannot work, or is not adequate, to secure a just distribution of the community's resources or the well-being of the community as a whole.[32]

When it comes to the struggle for recognition and protection of human rights across the globe, surely no figure in modern history looms larger than does Pope John Paul II. He has been a tireless crusader in this cause, working both publicly and privately, not merely for recognition of human rights in the abstract, but for the protection of human rights in specific cases. While stressing the need to respect legitimate cultural pluralism, he has vigorously asserted the absoluteness or nonrelativity of basic human rights.[33] Whether the issue concerns the mistreatment of religious believers in China, the abuse of refugees in war-torn nations of eastern Europe, genocide in Africa, economic exploitation in Latin America, abortion and euthanasia in the United States and Western Europe, or terrorism and oppression in the Middle East, the Pope has stressed the need to place protection of human rights at the top of the list of political priorities. He teaches that human rights are fundamental in such a way that they may never legitimately be sacrificed for the sake of other values or concerns, however important.[34]

Here, again, the Pope's old-fashioned liberalism is plainly in evidence. Although the concept of individual human rights is not unique to the liberal tradition, it is central to that tradition and strongly associated with it in the mind of the educated public. This association, if nothing else, makes "old-fashioned conservatives" and other critics of liberalism extremely nervous about "rights talk." Many critics of liberalism share the belief of contemporary liberals that the seeds of contemporary liberalism were planted by the older liberal tradition. To borrow a phrase from Wilfred McClay, they see "a straight line leading from the 'shot heard round the world' to endemic divorce, gangsta rap, and the North American Man-Boy Love

Association."[35] These critics condemn "the language of rights" as a way of speaking that incorporates into moral and political discourse the atomistic individualism and moral subjectivism characteristic of much contemporary liberal thought. To speak the language of rights, they contend, is to buy into the corrupt idea of human beings as "autonomous," "unencumbered," "imperial," selves—an idea, they insist, that lies at the very heart of all forms of liberalism.[36]

The Pope disagrees.[37] In line with his predecessors, John XXIII and Paul VI, John Paul II speaks unhesitatingly of the fundamental human rights of individual human beings.[38] Inasmuch as the Pope's "rights talk" is integrated into an account of the human person and human society that also stresses the importance of human solidarity, there is no real risk that his teachings will be misconstrued as an endorsement of atomistic individualism.[39] At the same time, his pleas for individual human rights are a powerful antidote to the corporatist tendency to absorb the interests of the individual into those of the larger society and/or the state. A central tenet of Christian faith is that men are saved or damned as individuals. They make the choices that constitute their acceptance or rejection of God's loving invitation to share in the divine life of the Holy Trinity as individuals. They have a profound and unique dignity as individuals. They have duties *and rights* as individuals. And, all of this is affirmed while at the same time recognizing that God calls us and relates to us as members of communities; that we are "selves" that are "encumbered," to use Michael Sandel's evocative term, by relationships and obligations—relationships and obligations that are not necessarily the results of choices we make; that, as persons, we are persons-in-relationships with other persons; that among the constitutive aspects of the well-being and fulfillment of every human person is the intrinsic—and not merely instrumental—good of friendship and living in harmony with others.[40]

I do not claim that a faithful Catholic must share the Pope's view of the utility of "rights talk." Although I myself believe that the language of rights can be of great value in articulating the requirements of social justice, there are responsible Catholics and others who judge the use of such language to be imprudent. I do not pretend to know with certainty that they are wrong. The matter is one about which reasonable people can disagree, for it is always possible to translate "rights claims" into other terms. What Catholics are bound to believe, however, are the propositions about the requirements of justice and political morality which the magisterium of the Church, and notably the Pope himself, has so powerfully asserted in the language of human rights. For example, no Catholic may deny the Pope's teaching regarding the right of Sudanese Christians—and all other human beings—not to be enslaved or tortured; or, the right of Bosnian women—and all others—not to be raped; or, the right of Chinese Christians, Tibetan Buddhists, and all believers freely to practice their faith; or, the right of the unborn child, the frail elderly person, the handicapped individual, and every innocent human being not to be directly killed.[41]

Catholic Faith and Contemporary Liberalism

THE old-fashioned liberalism of John Paul II and the modern Catholic Church is one thing. What I have called "contemporary liberalism" is something else. In this section, I shall highlight some key points of divergence.

First, however, I must acknowledge that there are significant points of overlap between the Pope's teaching and certain contemporary liberal positions. For example, many contemporary liberals share the Pope's views about a panoply of human rights questions, ranging from the evil of slavery in the Sudan to the injustice of religious persecution in China. Catholics of every stripe who are faithful to the Church's magisterium have joined forces with dissenting Catholics and with secular liberals in promoting these and other important human rights causes. Catholic conservatives and liberals tend to agree on these issues.

Moreover, on the issue of capital punishment, the Pope's development of the Church's teaching in *Evangelium Vitae* brings that teaching more closely into line with the anti-death penalty views held by many American liberals and opposed by most American conservatives—including Catholic conservatives. Although certain impeccably orthodox Catholic thinkers, most notably Germain Grisez and Joseph M. Boyle, Jr.,[42] have argued that capital punishment is *intrinsically* immoral and, therefore, may never legitimately be imposed, the Pope has stopped short of that position. Nevertheless, he has taught authoritatively that the circumstances in which the imposition of the death penalty could possibly be justified are today so rare as to be "practically non-existent."[43] The core of his teaching is that the death penalty cannot be justified, as Catholic thinkers have traditionally sought to justify it, on purely retributive grounds. While strongly reaffirming the retributive theory of criminal punishment—and plainly rejecting the utilitarian or consequentialist alternative justification—the Pope teaches that states "ought not go to the extreme of executing the offender except in cases of absolute necessity: in other words, when it would not be possible otherwise to defend society. Today, however, as a result of steady improvements in the organization of the penal system, such cases are very rare, if not practically non-existent."[44] Although some defenders of the death penalty have looked for "wiggle room" in the Pope's words about the possible use of the death penalty to "defend society," the context of these words makes clear, I believe, that the Holy Father does not accept generalized deterrence as a legitimate ground for the imposition of capital punishment. If the death penalty is ever justified, he is saying, it could be justified only when it is the only possible way of preventing *this* criminal from repeating *his* crimes.[45] In other words, *he* may not legitimately be executed as a means of deterring *others*.

Now, if the death penalty is an issue on which the Pope has developed the Church's teaching in a direction favored by many contemporary liberals and opposed by most conservatives, there is a wide range of subjects on which contemporary liberal positions, though compatible with the teachings of the magisterium, are not *favored* by that teaching over competing conservative positions. Although these issues are sometimes not highly morally charged—

for instance, the question of how much money should be spent on highway construction and how much on dam building—other times they concern matters of significant moral consequence. For example, liberals and conservatives in the United States are divided today over whether there should be federal governmental funding of the arts. This dispute arises, in part, from the fact that the National Endowment for the Arts (NEA) has supported, and, it appears, continues in some cases to support, "artistic" ventures that are blasphemous, obscene, or otherwise morally objectionable. Still, it would not be right for conservatives to claim that good Catholics cannot, under any circumstances, support the continuation of the NEA or the creation of other governmental programs offering financial support for artists. Although Catholic teaching condemns blasphemy and obscenity, there is nothing in principle contrary to morality, as it is understood and taught by the magisterium, that precludes absolutely governmental funding of the arts—even where there is a risk that such funding will sometimes be used for immoral purposes. (By the same token, of course, no principle of Catholic moral or social teaching *requires* governmental funding of the arts—even in affluent societies whose citizens can easily afford the increased tax burden it imposes.) Of course, a good Catholic would never support the use of governmental funds *for* blasphemous or obscene programs, performances, or exhibitions. Nor would a Catholic who understands the Church's moral and social teaching imagine that people have a moral right to produce obscene or blasphemous "art"—much less a right to do so at taxpayer expense. And, presumably a faithful Catholic who favored governmental funding of the arts would look for prudent ways to prevent abuses of arts funding programs by those who would produce immoral trash in the name of art.

On this issue and, as I say, a great many others, Catholic teaching simply does not resolve—though its moral principles will sometimes help properly to structure—debates between contemporary liberals and conservatives. On other issues, however, including some of the most urgent issues of justice and human rights at stake today in Western societies, Catholic teaching clearly and decisively favors one side or the other. We have seen that, on the issue of capital punishment, it favors what is regarded as the liberal side. However, when it comes to what the Pope himself has declared to be the most urgent issue of all in developed Western societies—namely, the right of the unborn child to protection against abortion—the position overwhelmingly favored by contemporary liberals, namely, the idea of a woman's "right" to abortion, is utterly incompatible with Catholic faith. And, this issue, above all, creates a dilemma for Catholic liberals.

Let us begin our analysis of this dilemma with some empirical facts. Every liberal member of the United States Senate, including every Roman Catholic liberal, and most liberal members of the House of Representatives, including again, most Catholic liberals, is considered to be a more or less reliable voter for the cause of abortion by lobbyists for the so called pro-choice movement. Indeed, the majority of Catholic Democrats in the Senate, and the overwhelming majority of Catholic liberals in that chamber, voted, in 1997, to uphold what the United States Conference of Catholic Bishops has described as President Clinton's "shameful veto" of the bill that would, if enacted, ban "partial-birth abortions." Among the self-identified Catholics whose votes in the Senate helped to preserve the practice of partial-birth abortion were Christopher Dodd (D-Conn.);[46] Tom Harkin (D-Iowa); John Kerry (D-Mass.); Carol Moseley-Braun (D-Ill.); Jack Reed (D-R.I.); Richard Durbin (D-Ill.); Edward Kennedy (D-Mass.); Barbara Mikulski (D-Md.); Patty Murray (D-Wash.); and Susan Collins (R-Maine).[47] It is true that a few Catholic liberals in the Senate, namely, Thomas Daschle (D-S.D.), Daniel Patrick Moynihan (D-N.Y.), and Joseph Biden (D-Del.), voted to override the president's veto. But, this was a departure from the norm for these senators, all of whom generally vote to protect abortion. (Moynihan explained his deviation from the "pro-choice" line on the partial birth abortion issue by saying that this particular method of abortion was just "too close to infanticide.") On the issue of abortion, it seems, there has been something very close to a complete collapse among Catholic liberals. Twenty-five years ago, pro-life liberals—especially pro-life Catholic liberals—were not uncommon; today, they are the political equivalent of an endangered species. Even in the House of Representatives only a handful remain.[48]

The Church's teaching on the inviolable right to life of every innocent human being from conception until natural death could not be clearer. Similarly, there is no room for doubt about the Church's absolute condemnation of deliberately induced abortion as a gross violation of this most fundamental of human rights. The practice of abortion has been condemned by the Church from its earliest days. This condemnation was reconfirmed in the most unambiguous terms by the Second Vatican Council, whose *Pastoral Constitution on the Church in the Modern World* declared abortion, no less than infanticide, to be an "unspeakable crime."[49] Indeed, this teaching has, I believe, long been infallibly proposed by the ordinary and universal magisterium of the Church. In case anyone had any doubts, Pope John Paul II formally confirmed the infallible status of the teaching in his 1995 encyclical letter *Evangelium Vitae*. Expressly invoking the authority "which Christ conferred upon Peter and his Successors, in communion with the Bishops—who on various occasions have condemned abortion and who...albeit dispersed throughout the world, have shown unanimous agreement concerning this doctrine," the Holy Father condemned all "direct abortion, that is, abortion willed as an end or as a means."[50] "This doctrine," he stated, "is based upon the natural law and upon the written Word of God, is transmitted by the Church's Tradition and taught by the ordinary and universal Magisterium."[51] And, to this statement he attached a footnote citing paragraph 25 of *Lumen Gentium*, the *Dogmatic Constitution on the Church* of the Second Vatican Council, which confirms the authority of the ordinary and universal magisterium of the Church to teach infallibly in matters of faith *and morals* and which sets forth the criteria for such infallible teaching.

How do Catholic liberals who support what they and other liberals call "abortion rights" square their position with the Church's unequivocal teaching regarding the right to life of the unborn child and the absolute moral impermissibility of direct abortion? Some, of course, make no effort to do so. Apparently, they do not take their faith seriously enough to be troubled by the inconsistency between their support for abortion and the Church's condemnation of the practice. Hadley Arkes describes liberal Catholics of this stripe as people who believe that their religious faith is so private a matter that they refuse to impose it even on themselves!

Other Catholic liberals, however, have struggled to show that their support for legalized abortion and even the public funding of abortion for indigent women is not, in fact, incompatible with adherence to the Church's teaching regarding the sanctity of unborn human life and the moral wrongfulness of abortion. Such people describe themselves as "personally opposed" to abortion, but "pro-choice." They profess to believe *both* that abortion is a grave moral evil *and* that women have a moral right to abortion. Their belief that abortion must be legal, they say, in no way rests upon or entails a denial of the Church's teaching that abortion is always morally wrong.

The most famous statement of the case for this position was made by Mario Cuomo, the former governor of New York, who addressed the question in a highly publicized lecture delivered at the University of Notre Dame in 1985.[52] Cuomo enjoys a reputation for being a serious and theologically sophisticated Catholic layman. Moreover, he is arguably the nation's most articulate defender of the contemporary liberal agenda. If it were possible to square contemporary liberalism's support for abortion with the Church's condemnation of the practice, he would be the man to do it.

Cuomo's argument went something like this: The Church herself does not teach that every moral offense must be prohibited by the law; in fact, only a certain subset of moral obligations can, or should, be legally enforced. In a pluralistic society, those practices which are condemned by some moral and religious traditions or authorities, yet permitted by others, are poor candidates for legal prohibition. Indeed, with respect to intimate, private matters, such as contraception and abortion, the principle of constitutional freedom itself requires that the law refrain from enforcing some people's moral views on other people who do not necessarily share them. To defend this freedom in the case of abortion, Cuomo insisted, is not to deny abortion's moral wrongfulness or the authority of the Church to declare that abortion is a grave sin. He assured his audience that he himself fully accepts the Church's teaching and that he and his wife have always lived by it. But, out of respect for the equal rights of religious conscience of others, he, as a public official, is bound under the Constitution to refrain from imposing that teaching on non-Catholics.[53]

As Cuomo presented the matter, then, abortion is fundamentally a matter of religion, and, as such, the right to abortion is a specific instance of the more general right to freedom of conscience in a religiously pluralistic society. This way of presenting the issue, however, fails to come to grips with the core of the very teaching that Cuomo claims to accept as a matter of his own religious conviction, namely, that abortion constitutes the unjust taking of an innocent human life. As such, abortion simply cannot be considered "private" in the sense that Cuomo attempts to depict it. It always involves the violation of the rights of another human being, namely, the unborn baby whose death is precisely what is sought in an act of direct abortion. Because the most fundamental of human rights is involved, the matter of abortion could not possibly be immune from legal regulation, since the protection of basic human rights is the primary justifying purpose of law and government. What Cuomo says about contraception and abortion might arguably be true about non-abortifacient methods of contraception, though, even here, the traditional view of the state's role in upholding public health, safety, and morals (the "police power") could provide the ground for the legal restriction of contraception. But, it cannot possibly be true of abortion.

In *Evangelium Vitae,* Pope John Paul II has addressed this point explicitly:

> [C]ivil law must ensure that all members of society enjoy respect for certain fundamental rights which innately belong to the person, rights which every positive law must recognize and guarantee. First and fundamental among these is the inviolable right to life of every innocent human being. While public authority can sometimes choose not to put a stop to something which—were it prohibited— would cause more serious harm, it can never presume to legitimize

as a right of individuals...an offense against other persons caused by the disregard of so fundamental a right as the right to life. The legal toleration of abortion or of euthanasia can in no way claim to be based on respect for the conscience of others....[54]

The Pope's logic here, I believe, is impeccable. Once one takes on board the central propositions informing the Church's teaching on abortion, it is impossible to believe that there could be a moral right to the legal freedom to have an abortion. Such a right would amount to a right to violate the fundamental human rights of others. As such, it would be ultimately incoherent and self-defeating.

The "personally opposed but pro-choice" position on abortion suggests the possibility that someone can *will* for others the freedom to have an abortion without being responsible in any morally significant way for the abortions sought or performed by people exercising that freedom. Cuomo and others purport to be willing not that anyone ever have an abortion, but only that they be free to choose whether or not to have an abortion. It is, of course, psychologically possible to will that others have the choice as to whether to have an abortion while, at the same time, *hoping* that they never choose that option. But, it is *not* possible—and here is the problem for liberal Catholics who support "abortion rights"—to will that someone have the freedom to abort without willing the injustice of abortion. A moment's reflection reveals the reason this is the case. A governor, legislator, or other public official who acts to establish or preserve a legal right to abortion necessarily wills that unborn human beings be denied the legal protection against direct (and other forms of unjust) killing that he wills for himself and others whom he considers to have lives worthy of the protection of the laws. Such a public official, therefore, acts in defiance of the Golden Rule of fairness in carrying out his public duties. In this way, he renders himself complicit in the injustice of those abortions that his actions help to make possible. However sincerely he may hope that women will forgo the freedom to abort and opt instead for pro-life alternatives, the blood of abortion's unborn victims is on his hands.[55]

Does this analysis imply that there is no room for differences of opinion among faithful Catholics as to the most prudent strategies for protecting the right to life of the unborn? In 1990, Vincent Schoemehl, a young Catholic Democrat of a moderate liberal persuasion who was then mayor of St. Louis and aspired to be governor of Missouri, announced that he was withdrawing his support for legal restrictions on abortion and would, if elected governor, veto any such restrictions enacted by the state legislature. He argued that, instead of making abortion illegal, he now favored "a comprehensive program" of education and health and family support services to help pregnant women in need and encourage them to bring their children to term. Schoemehl insisted that he had not changed his underlying pro-life commitments in any way. He had merely changed his views about the most prudent strategy by which to advance the pro-life cause.

No thoughtful pro-life advocate will deny that effective assistance to pregnant women in need is essential to the pro-life cause. Compassion for such women and justice for their children demand no less.[56] And, the Church herself has often taken the lead in providing what Marvin Olasky has called "effective compassion." Dioceses around the country, not to mention religious orders and institutes, such as the Missionaries of Charity and other organizations within the Church, have come to the aid of tens—perhaps hundreds—of thousands of women and their unborn and newborn children since abortion was legalized in this country. And, a great many pro-life politicians and citizens share Schoemehl's view that public, as well as private, efforts in this area are necessary and proper. They do not, however, believe that these efforts are a legitimate "alternative" to the legal protection of the right to life of the unborn child. Rather, they believe that a "comprehensive" pro-life program necessarily involves *both* the legal restriction of abortion and the effective provision of alternatives to abortion for women in need.[57]

It is certainly true that people who understand the injustice of abortion may legitimately differ as to strategies for responding to that injustice. It is also true, as Pope John Paul II makes it clear in

Evangelium Vitae, that faithful Catholics and other pro-life citizens may legitimately support legislation that falls short of all that justice requires for the unborn where, *but only where,* they prudently judge that no more fully just legislation is, in the circumstances, attainable and that the only viable alternative(s) would leave, or put, in place a regime of law even less protective of the right to life. Here is what the Pope says on the matter:

> A particular problem of conscience can arise in cases where a legislative vote would be decisive for the passage of a more restrictive law, aimed at limiting the number of authorized abortions, in place of a more permissive law already passed or ready to be voted on. Such cases are not infrequent.... In a case like the one just mentioned, when it is not possible to overturn or completely abrogate a pro-abortion law, an elected official, whose absolute personal opposition to procured abortion was well known, could licitly support proposals aimed at *limiting the harm* done by such a law and at lessening its negative consequences at the level of general opinion and public morality. This does not in fact represent an illicit cooperation with an unjust law, but rather a legitimate and proper attempt to limit its evil aspects.[58]

So, for example, a pro-life legislator who reasonably believes that there is, for the time being, no realistic hope of enacting laws that fully protect the unborn may, in good conscience, support reforms that would transform a regime of law, such as ours, that effectively permits abortion throughout the entire nine months of pregnancy and gestation into one that permits abortion only in the first trimester and forbids it from that point forward. Of course, even with these reforms, the law would remain unjust, and it would be the obligation of all pro-life citizens to work to make further reforms possible. The point is merely that, as the Pope teaches, a truly (and known by the public to be) pro-life official may support reforms that are less than perfect when (but, let us be clear, *only* when) his reason for supporting the proposed change in the law is precisely to bring into being the protections for the unborn it contains. Where one's reason for supporting the proposed legislation is precisely these protections, one *intends* only those aspects of the law and merely *accepts as an unintended side effect* those features of the law which remain unjust. Thus, one's intention—one's direct willing—bears no infection of injustice toward the unborn; the orientation of one's will toward them is in the direction of loving protection.[59]

The trouble with Vincent Schoemehl's position was evident in his promise to veto legal restrictions on abortion if they were enacted by the Missouri legislature. The "strategy" he was proposing was manifestly not compelled by circumstances that made it impossible to enact legislation more protective of the right to life. It, therefore, amounted to a denial of that right and collapsed into the sort of "personally opposed but pro-choice" view defended unsuccessfully by Mario Cuomo. Although Schoemehl's support for programs to help women choose life in the face of legal abortion was commendable, his promise to veto legislation to restore to the unborn the equal protection of the laws was unacceptable—unacceptable, let us be clear, because fundamentally unjust.

Efforts by notable Catholic liberals to square liberal ideology with Catholic teaching on abortion are plainly unavailing. Why, we must therefore ask, despite the Church's firm and constant teaching regarding the fundamental right to life of the unborn child, have so many Catholic liberals abandoned the pro-life cause? Support for "abortion rights" is plainly incompatible with fundamental tenets of Catholic faith. Is support for the pro-life cause similarly incompatible with basic tenets of modern liberalism? When it comes to abortion, does one have to choose between being a true liberal and being a faithful Catholic? If so, why have so many Catholics chosen to be faithful to liberal ideology rather than to the truths taught by the magisterium of the Church? If not, why is it that so few Catholics of a liberal persuasion have made an effort to establish the "pro-life" position as a viable one within the liberal camp?

In addressing these questions, one must distinguish two strands within what I have been calling "contemporary liberalism." The first

I shall refer to as the "Rooseveltian" strand. What is distinctive about Rooseveltian liberalism is its belief in what might be called "activist government." A Rooseveltian liberal need not believe that the particular programs championed by Franklin D. Roosevelt as part of his New Deal are just right for today, but such a person believes, as did Roosevelt, that government should design and implement programs to combat poverty, rectify economic and other forms of injustice, and promote the health, education, and general welfare of the people as a whole. The type of freedom that Rooseveltian liberalism is concerned to ensure is freedom from want: as President Roosevelt himself put it, "a necessitous people are not a free people."

I shall refer to the other strand of contemporary liberalism as the "personal liberationist" strand. What is distinctive about personal liberationism is its rejection of traditional norms of morality governing issues of sexuality and life and death. "Personal liberationists" object particularly to laws enforcing traditional morality or promoting it with governmental support. They believe that government should be "neutral" as to disputed questions of what they judge to be purely "personal" morality. Thus, they have championed the "reform" or "liberalization" of laws restricting contraception, abortion, divorce, pornography, homosexual sodomy, assisted suicide, and, in some cases, prostitution and drug abuse. Moreover, they oppose laws requiring parental consent for, or even notification of, abortions performed on minors, and they support the public funding of abortions for poor women. They favor "value-free" sex education in the schools and the distribution of birth control pills, condoms, and other forms of contraception to school children—again, without parental consent or notification. Recently, they have mounted an effort to secure the legal recognition of "marriages" between persons of the same sex. The type of "freedom" that "personal liberationism" is concerned with is freedom from interference with morally controversial "lifestyle choices."

The overwhelming majority of contemporary liberals, including Catholic liberals, combine Rooseveltian liberalism with belief in at least some of the central elements of personal liberationism. In my view, however, there is no necessary connection between these strands of liberalism. Personal liberationists can be—and more than a few are—economic libertarians who utterly reject what they denounce as "big government" health, education, and welfare programs and policies to ameliorate what Rooseveltians consider to be the unjust distribution of wealth. By the same token, Rooseveltians need not embrace the liberationist agenda. Whatever their personal failings in moral matters, "big government" liberals, such as Presidents Roosevelt, Kennedy, and Johnson, did not advance liberationist policies. Indeed, personal liberationism became a powerful force within liberalism only in the late 1960s (though, to be sure, a not insignificant number of liberals had come to embrace liberationism as early as the 1950s). And, to this day—though their numbers are dwindling—there remain Rooseveltians who reject liberationism.

Perhaps the most notable example of a contemporary Rooseveltian who rejects the liberationist agenda is former Pennsylvania Governor Robert P. Casey. As the Democrat governor of the nation's fifth largest state, Casey proposed to plead the pro-life cause to the delegates assembled for the 1992 Democratic National Convention. Despite giving a pro-abortion Republican woman from Pennsylvania (who had actively opposed Casey in his gubernatorial elections) an opportunity to address the convention, the party's leadership denied Casey's request for time to speak.[60] Addressing a pro-life rally outside the convention hall, Casey made the case for the unborn in Rooseveltian terms. He recalled the Democratic Party's heritage of support for the weak and vulnerable, for victims of exploitation and injustice. He retold the story of efforts by "progressives" within the Democratic Party to protect workers, abolish child labor, end segregation, and advance the civil rights of women and members of minority groups. He called upon those who identify with this great tradition of governmental activism in the cause of social justice to join him in protecting the unborn and assisting pregnant women in need. It is time, he said, for Democrats to once again "speak up for the little guy"—this time the littlest guy of all, the unborn child.

Casey's Rooseveltian case for the unborn fell on deaf ears. By 1992, most Democrats were liberals, and most liberals were not only Rooseveltians, but also liberationists. Although pro-life activism is compatible with the Rooseveltian conception of the role of government, it simply does not square with the liberationist view of morality and society. As liberationists view the world, the availability of abortion is essential, not only to the cause of women's equality, but also to the ability of men and women to lead the lives, including the sex lives, they prefer. Given the possibility of contraceptive failure, a world without the availability of abortion is one in which people must either practice sexual self-restraint or risk finding their lives dramatically altered by the responsibilities attached to having an "unwanted" child. Such a situation is simply unacceptable on liberationist terms. Abortion must remain lawful and, indeed, be made fully available to any woman who finds herself in need of the services of an abortionist.[61]

Contemporary liberals attempt to link the "pro-choice" position to the Rooseveltian tradition. That tradition, they say, is one of tolerance and compassion. Legal abortion is a matter of tolerance. Publicly funded abortion is a matter of compassion. Furthermore, they say, the availability of abortion completes—or, at least, makes more nearly complete—the efforts of the liberal tradition to bring about true equality between men and women.

Of course, these arguments could be persuasive only to someone who does not believe that abortion is what the Catholic Church says it is, namely, the taking of innocent human life. For people who recognize the literally homicidal nature of abortion, it can hardly be a matter of "tolerance," much less "compassion." And, no one who recognized the equal rights of the unborn would see fit to attempt to advance the cause of women's rights by authorizing abortion. Yet, Catholic liberals frequently join in promoting the idea that abortion, though evil, must be accepted as a matter of tolerance, compassion, and women's equality. Why is this so?

When it comes to abortion and other issues at the heart of liberationist ideology, sociologists, such as University of Virginia's

James Davison Hunter,[62] have noted that the lines of social division tend to run through religious communities rather than between them. More traditional or observant Protestants, Catholics, and Jews share with each other a wide range of moral convictions that are increasingly rejected by those among their co-religionists who have adopted a more liberal world view and understanding of their faith. What this suggests, I think, is that Catholic liberals have come to embrace the cause of abortion and other elements of the liberationist agenda because they have become "liberal Catholics." That is to say, they tend to differ with their fellow Catholics not only in matters of politics, but also in their understanding of what it means to hold the Catholic faith and, particularly, in their grasp of the authority of the Church's magisterium to teach truly in matters of faith *and morals.*[63]

At the end of the day, a Catholic liberal who supports legal abortion and its public funding simply cannot, at the same time, believe that the Church's teaching—the whole of the Church's teaching—about abortion is true. He, therefore, must not believe that the magisterium of the Church possesses the authority to teach truly in this matter. He certainly cannot believe that this teaching is infallibly proposed. And, if not this teaching, then what moral teaching could possibly be? Thus, as he understands the authority of the magisterium, what the Church offers in its moral teaching is guidance to be conscientiously considered, not truth to be relied on in the formation of conscience. He may very well feel obligated to thoughtfully reflect on the teachings of the Church and give them due consideration, but he will not judge himself to be bound to give to these teachings the religious assent of intellect and will that is called for by the Second Vatican Council.[64] And, with respect to an issue such as abortion, he will not consider that he is under any *obligation* to form his view of the requirements of justice and the common good of political society on the basis of the Church's teachings—even if he himself is inclined to believe that the Church might actually be right as to the immorality of deliberate feticide. Since the Church might also be wrong on the subject, it will seem to him best to leave the matter to individual consciences; indeed, it will seem to him "intolerant" and a violation of the principle of freedom of conscience not to do so.

This view of the Church and the authority of the magisterium understands the life of the Church as essentially that of a political society that is managed by bureaucratic institutions.[65] People who share it tend to view the papacy (together with the episcopate and the various Vatican congregations) as a concentration of power. Hence, they call for the radical democratization of ecclesiastical authority and the introduction of political-theoretical systems, such as checks and balances, to constrain power and soften its impact on those over whom it is exercised. However, this is contrary to the Church's own historical self-understanding and to the faith it informs. The Church is not primarily a bureaucratic institution— though there are, to be sure, bureaucracies to carry out many of the Church's activities; nor is the papacy or the magisterium a political office that exists primarily to carry out executive and legislative functions. Rather, the Church is the Mystical Body of Christ, the people of God. The papacy and the episcopate were established by Christ himself, not to legislate, but to teach Christ's saving truths to his people. Contrary to its depiction in the secular media, the magisterium does not "ban" abortion or contraception or homosexual activity; banning is a legislative act; rather, it teaches the truth that such acts are intrinsically immoral, contrary to Christ's saving truths, incompatible with the sharing of divine life. The Church does not "make law" on moral subjects; it teaches truth. In this, it is guided and protected by the Holy Spirit.

Understanding the nature of the Church and its authority makes all the difference when it comes to issues of moral consequence. People who view the Church as essentially a political body and the magisterium as a legislative office will chafe under the authority of decisions that strike them as restricting freedoms they enjoy. They will test these decisions by appeal to conscience—understood now, not as a judgment of what one is morally required to do or not do, but, rather, as one's feeling about whether a certain activity—abortion, premarital sex, or whatever—is in fact morally available for one's choice, the Church's teaching about the wrongfulness of that activity notwithstanding.[66] By contrast, people who understand the essentially mystical reality of the Church and the function of the magisterium as teacher of Christ's saving truths will adopt an attitude of humble— and grateful—submission to the Church's moral teachings, understanding those teachings as making known the mind of Christ and thus helping to make possible our salvation. Such people will treat these teachings as principles for the formation of their consciences.[67] And, they will struggle to live in accordance with them.

Will they "impose" them on others? That depends. We do not generally speak of the "imposing" of morality on people who believed in the right to own slaves or those who continue to believe in the right to practice racial discrimination. Semantics are of little importance, however. As I have already noted, *Dignitatis Humanae* declares the right of all people to be free from coercion in matters of religious belief and practice and in the dissemination of religious ideas. That great declaration further teaches that man "is bound to follow" his conscience.[68] But, this is no more to be interpreted as a license for anarchy than it is a brief for moral subjectivism. As the declaration itself makes clear, even the principle of freedom from coercion in religious matters is subject to the just requirements of public order, including the maintenance of public morality. The legal prohibition of injustices—particularly the prohibition of grave injustices, such as abortion and other violations of the right to life— is plainly legitimate and often demanded by justice itself. It is true that not every obligation of the moral law need, or should, be enforced by civil law. It would plainly be a mistake to make every sin a crime. Indeed, as we have seen, the Holy Father has himself observed that prudence dictates the toleration of certain vices, lest the effort to eradicate them by legal prohibition make matters worse, rather than better, for society as a whole.[69] But, this may not be interpreted as proposing a "right" to commit immoral acts, nor is it of any use to Catholic liberals or others who would countenance a regime of law that effectively denies to the unborn their fundamental right to life.

Conclusion

THERE is a sense in which every Catholic should be, as Pope John Paul II himself certainly is, an old-fashioned liberal. Every Catholic ought to support the right to religious freedom and other basic human rights. Every Catholic ought to believe in limited government, the rule of law, private property, and at least some significant sharing by all citizens in the process of political decision making.

Moreover, every Catholic should oppose the death penalty, even for those convicted of the most heinous murders and other atrocities. The development of Catholic doctrine on this subject has been in the direction of the view favored by contemporary liberals and generally opposed by conservatives. Although many faithful Catholics will find themselves allied with strange bed-fellows on this issue, there are no good grounds for doubting the meaning, authority, or truth of the Church's teaching that the death penalty, in modern societies, at least, may not rightly be imposed.

On questions of the role of government in providing programs for health, education, and welfare, Catholics may legitimately embrace the Rooseveltian liberal tradition, though they need not do so. All Catholics should, of course, share the concern of Rooseveltian liberals for social justice and the common good; there is, however, room for reasonable differences between Rooseveltian liberals and contemporary conservatives about the way these concerns are best addressed. Their debate should be structured by the principles of justice articulated in the tradition of Catholic social thought. It is imperative for Rooseveltians to bear in mind the importance of the principle of subsidiarity and the need to preserve individual initiative and the health of the family and other "mediating structures" of civil society. They must avoid the perversion of their view into socialism. By the same token, conservatives must remember the principle of solidarity and make sure that economic and social policy serves the interests of the entire community, especially those in need. They must avoid the perversion of their view into libertarianism.

Finally, no Catholic should embrace the agenda of personal liberationism. That strand of liberalism—and particularly its demand for legal abortion—is simply incompatible with the truths of the Catholic faith. To adopt the liberationist view of morality and politics is to support what the Pope has called "the culture of death." If that is what Catholics must do to remain in good standing as "liberals" today, then no Catholic should covet the label "liberal."

13

NATURE, MORALITY, AND HOMOSEXUALITY

I N *Virtually Normal: An Argument about Homosexuality,*[1] Andrew Sullivan, the young, "gay," British, Roman Catholic former editor of *The New Republic,* has argued eloquently and intelligently for dramatic revisions of natural law thinking and public policy regarding sexual morality and marriage. It is incumbent upon natural law theorists and, indeed, anyone who is inclined to support traditional ideas about sex and marriage to take Sullivan's challenge to the natural law tradition very seriously. My aim in this chapter is to engage his arguments about nature, morality, and homosexuality.

Homosexual acts have long been condemned as immoral by the natural law tradition of moral philosophy, as well as by Jewish and Christian teaching. Sullivan argues that these condemnations are rooted in a failure to recognize that, for somewhere between 2 percent and 5 percent of the population, homosexuality is, in a sense decisive for the moral evaluation of homosexual conduct and relationships, "natural." But (as Sullivan asks) what is a "homosexual"? And what, precisely, is the sense in which homosexuality is "natural"?

Being Homosexual

SULLIVAN approaches the first question autobiographically. At about age ten he began to feel what he describes as a "yearning" that "was only to grow stronger as the years went by." Although initially "not sexual," it was, nevertheless, "a desire to unite with another: not to possess but to join in some way; not to lose myself but to be given dimension." This is, of course, a perfectly normal experience. In Sullivan's case, however, there was something not entirely normal about the way this yearning developed, namely, as a desire to be united not only emotionally but also physically with a person of his own sex.

Sullivan recognizes that his experience may differ in various respects from that of other homosexuals. In particular, he observes that the experience of female homosexuals tends to differ from that of males in that "it is more often a choice for women than for men; it involves a communal longing as much as an individual one; and it is far more rooted in moral and political choice than in ineradicable emotional or sexual orientation." Nevertheless, he says, even many lesbians report experiences not entirely unlike his own. He concludes that homosexuality, whatever the form of its expression, "is bound up in that mysterious and unstable area where sexual desire and emotional longing meet; it reaches into the core of what makes a human being who he or she is."

Thus, Sullivan puts into place a crucial premise of his argument for the value and moral validity of homosexual conduct: namely, that for people like him the fulfillment of a longing for emotional and physical union with someone of the same sex is critical to the success of their lives. For a homosexual, such fulfillment is, Sullivan goes so far as to suggest, the very thing "which would most give him meaning." It is in this sense that homosexuality is "natural" for homosexuals.

So, Sullivan reasons, homosexual genital acts, far from being "unnatural," are, or at least can be, naturally fulfilling for people whose fundamental yearning is to unite with someone of the same sex. Such acts, Sullivan supposes, can be truly unitive, and thus valuable, in the same way that heterosexual intercourse can be unitive and valuable.

Many people believe that sexual intercourse has value only in the context of marriage, or at least that marital intercourse has special meaning and value. Until recently, Sullivan himself held this view.[2] When combined, however, with his proposition that some people are homosexual "by their nature" and with the proposition that he thinks follows from it (namely, that for such people homosexual genital acts can be unitive and fulfilling), it leads to the social and political conclusion that society should accept and provide for marriages between same-sex couples. And this conclusion is one that Sullivan presses with particular vigor.

If homosexuality is "natural" in a morally normative sense, then homosexuals are, as Sullivan says, "virtually normal": "virtually" in the sense that homosexual orientation is comparatively rare—certainly no more than one person in twenty, and perhaps as few as one person in fifty, is homosexual (so, in a merely statistical sense, heterosexuality is the "norm"); "normal" because being homosexual is no more *ab*normal than, say, being black, or Jewish, or having red hair.

If, as Sullivan argues, homosexual relationships and conduct are naturally fulfilling and as such morally good, then it follows not only that "marriage should be made available to everyone, in a politics of strict neutrality," but also that military positions should be made available to homosexuals and heterosexuals on a nondiscriminatory basis, as should positions as teachers, coaches, and counselors in public schools. In Sullivan's view, law and government may no more legitimately draw distinctions between homosexuals and heterosexuals than they may distinguish between blacks and whites, Jews and gentiles, or redheads and brunettes. Thus, Sullivan calls for more than the mere *toleration* of homosexuality in and by the institutions of public life. As his demand for "gay marriage" makes clear, he believes that these institutions are morally obliged to treat homosexual relationships as equal in worth and dignity to socially approved heterosexual relationships.

The Limits of Legislation: Alternative Political Views

AT the same time, Sullivan opposes extending civil rights laws to forbid discrimination based on sexual orientation into the private realms of housing and employment. He argues that liberals, who would bring the coercive force of law to bear to overcome intolerance of homosexuality in the larger society, have strayed from liberalism's own principles. "Liberalism," he declares, "is designed to deal with means, not ends; its concern is with liberty, not a better society." Contemporary liberals, in their zeal to free homosexuals (and members of other minority groups) from the consequences of prejudice, have, Sullivan suggests, "created a war within [liberalism] itself." They have breached the traditional liberal commitment to public neutrality between competing visions of what makes for, and detracts from, a valuable and morally worthy way of life. In practice, then, liberalism has become a threat to the very idea of private liberty it celebrates in theory.

Sullivan's argument proceeds by engaging ideas and arguments about the morality and politics of homosexuality advanced not only by "liberals" and "conservatives," but also by more extreme parties on each side—viz., "prohibitionists" and "liberationists." While acknowledging that his categories are "ideal types" whose tenets few people subscribe to in pure form, he subjects each to detailed criticism. His own view, unsurprisingly, fits into none. Sullivan is, in the end, not so much a "neoconservative," as he is sometimes said to be, as a sort of conservative liberal, saying "yes" to "gay marriage" and to open homosexuals in the military and schools, and "no" to state-sponsored affirmative action and the legal prohibition of private discrimination based on sexual orientation.

Liberal Views

LIBERALISM, whether in the form Sullivan criticizes or in his own conservative version of it, contrasts sharply with "gay liberationism," which scoffs at bourgeois values and seeks to subvert mainstream institutions (such as marriage and the family), as opposed to integrating homosexuals fully into them. Sullivan's "liberationists" eschew the argument that homosexuality and homosexual conduct are natural. They refuse to grant to "conservatives" the proposition that human nature has determinate content or any sort of moral normativity. They celebrate the plasticity of human nature and practice a "queer politics" that goes in for "outings," "speech codes," "censorship," and "intimidation." As Sullivan depicts it, liberationism tends to philosophical nihilism and political authoritarianism. Gay liberationists are the sort of people who give homosexuality a bad name.

Conservative Views

"PROHIBITIONISTS" and "conservatives" are Sullivan's classifications for people who judge that homosexual conduct is morally bad and believe that social policy ought to reflect that judgment. Conservatives differ from prohibitionists mainly in their tolerant attitude toward acts of "private" immorality. They strongly oppose the vilification of homosexuals and typically favor the repeal of laws against sodomy. Moreover, conservatives tend not to be especially uncomfortable in dealing with homosexual friends and acquaintances who do not flaunt their homosexuality. The only real demand they make is that active homosexuals respect the sensibilities of others and be discreet about their sexual relationships to a degree that married people need not be.

At the same time, conservatives oppose "gay marriage" and other forms of official recognition and approbation of homosexual conduct and relationships. Although they tend to avoid the moralistic rhetoric of prohibitionists, conservatives share the moral belief that a life of active homosexuality should not be put forward as any sort of model of virtue.

Sullivan attacks the conservative view on two fronts. First, he challenges, as we have seen, the premise that homosexual acts and relationships integrated around those acts are morally bad or, indeed, morally inferior in any way to upright heterosexual conduct. (This challenge, obviously, cuts equally against the prohibitionists, who favor a more aggressive policy of discouraging homosexual activity. I shall therefore defer discussion of it until I turn to Sullivan's engagement with prohibitionism.) Second, he challenges the conservative belief that homosexuality can, much less should, be kept private. He claims that "the old public-private distinction upon which the conservative politics is based" has been eviscerated by the rise of the "gay rights" movement. With large numbers of homosexuals "out of the closet," the cultural basis of conservative politics is collapsing; "its bluff is being slowly but decisively called."

What is the conservative to do? One possibility is to join Sullivan and other non-liberationist proponents of "gay rights" (such as Bruce Bawer, Gabriel Rotello, and Stephen Macedo) in encouraging "conservative trends among homosexuals and a co-optation of responsible gay citizenship." To do this, however, the conservative must, in effect, lay aside moral qualms about homosexual conduct and accept something like Sullivan's ideal of the "virtuous homosexual" who reserves sex for stable, loving, monogamous relationships and embraces other "family values."

Above all, according to Sullivan, the conservative who takes this route should support the campaign for same-sex marriage as the best way to channel homosexual desire in the proper direction and encourage "a responsible homosexual existence." His only other option, Sullivan believes, is to join the prohibitionists and, especially, "the religious fundamentalists who do not share conservatism's traditional support of moderate and limited government."

Religion

CONTRARY to what this last comment, shorn of its context, may suggest to the reader, Sullivan's chapter on prohibitionists is mainly concerned with Catholic appeals to rational moral principles of natural law, rather than evangelical arguments from revealed truth. Sullivan treats these appeals with respect, noting that the tradition of thought about natural law (of which the Catholic Church is today the principal institutional exponent) "has a rich literature, an extensive history, a complex philosophical core, and a view of humanity that tells a coherent and at times beautiful story of the meaning of our natural selves." To his credit, Sullivan denies that prohibitionism's principled moral opposition to homosexual conduct can be dismissed as a "phobia" or written off as "bigotry." At the same time, he argues that neither philosophical nor theological arguments against homosexual acts can survive criticism.

Scripture

SULLIVAN concedes that both the Jewish and Christian scriptures appear to condemn homosexual genital activity. As he points out, however, in our own time, pro-"gay" critics have "reinterpreted" the relevant scriptural passages in efforts to show either that what is being condemned is something other than sexual misconduct or that the condemnation pertains only to ritual impurity and not to morality as such. Sullivan relies on the work of some of these critics, though he is forthright in acknowledging his own lack of professional competence to judge their claims. I, too, am no expert in biblical interpretation. Still, I would point out that some of the work on which he relies, particularly certain arguments advanced by the late John Boswell, has come in for scathing criticism from distinguished scholars (including some who share Boswell's and Sullivan's moral and political views about homosexuality) for "politically correcting" the Bible and Jewish and Christian history.[3]

Where Sullivan is prepared to concede that a biblical text condemns homosexual conduct on moral grounds, as in the case of St. Paul's Letter to the Romans, he argues that what is being condemned is not anything related to *homosexuality*—as we now know and understand it—but, rather, "the perversion of heterosexuality." According to this argument, St. Paul, being ignorant of the fact that some people are "by their nature homosexual" (this presumably having been a discovery of modern psychologists), perceives perversion in all homosexual acts, whereas, in truth, there is perversion only in the homosexual acts of persons who are by their nature heterosexual.[4]

The Meaning of Human Nature

THIS argument is dubious. Its premise, that Paul and the people of his time simply "assume that every individual's nature is hetero-sexual," trades on an equivocation on the meaning of the term "na-ture" and its cognates. It is implausible to suppose that Paul, as a Pharisaical Jew and a Christian, understood people's natures to be constituted, in any sense relevant to moral judgment, by their *desires* (even those deep and more or less stable emotional desires Sullivan calls "yearnings"), sexual or otherwise. (This is not to deny that Paul considered it "natural" for people to experience bad as well as good desires, including sexual desires.)

The view that human nature *is* ultimately constituted by emo-tional desires, while not unknown in the ancient world, is prominent today largely because of the profound influence of Thomas Hobbes[5] and, especially, David Hume[6] on the intellectual life of our culture. It was, however, rejected by the greatest pre-Christian philosophers, and I see no evidence of it in Paul's letters or in the writings of other Jews and Christians in the premodern world. So it is anachronistic for contemporary critics, such as Sullivan, to suppose that writers like Paul understood human nature to be constituted more or less as they believe it is—namely, by deep and fairly stable emotional de-sires—and then to claim that the early writers simply failed to under-stand that some people are "by their nature" homosexual.

In fact, Sullivan's whole argument against "the prohibitionists," and, by implication, much of his argument against "the conserva-tives," assumes that they understand people's "natures" to be consti-tuted in the essentially Humean way that Sullivan and other liberals believe human nature(s) to be constituted. In fact, however, the "conservatives" as well as the "prohibitionists" reject the Humean understanding of how human nature is constituted as a *mis*understanding. Thus they need not and—in my own case and in the cases of "prohibitionists" and "conservatives" cited by Sullivan with whose work I am familiar—do not deny, as Sullivan thinks we must deny, that genuine homosexual orientation exists.[7]

But if one's nature is not constituted by one's basic emotional desires, what is it constituted by? What is it that is fundamental about each of us as human persons and rightly motivating of us?

Let us get at these questions by considering Sullivan's analysis of natural law argumentation, particularly as it has been advanced in recent statements of the Catholic Church on homosexuality and homosexual genital acts. He thinks that he has caught the Magisterium of the Church in a contradiction. Unlike St. Paul (as Sullivan, Boswell, and others read him), contemporary churchmen recognize that homosexually oriented persons exist; such persons are not merely heterosexuals who, for whatever reasons, choose to engage in homosexual acts. But, Sullivan suggests, if the Pope and Cardinal Ratzinger acknowledge that some people's "natures" are homosexual, how can they continue to insist that homosexual acts violate natural law?

The answer is that the Church has a view about human good and the constitution of human nature that is much more like St. Paul's (as I read him)—and Aquinas's and, for that matter, Plato's—than it is like Sullivan's or Hobbes's or Hume's. The Church teaches that a person's nature, in the sense relevant to moral judgment, is constituted by human goods that give him *reasons* to act and to refrain from acting, and not by *desires* that may, rightly or wrongly, also provide motivation.[8] These "natural goods" are "basic" inasmuch as they are ends or purposes that have their intelligibility not merely as means to other ends, but as intrinsic aspects of human well-being and fulfillment. Far from being reducible to desires, basic human goods give people *reasons to desire things*—reasons that hold whether they happen to desire them or not, and even in the face of powerful emotional motives that run contrary to what reason identifies as humanly good and morally right.[9]

This understanding of human nature and the human good has been applied to questions of homosexual conduct by John Finnis, among others, whose views Sullivan classifies as "conservative." For Finnis, as for the broader natural law tradition, the immorality of homosexual genital acts follows by implication from the intrinsic immorality of all forms of nonmarital sex.[10]

Marriage and Nonmarital Sex Acts

MARRIAGE, according to Finnis, is one of the basic human goods. As such, it provides a noninstrumental reason for spouses to unite bodily in acts of genital intercourse. This bodily union is the biological matrix of the multi-level (bodily, emotional, dispositional, and even spiritual) relationship that is their marriage. Marital acts, while (necessarily) reproductive in type, are not merely instrumental, as St. Augustine seems to have supposed, to the good of having children (or avoiding sin).[11] Nor are they mere means of sharing pleasure or even promoting feelings of closeness, as many contemporary liberals think.[12] Rather, such acts realize the intrinsic good of marriage itself as a two-in-one-flesh communion of persons.

> The union of the reproductive organs of husband and wife really unites them biologically (and their biological reality is part of, not merely an instrument of, their *personal* reality); reproduction is one function and so, in respect of that function, the spouses are indeed one reality, and their sexual union therefore can *actualize* and allow them to experience their *real common good—their marriage*....[13]

If this view, or something like it, is sound, then it is plain that oral or anal sexual intercourse, whether engaged in by partners of the same sex or opposite sexes, and, indeed, even if engaged in by marriage partners, cannot be marital. (This moral insight, if such it is, accounts for provisions of both civil and canon law according to which marriages cannot be consummated by such acts.)[14] Only acts of the reproductive type (whether or not, as Finnis explains, they are intended to be, or even can be, reproductive in effect) can actualize (and, in law, consummate) marriage. Other sexual acts cannot be maritally unitive because they do not unite the partners biologically, making them truly two-in-one-flesh.[15]

Moreover, masturbatory and sodomitical acts, by their nature, instrumentalize the bodies of those choosing to engage in them in a way that cannot but damage their integrity as persons. Inasmuch as nonmarital sexual acts cannot realize any intrinsic common good, such acts cannot but be willed for instrumental reasons. And in such willing, "the partners treat their bodies as instruments to be used in service of their consciously experiencing selves; their choice to engage in such conduct thus dis-integrates each of them precisely as acting persons."[16]

Moral Evaluation

OF course, this will not be considered morally problematic by people who hold an essentially dualistic conception of human beings as non-bodily persons who inhabit nonpersonal bodies which they "use" as "equipment."[17] (And dualists of a conservative bent will be quick to point out that they support not just any instrumentalized sex, but only that directed toward such valuable ends as emotional closeness and intimacy.) But those who reject the idea that the nature of human beings is constituted by their basic emotional desires tend to be the very people who reject person/body dualism. Start the list with John Finnis and Cardinal Ratzinger.

Sullivan devotes two or three pages to criticizing Finnis, whose bravery, honesty, and intelligence in arguing about homosexuality he praises. His focus, however, is on what Finnis says about the social and political implications of homosexuality and its legal treatment, rather than his more fundamental argument that homosexual conduct is intrinsically nonmarital and immoral. I have sketched that argument (all too briefly) here, not to defend it from its liberal critics—which I and others have done elsewhere[18]—but simply to show how it rejects—from start to finish—the conception of human nature as constituted by emotional desires, which Sullivan wrongly assumes is shared by natural law theorists who claim that homosexual acts are morally bad.

Catholic Teachings

ONCE we see that "prohibitionists," such as Cardinal Ratzinger, and "conservatives," such as John Finnis, in fact reject the Humean conception of how human nature is constituted, Sullivan's charge that the Church's recognition of the reality of homosexual orientation is inconsistent with its continued condemnation of homosexual acts loses its force. Indeed, it becomes clear that the Church's view of homosexual desire (and the homosexual condition) as "disordered" (in that it *inclines* people to sin) is perfectly consistent with its ringing affirmation of the intrinsic worth and dignity of *all* persons, not excluding those who happen to be homosexual. In this light, Cardinal Ratzinger's 1986 statement deploring "violence and malice in speech or action" against homosexual persons is hardly the "stunning passage of concession" Sullivan describes it as being. Rather, it is a simple reminder of the all-embracing scope of Christ's command: "Love thy neighbor."

Sexual Abstinence

IN the end, I think, Sullivan rejects the teaching of his Church (and mine) that homosexual acts are intrinsically immoral, because he has come to believe that the sublimation of sexual desire to which the Church calls those whose homosexual inclinations make marriage a psychological impossibility alienates people from themselves and "leads to some devastating loneliness." For Sullivan, it is celibacy that is "unnatural," at least for people from whom it is demanded because of a sexual orientation they did not choose, rather than, say, a religious vocation they did choose.

Of course, different people will consider (and even experience) the onerousness of sexual abstinence differently, depending upon their grasp of the reasons for exercising sexual self-restraint. And people's judgments as to whether such reasons obtain will likely vary, depending on their understanding, however informal and implicit, of the human good, of what is truly fulfilling of human persons.

It is entirely understandable that someone whose self-understanding is formed in accordance with the characteristically modern conception of human nature and the human good would be doubtful of the proposition that there are morally compelling reasons for people who are not married, who cannot marry, or who, perhaps, merely prefer not to marry, to abstain from sexual relations. For Sullivan and others who share this self-understanding, sexual abstinence seems not only pointless but emotionally debilitating and even, in some sense, dehumanizing.[19]

They should at least consider, however, that the modern conception does not hold a monopoly on the allegiance of thoughtful men and women. The alternative conception of human nature and its fulfillment articulated in the natural law tradition (and embedded in one form or another in historic Jewish and Christian faith) enables people who critically appropriate it to understand themselves and their sexuality very differently. Of course, the adoption of this (or any other) view, even if sound, cannot by itself effect a change of sexual orientation or simply eradicate homosexual or other morally problematic sexual desires. However, it can and does render intelligible and meaningful the struggle to live chastely, irrespective of the strength of such desires and regardless of whether one is "gay" or "straight," married or single.

14

BIOETHICS AND PUBLIC POLICY

Catholic Participation in the American Debate

A PROPER EXPLORATION of Catholic participation in America's bioethical debates requires historical and sociological, rather than philosophical, analysis, and I claim no expertise as a historian or sociologist. Still, the topic deeply interests me, for it seems to me that the American Catholic experience of contributing to major public policy debates about bioethical issues has been one marked by many disappointments and failures.[1] So I shall here give an account of the matter.

Let us take note of some fairly recent developments and work backward in time. This procedure has the advantage of enabling us to begin on a positive note. In June of 1997, the Supreme Court of the United States handed down two unanimous decisions rejecting constitutional challenges to state laws prohibiting people from assisting others in committing suicide. In *State of Washington v. Glucksberg* and *Vacco v. Quill,* not a single justice was prepared to endorse the proposition that the Constitution of the United States implicitly contains a general "right to die" analogous to the "right to abortion" the Court claimed to discover in the Constitution in the 1973 case of *Roe v. Wade.*

It is important to observe, however, that the Court has by no means ensured that the prohibition of assisting in suicide will remain in place in the American states. The practical effect of its decisions is to return the issue of assisted suicide to the individual states where it will be fought out in referenda and legislative contests.[2]

And here there is some rather alarming news: Polling data in many states show that substantial majorities favor changes in the laws to permit physicians to assist in the suicides of terminally ill patients. Even worse, it appears that throughout the country support for physician-assisted suicide among self-identified Roman Catholics closely parallels, and sometimes even exceeds, that of the population generally. Nevertheless, referenda in the states of Washington, Michigan, and California prove that effective public education campaigns—campaigns in which the Catholic Church has played critically important roles—can reverse a voting population's initial support for assisted suicide.[3] On the other hand, such a campaign failed—narrowly—to persuade a majority of voters in Oregon, which has adopted a policy permitting physician-assisted suicide.

The Church's ability to contribute effectively to the resistance to physician-assisted suicide in the United States is significantly enhanced by the fact that America's cultural elites—leading journalists, academics, television and film personalities, professionals and their associations, etc.—have not (yet) united in the cause of assisted suicide as they have in the cause of, say, abortion. Indeed, in asking the Supreme Court to deny the existence of a fundamental constitutional "right to die," the United States Catholic Conference (USCC) found itself in the company of many individuals and groups—including the Solicitor General of the United States, on behalf of the Clinton administration, and the American Medical Association (AMA), with whom the Conference has been in conflict over abortion and other bioethical issues. I do not mean to disparage in any way the Church's contribution to the political struggle against assisted suicide, much less her powerful witness in the cause of human life, when I observe that the Court's unwillingness to invent a right to physician-assisted suicide probably had more to do with the AMA's opposition, than with that of the USCC.

Furthermore, I am personally pessimistic about the prospects that the AMA and other elite institutions will maintain their opposition to physician-assisted suicide and euthanasia over the long term. Indeed, I will be surprised if, a decade from now, America's cultural elites are not firmly united in support of these practices. The logic of a commitment to an unqualified right to abortion on demand virtually compels such an outcome—a fact that has not been lost on scholar-activists such as Professor Ronald Dworkin, not to mention jurists such as Ninth Circuit Court of Appeals Judge Stephen Reinhardt (whose invalidation of a state law prohibiting assisting in suicide was overturned by the Supreme Court in the *Glucksberg* case). Reinhardt pressed the logic of the Supreme Court's abortion holdings[4] relentlessly in seeking to induce the justices to create a right to physician-assisted suicide. If I am correct, then the true struggle over assisted suicide and euthanasia—a struggle in which the Church will once again find herself in opposition to the most powerful constituencies and interests in American society—is yet to come.

In an important development in the struggle over abortion, the United States Congress has twice voted to ban dilation and extraction, better known as "partial-birth," abortions. Apparently because of the graphically barbaric nature of this procedure, public support for such a ban is particularly high. However, President Clinton vetoed the ban both times—claiming, utterly implausibly, that partial-birth abortions are sometimes necessary to protect the health and preserve the future fertility of pregnant women.[5] Although his vetoes were overridden in the House of Representatives, they were sustained in the Senate, where ten of the thirty-three votes needed to prevent an override of the veto were provided by self-identified Catholics.[6]

The night before the president's first veto, hundreds of Roman Catholics gathered in the pouring rain outside the White House in a silent, candlelight vigil to pray that Clinton would reconsider his announced opposition to banning partial-birth abortions. Present were several American cardinals. The American hierarchy had placed a very high priority on banning partial-birth abortions as a modest first step in the direction of bringing the unborn within the protection of American law. A few weeks after the veto, *all* of the active American cardinals came to Washington to urge Congress to override the veto. This was the first—and only—time in the history of the United States that all of the nation's active cardinals have appeared together to speak out on a matter of public policy. Yet their witness appears to have had no impact on President Clinton (who, as it happens, as a Georgetown University graduate is the first president ever to hold an earned degree from a Catholic institution of higher learning) or on those Catholic members of Congress who supported the president. Indeed, Clinton went so far as to refuse the cardinals the courtesy of an invitation to the White House. It is conceivable that he and his advisers believed—perhaps rightly—that he had more to gain politically from publicly snubbing the American Catholic leadership than he had to lose.

However that may be, Clinton and the Catholic members of the House and Senate who acted to protect partial-birth abortion received valuable "cover" for their deeds from a politically prominent Catholic clergyman whose actions had long served the pro-abortion cause. At a critical moment, Fr. Robert Drinan published articles in the *New York Times* and the *National Catholic Reporter* supporting Clinton's decision to veto the ban on partial-birth abortions and urging members of Congress to sustain that veto. Drinan is a Jesuit priest, a law professor at Georgetown University,[7] and a former member of Congress. He gained wide public recognition in the early 1970s as an outspoken Democratic member of the House Judiciary Committee, which recommended the impeachment of President Richard Nixon. What received less attention at the time was the fact that he was one of the first notable Catholic politicians in the country to begin opposing pro-life initiatives and voting in favor of legalized abortion and its public funding.[8] This happened at a time when even Senator Edward Kennedy, brother of the late president, scion of the most celebrated Roman Catholic family in the country, and since the mid-1970s one of the nation's most aggressively pro-abortion politicians, was professing implacable opposition to legal abortion and a desire for America to "fulfil its responsibility to its children from the very moment of conception."[9]

Unfortunately, Drinan did worse than set a bad example for Catholic politicians—particularly political liberals who were coming under increasing pressure to cast pro-abortion votes. He enabled them to rationalize support for pro-abortion legislative initiatives, and justify their votes to others, on the ground that they were doing nothing that a Catholic priest in good standing was not able and willing to do. Moreover, Drinan provided a much-imitated model for Catholic politicians who wished to support the pro-abortion movement while claiming to be faithful to Catholic moral teaching. When a constituent would write to his office expressing pro-life views, Drinan would respond with a letter giving assurances of his full agreement with the Church's teaching that abortion is gravely wrong. The letter would reveal nothing of Drinan's consistent support for pro-abortion legislative initiatives and opposition to pro-life initiatives. Drinan's legislative record on the subject was mentioned only when he replied to constituents whose letters to his office expressed pro-abortion sentiments.[10] What Drinan was developing in practice was the "personally opposed but pro-choice" position that was later to be defended formally in a famous speech by New York Governor Mario Cuomo at Notre Dame University.[11]

Drinan became a recognized leader of the "pro-choice" forces. For instance, a fund-raising letter from the National Abortion Rights Action League in 1980 identified Drinan as a friend of the movement whose re-election to the House of Representatives was critical to the "pro-choice" cause. He left Congress in 1980 only after the Holy See issued a general order requiring all priests to abstain from seeking or holding political office. He went on to become president of Americans for Democratic Action, a leading liberal advocacy group. In that connection, he sent out a fund-raising letter urging the moral necessity of electing candidates to Congress who favored legal abortion and its public funding.[12]

Drinan continued this line of argument in his articles supporting

Clinton's veto of the ban on partial-birth abortions. He claimed that the ban "would allow federal power to intrude into the practice of medicine." Further, he argued that banning these abortions would "detract from the urgent need to decrease abortions." Repeating the pro-abortion line on which Clinton had relied in justifying his veto, Drinan suggested that partial-birth abortions are rarely performed in the United States and then only when necessary to save women's lives or prevent grave injury.

This time, however, Drinan's efforts landed him in trouble, forcing him in the end into a humiliating retreat. First, a coalition of physicians, including former U.S. Surgeon General C. Everett Koop (who is not a Catholic), blasted apart the claim that partial-birth abortions are sometimes therapeutically indicated. Shortly thereafter, a leading lobbyist for the abortion movement publicly admitted lying about this and other issues pertaining to partial-birth abortion, including its frequency. At the same time, Drinan finally began to feel some heat from ecclesiastical sources. *The Pilot,* Boston's archdiocesan newspaper, published an editorial denouncing Drinan's defense of partial-birth abortion as "shocking, schizophrenic, and even scandalous." New York's John Cardinal O'Connor, writing in his own archdiocesan newspaper, dramatically called Drinan to account: "You could have raised your formidable voice for life; you have raised it for death.... Hardly the role of a lawmaker. Surely, not the role of a priest."

James Cardinal Hickey, archbishop of Washington, D.C., where Drinan resides and teaches, demanded that Drinan "clarify" his position since his published comments had, the Cardinal's spokesman said, "caused public confusion about Church teaching on abortion." Not long thereafter, Drinan issued a statement "withdrawing" what he had said in the *New York Times* and the *National Catholic Reporter.* After noting that he had relied on what turned out to be false information concerning "the true nature and widespread use of partial-birth abortion." Drinan reaffirmed his "total support" for the Church's "firm condemnation of abortion." I shall quote in full the concluding paragraph of his statement:

I do not believe that every moral evil should be outlawed. I do, however, see abortion—particularly partial-birth abortion—as a grave evil and can understand why Church leaders are urging lawmakers to ban it. I do not want anything to impede that effort. On the contrary, I join that effort and stand ready to promote laws and public policies that aim to protect vulnerable human life from conception until natural death. I support the Catholic bishops in their efforts to exercise moral leadership in the fight against abortion.[13]

Quite a satisfactory statement, I think. It would be interesting, and, indeed, instructive, to know what went on behind the scenes to produce it. The sad truth, however, is that it came more than twenty-five years too late. For, by 1997, Drinan's efforts, his bad example, and the profound scandal he had given, beginning in the early 1970s, had done immeasurable damage to the pro-life cause. The Church's failure to find a way effectively to meet the challenge presented by a notable priest's public activities and advocacy on behalf of abortion is among the most disappointing chapters in the story of the Church's participation in public policy debates on bioethical issues in the United States.

In the early 1970s, while Father Drinan was doing grave mischief in Congress, a prominent Catholic layman was doing similar harm in the far less public setting of the Supreme Court. Although it is difficult to obtain perfectly reliable information about the justices' deliberations, by all accounts Associate Justice William J. Brennan, who recently died at the age of 91, was a key player in creating a constitutional right to abortion in *Roe v. Wade.* Not only was Brennan a Catholic, he was appointed to the Court in the 1950s by President Eisenhower *precisely because he was a Catholic*—he filled the so-called "Catholic seat" on the Court. For most of his tenure on the Court, he was its only Catholic member. Yet, Brennan consistently worked to manufacture constitutional rights to activities condemned by the Church on moral grounds: pornography, contraception, sodomy, and abortion. Like Drinan, he claimed to be a faithful Catholic, fully

supportive of the Church's moral teaching. Nevertheless, he repeatedly acted to undermine principles of public morality that the Church
teaches are central to justice and the common good. Each time, he
would rationalize his actions by claiming that his judicial decisions
reflected, not his own political views, but the constitutional principles he was sworn as a federal judge to uphold. However, his extreme view of individual liberty (on issues such as abortion) is simply
not compelled by the Constitution itself.[14] In addition, one cannot
help but wonder why someone who "defined" the Constitution as
the protection of "the dignity" and "fundamental rights" of "the
human being,"[15] and who used that understanding of the Constitution to protect the poor, prisoners, the mentally retarded, and others, could not find within that same document protection for the
dignity and fundamental rights of the vulnerable and defenseless
unborn. After the opinion in *Roe,* which Brennan formally joined,
was handed down, Catholics—including Catholic politicians—who
wished publicly to join the elite consensus supporting abortion, while
claiming to be faithful to the Church's moral teaching, could point
to another prominent person—in this case the nation's highest rank-
ing Catholic jurist—as a model.

It was even more difficult for the Catholic hierarchy to deal with
Brennan and other Catholic laymen than it was to deal with Drinan.
Public criticism of them, and *a fortiori* public action against them,
was all but ruled out because of the likelihood that it would backfire. Anti-Catholicism remained, and remains, a fact of American
life—especially among American elites.[16] Powerful individuals and
interests who remain contemptuous and suspicious of the Church,
particularly for her moral teachings, are always ready to make a hero
of any Catholic public figure who defies the bishops. This is particularly true when they can depict the bishops as intervening in political affairs and attempting to tell Catholics how to vote.[17] Many American Catholics have themselves internalized a (mis)conception of the
constitutional "separation of church and state" according to which
religion, and religious authorities, should have nothing to say about
the conduct of public life. Non-Catholics and Catholics alike seem

to believe that full Catholic participation in public affairs is conditioned upon the bargain struck by John F. Kennedy—the first (and, so far, only) Roman Catholic president—when he spoke to a group of Protestant ministers in Houston during his campaign for the presidency in 1960:[18]

> I believe in an America where the separation of church and state is absolute—where no Catholic prelate would tell the President (should he be a Catholic) how to act and no Protestant minister would tell his parishioners for whom to vote—where no church or church school is granted any public funds or political preference...where no public official either requests or accepts instructions on public policy from the Pope, the National Council of Churches or any other ecclesiastical source—where no religious body seeks to impose its will directly or indirectly upon the general populace or the public acts of its officials.[19]

Kennedy went on to say that "Whatever issue may come before me as President...on birth control, divorce, censorship, gambling, or any other subject—I will make my decision in accordance with...what my conscience tells me to be in the national interest, and without regard to outside religious pressure or dictate. And no power or threat of punishment could cause me to do otherwise." Thus, at least as this speech was interpreted, Kennedy embraced the enduring, popular misconception that the Catholic Church seeks to "impose" its views on (rather than reason with) Americans, and declared his independence from any such interference with his conscience, which was itself apparently free to disregard Church teachings. He gave no positive account of how his Catholic faith would help make him a good president; rather, he accepted the view that religion should be separated from public life.

Kennedy effectively declared his Catholic faith to be irrelevant to his public life. For this and other reasons, few today cling to the old image of John F. Kennedy as a model Catholic. Still, he was a very public Catholic whose campaign and election largely set the terms of the American electorate's understanding of the relationship of politics and religion—at least as far as Roman Catholicism was concerned. And these terms—though they have been altered a bit in recent years and certainly are subject to further alteration—are realities with which faithful American Catholics and their ecclesiastical leaders have had to deal. And they make the job of bringing Catholic witness to bear in public debates over bioethical issues very difficult indeed—especially where the Church finds itself in sharp opposition to elite opinion.

With these facts in mind, let us examine the efforts of the United States Catholic Conference to influence these debates. Its approach to public policy matters has developed over the years, and we can understand its efforts best, I think, by dividing our analysis into certain periods, as follows: first, let us examine the period from the Second Vatican Council up to the preparation of the bishops' pastoral letter on nuclear war; second, let us look at the period from 1983 through 1987 when the nuclear pastoral was issued and the late Joseph Cardinal Bernardin of Chicago developed his widely publicized idea of a "seamless garment" or a "consistent ethic of life"; and third, let us focus on the period from 1988 to Father Drinan's retraction. After reviewing the development of the USCC's approach, I shall conclude by raising the question whether the bishops have recognized, and fully taken the measure of, the central problems they confront.

Preliminarily, let me make two points. First, the American Catholic experience of participating in public policy debates on bioethical issues cannot be accurately recounted if we focus on bioethical issues in isolation from other public policy debates. So it will be necessary for us to consider how the USCC has addressed a broad range of issues of public policy. Second, in undertaking this analysis, I have relied in large part on collections of official documents which the USCC itself publishes. Unfortunately, these publications are not entirely up-to-date.[20] Nevertheless, I think we can reach some fairly secure conclusions.

The United States Catholic Conference was "born" in 1966, in the exhilarating wake of Vatican II.[21] As the popes and fathers of the council saw things, the Holy Spirit was moving in the Church to effect a much needed renewal. As the secular media saw things, however, the Catholic Church was preparing to accommodate itself to, if not fully to embrace, the "new morality" which was fast entrenching itself among Western elites. More than a few Catholics shared the secular media's view, or, at least, hoped that it would prove to be correct. In many countries, including the United States, change and the demand for novelty, even if heretical, exploded and overwhelmed some of the Church's pastors.

Within four years of the creation of the USCC, the American bishops, in their pastoral letter *Christians in Our Time,* acknowledged candidly that the period since the Council had been one of "extraordinary testing for the Church."

> Most of us expected a gradual, orderly process of change and renewal.... Instead, we have seen dissension, controversy, and turmoil.... The problems are real, profound, and vitally crucial. They must be viewed with grave concern.[22]

This, by the way, was three years before *Roe v. Wade* and the flight from the pro-life cause by many Catholic liberals and liberal Catholic politicians.

The demands for change within the Church and within the larger society—the coinciding of what was misleadingly called "the spirit of Vatican II" with the "liberationist spirit of 1968" (the latter of which was expressing itself in widespread political unrest, the expansion of the drug culture, and a leap forward in the sexual revolution)—confronted the bishops with a nearly impossible array of problems to which they felt called to respond. And respond they did. In the ten years preceding the opening of Vatican II (1951–1961), the American bishops issued roughly three pastoral letters or statements per year. In the decade following the conclusion of the council (1966–1976), they issued approximately seven per year.

Here is a listing of some of the topics of pastorals issued by the U.S. bishops within ten years of the council (many of which have been revisited in subsequent pastorals): "the government and birth control"; "peace and Vietnam"; "penance"; "race relations and poverty"; "war in the Middle East"; "clerical celibacy"; "the Church in our day"; "the national race crisis"; "human life in our day"; "farm labor"; "abortion"; "poverty"; "ecumenism"; "conscientious objection"; "parental rights and the free exercise of religion"; "Christian concern for the environment"; "population and the American future"; "Mary—woman of faith"; "human rights in Chile and Brazil"; "the world food crisis"; "Catholic charismatic renewal"; "Panama-U.S. relations"; "toward a U.S. domestic food policy"; "the introduction of the family viewing period during prime time"; "hand-gun violence"; "the United Nations and the Republic of South Africa"; "the Eucharist and the hungers of the human family"; "Catholic-Jewish relations"; and "society and the aged."[23]

During this period, the United States experienced the Vietnam War, the struggle for civil rights for African Americans, the flowering of the drug culture, and the brunt of the sexual revolution. Then, in 1973, came *Roe v. Wade,* which, though accurately described by dissenting Justice Byron White as nothing more than "an exercise of raw judicial power," was widely understood to commit the nation to a regime of abortion on demand as a matter of constitutional principle. (As discussed above, it seems that Catholic jurist William Brennan played a key role in creating this "right.") The Supreme Court's declaration that abortion—which had been restricted in varying but significant ways in all fifty states—was a federal *constitutional right* gave many politicians, including Catholic politicians, an excuse for unburdening themselves of the pro-life political cause which, even in the early 1970s, was unpopular with elites. Before *Roe v. Wade,* Teddy Kennedy, as we have seen, had taken the position that "the legalization of abortion on demand is not in accordance with the value which our civilization places on human life."[24] In the aftermath of *Roe,* he and many other Catholic politicians revised their positions to bring them into conformity with the allegedly authoritative constitutional ruling of the Supreme Court on the subject. By the time Kennedy challenged President Jimmy Carter, a self-described "born again Christian" and a sort of "centrist" on the abortion question, for the Democratic Party's nomination for the presidency in 1976, the most visible Catholic public figure in America was an unabashed political champion of the most extreme wing of the pro-abortion movement.[25]

To their credit, the U.S. bishops responded vigorously to the challenge of *Roe,* issuing three statements in less than a year denouncing the judicial imposition of the abortion license and calling for a constitutional amendment to protect unborn human beings.[26] In 1975, they developed a sophisticated "Pastoral Plan for Pro-Life Activities," in which emphasis was placed on educating and equipping people at the parish and diocesan levels to defend the right to life.[27] In several documents issued in this period, they linked abortion, the quintessential "bioethical" issue, to others, particularly euthanasia and poverty.[28] Nevertheless, supporters of abortion, including influential figures within the print and broadcast media, depicted the bishops, and the Church as a whole, as being solely concerned with the issue of abortion, and of struggling to impose their allegedly purely "religious" view of the matter on Catholics and non-Catholics alike.

The bishops responded in their 1976 statement, *Political Responsibility: Reflections in an Election Year.*[29] They began in something of a defensive mode by asserting that their speaking out on political topics posed no threat to the domestic political order. Then, echoing the words of John F. Kennedy in Houston that "I believe in an America...where there is no Catholic vote, no anti-Catholic vote, no bloc voting of any kind," the bishops declared that they did "not seek the formation of a voting bloc." At least partially, in my judgment, to blunt the claim that the Catholic Church is concerned about abortion and nothing else, the document went on to draw together USCC positions on *eight* issue "clusters": abortion, the economy, education, food policy, housing, human rights/U.S. foreign policy, the mass media, and military expenditures. This combination of defensiveness and eagerness to show that they were not preoccupied with abortion would continue to mark USCC statements to the present.

THE USCC's approach in this period was subjected to respectful but powerful criticism by J. Brian Benestad.[30] While acknowledging many strengths of the bishops' statements, Benestad noted several problems:

1. Instead of being integrated into education and evangelization, the pursuit of social justice became a separate, parallel concern of the bishops.

2. By proposing particular policy initiatives, the bishops failed to communicate the richness of Catholic social teaching as a whole.

3. The bishops' teachings failed adequately to instruct and involve the laity in ways envisioned by the Second Vatican Council.

4. Apart from abortion, the bishops permitted secular liberalism to set their agenda.

5. Contrary to the Church's teaching on subsidiarity, the bishops seemed to embrace the liberal political view that there was a federal governmental solution to every social problem.

Although Benestad has been accused of exaggerating the extent and seriousness of these problems, it cannot reasonably be denied that problems existed. A review of the documents confirms that the bishops seem to be taking something of a "scattershot" approach to issues, to be responding too much to the left-liberal agenda of secular elites, and to be emphasizing governmental and, indeed, *federal* governmental solutions where more creative reflection would have suggested local governmental, and even non-governmental, approaches. Dealing with a very wide array of social problems, and attempting to resolve questions on which faithful Catholics might differ (both in their assessment of relevant social facts and in their prudential judgments as how best to address the problems), the bishops set themselves up for respectful disagreement by manifestly faithful Catholics on issues of social fact and prudential judgment on which the bishops could claim no special expertise or teaching authority. This was to be exploited aggressively by manifestly less faithful Catholics—particularly pro-abortion politicians—who sought to justify their dissent from the bishops' authoritative teachings on the right to life by depicting those teachings as matters of prudence on the order of the bishops' recommendations on, say, taxation and housing policy.

Let us next turn to the crucial period from 1983 to 1987. The key figure in our story now becomes the late Joseph Cardinal Bernardin of Chicago. Bernardin, who had been general secretary of the conference from 1968 through 1972 and its president from 1974 through 1977, was thoroughly familiar with its operations. He agreed with critics such as Benestad that Catholic teaching as a coherent whole had not been adequately communicated in previous pastoral letters and statements. He was aware that the bishops' approach had been too "scattershot." When, in January of 1981, he was appointed chairman of an *ad hoc* committee to draft a pastoral letter on the arms race, he sought to avoid replicating these problems. As Bernardin saw it, the goal of the pastoral was to "present a theory which is in conformity with the totality of the Church's moral teaching."[31]

Bernardin designed a "consultation" process with "experts" and laity far more extensive than the USCC had previously undertaken. Partially due to this consultation, and partially due to the fact that the first draft was leaked to the press, "it would be difficult to find a document more widely researched and discussed during its formation, from the very beginning."[32]

The pastoral went through three drafts, numerous meetings and consultations, and scores of amendments. *The Challenge of Peace,* as it was called, was finally issued in May of 1983. It was controversial from the outset. While some objections were spurious (such as the demand—this time heard more often from political conservatives than from liberals—that "religion be kept out of politics"), I believe there is at least one valid objection, an objection that may justly be made to many of the USCC's documents. Although the bishops "set forth...the principles of Catholic teaching on war," including, quite rightly, the Church's strict teaching regarding the absolute immunity of non-combatants from direct attack, they went on to make "a series of judgments, based on these principles, about concrete policies."[33] Many of these judgments involved assessments of fact and prudential judgments on which reasonable people and faithful Catholics can, and do, legitimately disagree. This was a recipe for confusing the faithful about which teaching of the bishops is binding in conscience and which is not. And, as I have already suggested, this confusion is bound to be—and, undeniably, has been—promoted and exploited by people who, in varying degrees of bad faith, have sought to rationalize their support for abortion and their efforts in its cause.

Cardinal Bernardin's famous initiative for a "seamless garment" or "consistent ethic of life" appears to have grown out of his experience with *The Challenge of Peace*. A few months after that document was issued, the cardinal used the occasion of a lecture at Fordham University in New York to announce the "seamless garment" initiative.[34] It was to have important ramifications for the development of a Catholic bioethic in America.

At that time, the pro-life movement was in the doldrums. Efforts to reverse or even substantially modify *Roe v. Wade* had failed. Commitment to the pro-life cause had steadily eroded among Catholic elites, and many Catholics in the pro-life movement had grown disheartened. Among "progressive" Catholics, many of those who remained formally pro-life came to view abortion as a side issue—an issue, indeed, inferior in importance to others. In this atmosphere, Cardinal Bernardin's effort may be seen in the most positive light as trying to unite Catholics of all stripes in a revivified effort to protect human life from the range of contemporary threats to it.

During his lecture at Fordham, the cardinal noted that *The Challenge of Peace* provides a "starting point" for shaping a consistent ethic of life inasmuch as it

> links the questions of abortion and nuclear war.... No other major institution presently holds these two positions in the way the Catholic bishops have joined them. This is both a responsibility and an opportunity.[35]

He went on to argue that "the long term ecclesiological significance of the pastoral rests with the lessons it offers about the Church's capacity for dialogue with the world in a way which helps to shape public policy on key issues." In proposing the "seamless garment" initiative, his purpose, he said, was to "argue that success on any one of the issues threatening life requires concern for the broader attitudes in society about respect for human life."

There is not a great deal to disagree with in what Cardinal Bernardin said thus far. But then he made the intellectual move that would bedevil the seamless garment initiative, and, eventually, rend the garment.

> The issue of consistency [of application of moral principle] is tested...when we examine the relationship between the "right to life" and the "quality of life" issues.... Those who defend the right to life of the weakest among us must be equally visible in support of the quality of life of the powerless among us.... Such a quality of life posture translates into specific political and economic positions on tax policy, employment generation, welfare policy, nutrition and feeding programs, and health care.

Bernardin's analysis here has been subjected to searching criticism by John Finnis.[36] As Finnis observed, it is at best tendentious to assert that people active in the pro-life cause must be "equally visible" in other good causes. Moreover, the cardinal's suggestion that a sound "quality of life posture translates into *specific* political and economic positions" is ambiguous to the point of being misleading. On a great many political and economic issues, choice is between, or among, not (or not only) good and bad policy options, but (also) between, or among, a range of choices all of which are consistent with a morally proper "posture." And even with respect to certain issues that do admit of a uniquely "best" policy option, the identification of that option may depend upon empirical and prudential judgments that are reasonably in dispute among people who share a sound "posture."

Questions of tax and welfare policy in the United States are good examples of political and economic issues of the sort I have in mind.

Unlike the question whether abortion ought generally to be permitted by law or forbidden, the question whether the income tax should be replaced or supplemented by a national sales tax, or whether welfare responsibilities ought to be shifted from the federal government to the states, requires many judgments of fact and prudence. In a very general sense, perhaps, we could say that a proper concern for justice and the common good must be "translated" into a fair program of tax or welfare reform, but it will hardly do to suggest that such a concern translates into "*specific* political and economic positions" in these areas. But the intellectual weaknesses of Bernardin's initiative are less important to the story of Catholic participation in public policy debates in the United States than are its actual political consequences.

Let me state clearly that I do not believe that the purpose of Cardinal Bernadin's seamless garment initiative was to provide "cover" to Catholic politicians (and others) who wished to advance the pro-abortion agenda while claiming to be faithful (or, at least, friendly) to Catholic social teaching generally.[37] Unfortunately, however, a side effect of the initiative was that it provided precisely such cover. The best example of someone seizing it is that of Mario Cuomo, the very publicly Catholic politician who served two terms as governor of New York.

On September 13, 1984, barely one year after Cardinal Bernardin had announced his seamless garment project, Cuomo delivered his famous speech on abortion at the University of Notre Dame.[38] At the time, Cuomo was the leader of the liberal wing of the Democratic Party and a much-touted presidential possibility. The central point of his speech was to claim that while he "personally" accepted, and lived by, the Church's teaching on abortion, he considered it wrong to deny his fellow citizens, including many who did not accept the teaching authority of the Catholic Church, the choice as to whether to have an abortion.

Noting that the Church does not insist that every immoral action be prohibited by law,[39] Cuomo depicted the question of abortion's legal treatment as a matter of prudence akin to the range of questions with which the seamless garment was concerned. It was a question on which, he suggested, reasonable people, including reasonable Catholics, could disagree. According to Cuomo, what made a politician truly pro-life, and truly someone who was prepared to act in the spirit of the Catholic teaching, was not his opposition to legal abortion or its public funding, though Cuomo acknowledged the bishops' clear teaching on those issues; it was, rather, the politician's stance on the whole range of sanctity and quality of life issues. And here, he implied, liberal Democrats such as himself, who shared the bishops' stated positions on capital punishment, welfare, housing, taxation, defense spending, international human rights policy, etc., had records far superior to those of pro-life conservatives whose only specific areas of policy agreement with the bishops had to do with abortion and related issues.[40]

Cuomo prides himself on being something of an intellectual. And there is no denying that he is a bright fellow. He must know, then, that, at its root, this is utter nonsense. He must be aware that the Church's teaching on abortion truly does "translate" straightforwardly into a specific public policy—the unborn, like the rest of us, are to be afforded the equal protection of the laws; abortion is to be generally prohibited and never publicly promoted—in a way that her teachings regarding care for the poor or the requirement of fairness in distributing tax liability, for example, simply do not.[41] But the fact is that Cuomo brilliantly exploited Bernardin's seamless garment teaching, and the USCC's practice of adopting specific positions on a wide range of policy questions, to undermine the bishops' efforts to give the right to life the priority it deserves in a society in which more than one million unborn human beings are destroyed by abortion every year.[42]

Cuomo's Notre Dame speech provided a virtual playbook for pro-abortion Catholic politicians who wished to claim that their public support for the "the right to choose" abortion was not inconsistent with their personal moral opposition to deliberate feticide. It taught liberal politicians of every religious persuasion how to explain to Catholic constituents that their differences with the bishops over the particular issue of abortion are overshadowed by their broad agreement with the bishops across the wide range of "quality of life" issues. It relieved much of the tension—internal as well as external— experienced by public men and women—Catholic and non-Catholic alike who wanted to be "pro-life" and "pro-choice" at the same time.

By 1986, pro-life Democrats were an endangered species and pro-life liberals were virtually extinct. It was in November of that year that the USCC issued what is probably its most famous pastoral, *Economic Justice for All*.[43] However it might have been intended by the bishops, for liberal politicians it was an early Christmas present. Although the pastoral began by denying that it was "a blueprint for the American economy,"[44] it undercut that claim by offering specific prescriptions on a host of issues. Again, though the bishops state that "we do not claim to make these prudential judgments with the same kind of authority that marks our declarations of principle," they "feel obliged to teach by example how Christians can undertake concrete analysis and make specific judgments on moral issues."[45] But why, if their prudential judgments are no more binding on the faithful than are mine or yours, do the bishops "feel obliged" to offer them? Is prudential political judgment of this sort not precisely the business of the laity? Is the failure to leave it to the laity not confusing and ultimately undermining of the bishops' proclamations of principle and their public witness on specific moral evils such as legal abortion? "We look for a fruitful exchange among differing viewpoints," the bishops say. "[T]ogether we will test our views by the Gospel and the Church's teaching...."[46]

The bishops apparently failed to see how their general approach and specific statements such as those I just quoted would be exploited by the enemies of their pro-life witness. What should they have done? More to the point: What should they do?

The bishops should say what they can say as a matter of moral principle consistent with their authority and responsibility to preach the Gospel.[47] Beyond that, politics should be left to the laity. That, as I understand it, is the teaching of Vatican II. It is what the American bishops themselves seemed to recognize in their 1980 pastoral, *Called and Gifted: The American Catholic Laity,* in which they wrote that "it is [the laity] who engage directly in...relating Christian values...to complex questions."[48] Yet, in continuing to speak out on matters on which they can claim no special expertise or authority, the bishops diminish their public standing and, unintentionally, risk impeding potentially valuable lay initiatives. So, though there are faithful, pro-life Catholics who deeply disagree with me about this, I believe that the bishops should desist from pronouncing specific prescriptions on matters that are subject to honestly disputed questions of fact and prudential judgments. (This extends, by the way, to questions of *strategy* disputed among committed pro-life activists, such as whether to move forward in Congress with a partial-birth abortion ban before attempting to ban late-term abortions, or whether the goal of pro-life political action should be a Human Life Bill invoking Congress's power under section 5 of the Fourteenth Amendment as opposed to a constitutional amendment to overturn *Roe v. Wade.*)

In the first two years after the publication of *Economic Justice for All,* the USCC issued statements on topics ranging from "biblical fundamentalism" to "the Ku Klux Klan," and from "principles for legal immigration policy" to "food, agriculture, and rural concerns."[49] As the foreword to one volume of the USCC's pastoral letters put it: "There is scarcely a serious international or domestic problem involving the United States during these years that the National Conference of Catholic Bishops and the United States Catholic Conference have not touched with a thoughtful statement."[50] Certainly, some—perhaps many—of the USCC's statements qualify as "thoughtful." But, thoughtfully or not, the USCC is talking too much, and the consequences of this excessive talking are part of the disappointing story of Catholic efforts to influence public policy regarding bioethical issues in the United States.

All this talk—all this taking of positions on specific policy proposals about which faithful Catholics (together with other men and women of goodwill) reasonably disagree—creates the image of the Catholic Church and its leadership as an *interest group.* This is the perception of the media, of politicians, and of many of the Catholic faithful themselves. In my view, the linking of its pro-life witness with advocacy on a wide range of "quality of life" issues has failed to accomplish the Church's goals in any area. It has not produced particularly valuable initiatives in areas such as tax and welfare, and it has arguably put the Church on the wrong side of several important debates. And who can blame politicians and others for perceiving, and treating, the Church much like any other interest group? The USCC's own documents report that it had over fifty congressional "legislative priorities" for 1991–92. And in teaching on such a bewildering variety of subjects, the USCC is in danger of "failing to see the forest for the trees." For instance, in testimony to the Democratic and Republican platform committees in 1988, the USCC mentions civil rights protection against every form of invidious discrimination and denial of liberty except that practiced against people of faith![51] The Holy Father travels the world stressing the importance of religious freedom, what he calls the "first freedom"—yet, the USCC forgets to mention it.

Let me tell a related story. According to USCC materials,

On March 22, 1988, the United States Congress voted to override President Reagan's veto of the Civil Rights Restoration Act. Almost angrily, Msgr. Daniel Hoye, then general secretary of the United States Catholic Conference declared that the President had vetoed one of the most important pieces of civil rights legislation in many years. Once the veto was overridden, Msgr. Hoye issued a *Statement on Civil Rights* [on behalf of the USCC]....[52]

Now, having served as a member of the United States Commission on Civil Rights, I can assure you that the intelligent assessment of the desirability of enacting any proposed piece of contemporary civil rights legislation requires prudential judgments of precisely the sort *lay people* are called to make in light of an evaluation of the complex facts of race relations in the United States. Calling something a "civil rights bill" or a "civil rights restoration act" is no guarantee of its soundness or justice. In fact, it will rarely make sense for the USCC to claim that *Catholic moral teaching* requires a particular judgment on a proposed piece of contemporary civil rights legislation. The question, mind you, is not whether racial discrimination is good or bad, or whether it should be permitted or forbidden. It is, rather, whether a particular policy (say, "affirmative action") constitutes racial discrimination, or, even more frequently, what is the best way, among a range of possible ways (all of which have drawbacks as well as advantages), to prevent racial discrimination or ameliorate its effects. When the bishops insist on weighing in with an opinion on issues of this sort, their views in Washington (and beyond) will "receive mostly a politically partisan reaction" (as did the one in question). And the reason for this, I would dare to suggest, is that the USCC's statement is in truth, however inadvertently, a politically partisan statement.

There are signs that the USCC is becoming aware of these problems. For instance in marking the tenth anniversary of its pastoral on economic justice, the USCC issued a one-page document called *Economic Justice for All: A Catholic Framework for Economic Life*. It is obviously much shorter than was the 185-page *Economic Justice* pastoral. It is also much better. It lists ten principles which it "urge[s] Catholics to use...as principles for reflection, criteria for judgment, and directions for action." It does not advocate specific fiscal, monetary, or tax policies.

In addition to talking too much about too many issues, the USCC's efforts to advance an effective Catholic bioethic in the United States have been hampered, as I have already suggested, by a certain defensiveness in engaging the opposition over the question of abortion. This criticism must, however, be tempered in two ways. First, people in the Pro-life Office of the USCC have been courageous to the point of heroism in their defense of the right to life. Nothing in my remarks should be taken to imply anything negative about these Evangelists of Life. Second, I must applaud the specific courageous acts of the USCC in criticizing the Supreme Court for its abominable abortion rulings. It has been in the great tradition of St. Ambrose, who defied and called to public penance the Emperor

Theodosius after he had ordered the massacre of innocent civilians, that the USCC has denounced the immoral and unconstitutional acts of judges who abuse their authority.

Having said that, I must return to the defensiveness with which the conference has often engaged the opposition in the debate over abortion. I fear that the factors that account for the temptation to go overboard in linking the Church's pro-life witness to other issues also account for this defensiveness. The bishops and their staff must be brought to see that no matter how reasonable the terms in which they couch their pro-life witness, no matter how extensively they link abortion to other issues, no matter how careful they are to avoid sounding as though stopping abortion is the only thing they care about, American cultural elites, for whom the ready availability of abortion is critical as a matter of self-interest as well as ideology, will viciously attack them. A tenor of defensiveness will not facilitate "dialogue" with these people. It will be taken by them, rather, as a sign of weakness or irresolution.

Furthermore, in constructing, as the Holy Father calls us to do, a new "culture of life," the USCC should be clear-headed about who are our friends and who are our enemies. As pleasant as it is to enjoy terms of cordiality with well-to-do, influential people who "happen" to be "pro-choice," our true friends are the ones we have encountered in the trenches of the pro-life movement—evangelical Protestant Christians, black and white. Instead of disavowing any attempt to form a voting bloc, we lay Catholics, inspired by the witness of our bishops, should be joining with our evangelical brethren in a voting bloc *for* life. The bishops, and the priests who preach with their authority, should, moreover, instruct the faithful that every single one of them is called by the Holy Father in *Evangelium Vitae* to be involved at some level in building the culture of life.[53] The indispensable first step in building that new culture is to oppose abortion, euthanasia, and all unjust killing. Teachers of the faith should make it clear that never may a faithful Catholic support a candidate even in part because he is pro-choice; only in the most extraordinary circumstances could it ever be legitimate to support a pro-abortion candidate over a reasonable pro-life candidate who presents himself as an alternative.[54] The urgent priority of the pro-life cause demands at least this much, and our pastors should be prepared to say so.[55]

NOW, a moment ago I praised the heroic efforts of the USCC's Pro-life Office. That Office has been very effective in promoting Catholic values in public policy debates in Washington concerning abortion and other bioethical issues. It has consistently made the case for desirable legislation and often played a central role in preventing bad legislation from being enacted. It is a sophisticated Catholic voice in media debates. And the office also works vigorously to assist pro-life leaders at the diocesan and parish levels. Yet, if you ask people in the Pro-life Office why, in light of the continuation of abortion on demand in America, the bishops have not issued a pastoral letter on abortion recently, they will tell you, I am sure, that Catholics already know very well the Church's teaching on this issue. And, of course, they are right. The real question is why so many Catholics disobey it. The abortion rate among self-identified Catholics appears to be equal to (or greater than!) that of the general population. And Catholic politicians are at least as likely to be pro-abortion as pro-life in their public advocacy and action. Why are Catholics not living as "signs of contradiction" to the "culture of death"?

If lay Catholics could be energized on the issue of abortion, if they could be inspired to make it a *primary* factor in their political considerations, then we could truly begin rolling back the abortion license in the United States. Bill Clinton, or some future president, would then find it politically disastrous to veto a ban on partial-birth abortion. And, even if he were prepared to fly a kamikaze mission in the cause of "abortion rights," the Congress would immediately override his veto. The question is: What stands in the way of energizing and inspiring lay Catholics in the cause of human life?

When he retired as president of the USCC in 1977, Cardinal Bernardin identified three "continuing, long-term problems" for the Catholic Church in America: (1) the difficulty many Catholics have in accepting the teaching authority of the Church; (2) the legality of

abortion on demand; and (3) the refusal to accept the Vatican's position on the question of ordaining women to the priesthood.[56] As the
third is simply an example of the first, we could say he identified two
problems—abortion and disobedience to the teaching authority of
the Church. Further, if I am correct in suggesting that the consequences of a unified, energized Catholic witness on abortion would
be the rolling back of the abortion license, there is, at bottom, one
"continuing, long-term problem"—refusal to accept the teaching of
the magisterium.

In my judgment, the single factor most responsible for undermining the laity's understanding of, and willingness to be guided by, the
teaching authority of the Church is the scandalous defiance of this
authority by theologians, especially priest-theologians and members
of women's religious orders. Above all, the suggestion—sometimes
formal, often merely implicit—that theologians represent a parallel,
or even superior, magisterium has had a devastating effect on the
faith of many lay Catholics. If there are two, equally valid sources of
authoritative teaching, and these sources disagree, then the individual believer is free to choose between them. The public dissent of
theologians becomes a licence for the very practical dissent of ordinary Catholics on issues ranging from contraception and in vitro
fertilization, to divorce and remarriage, and, of course, abortion.

Commenting with approval on the strategy of dissident theologian Hans Küng, the American pro-abortion, feminist theologian
Rosemary Radford Reuther explained in 1981 that

> [a] new consensus could only come about if this traditional power
> [i.e., the authority of the magisterium] could be deposed and the
> Church restructured on conciliar democratic lines accountable to
> the people. Then the theological consensus in the academy could
> serve as a guide for the pastoral teaching of the Church. This is
> really what Küng is calling for: *that the academy replace the hierarchy*
> *as the teaching magisterium of the Church.* This cannot be accom-
> plished by the academy itself. It entails the equivalent of the
> French Revolution in the Church, the deposing of a monarchical

for a democratic constitution of the Church.... In the immediate future we cannot hope for a new consensus that will overcome the theological split between the academy and the hierarchy. Rather the best we can hope for is the defence of pluralism.... Pluralism can be defended only by making sure that this hierarchical power structure is not strong enough to repress successfully the independent institutional bases of conciliar and liberation theology.[57]

And so we find as recently as June 8, 1997, the Catholic Theological Society of America (CTSA) voting overwhelmingly to urge not that the magisterium reverse its teaching regarding the reservation of the ordained priesthood to males—liberal theologians do not expect that to happen any time soon—but that discussion of the question be continued despite the Holy Father's teaching in *Ordinatio Sacerdotalis* that the matter is settled and that discussion of the possibility of ordaining women harms the Church and should cease. So, the laity must choose whom to believe, the Pope or the theologians. The call by the CTSA to keep the issue open for discussion in defiance of the Pope's solemn teaching is precisely the sort of thing Reuther had in mind in calling for "pluralism" as the strategy best suited to the period prior to the one in which a French-style revolution can be made to destroy the teaching authority of the magisterium and replace it with a new "magisterium" of the theologians. Does anyone doubt that the real goal of those CTSA theologians who voted with the majority is to reverse the magisterium's teaching regarding the reservation of the priesthood to males? Does anyone doubt that these theologians, in their hearts, simply do not believe that the magisterium possesses authority superior to their own to settle issues such as women's ordination?

Theological dissent and defiance of this sort is largely, though, of course, not exclusively, to blame for the fact that many—perhaps most—American Catholics today embrace secular liberal understandings of marriage and sexual morality. The U.S. bishops' efforts to reinforce an authentically Christian understanding of these matters among the faithful in documents such as *Human Life in Our Day*

(1968), *To Live in Christ Jesus* (1976), and *Statement concerning Human Sexuality* (1977)[58] have been constantly undercut by the scandal of theological dissent. Sometimes, as in the famous press conference of July 30, 1968, at which Charles Curran and eighty-six other theologians issued a statement dissenting from Pope Paul VI's teaching in *Humanae Vitae,* theologians' attempts to undermine authoritative teachings of the magisterium are explicit, public, and orchestrated. More often, however, their efforts are informal, subtle, and dispersed. And the consequences extend beyond questions of sex, marriage, and the sanctity of human life. Many of us were shocked—though perhaps we should not have been—by recent polling data revealing that significant numbers of self-identified (and in many cases active) American Catholics reject the Church's teachings on such matters as the bodily resurrection of our Lord and his real presence in the Eucharist. Dissenting theologians have won the hearts and minds of many, many American Catholics. It is only a bit of an exaggeration to say that heresy is so widespread that it threatens to become the norm. It is almost as if, to paraphrase St. Jerome, "the whole world groaned *again* to find itself Arian."

In responding to this challenge, the bishops should, I believe, follow the Pope's lead in *Evangelium Vitae* by formally and publicly identifying abortion, euthanasia, and other threats to life as issues of the highest priority for faithful Catholics.[59] The Church's firm, constant, and—in my judgment and, apparently, the Pope's—*infallibly proposed* teachings on these matters should be resoundingly reaffirmed,[60] and it should be made clear by individual bishops throughout the land that public dissent from these teachings by anyone speaking with their authority or as a Catholic theologian or teacher in their dioceses will not be tolerated.[61]

Perhaps most importantly of all, the bishops should firmly implement *Ex corde Ecclesiae,* the constitution for Catholic colleges and universities which John Paul II has given as a gift to the Church. As the bishops recognized in their 1980 pastoral, *Catholic Higher Education and the Pastoral Mission of the Church,*[62] it is crucial for Catholic colleges and universities to maintain their Catholic identity. In the cases of most major Catholic institutions, that identity has been seriously compromised by, among other things, the presence (often as teachers) of theologians who publicly dissent from the Church's firm and constant teachings on a variety of moral and doctrinal questions. As *Ex corde Ecclesiae* makes clear, it is the diocesan bishop's responsibility to ensure that Catholic institutions in his diocese retain their Catholic character and enrich, rather than undermine, the faith of Catholic students. The occasion of implementing *Ex corde Ecclesiae* provides an excellent opportunity for the bishops to restate the Catholic vision of education, a vision that inspires young people to lead lives of fruitful and faithful service to Christ and his Church. The juridically firm implementation of *Ex corde Ecclesiae* is critical, for, to a very large extent, it is on Catholic campuses that the future of the Church in America, and of a Catholic bioethic, will be decided. Let us be under no illusions: much of this ground is currently under enemy occupation.

Now, what can the bishops do about Catholic public officials who publicly support such evils as abortion and euthanasia? What can be done about Catholics in the legislative, executive, and judicial branches of government whose public advocacy and action in support of these evils gives scandal to the faithful and undermines the Church's witness for life? In most cases, it would likely be a mistake for bishops to excommunicate individual office holders or formally deny them access to the Eucharist pursuant to provisions of canon law authorizing such a denial to those who persist in manifest, grave sin. The reason is that such action by the bishops would often backfire by enabling the media to depict the "pro-choice" politician as a "martyr for freedom" in the way I have already indicated. There are two things I would suggest as alternatives. First, bishops should not hesitate to publicly criticize the anti-life activities of specific politicians, nor should they refrain from pointing out the inconsistency of these activities with any profession of Christian faith. Second, I would urge bishops to revive the ancient and honorable practice of shunning. Individual bishops should refuse to share the head table at any Catholic event (not just those sponsored by the NCCB) with pro-abortion politicians (including jurists), or the dais at events at Catholic colleges and universities or other institutions. They should refuse to be photographed with such people or permit themselves to be used by them to any political advantage. They should ensure that such persons are never honored by Catholic institutions in their dioceses or given the podium in any context other than one designed to highlight the disgracefulness of their support for the "culture of death." The shunning of such politicians would vividly remind ordinary lay Catholics of the seriousness of the church's teachings regarding the sanctity of human life and would send the clear message that Catholics (and other Christians) who serve the "culture of death" are tragically weakening their relationship with Christ and alienating themselves from the community of Christian faith.

Let me conclude, as I began, on a positive note. In the summer of 1997, the USCC issued *Living the Gospel of Life: A Challenge to American Catholics* (December 1998). That statement powerfully criticizes the abuse of the "seamless garment" metaphor to, in the words of Father Richard John Neuhaus, "relativize the enormity of taking innocent human life by making it one item on a long list of concerns." The statement properly recognizes the principle of respect for the right to life of the unborn as the foundation of a sound Catholic bioethic in America. One hopes that the bishops will spread its message widely and reiterate it ceaselessly, calling upon all Catholics, but particularly Catholic political officials, to inform their consciences in the light of its teaching.

15

ON *FIDES ET RATIO*

I N THE YEARS that have passed since the release by Pope John Paul II of his encyclical letter *Fides et Ratio* (Faith and Reason), theologians, philosophers, scientists, and other scholars have pondered its meaning and significance. One thing has become clear: a full appreciation of the teaching set forth in this extraordinarily rich and suggestive document requires multiple readings and, in all probability, many more years of reflection and discussion. As befits the profound and ancient topic it addresses—the relationship between religious faith and intellectual inquiry—*Fides et Ratio* is an encyclical for the ages.

"Each time I work through the encyclical," Father Richard John Neuhaus reports, "I do so with quite different sensations—ranging from intellectual excitement to puzzlement to wonder that such a thing should be attempted and, finally, to a humbling awareness that there is more going on in this text than I understand." I sympathize with Father Neuhaus, for I have experienced very similar sensations, leading to precisely the same "humbling awareness." Still, I shall venture some thoughts about the aims and significance of the encyclical.

Perhaps the first thing to notice about *Fides et Ratio* is to whom it is addressed, namely, "the Bishops of the Catholic Church." In this respect, the encyclical differs strikingly from, say, the 1995 encyclical *Evangelium Vitae,* on the value and moral inviolability of human life, which was addressed not only to "the Bishops," but also to "Priests and Deacons, Men and Women Religious, Lay Faithful," and, indeed, "all people of Good Will." The latter encyclical was concerned with very practical moral and political questions facing contemporary societies, such as abortion and infanticide, suicide and euthanasia, war and capital punishment, poverty and oppression. These are, of course, pressing and nearly universal issues. Still, the issues taken up by Pope John Paul II in *Fides et Ratio,* are certainly no less universal, and in important ways no less pressing. So why the much more limited scope of address?

I suspect that the answer is that the Pope's principal concern in *Fides et Ratio* is with the moral and spiritual health of the Church herself. In particular, it seems to me, he wishes to instruct his brother bishops regarding the importance of the intellectual, as well as spiritual, formation of priests. It is, I believe, the Pope's view—it is certainly mine—that the Church's essential tasks of catechesis and evangelization are severely hampered by what he perceives to be widespread intellectual weaknesses in seminaries and other Catholic institutions of learning. If I am getting his drift, these weaknesses are simultaneously causes and effects of various intellectual vices as well as methodologies and ideologies that are hostile to, or, in any event, incompatible with, a proper understanding of the truths of the Gospel.

Of course, the Pope is a former philosophy professor, and the encyclical is, at one level, a sort of celebration of the dignity and importance of philosophy and an exhortation to philosophers to "think big." And so the Pope denies the self-sufficiency of faith: quoting St. Augustine, he declares that "if faith does not think, it is nothing." Indeed, faith itself points to the indispensable role of reason and, thus, of philosophy. "In the light of faith," the Pope says, "I cannot but encourage philosophers—be they Christian or not—to trust in the power of human reason and not to set goals that are too modest in their philosophizing." And while he stresses the role (and profound importance) of philosophy in the theological enterprise, he also insists on the autonomy of philosophy as a scholarly and intellectual discipline.

It would be a mistake, however, to read *Fides et Ratio* as fundamentally a professional philosopher's celebration, or even defense, of the importance and autonomy of his beloved discipline. John Paul II is writing not as Karol Woytila, the philosopher, but as Peter, the Rock on which Christ builds his Church. As supreme pontiff and pastor of the Catholic Church, he is addressing problems in the Church that impede the successful prosecution of her divine mission. He is concerned to promote a proper understanding of the relationship between theology and philosophy, between faith and reason, not, primarily, for the sake of solving what is, admittedly, an intriguing intellectual problem, but rather because the salvation of souls is at stake. He is moved to offer instruction to his brother bishops precisely with a view to renewing the intellectual life of the Church *for the sake of her saving mission.*

Now, please do not misunderstand me. The Pope does not suggest that anyone is going to go to hell for the "sin" of holding an incorrect understanding of the relationship between faith and reason. He does believe, however, that the widespread misunderstanding of this relationship, particularly among those primarily responsible for catechesis and evangelization, weakens the ability of the Church to transmit saving faith. Indeed, the faith that Christians attempt to transmit, when they badly misunderstand the relationship, is Christian faith only in a weak and defective sense. It may, for example, be an overly rationalistic faith, or an overly emotional one. The Jesus in whom people are invited to have faith may be, not the Christ of the Gospels—the Word made flesh who suffered and died for our sins and whose resurrection makes possible our own salvation—but rather a magician, or a comforting teddy bear, or a mere example of ethically upright living, or what have you.

So far, in discussing the Pope's emphasis on reason and its importance to the life of faith and the mission of the Church, I have spoken only of philosophy. And it is true that the Pope himself—rightly, in my view—stresses the role of philosophy in the theological enterprise and, therefore, the need for priests and other evangelists to be trained heavily and rigorously in philosophy. And he is plainly alarmed that indispensable philosophical work is widely neglected—both in theological research and in priestly formation—in favor of psychological and sociological approaches to theological subjects, approaches that are often (not inevitably, not always, but often) reductionistic and, as such, incompatible with the very faith in whose service they are putatively placed. But the Pope also recognizes the legitimacy, autonomy, and importance of non-philosophical methods of inquiry and intellectual disciplines, including psychology and sociology, and, especially, the natural sciences. Scholars and students in these disciplines rightly, in the Pope's view, pursue knowledge of their subject matters for its own sake, as well as for its practical use in the improvement of the conditions of human life.

Here, perhaps, it is worth pausing to take note, however, of the Pope's warning against possible corruptions of these fields that render them incompatible with Christian faith. The first of these warnings is that the legitimate autonomy of the sciences can be misinterpreted as somehow liberating them from the overarching requirements of the moral law. So what the Pope calls the "scientistic [as opposed to scientific] mentality" can lead people "to think that if something is technically possible it is therefore morally permissible." The second warning is against "scientism" as such, that is, "the philosophical notion which refuses to admit the validity of forms of knowledge other than those of the positive sciences." This notion—a philosophical, and not itself scientific one, you will note—"dismisses values as mere products of the emotions" and "consigns all that has to do with the question of the meaning of life to the realm of the irrational or imaginary."

The reality of scientism (whether or not it is quite as widespread as the Pope believes it is) reveals not only the possibility of philosophical error, about which no one needs convincing, but also the way in which philosophy can become anti-philosophical. The positivism at the heart of scientism was devised by philosophers as part of their philosophical enterprise—reason itself in the critique of what were perceived to be the pretensions of reason. By instrumentalizing reason—viewing it as, in Hume's famous phrase, the mere "slave of the passions"—it reconceived philosophy, not as the search for wisdom (what the Pope calls the pursuit of sapiential knowledge), but as a purely analytic enterprise. But when reason is instrumentalized, it soon turns on itself in utter distrust. Then, as even the analytic value of reason is denied, positivism collapses into the darker phenomenon of nihilism, the critique of which is impossible from the purely analytic perspective. To overcome nihilism, philosophy must return to its original Socratic status as both an analytic *and* sapiential pursuit. If the Pope believes that the restoration of philosophy in Catholic intellectual life is essential to the catechetical and evangelical mission of the Church, it must be philosophy restored to its Socratic status and thus revivified. Obviously anti-philosophical philosophy won't do. So the Church herself, as the Pope sees it, has a stake in the renewal of philosophy in *both* its analytical and sapiential aspirations.

John Paul II, whose own philosophical commitments and methods are drawn from the phenomenological tradition associated with such thinkers as Husserl and Scheler, is at pains to observe that the Church herself does not *choose* among those philosophical systems and methods which are compatible with Christian faith (whether or not their origins are in the work of Christian thinkers). More than one system, he plainly supposes, can be valuable in the pursuit of truth and the understanding of faith. True, as the Pope acknowledges in a subsection of the encyclical entitled "The Enduring Originality of the Thought of St. Thomas Aquinas," Thomism has a special standing—a sort of pride of place—in the intellectual life of the Church, at least since the publication of the encyclical letter *Aeterni Patris* by Pope Leo XIII. But in commending this philosophical approach, and Aquinas himself as a model of intellectual rigor and philosophical and theological attainment, the Church does not confer upon Thomism standing as the "one true philosophy." Indeed, John Paul II says explicitly and emphatically that "no historical form of philosophy can legitimately claim to embrace the totality of truth, nor to be the complete explanation of the human being, of the world and of the human being's relationship with God."

At the same time, the magisterium of the Church, and this Pope himself, as we have already seen in *Fides et Ratio* itself, claims the authority to "intervene," as the encyclical puts it, in philosophical matters to "respond clearly and strongly when controversial philosophical opinions threaten right understanding of what has been revealed, and when false and partial theories which sow the seed of serious error, confusing the pure and simple faith of the people of God, begin to spread more widely." So: although diverse philosophical systems may legitimately be embraced by Catholics, and while various systems can contribute to the project of understanding faith, the Church's view of philosophy is not an utterly relativistic one. For there are also false and destructive philosophies, false and dangerous philosophical claims. And the Pope lists among these not only scientism and nihilism but also "eclecticism," a position that ignores the logical requirement of internal coherence and sometimes abandons even the principle of the unity of truth; "historicism," which relativizes truth by denying its "enduring validity"; and "pragmatism" of the sort that sacrifices moral principle to perceived interests and expediency. Philosophical errors are possible in part because of the weakening of reason itself by sin. Thus, in the absence of revelation and faith, even those aspects of the moral life that can, in principle, be grasped and understood by reason would, to some extent, remain hidden from view. Reason needs faith to illuminate even those truths to which it has access. But more on this point later.

The point I wish to focus on now—a point more central to the encyclical—is that faith also needs reason. Just as there are philosophical errors, so too are there theological ones. And the abandonment of philosophy, or the failure to develop and deploy sound philosophical methods, results according to *Fides et Ratio* in some of the errors characteristic of contemporary theology—including Catholic theology. Above all, fideism—particularly as it manifests itself in what the Pope labels biblicism—is the consequence of a theological error about philosophy, indeed, the theological error of supposing that theology can *do without* philosophy, that faith can get along without *rational* inquiry, understanding, and judgment.

Now, perhaps this is puzzling. For, in a certain sense, is Catholic doctrine anything other than the Church's understanding of biblical revelation? How, then, can biblicism be a vice? How, indeed, can fideism, an utter reliance on faith, be an error?

The Pope describes "biblicism" as a view that

> tends to make the reading and exegesis of Sacred Scripture the sole criterion of truth. In consequence, the word of God is identified with Sacred Scripture alone, thus eliminating the doctrine of the Church.... Scripture is not the Church's sole point of reference. The "supreme rule of faith" derives from the unity which the Spirit has created between Sacred Tradition, Sacred Scripture and the Magisterium of the church in a reciprocity which means that none of the three can survive without the others.

The Pope notes that, when unpurified by rational analysis, religion degenerates into superstition. He says that, "deprived of reason, faith has stressed feeling and experience, and so runs the risk of no longer being a universal proposition." More to the point, Scripture itself is not self-interpreting. And the required interpretation proceeds according to canons of rationality that one must bring to the scriptural text. Of course, an interpreter may wish to let the sacred text speak for itself, free of the alleged distortions that would be introduced by human philosophical principles. Indeed, he may emphatically deny that he brings any philosophical assumptions whatsoever to the text. But, of course, he cannot escape the problem of the need for philosophy. The most any interpreter can hope for is to bring philosophically *sound* principles of interpretation to the text. It is only in the light of such principles, or so the Pope—in line with the entire Catholic tradition—teaches, that the word of God may be accurately understood.

Furthermore, philosophy and other forms of rational human

inquiry are often indispensable to understanding the full practical implications of propositions revealed in Scripture. On this point, the Pope is crystal clear:

> Without philosophy's contribution, it would in fact be impossible to discuss theological issues such as, for example, the use of language to speak about God, the personal relations within the Trinity, God's creative activity in the world, the relationship between God and man, or Christ's identity as true God and true man. This is no less true of the different themes of moral theology, which employ concepts such as the moral law, conscience, freedom, personal responsibility and guilt, which are in part defined by philosophical ethics.

The soundness of what the Pope says in this regard is clearest today, I think, in the moral sphere, where rational inquiry—and, again, particularly philosophical analysis—is crucial to understanding revealed truths that are the data and content of faith. Take the question of marriage, for example. Philosophical work is indispensable to working out the full meaning of the proposition, revealed in the book of Genesis and the Gospels, that marriage is a "one-flesh communion" of a man and a woman. I wish to stress that it is not merely that philosophical work is needed to defend the Jewish and Christian understanding of marriage against the critique currently being waged against it with great force (sometimes, of course, from within the Church) by liberal secularism. That is true and important. More than that, however, the meaning of the proposition cannot be fully understood—even apart from the liberal critique—without philosophical reflection. What does it mean for a man and woman to become "one flesh"? Is the biblical notion of "one-flesh union" merely a metaphor? If not, do married couples become "one flesh" only in the sense that they are genetic contributors to their biological offspring? Are marriages between infertile spouses truly marriages? Can an infertile man and his wife become "one flesh"? If so, why not two persons of the same sex? Why not more than two persons?

THERE are, I submit, answers to these questions. But one cannot simply look up the answers in the Bible. To achieve an adequate understanding of the biblical teaching, one must advert to philosophical truths. To grasp the profound, and quite literal, sense in which spouses in marriage truly become one flesh—and not merely in their children, and, indeed, even if they cannot have children—one must think through the matter philosophically. One must understand correctly, for example, the status of the human being as an *embodied person,* rather than a *non-bodily person who merely inhabits and uses a nonpersonal body.* For the biological ("organic") unity of spouses in reproductive-type acts (even where the nonbehavioral conditions of reproduction happen not to obtain) unites them interpersonally—and such interpersonal unity provides the bodily matrix of a comprehensive (and, thus, truly marital) unity—only if persons *are* their bodies (whatever else they are) and do not merely inhabit them. Is the body part of the personal reality of the human being? Or is it merely an instrument of the conscious and desiring part of the self? These are *philosophical* questions that cannot be evaded if we are to understand, much less defend, the biblical view of marriage.

But if reason is, as the Pope concedes, weakened by sin in the fallen condition of humanity, how can we trust it not to corrupt the interpretation of Scripture? Well, we, as individuals, have no guarantee that we will understand Scripture correctly. For us there is only the honest trying. No philosopher as such enjoys the charism of infallibility. No Catholic, certainly no Catholic philosopher, can be certain that he has interpreted the data of revelation correctly, or worked out its true implications, before the magisterium of the Church—drawing on all of her resources, including the work of exegetes, theologians, and philosophers—resolves the issue definitively. It is in the Church herself and her magisterium that authority and the charism of infallibility reside. Or so Catholics believe.

But fallibility, while demanding of philosophers—both professional and lay (and all of us, as the Pope says, are lay philosophers)—an attitude of humility and a policy of rigorous self-criticism, should not be taken as vindicating the radical distrust, much less the fear, of reason. Philosophical fallibility is no ground for fideism—biblicist or otherwise—much less does it warrant the anti-philosophical positions of positivism and nihilism. It is not as if there were a reliable, or more reliable, *alternative* to philosophy for the Christian or anyone else.

Nor, from the Catholic viewpoint, can the magisterium of the Church herself do without the contributions of philosophy. To settle the mind of the Church on disputed questions in exercising her own teaching office, philosophical reflection on the data of revelation is often necessary. And so the Pope, speaking of "the fundamental harmony between the knowledge of faith and the knowledge of philosophy," says that "faith asks that its object be understood with the help of reason; and at the summit of its searching, reason acknowledges that it cannot do without what faith presents."

There are, of course, from any Christian viewpoint certain truths of faith that cannot be known by unaided reason. For example, the truth that the one and only God is three persons—Father, Son, and Holy Spirit. Were this truth unrevealed, it could not be known—even "in principle," and even if reason were unweakened by sin. Still, even with regard to this truth of faith, as *Fides et Ratio* explicitly teaches, philosophy plays a central role in theological understanding. If the one God is three persons in perfect unity, then what is their relation to one another? How could the Church even begin to understand the relations of the persons within the Holy Trinity without an adequate understanding of the concept of a person? And while such an understanding is necessarily, as the Pope says of all talk of God, analogical, *where but to philosophy can the Church go in seeking its understanding?*

It is sometimes said, most recently, I believe, in a book by Stephen Jay Gould on science and religion, that so long as science and religion remain in their proper spheres there need be no conflict between them. Peace (if not always mutual respect) is ensured by separation. And there is truth in this. Religion and science have all too often invaded each other's spheres. But faith and reason, while enjoying, as the Pope says, a legitimate independence or autonomy from each other, are also profoundly *inter*dependent in the ways that I have indicated in explicating the teaching of *Fides et Ratio.*

This interdependence is signaled in the encyclical's magnificent opening sentence: "Faith and reason are like two wings on which the human spirit rises to the contemplation of truth." This is not to say that there are two truths: that something can be true as a matter of faith, yet false as a matter of science, history, or philosophy. As I have already remarked, the Pope firmly reasserts the unity of truth. (So, for example, if Christ is not risen bodily from the dead as a matter of historical and scientific fact, he is not risen as a matter of faith; and if his resurrection is indeed, as the Church teaches, a truth of faith, then it is true historically and scientifically as well.) Nor, as I have also remarked, is this to deny the autonomy of theology and philosophy or, indeed, faith and reason. Faith and reason, the Pope says, are two orders of knowledge. But they are linked, and, to some extent, overlapping, orders. Some truths are known only by revelation; others only by philosophical, scientific, or historical inquiry. Those known by revelation are often, however, fully understandable, or their implications fully knowable, only by rational inquiry. And often the full human and cosmic significance of those knowable by philosophical, scientific, and historical inquiry only becomes evident in the light of faith. And then there is the category of truths, particularly in the moral domain, knowable, in principle, at least, by philosophical inquiry but also revealed. Here revelation illuminates the truths of natural law, bringing into focus their precise contours, and making apparent to people of faith their supernatural significance. At the same time, natural law principles inform the Church's understanding of the content of revelation (as in the example of marriage) and enable the believer more fully to grasp the meaning and implications of what is revealed. *Thus it is* that on the "two wings" of faith and reason the human spirit rises to the contemplation of truth.

Of course, on any biblical understanding—Jewish or Christian, Protestant, Orthodox, or Catholic—faith is not merely a way of *knowing.* It is also a kind of trusting. As "the assurance of what is hoped for and the conviction of things unseen," in the words of the New Testament Letter to the Hebrews, faith is a placing of oneself in God's hands. Thus it is, for Jews, Christians, and, I believe, Muslims alike, that Abraham is our "father in faith." (Indeed, as John Paul II has observed, thus it is for Christians that Jews are our *elder* brothers in faith.) But on the Catholic understanding—and here again the Pope is in line with the entire Catholic tradition—faith is also reasoned and reasonable. Faith is trusting and believing, but not entirely without reasons and reasoning.

By the same token, reason itself is supported by faith. It is in the light of faith, as the Pope says, that we can trust reason despite our acknowledged human fallibility. And those traditions of faith which resist the collapse into fideism provide critical resources for understanding *practical* reason as a *moral* truth-attaining faculty or power. Although, in principle, anyone ought to be able to see that reason can be more than merely instrumental, more than emotion's ingenious servant ("the slave of the passions"), it is no accident that resistance to the positivistic reduction of reason (or the nihilistic denial of rationality) comes, in the main, from philosophers firmly rooted in traditions of faith. If, as the Pope says, faith has nothing to fear, and much to gain from, reason, then it is also true that reason has nothing to fear, and much to gain from, faith.

But, of course, there are different, and competing, traditions of faith. And their engagement has often been less than friendly. Indeed, it has sometimes been bloody. No pope in history—indeed, few religious leaders of any kind—have been more candid than John Paul II in acknowledging this sad fact. But from this fact, the Pope, who is by far the greatest ecumenist in the history of the papacy, does not draw the conclusion that the Church should avoid engagement of issues of theological principle with those who do not share the Christian faith, or her version of the Christian faith. On the contrary, it is the quest for truth—on the "wings" of faith and reason—that provides the "common ground" of honest theological engagement and ecumenical cooperation. And here philosophy is crucial precisely because of a lack of shared faith. "Philosophical thought," the Pope says, "is often the only ground for understanding and dialogue with those who do not share our faith." And he makes abundantly clear that by philosophy here he means the real sapiential and analytic thing: not ideology, not apologetics, not sophistical techniques of persuasion. Without abandoning the truth-claims of Christianity—indeed, while vigorously reaffirming them—*Fides et Ratio* eschews triumphalism and the intellectual or spiritual denigration of non-Christian traditions:

> When they are deeply rooted in experience, cultures show forth the human being's characteristic openness to the universal and transcendent. Therefore they offer different paths to the truth, which assuredly serve men and women well in revealing values which can make their life ever more human. Insofar as cultures appeal to the values of older traditions, they point—implicitly but authentically—to the manifestation of God in nature.

And, the Pope continues, the Gospel—while demanding all who hear it the adherence of faith—must be understood to allow people to preserve their own cultural identity. "This means," he says, "that no one culture can ever become the criterion of judgment, much less the ultimate criterion of truth with regard to God's Revelation."

Of course, the Pope is no cultural or moral relativist. Still less does he relativize the truths of the Gospel. His point is that these truths *transcend* particular cultures just as they cannot be captured in any one, final, ultimately and definitively *true* philosophical system. Yet, just as faith cannot do without philosophy, it cannot do without cultures—which, like philosophies, are (even at their best) particular and limited. People understand, appropriate, and live the truths of faith in light of particular cultures—or they understand, appropriate, and live these truths *not at all.* So faith is, unavoidably, mediated by and through cultural structures—if it is present at all—even as it necessarily transcends every culture.

The transcendence of the truths of faith to cultures and cultural structures in the teaching of John Paul II and the Catholic tradition follows from the nature of truth as understood by the Pope and the Church. Truth is, in Christian teaching, both universal and universally longed for. God *is* truth—Jesus Christ, as the Son of living God, is "the way, *the truth,* and the life." And "God has," as the Pope says in the second half of the opening sentence of *Fides et Ratio,* "placed in the human heart a desire to know the truth—in a word, to know *himself*—so that by knowing and loving God, men and women may also come to the fullness of truth about themselves."

So, whoever sincerely pursues truth, existentially as well as in the scholarly disciplines, seeks—and thereby honors—the God who is Truth. Whoever, in whatever cultural context and drawing on the resources of whichever cultural structures, exhibits "the human being's characteristic openness to the universal and transcendent" is indeed on *a* path to the truth. And God, as he is understood by the Pope and in Catholic tradition, is (like the father of the prodigal son in the Gospel parable) already calling out to him in welcome, ready to place a ring on his finger and prepare the fatted calf, for it is, as John Paul II said in the encyclical *Veritatis Splendor*—the Splendor of Truth—"on the path of the moral life that the way of salvation is open to all."

AFTERWORD

We Should Not Kill Human Embryos–
For Any Reason: The Ethics of Embryonic
Stem Cell Research and Human Cloning

ANYONE WHO has been paying attention to public affairs knows that the United States and many other nations are grappling with two big bioethical issues: human embryonic stem cell research and human cloning. Although I have the honor to serve on the President's Council on Bioethics, the opinions I will express in this epilogue are my own, not those of the President, and certainly not those of the President's Council. While my personal views happen to be closely in line with those of President Bush, the fact is that the members of the council are not of a single mind on these issues. The President has chosen to appoint to the council people representing quite a wide spectrum of views—including views sharply at odds with his own.

First some background: Stem cells are primitive cells that are capable of forming diverse types of tissue. Because of this remarkable quality, *human* stem cells hold tremendous promise for the development of therapies to regenerate damaged organs and heal people who are suffering from terrible diseases.

Embryonic stem cells are derived from human embryos. Their use is controversial because, unfortunately, such stem cells cannot be harvested without destroying the living embryo. Other sources of stem cells are available, however, and can be harvested from umbilical cord blood as well as from fat, bone marrow, and other adult tissue without harm to the donor. An enormous amount of research involving adult stem cells is currently going on in laboratories in the United States. This research is ethically uncontroversial and has generated a number of exciting discoveries on the therapeutic front.

For many therapeutic purposes, adult stem cells are superior to embryonic stem cells because of their comparative stability. (In certain cases, adult stem cells are clearly preferable because of the risk that the use of volatile embryonic stem cells will cause tumors of various types.) However, no one knows with certainty whether adult stem cells can be obtained that possess the versatility or flexibility to do everything that embryonic stem cells hold out the promise of doing. Recently, Dr. Catherine Verfaille and her co-workers at the University of Minnesota discovered "multipotent adult progenitor cells" in bone marrow which can, some have claimed, "differentiate into pretty much everything that embryonic stem cells can differentiate into," and, indeed, "turn into every single tissue in the [human] body." What remains to be seen is whether Dr. Verfaille's results can be replicated and her findings confirmed. It is possible, though by no means certain, that the debate over embryonic stem cell research can be obviated by the development of equally good (or even superior) alternatives that are ethically unproblematic.

Because embryonic stem cell research involves the destruction of the embryos from whom stem cells are harvested, federal funding for it was banned by an act of Congress. Under President Clinton, however, the Department of Health and Human Services reinterpreted the provisions of that act to permit the funding of research using stem cells harvested from embryos destroyed with private money. When President Bush came into office, he was faced with a decision whether to uphold the ban as originally understood or stick with the Clinton administration's interpretation. In August, after a period of deliberation marked by intense lobbying and public relations campaigns by both sides, the President announced that he would not permit funding of research involving stem cells harvested from embryos destroyed in the future; he would, however, permit continued funding of research on existing cell lines derived from embryos from which stem cells had been harvested. Some hailed the President's decision as a principled compromise that maintained the norm against deliberate embryo destruction but allowed funding for research to continue where the embryos from which stem cells had been harvested were already dead and could not be restored to life. Others were, however, disappointed. Those in favor of embryonic research argued that too few good cell lines existed to enable scientists to fulfill what they asserted was the enormous and unique promise of embryonic stem cell research. As a result, they contended, many people would continue to suffer from horrible diseases that might be cured, or whose painful and damaging effects might be mitigated, by therapies and technologies deriving from embryonic stem cell research. People on the other side, while approving the President's ban on funding of research involving further embryo destruction, disagreed with his permission of funding for research on existing cell lines. They worried that this might down the line lead to further embryo killing; some went further, arguing that just as it would be wrong to make use of knowledge derived by unethical experimentation by German scientists in the Nazi period, it is unjust for people to make research use of material derived from the destruction of embryonic human beings.

But are they human beings? Here we reach the central question. It is also the question at the heart of the current debate over human cloning. Now, some readers may be surprised to hear this. Isn't cloning a matter of the asexual reproduction of human beings as genetic copies (or near copies) of other human beings? What does that have to do with the human status of embryos and the rightness or wrongness of destroying them?

Well, cloning is indeed the bringing into being by asexual processes genetic copies (or near copies) of existing beings. When, to international fanfare, Dolly the sheep was cloned a few years ago, here is how it was done. The nucleus of a somatic cell of an adult ewe was transferred to a sheep ovum (or oocyte) whose nucleus had been removed. Electrofusion was then employed to produce a distinct, self-integrating, new organism possessing the genome of the original ewe (of which Dolly could be considered a sort of younger twin). This organism—Dolly—developed from the embryonic stage through the fetal and other stages of her development as an otherwise ordinary sheep, and finally matured into adulthood.

Now, in principle (some claim that it has already been done in fact) it should be scientifically possible to generate new human beings by the same procedure—a technique called "somatic cell nuclear transfer." Some people think that this would be a good thing; most people do not.

Those who favor the reproduction of human beings by cloning argue that it would enable people to have a desirable control over the qualities and genetic characteristics of the children they have. They suggest that it would enable certain people who might otherwise not have children to have them. They say that it would make it possible for people who suffer the loss of a child to have the comfort of a genetic copy of the child. They maintain that cloning is a matter of "reproductive choice" and ought to be freely permitted.

Those who oppose the reproduction of human beings by cloning—I among them—insist that it is a dehumanizing procedure that will lead our culture down the road—or further down the road—to the commodification of human life. They argue that it constitutes treating children as products of manufacture—"made" rather than "begotten"—compromising their individuality and raising a knot of serious problems pertaining to kinship, identity, and self-image. They warn that it will exacerbate the difficulty children already have when parents become obsessive in their expectations for their children and seek to live vicariously through them.

This is an important debate; and someday we will almost certainly have it. Not now, though. There is overwhelming support in the public at large and in both houses of Congress for a ban on cloning human beings for reproductive purposes. Even many people who do not oppose what is called "reproductive cloning" as a matter of strict moral principle favor a ban for now. University of Chicago Professor Leon Kass, Chairman of the President's Council on Bioethics, sums up the reasons:

> Any attempt to clone a human being would constitute an unethical experiment upon the resulting child-to-be. In all the animal experiments, fewer than two to three percent of all cloning attempts succeeded. Not only are there fetal deaths and stillborn infants, but many of the so-called "successes" are in fact failures. As has only recently become clear, there is a very high incidence of major disabilities and deformities in cloned animals that attain live birth. Cloned cows often have heart and lung problems; cloned mice later develop pathological obesity; other live-born cloned animals fail to reach normal developmental milestones. *

As if to confirm Dr. Kass's concerns, we were recently informed that Dolly the sheep has been diagnosed with a severe and premature arthritis.

So across the spectrum people oppose cloning for baby-making, at least for now. But that does not mean that everybody opposes cloning as such. Many people favor legislation that would ban human cloning for reproductive purposes *but permit it for purposes of biomedical research*. This position has been endorsed by the National Academy of Sciences and a number of other groups. Commonly, cloning for biomedical research purposes is called "therapeutic" cloning, though that language is controversial. I myself reject the term "therapeutic" in this connection because the cloning in question is not for the benefit of the embryo brought into existence by it. In fact, that embryo will be destroyed. Thus, the President's Council, seeking a morally neutral term, refers to such cloning as "research cloning"—a label that can be accepted by supporters and critics alike.

---

* Dr. Kass himself, I should point out, opposes reproductive cloning as a matter of principle and supports a legislative prohibition of all human cloning.

Here, the procedure of nuclear somatic cell transfer is used to create an embryo that will be used for research and in the process destroyed rather than implanted in the prepared uterus of a woman and permitted to develop into a fetus, infant, child, adolescent, and adult.

There are significant scientific and potential therapeutic advantages (though not, of course, to the cloned embryos themselves) to research cloning. In particular, in the area of regenerative medicine there is the possibility of harvesting material from embryonic clones that, because of the nearly perfect genetic match to the patient, will not be prone to rejection. Anyone familiar with transplantation surgery, for example, knows that rejection is the great bane of the field. Suppressing the human immune system to prevent rejection of implanted organs is difficult, dangerous, and all-too-often unsuccessful. If cloning could help to solve the problem, it would be a genuine leap forward. It is little wonder that people who do not have moral objections to the deliberate destruction of human embryos are very excited about the promise of research cloning.

But then again, it is little wonder that those who do oppose the deliberate destruction of human embryos find research cloning particularly appalling. Critics contend that it constitutes bringing new human beings into existence precisely for the purpose of killing them and harvesting their body parts. This, they say, is the ultimate in the commodification of human life and the dehumanization of man in the name of scientific progress. Worse yet, if this is combined with a ban on implanting these embryos in women's wombs—a ban designed to prevent the "reproductive cloning" that almost everybody opposes—it creates a bizarre state of affairs: Society would permit new human beings to be brought into existence but forbid people from doing what is necessary for them to survive and grow. In effect, the law would define a class of developing human beings that it is illegal *not* to discard or destroy. Since what would be banned, strictly speaking, would be *implantation* rather than cloning itself, it would amount to *legally mandated human embryo destruction*.

Now, all of this should make clear why it is that the question of the humanity of the embryo is central not only to the debate about embryonic stem cell research but also to the debate about human cloning. If human embryos *are not* human beings, then (1) the promise of advances in scientific knowledge, (2) the prospect of developing useful therapies, and (3) the general principle of liberty of scientific inquiry would make an overwhelming case for funding research involving embryo destruction. If, however, human embryos *are* human beings, then the case for a ban on funding destructive embryo research—and, indeed, a ban on the research itself—would be powerful. To dislodge it, advocates of the research would have to show either that the deliberate killing of some human beings to benefit others can be justified by some sort of utilitarian calculus; or they would have to demonstrate that human beings do not have a right to life throughout their existence, but acquire such a right only at some point in their development.

Those who argue that human embryos are not human beings point out that the five or six-day-old embryo is very small—smaller than the period at the end of a sentence on a printed page. It looks nothing like what we ordinarily think of as a human being. It has not yet developed a brain—so it does not exhibit the human capacity for rationality. Indeed, it has no consciousness or awareness of any sort. It is not even sentient. Of course, people who deny that human embryos are human beings acknowledge that the entities in question possess a human genome. They point out, however, that the same is true of ordinary somatic cells, such as skin cells, millions of which each of us rubs or washes off our bodies on any given day. Plainly these cells are not human beings; nobody supposes that there is anything wrong with destroying them or using them in scientific research.

In defending research involving the destruction of human embryos, Ronald Bailey, a science writer for *Reason* magazine, has developed the analogy between embryos and somatic cells in light of the possibility of human cloning. Bailey claims that every cell in the human body has as much potential for development as any human embryo. Embryos therefore have no greater dignity or higher moral status than ordinary somatic cells. Bailey observes that each cell in the human body possesses the entire DNA code; each has become specialized (as muscle, skin, etc.) by most of that code being turned *off*. In cloning, those portions of the code previously deactivated are reactivated. So, Bailey says, quoting Australian bioethicist Julian Savulescu: "If all our cells could be persons, then we cannot appeal to the fact that an embryo could be a person to justify the special treatment we give it." Since plainly we are not prepared to regard all of our cells as human beings, we shouldn't regard embryos as human beings.

What do opponents of embryo destruction say in reply to these points and arguments? To claims about the size and appearance of the embryo, they observe that it merely begs the question about the humanity of the embryo to say that it does not resemble (in size, shape, etc.) human beings in later stages of development. The five-day-old embryo looks exactly like what human beings look like at five days old. Each of us once looked like that. The morally relevant consideration is not appearance; rather, it is the fact that from the beginning the embryo possesses the epigenetic primordia for self-directed growth and maturation through all the stages of human development, from the embryonic through the fetal, infant, child, and adolescent stages, and finally into adulthood, with its distinctness and identity fully intact. As such, the embryo is a whole, living member of the species homo sapiens that is already—and not merely potentially—developing itself (actually himself or herself since sex is already determined) to the next more mature stage along the continuum of development of a determinate and enduring human life.

The point was illustrated rather vividly at the second meeting of the President's Council on Bioethics, at which we had a presentation by, and discussion with, Dr. Irving L. Weissman, chairman of the committee of the National Academy of Sciences that drafted the academy's recent report on human cloning. Dr. Weissman, one of the nation's most distinguished research scientists and a leader in the field of adult stem cell research, personally favors funding of embryonic research as well as cloning for research purposes. He was with us, however, to answer *scientific* questions, and (as he made very clear) not to offer opinions on ethics, a subject matter in which he claims no particular expertise. He was very candid with us, and informative. Let me paraphrase our exchange. I asked Dr. Weissman whether the chairman of the President's Council, Dr. Leon Kass, who was presiding at the meeting, is as a matter of fact the same human being who, at an earlier stage of his development, was an adolescent and before that an infant. "Yes," Dr. Weissman replied. "And before that was he in the fetal stage of his development?" "Yes." "And before that"—at this point Dr. Weissman was under no illusions about where this line of questioning was heading—"was he in the blastocyst stage?" "For sure." "When we speak of 'the blastocyst' (or 'the embryo'), then, we are referring not to a being or entity different or distinct from the 'human being'; we are referring rather to a developmental stage?" "Right."

But if this is true, one might ask, wouldn't we have to conclude by the same train of logic that an adult who came into existence by a process of cloning from a human skin cell was once a skin cell (just as Leon Kass—like all the rest of us—was once an embryo), and that skin cells are therefore nascent human beings? Ronald Bailey's argument in the form *reductio ad absurdum* was designed to show that those who hold for the humanity of the embryo are driven to this obviously false conclusion. However, Bailey's analogy between somatic cells and human embryos collapses under scrutiny. The somatic cell is something from which (together with other causes) a new organism can be generated; it is certainly not, however, a distinct organism. A human embryo, by contrast, already is a distinct, self-developing, complete (though immature) human organism.

Bailey suggests that the somatic cell and the embryo are on the same level because both have the "potential" to develop to a mature human being. The kind of "potentiality" possessed by somatic cells that might be used in cloning differs profoundly, however, from the potentiality of the embryo. In the case of somatic cells, each has a potential only in the sense that something can be done to it so that its constituents (its DNA molecules) enter into a distinct whole human organism, which is a human being, a person. In the case of the embryo, by contrast, he or she already is already actively—indeed dynamically—developing himself or herself to the further stages of maturity of the distinct organism—the human being—he or she already is. True, the whole genetic code is present in each somatic cell; and this code can be used for guidance of the growth of a new entire organism. But this point does nothing to show that its potentiality is the same as that of a human embryo. When the nucleus of an ovum is removed and a somatic cell is inserted into the remainder of the ovum and given an electric stimulus, this does far more than merely place the somatic cell in an environment hospitable to its continuing maturation and development. Indeed, it generates a wholly distinct, self-integrating, entirely new organism—indeed, it generates an embryo. The entity—the embryo—brought into being by this process, is quite radically different from the constituents that entered into its generation.

Somatic cells, in the context of cloning, then, are analogous not to embryos, but to the gametes whose union results—in the case of ordinary sexual reproduction—in the generation of a distinct, self-integrating, new organism. Sperm cells and ova are not distinct, complete, self-integrating human organisms; they are properly speaking parts of human organisms—the men and women whose gametes they are. Their union can generate a new organism, an entity that is not merely part of another organism. That organism was never, however, a sperm cell or an ovum. Nor would a person who was brought into being as an embryo by a process of cloning have been once a somatic cell. Dr. Kass and you and I, as Dr. Weissman made clear, were once embryos, just as we were once children, and before that infants, and before that fetuses. But none of us were ever sperm cells, or ova, or somatic cells. To destroy an ovum or a skin cell whose constituents might have been used to generate a new and distinct human organism is not to destroy a new and distinct human organism—for no such organism exists or ever existed. But, in line with Dr. Weissman's logic, for someone to have destroyed the human being who is now you or me during the embryonic stage of our existence and development would have been to destroy you or me.

Or would it have been? After all, Dr. Kass and you and I really are remarkably different today than we were as embryos. We have developed and changed in profound ways. Perhaps we are the same organism that existed then, but perhaps we were at that stage of our development not yet *persons*—that is, human beings with dignity and rights, including a right to life. Perhaps we acquired dignity and rights not by merely coming into existence, but by developing certain qualities, or capacities, or traits. In fact, perhaps "you" and "I" were never really embryos; perhaps "you" and "I" are not the physical, material realities that come into being by fusion of gametes or by cloning, but are rather the psychological or spiritual realities—the "centers of consciousness"—somehow associated with our material bodies but distinct from them. Perhaps "I" am not the physical organism you see before you and hear speaking. Perhaps "I" did not come into existence until sometime after that organism (which I merely inhabit or with which I am somehow otherwise associated) came into existence; and perhaps "I" may cease to be before my physical body dies (for example, by going into a permanent coma or persistent vegetative state).

Michael Gazzaniga, a member of the President's Council who favors embryo research, is a distinguished brain scientist at Dartmouth College. He argues that the human person comes into being with the development of a brain and that prior to that point we have a complete human organism, but one lacking the dignity and rights of a person. Human embryos may therefore legitimately be treated as we would treat organs available for transplantation (assuming, as with transplantable organs, that proper consent for their use was given, etc.). In developing his case, Dr. Gazzaniga observes that modern medicine treats the death of the brain as the death of the person—authorizing the harvesting of organs from the remains of the person, even if some physical systems are still functioning. But if a human being is no longer a person with rights once the brain has died, then surely a human being is not yet a person prior to the development of the brain.

Critics, however, and again I am one, call attention to a damning

defect in this argument. Under prevailing law and medical practice, the rationale for "brain death" is not that a brain-dead body is
a living human organism but no longer a person. Rather, brain
death is accepted because the irreversible collapse of the brain de-
stroys the capacity for self-directed integral organic functioning of
human beings who have matured to the stage at which the brain
performs the key role in integrating the organism. What is left is
no longer a unitary organism at all. Obviously, the fact that an
embryo has not yet developed a brain (though its capacity to do so
is inherent and active, just as the capacity of an infant to develop
its brain sufficiently for it to actually *think* is inherent and active)
does not mean that it is incapable of self-directed integral organic
functioning. Unlike a corpse—which is merely the remains of what
was once a human organism but is now dead, even if particular
systems may be mechanically sustained—a human being in the
embryonic stage of development is a unified, self-integrating human organism. It is not dead, but very much alive. A factor or
factors other than the brain make possible its self-integration and
organic functioning. Its future lies ahead of it, unless it is cut off or
not permitted to develop its inherent capacities. Thus it is that I
and other defenders of embryonic human life insist that the embryo is not a "potential life" but is rather a life *with potential*. It is a
potential *adult*, in the same way that fetuses, infants, children, and
adolescents are potential adults. It has the potential for agency,
just as fetuses, infants, and small children do. But, like human
beings in the fetal, infant, child, and adolescent stages, human
beings in the embryonic stage are already, and not merely potentially, *human beings*. All of these stages are, as Dr. Weissman made
clear, developmental stages in the life of a being who comes into
existence as a single cell human organism and develops, if all goes
well, into adulthood by a gradual and gapless process over many
years. An embryo (or fetus or infant) is not something distinct
from a human being; it is a human being at the earliest stage of its
development.

But what about the possibility that I mentioned a few minutes ago that we are not really our bodies anyway; we are centers of consciousness—minds, or souls, or what have you—inhabiting bodies or somehow, perhaps mysteriously, associated with them. If this is true, then it is not enough for defenders of embryonic life to prove that embryos are whole living members of the species homo sapiens; that the embryonic stage is simply the earliest stage of the development of a distinct and determinate organism; and that that organism in the embryonic stage is directing its own integral organic functioning as it develops itself into and through the next more mature stage on the continuum of human life.

Well, this conception of the human being as a nonbodily person who inhabits and uses a nonpersonal body—a conception known in the philosophical literature as "person-body dualism"—moves us into deep metaphysical waters. It presents a clear alternative to the view of the human being as a dynamic unity of body, mind, and spirit. Is it sound?

Elsewhere in this book I argue that the separation of "person" and "body"—the conception of the body as a subpersonal instrument rather than as a part of the personal reality of the human being—is at the heart of the liberal secularist worldview. It is person-body dualism, I suggest, that underwrites orthodox liberal positions on "life issues" such as abortion and euthanasia, as well as on issues of marriage and sexual morality. Oxford University philosopher John Finnis has summed up the case against person-body dualism:

> [It] suffers the fate of every account of our being, life, and activity which treats *human person* and *human life*, or *conscious self* and *human organism*, or *acts of the human organism* and *acts of the person*, as other and other. That fate is: to overlook, or render inexplicable, a unity which we know more intimately and thoroughly than any other unity in the world, indeed the very paradigm (for us) of substantial unity and identity through time. For this dualism renders inexplicable the unity (and continuity) in complexity, which

one is aware of in each of one's conscious acts. Every dualism undertakes to be a theory of something (of *my personal identity* as a unitary and subsisting, *intermittently* self-conscious and freely self-directing organism), but ends up unable to pick out any *one* something of which to be the theory.

People—you and I and everybody else—are (whatever else we are) *essentially* human, physical organisms. The person that is writing these words is not an unseen consciousness somehow inhabiting the physical organism sitting at the word processor; I am, rather, a unified rational animal organism. It is not that I—considered as something apart from the organism—*have* an organism; it is that I *am* a rational animal organism. Therefore, I—that is the human being, the person I am—came to be precisely when the animal organism I am came to be. I did not come to be first and then become a person later; nor will I cease being a person without ceasing to be (by dying).

Some people admit that human beings are (whatever else we are) physical organisms, and so concede that you and I once were embryos and fetuses, but argue, nonetheless, that we became intrinsically valuable (and bearers of a right to life) only at some point in time after we came to be, when we acquired some characteristic such as mental functioning, consciousness, or self-awareness. They believe that human beings are valuable in a sense that makes it wrong to kill them not in virtue of the *kind of entity* (i.e., the "substance") they are, but in virtue of some *accidental characteristic*—some quality or attribute that they may (or may not) acquire (and may eventually lose).

A serious problem with this view is that the characteristics or qualities it proposes as necessary for moral worth and a right to life all come in varying degrees. So the following questions naturally arise: What degree of the characteristic or quality is required? Can the answer to that question be anything other than arbitrary? Aren't people who have the characteristic or quality to a greater degree more valuable than people who have it to a lesser degree? What then of the principle of the equality of persons?

These questions begin to suggest the central flaw in this position. If it is an accidental characteristic or quality that provides moral worth and a right to life—if it is not enough to be a substantial entity with a rational nature, as all human beings are—then the characteristic or quality will have to be a capacity for mental functions of some sort. It will have to be a *capacity* because obviously one cannot say that certain living human beings who are not now performing mental functions (because they are asleep, for example, or in a reversible coma) are not "persons" who possess intrinsic value and a right to life. It will have to be a capacity *for mental functions* of some sort because persons (on any account of the matter) are distinguished from entities that are not persons by some sort of relation to mental functions (such as reasoning and acting on the basis of deliberation and choice). But human beings even in the embryonic, fetal, and infant stages have real capacities for mental functions, though not immediately exercisable. The human embryo (or fetus or infant) possesses the capacity for such functions in virtue of the kind of entity he or she is, namely, a human being. Of course, the basic, natural capacity possessed by the embryo, fetus, infant, and in some respects even the toddler is not the capacity to exercise certain mental functions *now* in response to some stimulus. But even in the embryonic stage, the human being possesses the entirety of the positive reality needed actively to develop himself or herself to the point at which the basic natural capacity for the mental functions characteristic of human beings will be immediately exercisable. Indeed, the full development of the basic natural capacity for mental functioning is a process that will not be complete for many years. It will gradually develop as the human being matures through gestation, infancy, childhood, and adolescence into adulthood. (Indeed, even in those human beings who due to injury, retardation, or some other misfortune will not develop the capacity fully or even very far, the capacity itself is present.)

The development of the basic natural capacity of human beings for their characteristic forms of mental functioning is, then, a matter of degree. The difference between the adult and the child, or the

child and the embryo, is merely the gradual development of the
same basic natural capacity. But the difference between how we should
treat a person (i.e., a being who has intrinsic value and a right to life)
and how we may treat an entity that is not a person, and may therefore legitimately be used and even destroyed for the benefit of persons, is a difference that can be morally justified only in virtue of a
difference in *kind* between the person and the nonpersonal entity.
Mere differences of *degree* cannot bear the moral weight required to
justify treating some beings possessing the capacity (e.g., normal
adults or adolescents) as having dignity and rights while treating
other beings possessing the capacity in a lesser, or less developed,
degree (e.g., human beings in the embryonic, fetal, or infant stages,
mentally retarded people, victims of dementia or Alzheimer's disease) as lacking dignity and a right to life.

I conclude from the foregoing analysis that it is illegitimate to
deny dignity and a right to life on the basis of age, size, stage of
development, or condition of dependency, just as it is illegitimate to
deny dignity and a right to life based on race, sex, ethnicity, or any
other morally irrelevant factor. Because human beings in the embryonic, fetal, and infant stages do not differ in kind from more mature
human beings, but differ only in such morally irrelevant factors as
age, size, stage of development, and condition of dependency, they
are equally entitled to legal protection and may not legitimately be
reduced to the status of mere means to benefit others.

Of course, it flies in the face of strong "intuitions" that some
people have that, say, a single-cell human zygote, even conceding
that it is a human being at the earliest stage, is not—cannot be—the
equal in moral worth of an infant and even an adult human being.
People who possess these intuitions observe that we typically do not
mourn and hold funerals for embryos that die. Indeed, they point
out, even in natural sexual reproduction upwards of half of all preg-
nancies fail naturally—often before women even know they are pregnant; we do not treat the deaths of these embryos as we would the
loss of infants.

Defenders of embryonic life reply that reason, not emotion, must control ethical judgments—particularly where fundamental rights are concerned. It is perfectly understandable that the early embryo would not elicit from us the sympathy of more fully developed human beings—particularly in circumstances in which people with whom we do sympathize (because we emotionally regard them as "more like us") stand to benefit from their destruction.** It was, no doubt, ever thus in human affairs. Progress in civilization comes, however, from moving beyond reliance on imagination and sense impressions and the emotions they generate—particularly in respect to who is "like" and "unlike" us—to the rational understanding of who truly is a human being and in that crucial respect "like us." Whether or not we feel the need to mourn for a particular human being—or a particular class of human beings—is not the criterion of their worth, dignity, and right to life. No one who recognizes and honors the rights of another need feel any guilt for failing to feel a need to mourn his death—especially where, either as a contingent matter or in the nature of the case, opportunities of forming emotional attachments did not present themselves.

How about the fact that large numbers of embryos die in natural failures of pregnancy? Does this mean that it is reasonable to treat human embryos as research material? The problem with this argument is that its principle would seem to lead to perverse results when applied in other contexts. Up until a little more than a century ago, infant mortality rates from natural causes were very high. In some times and places they were as high as embryonic deaths in pregnancy failures are today. (This is true even if we count all preg-

---

** On the other hand, it should not be ignored that many women do grieve when they experience a miscarriage, even a very early one. Moreover, internet "chat rooms" on use of the morning-after pill include anguished contributions by women who have learned only after the fact that what they were told was "emergency contraception" may actually have worked by ensuring the death of an early embryo. Couples and even staff at IVF clinics show considerable emotional resistance to discarding "spare" embryos—which is one reason why so many thousands of embryos have survived for years in a frozen state. And several states have dealt with intense court battles in which one party in an estranged or divorced couple sues for "custody" of the embryonic offspring the couple produced together.

nancy failures as involving the deaths of true embryos. In fact, there is evidence that in many cases early pregnancy loss is the result of failures in conception and the resulting formation of entities possessing a human genome but lacking the epigenetic primordia for maturation as human beings, e.g., hydatidiform moles.) It would be absurd to conclude that in these circumstances human infants are not human beings and that they can therefore be destroyed for the purpose of harvesting organs for the benefit of others.

There is one more argument sometimes advanced by advocates of embryonic stem cell research and research cloning. While conceding that the human embryo is a complete human organism, they claim that in the early stages it is not really a human being because it is not a human individual. Why not? Because up until approximately fourteen days, it may divide into identical twins. Up until the point at which monozygotic twinning is no longer possible, they argue, the embryo is properly understood as a mere mass of cells—each cell totipotent (i.e., capable of becoming a complete individual) but independent of the others.

It is certainly true that at the earliest stages a cell or cells detached from the whole can develop into a complete organism. But it is fallacious to infer from that fact that *before* detachment the cells of the human embryo constitute merely an unintegrated, and thus incidental, mass. Just as separated parts of a flatworm have the potential to become a whole flatworm when isolated from the present whole of which they are a part, separated parts of the embryo at the earliest stages of development (before specialization by the cells has progressed very far) can become whole and distinct embryonic human beings. No one supposes that the possibility of producing separate flatworms by dividing a single creature means that flatworms that could be separated, but have not been, are anything other than unitary individual organisms. Similarly, it would be wrong to suppose that the totipotency of the (cells of the) early embryo means that it is other than a distinct, unitary, complex, actively self-integrating, human organism—a developing human being.

Patrick Lee has made the following points in reply to the claim that the early embryo is a mere mass of totipotent cells:

> From the very beginning, even at the zygote stage, the cells of the new organism are cytoplasmically and positionally differentiated. In mammals, even in the unfertilized ovum, there is already an "animal" pole (from which the nervous system and eyes develop) and a "vegetal" pole (from which the future lower organs and the gut develop). After the first cleavage, the cell coming from the "animal" pole is probably the primordium of the nervous system and the other senses, and the cell coming from the "vegetal" pole is probably the primordium of the digestive system. Moreover, the relative position of a cell from the very beginning (that is, from the first cleavage) does make a difference in how it functions. Again, most (identical) twinning occurs at the blastocyst stage, in which there clearly is a differentiation of the inner cell mass and the trophoblast that surrounds it (from which the placenta develops).

Lee goes on to observe that if the cells within the human embryo prior to twinning were each independent of the others, as the argument under consideration presupposes, then each would be expected to develop on its own. But that is not what happens.

> Instead, these allegedly independent, non-communicating cells regularly function together to develop into a single, more mature member of the human species. This fact shows that interaction is taking place between cells within the zona pellucida, restraining them from individually developing as whole organisms and directing each of them to function as a relevant part of a single, whole organism continuous with the zygote. Thus, prior to an extrinsic division of the cells of the embryo, these cells together do constitute a single organism, and twinning is a phenomenon biologically equivalent to cloning.

It seems to me rationally undeniable that human embryos are, from the beginning, human beings with inherent dignity and rights. Having reflected as carefully as I can on the arguments advanced by those who would license embryo destruction for research purposes, I do not believe that their position can be morally justified. I understand, appreciate, and share their desire to advance scientific knowledge and produce new therapies; like them, I want to see science move ahead wherever it ethically can, adding to the sum of human knowledge and enhancing human health. The great moral principle of respect for the equal dignity of every human being places limits, however, on what we can do to some for the benefit of others. It forbids our treating living human beings at any stage or in any condition as exploitable and expendable "research material."

NOTES

Chapter 1

1. Samuel P. Huntington, "The Clash of Civilizations," *Foreign Affairs* 72 (summer 1993). Interest in Professor Huntington's thesis has revived in light of recent attacks against our fellow citizens and our nation by terrorists claiming to act in the name of Islam.
2. James Kurth, "The Real Clash," *The National Interest* 3 (fall 1994): 3–15.
3. A minority party within the secularist camp defends secularist ideology not on the ground that its tenets are true or vindicated by reason—secularists of this stripe deny the possibility of moral truth or the power of reason to make sound moral judgments of any type—but on the purely prudential ground that the official commitment of public institutions to secularism is the only way of preserving social peace. Ultimately, this is a hopeless strategy for defending secularism. It must implicitly appeal to the idea of moral truth and invoke the authority of reason (if, for no other purpose, than to establish the value of social peace) even as it officially denies that moral truth is possible and that reason has any real authority.

    Moreover, there is simply no warrant for believing that social peace is likely, or more likely, to be preserved by committing our public institutions to secularist ideology. Partisans of worldviews that compete with secularism are, to say the least, unlikely to surrender these institutions to the forces of secularism without a fight; nor is there any reason for them to do so. Consider the issue of abortion: Christians, observant Jews, and others who oppose the taking of unborn human life do not consider a circumstance in which more than a million elective abortions are performed each year to be a situation of "social peace." They quite reasonably reject secularism's claim to constitute nothing more than a neutral playing field on which other worldviews may fairly and civilly compete for the allegiance of the people. As the example of abortion makes clear, secularism is itself one of the competing worldviews. We should credit its claims to neutrality no more than we would accept the claims of a baseball pitcher who in the course of a game declares himself to be umpire and begins calling his own balls and strikes.

4. For the full defense of this claim, see Robert P. George, "Public Reason and Political Conflict," *Yale Law Journal* 106 (1997): 2475–2504.

5. For a more complete account of the kind of critique of person/body dualism I will present here, see Patrick Lee, "Human Beings Are Animals," in *Natural Law and Moral Inquiry*, ed. Robert P. George (Washington, D.C.: Georgetown University Press, 1998), 135–151.

6. It is true that some Christians embrace a certain form of person/body dualism, believing it necessary to identify the human person with the soul as distinct from the body in order to avoid materialism and/or affirm the existence of the immaterial human soul or its immortality. According to this form of dualism, the body, though not an intrinsic part of the person, may nevertheless enjoy a certain dignity by virtue of its association with the soul so that the deliberate destruction of the body, as in suicide, euthanasia, and abortion, may therefore be morally wrongful. Still, the body remains an essentially subpersonal reality and does not in itself participate in the dignity of the person. A homicidal act does not actually destroy a person, though it may nevertheless constitute the wrongful destruction of a person's body. This view, whose proponents can claim the patronage of Plato and Descartes, was rejected by Aquinas and other great Christian thinkers for what I believe to be excellent reasons. They saw that it is by no means logically (or, for that matter, theologically) necessary to identify the human person with the soul as distinct from the body, and thus to deny that bodily life is intrinsic to the human person, in order to avoid materialism or to affirm the soul's existence and immortality. One needn't deny the soul's existence or immortality in order to affirm that the human person is a unity of body and soul—both being intrinsic parts of the person. As the doctrine of the resurrection of the body makes clear, human beings are saved and exist in eternity as bodily persons, not as disembodied souls.

7. For a more complete presentation of the argument I here present, see Robert P. George and Gerard V. Bradley, "Marriage and the Liberal Imagination," *Georgetown Law Journal* 84 (1995): 301–320.

8. For a more complete presentation of the argument presented here, see Patrick Lee and Robert P. George, "What Sex Can Be: Self-alienation, Illusion, or One-Flesh Union," *American Journal of Jurisprudence* 42 (1997).

9. John Finnis, "Law, Morality, and 'Sexual Orientation,'" in *Same Sex: Debating the Ethics, Science, and Culture of Homosexuality*, ed. John Corvino (Lanham, Md.: Rowman & Littlefield, 1997), 1049.

10. These objections are confronted and treated in detail in works cited in previous notes.

11. *A Treatise of Human Nature* (1740), Book 2, pt. 3, iii.

12. For a complete account of the view I endorse in this paragraph, see John Finnis, Germain Grisez, and Joseph M. Boyle, Jr., "Practical Principles, Moral Truth, and Ultimate Ends," *American Journal of Jurisprudence* 32 (1987): 99–151.

13. See Germain Grisez, Joseph M. Boyle, Jr., and Olaf Tollefsen, *Free Choice: A Self-Referential Argument* (South Bend, Ind.: University of Notre Dame Press, 1976).

This work provides a complete account of the argument I sketch here and fully addresses possible lines of counterargument.

14. Joel Feinberg, *Harmless Wrongdoing: The Moral Limits of the Criminal Law* (Oxford: Oxford University Press, 1988), 305.

15. Alasdair MacIntyre, *Whose Justice, Which Rationality?* (Notre Dame, Ind.: University of Notre Dame Press, 1988).

16. Ibid.

Chapter 2

1. The Supreme Court unanimously rejected claims to a constitutional right to assisted suicide *in Washington v. Glucksberg* and *Vacco v. Quill.*

2. On the application of the principle of reciprocity in these circumstances, see Robert P. George, "Law, Democracy, and Moral Disagreement," *Harvard Law Review* 110, no. 7 (May 1997): 1388–1406, esp. 1397–1400.

3. Ronald Dworkin, *Life's Dominion: An Argument About Abortion, Euthanasia, and Individual Freedom* (New York: Knopf, 1993), 3.

4. Ibid.

5. Luke Gormally, *Euthanasia, Clinical Practice and the Law* (London: Linacre Centre, 1994), 111–166.

6. John Rawls, *Political Liberalism,* paperback edition (New York: Columbia University Press, 1996), xlii.

7. Ibid., 1.

8. Ibid., xx.

9. Ibid., xvii.

10. Ibid., xlii, 388, 390, and 392. Rawls's emphasis on the need for social stability in the face of moral pluralism should not lead the reader to suppose that his argument for "political liberalism" is merely pragmatic. A "strictly political" conception of justice is, he maintains, the *fairest* and *most reasonable* way of resolving questions of constitutional essentials and matters of basic justice.

11. Rawls introduces this "wide view" of public reason in the introduction to the paperback edition of *Political Liberalism,* p. lii. It represents a broadening of the more restrictive view set forth in the text (see pp. 247–252).

12. Rawls says that appeals to comprehensive doctrines are never legitimate in legislative assemblies or in the public acts and pronouncements of executive officers. Nor may judges in interpreting the Constitution or justifying their interpretations rely upon or invoke principles drawn from comprehensive doctrines. See *Political Liberalism,* p. 215.

13. Ibid., xl.

14. Ibid., xl.

15. Ibid., xxi.

16. Ibid., xxi.

17. In what has become a famous footnote in *Political Liberalism,* Rawls defends what he describes as a "duly qualified" right to abortion in the first trimester (and possibly beyond). See n. 32, pp. 243–244. He treats the matter as a falling within the category of constitutional essentials and matters of basic justice to which his doctrine of "public reason" applies, concluding that "we would go against the ideal of public reason if we voted from a comprehensive doctrine

that denied this right." This by itself should raise doubts in the minds of serious Catholics, Protestants, and Jews who consider whether their views have a place in Rawls's "overlapping consensus." For a detailed critique of Rawls on abortion, see Robert P. George "Public Reason and Political Conflict: Abortion and Homosexuality," *Yale Law Journal* 106 (1997): 2475-2504. (These pages are reproduced below as the appendix to the current essay.)

18. Rawls, *Political Liberalism,* xliv.
19. Ibid.
20. Ibid., 137.
21. See St. Thomas Aquinas, *Summa Theologiae,* I-II, q. 71, a. 2c: "The good of the human being is in accord with reason, and human evil is being outside the order of reasonableness." On the proper interpretation of Aquinas on this point, see John Finnis, *Natural Law and Natural Rights* (Oxford: Clarendon Press, 1980), 36. See also Finnis's more detailed account in *Aquinas: Moral, Political, and Legal Theory* (Oxford: Oxford University Press, 1998).
22. Rawls, *Political Liberalism,* 137 (emphasis supplied).
23. Ibid., 152–153.
24. Ibid., 153.
25. Ibid.
26. In fairness to Rawls, I should acknowledge here his treatment of the sources of moral disagreement in connection with what he calls "the burdens of judgment" in *Political Liberalism,* p. 58. However, to preserve the integrity of his political liberalism, we must read his account of the sources of disagreement in such a way as to avoid its collapse into relativism. If we do, then Rawls's idea of "fully reasonable," and even "perfectly reasonable," though erroneous, views refers to false beliefs that are formed without subjective fault. I think that this is what people generally have in mind when, though fully persuaded of the truth of a certain view, they allow nevertheless that "reasonable people" can disagree with them. The fact of "reasonable disagreement" in this sense is certainly not a valid warrant for ruling out argument as to the truth of matters in dispute on the ground that reasons adduced in any argument "on the merits" cannot qualify as "public reasons."
27. Rawls, *Political Liberalism,* 225.
28. See Robert P. George (with William L. Saunders), "Religious Values in Politics: A Liberal Perspective," in *Religious Values at the Threshold of the Third Millennium,* ed. Francis Eigo (Villanova, Pa.: Villanova University Press, 1999), 103–133.
29. Ibid., 214–215.
30. Ibid., lii.
31. Ibid., 243.
32. Ibid., n. 32.
33. Ibid.
34. See especially Thomas McCarthy, "Kantian Constructivism and Reconstructivism: Rawls and Habermas in Dialogue," *Ethics* 105 (1994): 44, 53 n. 16.
35. See, for example, Kent Greenawalt, *Religious Convictions and Political Choice* (New York: Oxford University Press, 1988).
36. Ibid., lv–lvi, n. 31.
37. The article to which Rawls plainly is referring appeared under the title "Abortion" in *Boston Review* 20 (1995): 11–15.

38. Ibid., 15.
39. Ibid. Thomson's rhetoric here, referring to "Catholic doctrine" on abortion, helps her case along by presenting the pro-life position, at least as it figures as part of Catholic moral teaching, as a sectarian matter that relies on religious premises that are somehow unavailable to non-Catholics. The "Catholic doctrine" on the subject, however, condemns abortion as homicidal and unjust as a matter of publicly accessible scientific fact and rational (natural law) morality.
40. Ibid.
41. Moreover, it would undercut the support Thomson's argument supplies to what many find to be the politically attractive (though obviously questionable) idea that people can accept pro-life claims as a basis for being "personally opposed to abortion," yet affirm at the same time support for a legal right to abortion on the ground that the *truth* of pro-life claims is not relevant to (or, at least, is not determinative of) the question whether women are morally entitled to the legal freedom to abort.
42. Ibid., 13.

Chapter 3

1. For a fuller development of my critique of Rawls's position, see George, "Public Reason and Political Conflict," 2475–2504. This article also develops much of the scientific material that I will discuss subsequently herein.
2. See Germain Grisez, *The Way of the Lord Jesus,* vol. 2: *Living a Christian Life* (Quincy, Ill.: Franciscan Press, 1992), ch. 9.
3. See John Connery, S.J., *Abortion: The Development of the Roman Catholic Perspective* (Chicago: Loyola University Press, 1997).
4. See St. Thomas Aquinas, *Summa Theologiae,* I-II, q. 91, a. 2.
5. For a fuller explanation, see Robert P. George, "Recent Criticism of Natural Law Theory," *University of Chicago Law Review* 55 (1988): 1371–1429.
6. See St. Thomas Aquinas, *Summa Theologiae,* I-II, q. 94, a. 2. For an effort by contemporary natural law thinkers to provide a more complete account, see Boyle, Grisez, and Finnis, "Practical Principles, Moral Truth, and Ultimate Ends," 99–151.
7. For a fuller explanation, see Robert P. George, "Natural Law Ethics" in *A Companion to Philosophy of Religion,* ed. Philip L. Quinn and Charles Taliaferro (Oxford: Blackwell Publishers, 1997), 460–65.
8. Stanley Fish, "Why We Can't All Just Get Along," *First Things* 60 (February 1996): 18–26.
9. See James Davison Hunter, *Before the Shooting Begins: Searching for Democracy in America's Culture War* (New York: Free Press, 1994), 104–5.
10. See Wolfe's "Our Bodies, Our Souls," *The New Republic* (1995), reprinted with commentaries by pro-life writers in *The Human Life Review* (winter 1996), and Thomson's "A Defense of Abortion," in *The Rights and Wrongs of Abortion,* ed. Marshall Cohen (Princeton, N.J.: Princeton University Press, 1974).
11. See Dworkin, *Life's Dominion.*
12. I explain this point more fully below. Also see Patrick Lee, *Abortion and Unborn Human Life* (Washington, D.C.: Catholic University of America Press, 1995); and Dianne Nutwell Irving, "Scientific and Philosophical Expertise: An Evalu-

ation of the Arguments on 'Personhood,'" *Linacre Quarterly* 60 (1993): 18–46.

13. See Finnis's paper, "Abortion, Natural Law, and Public Reason," and Reiman's paper, "Abortion, Natural Law, and Liberal Discourse," in *Public Reason,* ed. Robert P. George and Christopher Wolfe (Washington, D.C.: Georgetown University Press, 1999).

14. The following nine paragraphs are reprinted, with minor revisions, from my *Yale Law Journal* article "Public Reason and Political Conflict: Abortion and Homosexuality."

15. Dianne Nutwell Irving, "Scientific and Philosophical Expertise: An Evaluation of the Arguments on 'Personhood," *Linacre Quarterly* (February 1993).

16. *Stanford Law Review* 43 (1991): 599.

17. 476 U.S. 747 (1986).

18. Rubenfeld, "On the Legal Status of the Proposition that 'Life Begins at Conception,'" 599.

19. Once one recognizes that the scientific evidence establishes that the fetus, no less than the newborn, is a human being, one must logically treat the two the same in assessing the question of their rights and our duties toward them. And so Peter Singer, a leading advocate of abortion and a recent appointee to a distinguished professorial chair of bioethics in my own university, argues that infanticide is sometimes morally justifiable and ought, up to a certain point, to be legally permissible. While Singer's views have caused outrage and made his appointment at Princeton controversial, the truth is that he is merely following the logic of a pro-choice position in light of an honest assessment of the scientific facts. He recognizes that "birth" is an arbitrary dividing line when it comes to the humanity and rights of human beings in the early stages of their development. Hence, if abortion is morally justifiable, so is infanticide. Of course, I believe that Singer is tragically wrong in supposing that abortion and infanticide are morally justifiable; but he is right in claiming that either both of these practices are justifiable, or neither can be justified.

20. Rubenfeld, "On the Legal Status of the Proposition that 'Life Begins at Conception.'"

21. The efforts of Judith Jarvis Thomson and other philosophers to defend abortion as "justified homicide" are very ably criticized by Patrick Lee in *Abortion and Unborn Human Life.*

22. See John Finnis, "Abortion and Health Care Ethics II," in *Principles of Health Care Ethics,* ed. Raanan Gillon and Ann Lloyd (New York: Wiley, 1994), 547–57.

23. See Grisez, *The Way of the Lord Jesus,* vol. 2, 502.

Chapter 4

1. The late John Boswell, for example, claimed that brother/sister-making rituals found in certain early medieval Christian manuscripts were meant to give ecclesiastical recognition and approval to homosexual relationships. See *Same-Sex Unions in Premodern Europe* (New York: Villard Books, 1994). However, as Robin Darling Young has observed, "the reviews [of Boswell's work] after the early burst of hopeful publicity, have been notably skeptical—even from sources one would expect to be favorable" ("Gay Marriage: Reimagining Church History," *First Things* 47 (November 1994): 48). Darling herself concludes that

Boswell's "painfully strained effort to recruit Christian history in support of the homosexual cause that he favors is not only a failure, but an embarrassing one" (Ibid).

2. Germain Grisez, "The Christian Family as Fulfillment of Sacramental Marriage" (paper delivered to the Society of Christian Ethics Annual Conference, 9 September 1995).

3. Adulterous acts, for example, may be reproductive in type (and even in effect) but are intrinsically nonmarital.

4. Securely grasping this point, and noticing its significance, Hadley Arkes has remarked that "'sexuality' refers to that part of our nature that has as its end the purpose of begetting. In comparison, the other forms of 'sexuality' may be taken as minor burlesques or even mockeries of the true thing." Now, Arkes is not here suggesting that sexual acts, in what he calls "the strict sense of 'sexuality,'" must be *motivated* by a desire to reproduce; rather, his point is that such acts, even where motivated by a desire for bodily union, must be reproductive in type if such union is to be achieved. This, I believe, makes sense of what Stephen Macedo and other liberal critics of Arkes's writings on marriage and sexual morality find to be the puzzling statement that "[e]very act of genital stimulation simply cannot count as a sexual act." See Hadley Arkes, "Questions of Principle, Not Predictions: A Reply to Stephen Macedo," *Georgetown Law Journal* 84 (1995): 323.

5. This is by no means to suggest that married couples cannot instrumentalize and thus degrade their sexual relationship. See George and Bradley, "Marriage and the Liberal Imagination," 301–20, esp. 303, n. 9.

6. On person-body dualism, its implications for ethics, and its philosophical untenability, see John Finnis, Joseph M. Boyle, Jr., and Germain Grisez, *Nuclear Deterrence, Morality and Realism* (Oxford: Oxford University Press, 1987), 304–9; and Lee, "Human Beings Are Animals."

7. Finnis, "Law, Morality, and 'Sexual Orientation,'" sec. III.

8. See George and Bradley, "Marriage and the Liberal Imagination," 307–309.

9. See George and Bradley, "Marriage and the Liberal Imagination," 304.

10. I am not here suggesting that traditional ethics denies that it is legitimate for people to "desire" or "want" children. I am merely explicating the sense in which children may be desired or wanted by prospective parents under a description that, consistent with the norms of traditional ethics, does not reduce them to the status of "products" to be brought into existence at their parents' will and for their ends, but rather treats them as "persons" who are to be welcomed by them as perfective participants in the organic community established by their marriage. See George and Bradley, "Marriage and the Liberal Imagination," 306, n. 21. See also Leon Kass, "The Wisdom of Repugnance: Why We Should Ban the Cloning of Humans," *New Republic*, 2 June 1997, 17–26, esp. 23–24.

11. Stephen Macedo, "Homosexuality and the Conservative Mind," *Georgetown Law Journal* 84 (1995): 278.

12. Richard Posner, *The Problematics of Moral and Legal Theory* (Cambridge, Mass.: Harvard University Press, 1999), 77. Apparently having in mind accusations that he had in an earlier publication unfairly quoted fragments of Finnis's argument without providing their context, Posner goes on to say: "It may seem unfair of me to quote Finnis out of context. But the context is dominated by even stranger

sentences, which read as if they had been translated from medieval Latin and makes one wonder whether Finnis agrees with Aquinas that masturbation is a worse immorality than rape" (Ibid). This unfortunate and, indeed, unworthy sentence of Judge Posner's responds to a charge of implicit unfairness (i.e., not providing the essential context of quoted material to which one directs criticism) by manifesting explicit, indeed blatant, unfairness—and doing so in a way that has no evident purpose other than to appeal to prejudices that many of Posner's readers can be counted upon to share. Having thus dealt with Finnis, Posner turns his attention to the present author: "Robert George makes the same point in a more modern idiom, but I still can't make any sense of it."

13. Ibid., n. 143.
14. Germain Grisez proposes a thought experiment. Imagine a type of bodily, rational being that reproduces, not by mating, but by some act performed by individuals. Imagine that for these same beings, however, locomotion or digestion is performed not by individuals, but only by complementary pairs that unite for this purpose. Would anybody acquainted with such beings have difficulty understanding that in respect of reproduction the organism performing the function is the individual, while in respect of locomotion or digestion, the organism performing the function is the united pair? Would anybody deny that the union effected for purposes of locomotion is an organic unity?
15. See Robert P. George, "Can Sex Be Reasonable?" *Columbia Law Review* 93 (1993).
16. Macedo, "Homosexuality and the Conservative Mind," 278.
17. Ibid., 280.
18. Finnis, "Law, Morality, and 'Sexual Orientation,'" sec. 5.
19. Ibid.
20. John Finnis has carefully explained the point:

> Sexual acts which are marital are "of the reproductive kind" because in willing such an act one wills sexual behaviour which is (a) the very same as causes generation (intended or unintended) in every case of human *sexual* reproduction, and (b) the very same as one would will if one were intending precisely sexual reproduction as a goal of a particular marital sexual act. This kind of act is a "natural kind," in the morally relevant sense of "natural," not...if and only if one is intending or attempting to produce and *outcome,* viz. reproduction or procreation. Rather it is a distinct rational kind—and therefore in the morally relevant sense a natural kind—because (i) in engaging in it one is intending a *marital* act, (ii) its being of the reproductive kind is a necessary though not sufficient condition of its being marital, and (iii) marriage is a rational and natural kind of institution. One's reason for action—one's rational motive—is precisely the complex good of marriage. (Ibid.)

21. Stephen Macedo, "Reply to Critics," *Georgetown Law Journal* 84 (1995): 335.
22. Ibid., 335.
23. Joseph Raz, *The Morality of Freedom* (Oxford: Clarendon Press, 1986), 162.

Chapter 5

1. I've written at length about this question in *Making Men Moral: Civil Liberties and Public Morality* (Oxford: Clarendon Press, 1993); and in *In Defense of Natural*

Law (Oxford: Clarendon Press, 1999). I will avoid repetition here to the extent possible.

2. See *In Defense of Natural Law,* chs. 8, 9, 15, and 16. See also John Finnis, "Law, Morality, and 'Sexual Orientation,'" *Notre Dame Law Review* 69 (1994) and "The Good of Marriage and the Morality of Sexual Relations," *American Journal of Jurisprudence* 42 (1997).

3. Dworkin sets forth his view most fully in "Do We Have a Right to Pornography?" in *A Matter of Principle* (Cambridge, Mass.: Harvard University Press, 1985).

4. Ibid., 349.

5. See for example, John Finnis, "Is Natural Law Theory Compatible with Limited Government?" in *Natural Law, Liberalism, and Morality,* ed. Robert P. George (Oxford: Clarendon Press, 1996).

6. Ibid., 5.

7. Ibid.

8. Ibid., 6.

9. Ibid., 8.

10. Ibid.

Chapter 6

1. *Ginsberg v. New York,* 390 U.S. 629 (1968).

2. Ibid., 634.

3. Ibid., 635–37.

4. Ibid., 636.

5. Ibid., 638–43.

6. Ibid., 639 (quoting *Prince v. Massachusetts,* 321 U.S. 158, 166 (1944) (upholding in the face of constitutional challenge the conviction of the guardian of a minor child for permitting the child to sell religious tracts on the streets of Boston, in violation of Massachusetts' child labor laws).

7. Ibid., 639.

8. Ibid., 640.

9. 15 N.Y. 2d 311, 312 (1965).

10. *Ginsberg,* 390 U.S. 640–641 (quoting *Prince,* 321 U.S. 165).

11. Ibid., 641.

12. Ibid., 640–41.

13. A typical example: On January 22, 1997, a federal district court in New York City invalidated the Military Honor and Decency Act of 1996, which prohibited the sale of pornographic magazines and videotapes on military bases. The judge, Shira A. Scheindlin, ruled that the ban violated constitutionally protected free speech rights. "While the majority of Americans may wish to ban pornography," she wrote, "in the final analysis, society is better served by protecting our cherished right to free speech, even at the cost of tolerating speech that is outrageous, offensive, and demeaning" (*General Media Communications, Inc. v. Perry,* 952 F. Supp. 1072, 1074 [S.D.N.Y. 1997]). Predictably, she went on to assure her readers that she shared the view that "the result of permitting such speech is often unfortunate and unpleasant" (Ibid). It is plain, I think, that Judge Scheindlin supposes that the motivating purpose of the

Military Honor and Decency Act was, above all, to prevent offense. But this supposition is gratuitous and almost certainly incorrect. The purpose, rather, was to uphold public morality on military bases by protecting people (and the moral environment in which they live) from the morally corrosive effects of pornography. (One may, of course, deny that pornography has "morally corrosive" effects, but that denial does not entitle one to suppose that the people responsible for laws against pornography share one's own view of the matter and must therefore be motivated, in reality, not by a concern to protect public morality, but rather by a desire to prevent offense.) Scheindlin's supposition is connected to other highly questionable aspects of her reasoning. For example, why should her views, or those of other judges, about what is, after all, the factual question of whether society is "better served" by permitting pornography than prohibiting it prevail over the contrary opinions of the American people or their elected representatives? It simply begs the question to say that her views should prevail because she is a judge and is therefore responsible for enforcing constitutional guarantees.

14. *Ginsberg*, 390 U.S. 655 (Douglas, J., dissenting).
15. Ibid.
16. Ibid.
17. On what the First Amendment was designed to do—and how far prevailing free speech doctrine diverges from that design—see Walter Berns, *The First Amendment and the Future of American Democracy* (New York: Basic Books, 1976).
18. Morton A. Hill and Winfrey C. Link, "Separate Statements by Commission Members," in *The Report of the Commission on Obscenity and Pornography* (1970), 456, 457 [hereinafter, *Commission Report*].
19. *Ginsberg*, 390 U.S. 655 (Douglas, J., dissenting).
20. Harry M. Clor, *Public Morality and Liberal Society: Essays on Decency, Law, and Pornography* (Notre Dame, Ind.: University of Notre Dame Press, 1996), 190.
21. Ibid.
22. Ibid.
23. John Finnis, *Pornography* (1973), 19 (unpublished manuscript, on file with author).
24. Clor, *Public Morality and Liberal Society,* 190–91.
25. Eric Schlosser, "The Business of Pornography," *U.S. News & World Report,* 10 February 1997, 4.
26. John Finnis, *Natural Law and Natural Rights* (Oxford: Clarendon Press, 1980), 217.
27. The sexual intercourse of spouses is the biological matrix of the multi-level (bodily, emotional, dispositional, spiritual) relationship and good of their marriage. The climactic one-flesh union of husband and wife in marital intercourse not only expresses, but enables them to consummate, actualize, and experience the uniquely sexually unitive form of friendship that marriage is. Sex is not a "necessary evil" that good people need to engage in and tolerate in order to continue the human race; rather, it is a central and more-than-merely-instrumental aspect of the great and intrinsic good of marriage. This view of sexual morality differs from both the strict Augustinian view that understands sex as instrumental to procreation and the dominant liberal view that understands sex as instrumental to procreation (if that is the wish of the persons involved), or to pleasure, or as a means of promoting emotional close-

ness or expressing affectionate feelings. See generally George and Bradley, "Marriage and the Liberal Imagination," 301.

28. John Finnis provides a valuable explication and defense of Aquinas's account of this dependency in *Aquinas: Moral, Political, and Legal Theory* (Oxford: Oxford University Press, 1998), ch. VII, sec. 2.

29. For the defense of these claims, see George and Bradley, "Marriage and the Liberal Imagination"; see also John Finnis, "Law, Morality, and 'Sexual Orientation,'" 1049; and John Finnis, "The Good of Marriage," *American Journal of Jurisprudence* 42 (1997).

30. D. A. J. Richards, *The Moral Criticism of Law* (Encino, Calif.: Dickenson Publishing, 1977), 71 (footnote omitted).

31. *Commission Report*, 458.

32. Ronald Dworkin, "Do We Have a Right to Pornography?" 335, 349.

33. Ibid.

34. John Stuart Mill, "On Liberty," in *Utilitarianism, Liberty, Representative Government*, ed. H. B. Acton (1972), 82.

Chapter 7

1. A little while back, Tom Edsall of the Washington Post, having read my essay "The Tyrant State," sent me a message asking me whether the United States had, in my opinion, degenerated into a tyrant state. I answered him as follows:

> Dear Tom:
>
> I don't want to appear to be evading your question, so let me say plainly that my answer is "no, the United States of America is not a tyrant state." The question that the Pope sets before us and other democratically constituted nations intends, however, not a simple "yes" or "no" answer, but deep reflection on the extent to which we permit injustices to flourish and even employ the institutions of law and democratic government to insulate wrongs from rectification.
>
> We Americans can put the question in terms of our fidelity or lack of fidelity to the founding principles of our republic, principles according to which each and every human being is possessed of a profound worth and dignity that is to be respected and protected by law. All of us are created equal and endowed by our Creator with certain unalienable rights. None of us is a natural slave or master. None may be disposed of, or used, merely to advance the interests of another. Human beings are ends-in-themselves, not mere means to other ends. Our lives enjoy a certain sanctity.
>
> No society could live up to such ideals perfectly; certainly ours hasn't. Slavery blighted our record from the beginning. And even after its abolition, we shamed ourselves by the practice of segregation and other forms of racial injustice. Today we mock our founding principles by treating the unborn and sometimes even the newly born as "human nonpersons" lacking any rights that the rest of us are bound to respect. Going beyond the issue of elective abortion, there are those who would move us in the direction of creating new human beings precisely for the purpose of "harvesting" their body parts to benefit others. Of course, the goal of curing people with horrible illnesses is a very worthy one. But the means now being proposed are antithetical to the

principles of human dignity and equality for which our nation, in its found-ing principles, stands.

On the positive side, as I see it, we have not gone down the road towards euthanasia, as we appeared to be doing in 1996 when the *First Things* sympo-sium (in which "The Tyrant State" appeared) was published. The Supreme Court reversed the decision of the U.S. Court of Appeals for the Ninth Circuit creating a right to assisted suicide, a right that almost certainly would have evolved in short order into something along the lines of what is now common in the Netherlands. Of course, Oregon has by democratic means decided to permit physician-assisted suicide; but referenda in other states have gone the other way, despite early polling that indicated fertile ground for the assisted suicide movement.

Now, I recognize that people who believe, as my colleague Peter Singer, for example, believes, that the "sanctity of human life" ethic is a mere relic of outmoded religion (or what have you) will view these matters entirely differ-ently. They do not believe that all human beings are persons, or have funda-mental rights. They are not scandalized by the concept of a "human nonper-son." On the contrary, they believe that there are "pre-personal" and "post-personal" human beings (as well as severely retarded human beings who never were and never will be "persons," as they are pleased to define the term) to whom the promises of basic rights and equality under the law do not apply. Although I deeply disagree with these people, at least they engage the issues straightforwardly and do not pretend to ignorance about when human life begins (or ends). Professor Singer himself, in defending abortion (and infan-ticide), does not try to hide the fact that it is killing and, indeed, killing a human being. He does not feign a belief in the equality of all human beings while advocating policies and practices that simply cannot be squared with such a belief. In any event, I do not expect people who do not believe that the unborn, or newly born, or the profoundly handicapped, or demented are persons with rights to share the Pope's worries and mine about what the acceptance of abortion, infanticide, and euthanasia does to democracy. So I was not writing in *First Things* to engage the basic moral issues with them. (I've done that elsewhere.) My thoughts were directed on that occasion (at the request of the editors) to those who share the sanctity of life ethic but, perhaps, had not reflected, as the Pope has, on the question of what its abandonment does to democracy.

Yours sincerely,

Robert P. George

Chapter 8

1. Pope John Paul II, Encyclical Letter *Evangelium Vitae* (25 March 1995), 2.
2. Ibid., 73.
3. Ibid., 56. This language seems clearly to exclude the possibility of a purely retributive justification for the death penalty. In the sentence immediately following it, the encyclical also seems to rule out as a matter of moral prin-ciple, and not merely on the basis of sociological considerations, a justifica-tion based on the belief that punishing some criminals with death deters

others: "Today however, as a result of steady improvements in the organization of the penal system, such cases [i.e., cases in which the execution of a
wrongdoer is absolutely necessary for the protection of society] are very rare, if
not practically non-existent" (Ibid.).

4. See "The Authoritative Catechism," *Catholic World Report,* October 1997, 6–7.

5. See *Evangelium Vitae,* 68–74.

6. See *Vacco v. Quill.*

7. See *Evangelium Vitae,* 70.

8. On these critics, see Richard John Neuhaus, "The Liberalism of John Paul II,"
First Things, May 1997, 16.

9. See Pope John Paul II, Encyclical Letter *Centesimus Annus* (1 May 1991), 46.

10. Ibid.

11. *Evangelium Vitae,* 70.

12. Ibid.

13. Ibid.

14. See John M. Finnis, "Law as Co-ordination," *Ratio Juris* 2 (1989): 97 (citations
omitted).

15. Ibid.

16. See St. Augustine, *The Problem of Free Choice: De Libero Arbitrio* I, 5.11, trans.
Dom. Mark Pontifex (Westminster, Md.: Newman Press, 1955) (stating that an
unjust law seems not to be law); St. Thomas Aquinas, *Summa Theologiae* I-II, q.
95, a. 2, trans. Fathers of the English Dominican Province (Benziger Bros.,
1947) (stating that an unjust law is not a law but a corruption of law); Ibid., I-
II, q. 96, a. 4 (stating that unjust laws are not so much laws as they are acts of
violence); Plato, *The Laws* IV, 715, trans. A. E. Taylor (Aidine Press, 1966);
Aristotle, *The Politics* III, 6: 1279a8, trans. Ernest Barker (Oxford: Oxford University Press, 1995); and Cicero, *Laws: De Legibus* II, v. 11–13, trans. Clinton
Walker Keyes (Cambridge, Mass.: Harvard University Press, 1966).

17. See *Evangelium Vitae,* 72.

18. Ibid.

19. Ibid., 72. John Paul II goes on to argue that such laws call for disobedience and
even "conscientious objection." Ibid., 73.

20. See *Evangelium Vitae,* 71.

21. Peter L. Berger, "On the Future of Conservatism: A Symposium," *Commentary*
103 (February 1997): 17, 18. A similar point is made by Gertrude Himmelfarb
in her contribution to the same symposium. See Gertrude Himmelfarb, "On
the Future of Conservatism," *Commentary* 103 (February 1997): 29, 31.

22. Berger, "On the Future of Conservatism," 18.

23. See Robert H. Bork, *Slouching Towards Gomorrah: Modern Liberalism and American Decline* (New York: Harper Collins/ReganBooks, 1996), 173–85.

24. See Justice Antonin Scalia, "Of Democracy, Morality, and the Majority," *Origins* 26 (1996): 81 [hereinafter, "Of Democracy"].

25. *Planned Parenthood v. Casey,* 505 U.S. 833, 997–1000 (1992) (Scalia, J., concurring in part and dissenting in part); *Webster v. Reproductive Health Servs.,* 492
U.S. 490, 532–37 (1989) (Scalia, J., concurring).

26. See Scalia, "Of Democracy," 87.

27. See *Webster,* 492 U.S. 532–37.

28. See Scalia, "Of Democracy," 87.

29. See Robert P. George, "Natural Law and Positive Law," in *The Autonomy of Law:*

Essays on Legal Positivism, ed. Robert P. George (Oxford: Clarendon Press, 1996), 321, 330–32,

30. U.S. Const. amend. XIV, § 1.
31. *Roe v. Wade,* 410 U.S. 113.
32. Ibid.
33. Ibid, 156–57.
34. U.S. Const. art. II. § 1, cl. 5; *Roe,* 410 U.S., 157.
35. *Roe,* 410 U.S., 157.
36. Ibid., 159.
37. See Irving, "Scientific and Philosophical Expertise" 18.
38. *Roe,* 410 U.S. 222.
39. See *Casey,* 505 U.S. 979.
40. See Germain Grisez, "When Do People Begin?" *Proceedings of the American Catholic Philosophical Association* 63 (1989), 27, 31.
41. See Patrick Lee, *Abortion and Unborn Human Life.*
42. See John Rawls, *Political Liberalism,* 243 n. 32.
43. Finnis, "Abortion, Natural Law, and Public Reason," 11.
44. For a valuable account of such reasons, see generally Cass R. Sunstein, *Legal Reasoning and Political Conflict* (New York: Oxford University Press, 1996).
45. Mary A. Glendon, "Comment in 'The End of Democracy?' A Discussion Continued," *First Things* 69 (January 1997): 23, 23.
46. *Dred Scott v. Sandford,* 60 U.S. (19 How.) 393 (1857).
47. It was to secure fully this protection that the Fourteenth Amendment, after the abolition of slavery throughout the nation by the Thirteenth Amendment, introduced into the Constitution a guarantee of equal protection to be enforced by Congress against the states. U.S. Const. amend. XIV.
48. *Dred Scott,* 60 U.S., 393.
49. Ibid., 400–403.
50. See Robert H. Bork, *The Tempting of America: The Political Seduction of the Law* (New York: Free Press, 1990), 28–34 (discussing the political climate surrounding the *Dred Scott* decision).
51. 410 U.S. 113.
52. Archibald H. Grimke, *William Lloyd Garrison: The Abolitionist* (New York: Funk & Wagnalls, 1891), 310.
53. See Abraham Lincoln, "First Inaugural Address," in *Speeches and Letters of Abraham Lincoln,* ed. Merwin Roe (New York: E. P. Dutton, 1919), 165.
54. Ibid., 171–72.
55. *Casey,* 505 U.S., 867.
56. This familiar phrase, which was inserted into the Pledge of Allegiance in the 1950s, derives from President Abraham Lincoln's Gettysburg Address. See Abraham Lincoln, "Gettysburg Address," in *Speeches and Letters of Abraham Lincoln,* 214.

Chapter 9

1. Jeremy Bentham, "Anarchical Fallacies," in *The Works of Jeremy Bentham,* vol. 2, ed. John Bowring (New York: Russell & Russell, 1962), 489, 501.
2. 60 U.S. (2 How.) 393 (1857).

3. Abraham Lincoln, "Speech at Springfield, Illinois (June 26, 1857)," in *The Collected Works of Abraham Lincoln,* vol. 2, ed. Roy P. Basler et al. (New Brunswick, N.J.: Rutgers University Press, 1953), 398, 405–6.

4. *Natural Law Theory: Contemporary Essays,* ed. Robert P. George (Oxford: Clarendon Press, 1992).

5. Interview with Clarence Thomas, Judge, United States Court of Appeals for the District of Columbia Circuit, in Princeton, N.J. (June 1991).

6. *The Declaration of Independence* para. 1 (U.S. 1776).

7. Ibid., para. 2.

8. "Letter from Thomas Jefferson to Henry Lee (May 8, 1825)," in *The Political Writings of Thomas Jefferson,* ed. Edward Dumbauld (1955), 88.

9. See generally Robert P. George, "Natural Law and Human Nature," in *Natural Law Theory,* 31 (arguing that human nature is not a closed nature).

10. See generally Germain Grisez et al., "Practical Principles, Moral Truth, and Ultimate Ends," *American Journal of Jurisprudence* 32 (1987): 99 (responding to criticisms of natural law theory).

11. On practical reasonableness, see generally John Finnis, *Natural Law and Natural Rights,* 100–133.

12. Versions of this argument are advanced by Melville J. Herskovits, *Cultural Relativism,* ed. Frances Herskovits (New York: Random House, 1972); and J. L. Mackie, *Ethics: Inventing Right and Wrong* (Harmondsworth, N.Y.: Penguin, 1977). For powerful defenses of natural law and natural rights against arguments for relativism and skepticism that appeal to moral diversity, see Hadley Arkes, *First Things: An Inquiry into the First Principles of Morals and Justice* (Princeton, N.J.: Princeton University Press, 1986); and John Finnis, *Fundamentals of Ethics* (Oxford: Clarendon Press, 1983).

13. Leo Strauss, *Natural Right and History* (Chicago: University of Chicago Press, 1953), 10.

14. This objection is asserted against the natural law theorizing of Germain Grisez and John Finnis in Bernard Hoose, "Proportionalists, Deontologists and the Human Good," *Heythrop Journal* 33 (1992): 172. For a defense of this sort of theorizing against Hoose's critique, see Robert P. George, "Liberty Under the Moral Law: On B. Hoose's Critique of the Grisez-Finnis Theory of Human Good," *Heythrop Journal* 34 (1993): 175.

15. On the compatibility of natural law theory with recognition of legitimate pluralism and diversity, see generally Robert P. George, *Making Men Moral: Civil Liberties and Public Morality.*

16. For two excellent analyses of Nietzschean nihilism, see Stanley Rosen, *Nihilism: A Philosophical Essay* (New Haven, Conn.: Yale University Press, 1969), xiii–xx; and Werner J. Dannhauser, "Friedrich Nietzsche," in *History of Political Philosophy,* 3d ed., ed. Leo Strauss and Joseph Cropsey (Chicago: University of Chicago Press, 1987), 829, 842.

17. In the original debate about natural justice in the Western philosophic tradition, Thrasymachus in Plato's *Republic* anticipates Nietzsche's "transvaluation of values" when he declares under Socrates' relentless questioning that "the just is nothing other than the advantage of the stronger." Plato, *Republic,* 338c. Cf. Friedrich W. Nietzsche, *The Antichrist,* reprinted in *The Portable Nietzsche,* ed. and trans. Walter Kaufmann, (New York: Viking Press, 1954), 565, 568; and Friedrich W. Nietzsche, "On the Genealogy of Morals" II.17, app. 92, reprinted in *On the*

Genealogy of Morals and Ecce Homo, ed. Walter Kaufmann, trans. Walter Kaufmann and R. J. Hollingdale (New York: Vintage Books, 1967), 1, 86, 168–69.

18. Plato, *Republic*, 501b.
19. Plato, *Minos,* 314e.
20. Xenophon, *Memorabilia and Oeconomicus* IV.iv.17–23.
21. Aristotle, *On Rhetoric* I.1373b.
22. Cicero, "On the Laws" I.vi.12–19.
23. On natural law in the Jewish tradition, see David Novak, *Jewish Social Ethics* (1992): 22–44.
24. Romans 2:13–15.
25. St. Thomas Aquinas, *Summa Theologiae* Ia IIae Q. 91, art. 2.
26. See Duncan B. Forrester, "Richard Hooker," in *History of Political Philosophy,* 3d ed., ed. Leo Strauss and Joseph Cropsey (Chicago: University of Chicago Press, 1987), 356, 358–59.
27. Martin Luther, "Commentary on Psalm 101," in *Luther's Works,* vol. 13, ed. Jaroslav Pelikan and Helmut T. Lehmann, trans. Alfred von Rohr Saver (St. Louis, Mo.: Concordia Publishing House, 1956), 146, 161.
28. John Calvin, *Institutes of the Christian Religion* (1536), trans. Henry Beveridge (1966), 16 (construing Romans 2:1–16).
29. "Letter from Thomas Jefferson to Henry Lee," 8.
30. John Locke, *Two Treatises of Government* (1698), 2d ed., ed. Peter Laslett (Cambridge: Cambridge University Press, 1967), 289.
31. Ibid., 290.
32. Sir Robert Filmer, *Patriarcha and Other Writings* (1679), ed. Johann P. Sommerville (Cambridge: Cambridge University Press, 1991).
33. Algernon Sidney, *Discourses Concerning Government* (1698) ii. 20, ed. Thomas G. West (Indianapolis: Liberty Classics, 1990).
34. "Letter from Thomas Jefferson to William S. Smith (November 13, 1787)," in *The Political Writings of Thomas Jefferson,* 68, 69.
35. See George, *Making Men Moral.*
36. *The Federalist No. 43* (James Madison), ed. Benjamin F. Wright (1961), 316.
37. Martin Luther King, Jr., "Letter from Birmingham Jail," in *What Country Have I? Political Writings by Black Americans,* ed. Herbert J. Storing (New York: St. Martin's Press, 1970), 117, 130.
38. Ibid., 121.
39. See Finnis, *Natural Law and Natural Rights.*
40. King, "Letter from Birmingham Jail," 121–22.
41. Ibid., 122.
42. Ibid.

Chapter 10

1. See George, "Natural Law Ethics," 453–65.
2. Romans 2:14–15.
3. *The Declaration of Independence* para. 1 (U.S. 1776).
4. For a valuable summary of, and important contribution to, the debate, see Philip A. Hamburger, "Natural Rights, Natural Law, and American Constitutions," *Yale Law Journal* 102 (1993): 907

5. 381 U.S. 479 (1965).

6. Ibid., 484.

7. Ibid.

8. Ibid., 524 (Black, J., dissenting).

9. Ibid., 509–10 (Black, J., dissenting).

10. Ibid, 512–13 (Black, J., dissenting).

11. "We do not sit as a super-legislature to determine the wisdom, need, and propriety of laws that touch economic problems, business affairs, or social conditions" (ibid., 482).

12. Douglas listed "[t]he right of association contained in the penumbra of the First Amendment;" the Third Amendment's prohibition of quartering soldiers in private houses in peace time; the Fourth Amendment right against unreasonable searches and seizures; the Fifth Amendment right against self-incrimination; and the Ninth Amendment's concept of rights "retained by the people." See ibid., 484. In a famous concurring opinion, Justice Arthur Goldberg (a Kennedy appointee), joined by Chief Justice Earl Warren and Justice William J. Brennan (both Eisenhower appointees), expounded a due process theory of the case, one buttressed by the invocation of the Ninth Amendment, which, according to Goldberg, "lends strong support to the view that the 'liberty' protected by the Fifth and Fourteenth Amendments . . . is not restricted to rights specifically mentioned in the first eight amendments" (Ibid., 493 (Goldberg, J., concurring)). Justice John Marshall Harlan (another Eisenhower appointee), in a separate concurrence, announced his preference for a more straightforward Fourteenth Amendment due process theory. See ibid., 499–502 (Harlan, J., concurring in judgment).

13. See, e.g., *Lochner v. New York,* 198 U.S. 45 (1905) (invalidating a New York statute limiting the number of hours employees in a bakery could be required or permitted to work); *Adair v. United States,* 208 U.S. 161 (1908) (striking down a federal law against "yellow dog contracts" on interstate railroads); *Adkins v. Children's Hospital,* 261 U.S. 525 (1923) (citing *Lochner* to invalidate legislation setting minimum wages for women workers in the District of Columbia).

14. *Pierce v. Soc'y of Sisters,* 268 U.S. 510 (1925).

15. *Meyer v. Nebraska,* 262 U.S. 390 (1923).

16. Roosevelt's criticisms of the Court have come to be widely accepted as valid by liberal and conservative constitutional scholars alike. A notable exception is Hadley Arkes, whose recent writings offer a vigorous defense of the "natural rights" approach taken by the Justices in *Lochner, Adair, Adkins,* and other leading "*Lochner* era" cases. See, in particular, Hadley Arkes's essay, "*Lochner v. New York* and the Cast of Our Laws," in *Great Cases in Constitutional Law,* ed. Robert P. George (Princeton, N.J.: Princeton University Press, 2000); and his book, *The Return of George Sutherland: Restoring a Jurisprudence of Natural Rights* (Princeton, N.J.: Princeton University Press, 1994).

17. In his radio address of March 9, 1937, Roosevelt defended his "court packing plan" as necessary to "save the Constitution from the Court and the Court from itself."

18. Pro-contraception groups had attempted to challenge anti-contraception statutes in the courts beginning in the 1940s. Prior to *Griswold,* however, these constitutional challenges had ultimately been dismissed on procedural grounds. See *Poe v. Ullman,* 367 U.S. 497 (1961); and *Tileston v. Ullman,* 318 U.S. 44 (1943).

19. See Pope Paul VI, *Humanae Vitae* (1968).

20. The dubiousness of some of these suppositions was not evident in 1965, though opponents of contraception warned that the social consequences of its widespread availability and acceptance would be dire. The *Griswold* court barely considered these warnings. In the end, Douglas's opinion rests on the essentially undefended assertion that the availability of contraceptives is good for the institution of marriage. But that was a debatable proposition even in 1965. Supporters of Connecticut's law argued that access to contraceptives, far from strengthening the institution of marriage, would weaken it by fueling a revolution in sexual mores leading to increased family breakdown, abandonment, divorce, adultery, fornication, and other evils. Some maintained that these social pathologies were predictable consequences of the intrinsically anti-marital nature of contraception as a severing of the link between spousal love and openness to procreation that gives marriage its intelligible purpose and specifies its essential requirements (e.g., permanence of commitment, exclusivity [fidelity], obligations of mutual support). If, indeed, the question ultimately turns on empirical, and even moral judgments as to whether contraception strengthens or weakens the institution of marriage, it is difficult to see how a court could be justified in displacing a legislative judgment of the matter one way or another. It obviously won't do to say that the invalidation of laws restricting contraception simply leaves the question of the goodness or badness of the practice to the conscientious judgment of individuals and married couples. The question, as Douglas seemed to grasp clearly enough, is whether the availability of contraception is good for the institution of marriage. The decision is an inherently social one. To recognize this fact is not necessarily to conclude that contraception is bad for marriage or that laws against it will do more good than harm; it is merely to suggest that these questions are unavoidably political. To endorse the political proposition that contraception should be left to individual judgment is to answer the questions in a particular way. And even if one is prepared to answer them in precisely this way, the question remains as to whether courts should have the authority to displace contrary legislative judgments. Thus, Black and Stewart, basing their dissenting opinions solely on the denial of judicial authority, could denounce the Connecticut law as "offensive" and "silly" yet judge it to be constitutionally permissible.

21. Anti-contraception laws in Connecticut and other states had been enacted by legislatures in the mid-nineteenth century—a time when religious and moral opinion was largely united in opposition to the practice of contraception. The pro-contraception movement, beginning with Margaret Sanger's crusade for birth control and sexual liberation in the early twentieth century, attempted to persuade state legislators to repeal anti-contraception statutes. When, as in Connecticut, their efforts in the legislatures failed or stalled, they turned to the courts in the hope of persuading judges to do what public opinion, still clinging at some level to the older sexual morality, prevented elected representatives from doing. As Justice Douglas's opinion for the majority in *Griswold* makes clear, the pro-contraception parties suggested that a decision invalidating the Connecticut statute could be based explicitly on precisely the doctrine which Black would accuse the majority of surreptitiously reviving, namely, the "natural law [substantive] due process philosophy" of the "*Lochner*

era." After all, *Lochner* itself, though in gross disrepute, had never been expressly reversed. Although most commentators were (and are) of the view that *Lochner* had been implicitly overruled in *West Coast Hotel Co. v. Parrish*, 300 U.S. 379 (1937)—a case officially overruling the decision in *Adkins v. Children's Hospital*, which, in turn, had relied on *Lochner*—the *Griswold* majority could, presumably, have invoked the basic principle of *Lochner* while arguing that the court in *Adkins* had misapplied it to the facts in that case. Indeed, they could have argued that the *Lochner* court itself had erroneously applied a perfectly sound principle of constitutional interpretation to the facts before it. However that may be, Douglas plainly wanted no part of such a strategy: "Overtones of some arguments suggest that *Lochner v. New York* should be our guide. But we decline that invitation as we did in *West Coast Hotel Co. v. Parrish*..." (*Griswold*, 381 U.S. 481–82 (1964) (citations omitted)). In the very next paragraph he introduced the "penumbras formed by emanations" (ibid. 482). Interestingly, Douglas's original proposal was to invalidate the Connecticut statute on the ground that it violated the First Amendment right to freedom of association. He could not, however, put together a majority for that remarkable proposition.

22. *Griswold*, 381 U.S. 507 (Black, J., dissenting).
23. Ibid., 527 (Stewart, J., dissenting).
24. One suspects that the "penumbras formed by emanations" rhetoric was designed to suggest that the alleged marital right to use contraceptives is somehow derivable from the "logic" or "structure" of the Constitution, and does not depend on any independent moral-political judgment that married couples ought to be free from legal interference in deciding whether to use contraceptives. But this suggestion is dubious. Someone who happens to believe that contraception is morally wrong and damaging to the institution of marriage, and that the legal permission of contraception would harm public morals and exacerbate various social ills, simply has no reason to affirm a constitutional right to contraception. It is only by bringing belief in a right to marital contraception (with all that it presupposes and entails) to the enterprise of constitutional interpretation that one can find such a right in the "logic" or "structure" of the Constitution.
25. See *Griswold*, 381 U.S. 511–12 (Black, J., dissenting).
26. Edward S. Corwin, "The Debt of American Constitutional Law to Natural Law Concepts," *Notre Dame Law Review* 25 (1950): 258.
27. Ibid. Corwin's lecture builds on his famous essay, "The 'Higher Law' Background of American Constitutional Law," *Harvard Law Review* 42 (1928): 149–85 (pts. I–II), 365–409 (pt. III).
28. Corwin, "The Debt of American Constitutional Law," 259.
29. Ibid., 261.
30. See John Finnis, "The Truth in Legal Positivism," in *The Autonomy of Law: Essays on Legal Positivism*, ed. Robert P. George (Oxford: Clarendon Press, 1996), 195, 202.
31. Corwin, "The Debt of American Constitutional Law," 262 (quoting what is cited by Corwin as 8 Rep. 113b, 77 Eng. Rep. 646 (1610)).
32. Ibid., 258.
33. Ibid., 263.
34. Ibid., 266 (emphasis in original).

35. Ibid.
36. Ibid. (emphasis in original).
37. Ibid. (citing *The Federalist No. 78* [Alexander Hamilton]).
38. Ibid., 267 (citing *Marbury v. Madison,* 5 U.S. (1 Cranch) 137 (1803)).
39. 3 U.S. (3 Dall.) 386 (1798).
40. Ibid., 388.
41. Ibid., 398 (Iredell, J., dissenting).
42. Corwin, "The Debt of American Constitutional Law," 268.
43. Ibid., 269.
44. See George, "Natural Law and Positive Law," 321.
45. St. Thomas Aquinas, *Summa Theologiae* I-II, q. 95, a. 2c., on which see Finnis, *Natural Law and Natural Rights,* 284–89; and Finnis, *Aquinas,* 266–74.
46. Bork, *The Tempting of America,* 66. Of course, some people, including, it seems, Chief Justice William H. Rehnquist, reject what Black condemned as natural law jurisprudence precisely on grounds of skepticism about the existence of natural law and natural rights. The statement by Bork that I quote in the text was evidently intended to make clear to those who had interpreted his earlier writings as grounding his rejection of "judicial activism" in skepticism about natural law and natural rights that he is not of this view.
47. See Ronald Dworkin, *Freedom's Law: The Moral Reading of the American Constitution* (New York: Oxford University Press, 1996). See generally Ronald A. Dworkin, "'Natural' Law Revisited," *University of Florida Law Review* 34 (1982): 165.
48. See Stephen M. Krason, "Constitutional Interpretation, Unenumerated Rights, and the Natural Law," *Catholic Social Science Review* 1 (1996): 20, 25–26.
49. Ibid., 25–28.
50. See Scalia, "Of Democracy," 82.
51. Krason, "Constitutional Interpretation," 26.
52. See Robert P. George, "Free Choice, Practical Reason, and Fitness for the Rule of Law," in *Social Discourse and Moral Judgment,* ed. Daniel N. Robinson (San Diego: Academic Press, 1992), 123–32. I am assuming that the question at hand is that of the obligation of judges and other officials to respect the constitutionally established limits of their authority in reasonably just regimes. I do not here address issues of the rights and responsibilities of judges and others operating in regimes so unjust as to warrant subversion.
53. George has written or edited a number of books advocating reviving the natural law tradition. See, e.g., George, *In Defense of Natural Law*; George, *Making Men Moral*; *Natural Law and Moral Inquiry,* ed. Robert P. George; *Natural Law, Liberalism, and Morality,* ed. Robert P. George (Oxford: Clarendon Press, 1996); *Natural Law Theory,* ed. George. I recently also had the opportunity to respond to another, fundamentally different, leading proponent of a moral realist or natural law theory of constitutional interpretation, Michael Moore. See James E. Fleming, "The Natural Rights-Based Justification for Judicial Review," *Fordham Law Review* 69 (2001): 2119.
54. See Bork, *The Tempting of America,* 95–100 (criticizing *Griswold* but praising the dissent of Justice Black).
55. *Calder v. Bull,* 3 U.S. (3 Dall.) 386, 398–99 (1798) (Iredell, J., dissenting).
56. See, e.g., Edward B. Foley, "The Bicentennial of *Calder v. Bull*: In Defense of a Democratic Middle Ground," *Ohio State Law Journal* 59 (1998): 1599.
57. I do not mean politics in a crude or pejorative sense, but in the sense that his

position reflects political judgments about what institutions are most likely to realize his particular conservative conception of natural law.

58. See *Griswold v. Connecticut,* 381 U.S. 479, 522–24 (1965) (Black, J., dissenting) (criticizing the "natural law due process philosophy" of *Lochner v. New York,* 198 U.S. 45 (1905)).

59. See, e.g., Hadley Arkes, *The Return of George Sutherland: Restoring a Jurisprudence of Natural Rights* (1994).

60. That is, Black criticized the majority opinion in *Griswold,* not because he believed the Constitution embodied natural law but because he opposed judicial enforcement of it. He criticized the very idea that the Constitution embodied natural law. See *Griswold,* 381 U.S. 522 (Black, J., dissenting).

61. 410 U.S. 113 (1973).

62. 505 U.S. 833 (1992).

63. It is common for conservatives to blast *Roe* and *Casey* as illegitimate instances of "Lochnering." See, e.g., *Casey,* 505 U.S. 998 (Scalia, J., concurring in the judgment in part, and dissenting in part); *Roe,* 410 U.S. 174 (Rehnquist, J., dissenting). Some scholars have defended *Griswold, Roe,* and *Casey* (as distinguished from *Lochner*) on the basis of natural law or natural rights arguments. See, e.g., Charles A. Kelbey, *Natural Law and the Supreme Court* (unpublished manuscript on file with author).

64. 347 U.S. 483 (1954).

65. James E. Fleming, "Securing Deliberative Autonomy," *Stanford Law Review* 48 (1995): 1, 13 (drawing an analogy to *West Virginia State Board of Education v. Barnette,* 319 U.S. 624, 642 (1943)).

66. See Senate Committee on the Judiciary, *Nomination of Judge Clarence Thomas to Be Associate Justice of the Supreme Court of the United States: Hearings before the Senate Committee on the Judiciary,* 102d Cong. 225, 364 (1991); *Nomination of David H. Souter to Be Associate Justice of the Supreme Court of the United States: Hearings before the Senate Committee on the Judiciary,* 101st Cong. 172–76 (1990); *Nomination of Anthony M. Kennedy to Be Associate Justice of the Supreme Court of the United States: Hearings before the Senate Committee on the Judiciary,* 100th Cong. 135–36, 164–65 (1987). Even Scalia strains to say that *Griswold* was rightly decided according to his conception of the due process inquiry. See *Michael H. v. Gerald D.,* 491 U.S. 110, 128 n. 6 (1989) (plurality opinion).

67. *Griswold v. Connecticut,* 381 U.S. 479, 485 (1965).

68. Ibid., 485–86.

69. Ibid.,486.

70. I have defended such an interpretation of *Griswold* in terms of a theme of "deliberative autonomy." See Fleming, "Securing Deliberative Autonomy," 10–14.

71. See, e.g., *Baker v. State,* 744 A.2d 864 (Vt. 1999).

72. *Griswold,* 381 U.S. 484.

73. Kenneth L. Karst, "The Freedom of Intimate Association," *Yale Law Journal* 89 (1980): 624.

74. 468 U.S. 609 (1984).

75. Ibid., 617–19.

76. Ibid., 618.

77. See, e.g., Foley, "The Bicentennial of *Calder v. Bull*"; and Kelbey, *Natural Law and the Supreme Court.*

78. *Griswold v. Connecticut,* 381 U.S. 479, 524–25 (1965) (Black, J., dissenting) (quoting *Calder,* 3 U.S. 399 (Iredell, J, dissenting)).

79. Ibid., 500 (Harlan, J., concurring) (incorporating by reference his dissent in *Poe v. Ullman,* 367 U.S. 497, 541 (1961) (Harlan, J., dissenting) (quoting *Calder,* 3 U.S. 388 (Chase, J.)).

80. See, e.g, Fleming, "Securing Deliberative Autonomy."

81. Corwin, "The Debt of American Constitutional Law," 258.

82. See, e.g., *Michael H. v. Gerald D.,* 491 U.S. 110, 123–27, 127 n. 6 (1989) (plurality opinion).

83. I have developed this distinction elsewhere. James E. Fleming, "Constructing the Substantive Constitution," *Texas Law Review* 72 (1993): 211, 268–73.

84. For a work that conceives the enterprise of constitutional interpretation on the basis of these two fundamental interrogatives—along with a third, *How should the Constitution be interpreted?*—see Walter F. Murphy, James E. Fleming, and Sotirios A. Barber, *American Constitutional Interpretation,* 2d ed. (Westbury, N.Y.: Foundation Press, 1995).

85. *The Federalist No. 78* (Alexander Hamilton) (Clinton Rossiter ed., New York: New American Library, 1961), 467, 469.

86. *Marbury v. Madison,* 5 U.S. (1 Cranch) 137, 177–78 (1803).

87. See, e.g., *Planned Parenthood v. Casey,* 505 U.S. 833, 979 (1992) (Scalia, J., concurring in the judgment in part and dissenting in part); *Griswold v. Connecticut,* 381 U.S. 479, 507 (1965) (Black, J., dissenting); Hugo LaFayette Black, *A Constitutional Faith* (New York: Knopf, 1969); Bork, *The Tempting of America*; Antonin Scalia, *A Matter of Interpretation* (Princeton, N.J.: Princeton University Press, 1997); Antonin Scalia, "Originalism: The Lesser Evil," *University of Cincinnati Law Review* 57 (1989): 849.

88. See, e.g., Sotirios A. Barber, *The Constitution of Judicial Power* (Baltimore: Johns Hopkins University Press, 1993); Sotirios A. Barber, *On What the Constitution Means* (Baltimore: Johns Hopkins University Press, 1984); Michael S. Moore, "Justifying the Natural Law Theory of Constitutional Interpretation," *Fordham Law Review* 69 (2001): 2087; Michael S. Moore, "A Natural Law Theory of Interpretation," *Southern California Law Review* 58 (1985): 279; and Michael S. Moore, "The Semantics of Judging," *Southern California Law Review* 54 (1981): 151.

89. See, e.g., Dworkin, *Freedom's Law*; and Ronald Dworkin, "The Arduous Virtue of Fidelity: Originalism, Scalia, Tribe, and Nerve," *Fordham Law Review* 65 (1997): 1249.

90. I say "with some simplification" because Dworkin speaks of the Constitution as embodying abstract moral principles rather than natural rights as such.

91. Bork, *The Tempting of America*; Scalia, *A Matter of Interpretation*; and Scalia, "Originalism." Elsewhere, I have criticized the narrow originalists' claim to have a monopoly on concern for fidelity in constitutional interpretation. James E. Fleming, "Fidelity to Our Imperfect Constitution," *Fordham Law Review* 65 (1997): 1335; and James E. Fleming, "Original Meaning Without Originalism," *Georgetown Law Journal* 85 (1997): 1849.

92. Bork, *The Tempting of America,* 66, 209–10, 351–55; Scalia, *A Matter of Interpretation*; and Scalia, "Originalism."

93. See, e.g., Barber, *Judicial Power,* 157–58; and Dworkin, *Freedom's Law,* 72–83.

94. Here I do not mean "noninterpretive" in the common pejorative sense that

one thinks another's theory of interpretation is not really a theory of "interpretation" at all. Rather, I mean it in the sense that the argument against judicial review reflects or grows out of concerns that do not simply follow from a theory of interpretation.

95. See, e.g., Cass R. Sunstein, *The Partial Constitution* (Cambridge, Mass.: Harvard University Press, 1993), v–vi, 9–10, 138–40, 145–61, 350; Lawrence G. Sager, "Justice in Plain Clothes: Reflections on the Thinness of Constitutional Law," *Northwestern University Law Review* 88 (1993): 410; and Lawrence G. Sager, "Fair Measure: The Legal Status of Underenforced Constitutional Norms," *Harvard Law Review* 91 (1978): 1212.

96. Sunstein, *The Partial Constitution,* 9–10.

97. Ronald Dworkin, *Taking Rights Seriously* (Cambridge, Mass.: Harvard University Press, 1977), 131–49.

98. Dworkin, "Arduous Virtue," 1249–51, 1262–68.

99. See, e.g., *Planned Parenthood v. Casey,* 505 U.S. 833, 847–49, 901 (1992); and Dworkin, *Freedom's Law,* 72–83, 119, 124–29.

100. John Finnis, *Natural Law and Natural Rights,* 3.

101. See Hans Kelsen, "The Natural-Law Doctrine before the Tribunal of Science," in *What is Justice? Justice, Law and Politics in the Mirror of Science: Collected Essays* by Hans Kelsen (Berkeley, Calif.: University of California Press, 1971), 137, 141. I criticize Kelsen's thought in "Kelsen and Aquinas on 'The Natural-Law Doctrine,'" *Notre Dame Law Review* 75 (2000): 1625.

102. "I am far from denying that there is a natural law, but I do deny both that we have given judges the authority to enforce it and that judges have any greater access to that law than do the rest of us" (Bork, *The Tempting of America,* 66). Of course, my own view is that in enforcing the positive law of the Constitution, judges in many cases will be carrying out one of the Constitution's strategies for giving effect to principles of natural law and natural rights. I would be surprised if Bork disagreed, though I do not propose to put words in his mouth.

103. See Richard Posner, *The Essential Holmes* (Chicago: University of Chicago Press, 1992), 116. ("[V]alues are simply generalizations emotionally expressed.")

104. See *Griswold v. Connecticut,* 381 U.S. 479, 507–27 (1965) (Black, J., dissenting).

105. Ibid.

106. I set forth my defense of natural law against the skeptical critique in Robert P. George, "A Defense of the New Natural Law Theory," *American Journal of Jurisprudence* 41 (1996): 47, reprinted with corrections of multiple printer's errors in George, *In Defense of Natural Law,* 18–33.

107. Please note, however, that my willingness to acknowledge the force of Black's critique of the majority opinion in *Griswold* should not be interpreted as a wholesale endorsement of Black's constitutional jurisprudence, any more than it is an endorsement of his metaethical views, whatever they were. While I believe there is more to be said for Black's dissent in *Griswold* than Fleming allows, there are many points of constitutional law and theory on which I disagree with Black—in some cases profoundly.

108. See Dworkin, *Freedom's Law,* 3 (emphasis added).

109. Ibid.

110. Fleming insists not only that *Griswold* was rightly decided, but that it ought not even to be questioned. It is, he says, a "fixed star in our constitutional

constellation" right up there with *Brown v. Board of Education* (quoting his *Securing Deliberative Autonomy*). Indeed, he accuses me of "obstinacy" in going "against the grain of *our* constitutional practice by continuing to criticize *Griswold* as wrongly decided" [emphasis mine]. It is certainly true that liberal ideology, particularly on questions of sexual morality and the sanctity of human life, has achieved the status of orthodoxy in American law schools and in elite sectors of the legal profession (as manifested, for example, in the positions officially taken and advocated by the American Bar Association on issues pertaining to homosexuality and abortion). And this, in turn, gives *Griswold* the standing of a core doctrine in something like an established faith. Dissenters will therefore feel the chill force of what is packed into Fleming's reference to *our* constitutional practice and the putative illegitimacy of any dissent from it. *Our* practice is the practice of the people who are "in charge around here," who "run the show," who have the power to decide who is included and excluded from faculty posts and perhaps from judicial appointments, and which views may or may not be dissented from on pain of being declared "obstinate," "out of the mainstream," and "out of line with *our* constitutional practice." (I do not know whether Fleming himself believes it would be right to deny an otherwise well-qualified candidate a judicial appointment because the candidate is "obstinate" enough to believe that Black had the better argument in *Griswold*. I do know, however, and should here point out in fairness to him, that to his great credit he has been willing to support faculty appointments in his own law school of scholars who dissent from the liberal orthodoxy on social issues that less fair-minded scholars are willing to enforce ruthlessly.)

111. 410 U.S. 113 (1973).

112. I am baffled by Fleming's attribution to me of the view that "judges have no authority to enforce natural law and natural rights against legislative encroachment." That is not my view, nor do I assert such a thing in my paper or anywhere else. Often, by enforcing principles fairly discoverable in the constitutional text, its structure, logic, and original understanding, judges enforce natural law and natural rights, as embodied in the Constitution, against legislative encroachment. Thus, judicial review is among the strategies by which the Constitution gives effect to natural law and protects natural rights—though it is not the only one. As I said in my paper, judicial review, properly practiced, "help to make the natural law ideal of constitutional government a reality." I honestly do not see how I could have made myself clearer about this.

113. 468 U.S. 609 (1984).

114. The opinion is in Bernard Schwartz, *The Unpublished Opinions of the Warren Court* (New York: Oxford University Press, 1985), 231–36. Professor Schwartz, a scholar of liberal sympathies who plainly approves of the outcome in *Griswold*, states that "[i]t must be conceded that the Douglas draft *Griswold* opinion is not legally convincing" (ibid., 37).

Chapter 11

1.   Oliver Wendell Holmes, "The Path of the Law," *Harvard Law Review* 10 (1897), 458.

2. Ibid., 457.
3. Ibid.
4. Ibid.
5. Ibid.
6. Ibid., 458–62.
7. Ibid., 459.
8. Ibid., 464.
9. Ibid., 458.
10. Ibid., 359.
11. Ibid., 460–61.
12. Ibid., 461.
13. Ibid., 459.
14. Ibid.
15. Ibid., 473.
16. Ibid.
17. See ibid., 474.
18. Ibid., 465.
19. Ibid., 466.
20. Ibid.
21. Ibid., 469.
22. Ibid.
23. Ibid.
24. See H. L. A. Hart, "American Jurisprudence Through English Eyes: The Nightmare and the Noble Dream," in *Essays in Jurisprudence and Philosophy,* ed. H. L. A. Hart (Oxford: Clarendon Press, 1983), 123, 123–24.
25. Holmes, "Path of the Law," 467.
26. Ibid., 474.
27. Ibid., 476.
28. J. W. Harris, *Legal Philosophies* (1980), 94.
29. 198 U.S. 45 (1905).
30. See ibid.
31. Holmes, "Path of the Law," 468.
32. Ibid., 462.
33. Karl Llewellyn, *The Bramble Bush: On Our Law and Its Study* (New York: Oceana Publications, 1951), 12.
34. See generally Jerome Frank, *Law and the Modern Mind* (New York: Brentano's, 1931).
35. See Jerome Frank, *Law and the Modern Mind,* 6th ed. (New York: Coward-McCann, 1949).
36. See John Finnis, *Natural Law and Natural Rights,* 11–18. For a critique of Hart's idea of the importance of the internal point of view from a perspective sympathetic to Hart's legal positivism, see Jules Coleman, "Authority and Reason," in *The Autonomy of Law: Essays on Legal Positivism,* ed. Robert P. George (Oxford: Clarendon Press, 1996), 287.
37. H. L. A. Hart, *The Concept of Law* (Oxford: Clarendon Press, 1961), 95–96.
38. For a defense of Austin and Bentham against Hart's criticisms, see L. Jonathan Cohen, "Critical Notice: Hart, The Concept of Law," *Mind* 72 (1962): 395.
39. Hart, *Concept of Law,* vii.
40. Finnis, *Natural Law and Natural Rights,* 12.

41. See Patrick Devlin, *The Enforcement of Morals* (New York: Oxford University Press, 1965); and H. L. A. Hart, *Law, Liberty and Morality* (Stanford, Calif.: Stanford University Press, 1963).

42. See Kelsen, "The Natural-Law Doctrine before the Tribunal of Science," 137.

43. See generally Raz, *The Morality of Freedom.*.

44. Finnis, "The Truth in Legal Positivism," 195, 203–4.

45. See Lon L. Fuller, *The Morality of Law* (New Haven, Conn.: Yale University Press, 1969).

46. For Hart's response, see H. L. A. Hart, "The Morality of Law," *Harvard Law Review* 78 (1964–65): 1281.

47. Fuller, *Morality of the Law,* 106.

48. See Joseph Raz, The Rule of Law and Its Virtue, in *The Authority of Law: Essays on Law and Morality* (Oxford: Clarendon Press, 1979), 226.

49. See Joseph Raz, "Formalism and the Rule of Law," in *Natural Law Theory,* 339. See generally Neil MacCormick, "Natural Law and the Separation of Law and Morals," in *Natural Law Theory,* 105.

50. Finnis, *Natural Law and Natural Rights,* 14.

51. I develop these thoughts at greater length in "Natural Law and Positive Law," 321.

Chapter 12

1. See, e.g., Mario Cuomo, "Religious Belief and Public Morality: A Catholic Governor's Perspective," *Journal of Law, Ethics & Public Policy* (1984): 13–31.

2. "The Liberalism of John Paul II," *First Things* (May 1997): 16–21.

3. *Evangelium Vitae,* 70.

4. He rejects any notion that democracy should, or must, rest on ethical relativism:

> At the basis of all these [modern] tendencies lies the *ethical relativism* which characterizes much of present-day culture. There are those who consider such relativism an essential condition of democracy, inasmuch as it alone is held to guarantee tolerance, mutual respect between people and acceptance of the decisions of the majority, whereas moral norms considered to be objective and binding are held to lead to authoritarianism and intolerance.
>
> But it is precisely the issue of respect for life which shows what misunderstandings and contradictions, accompanied by terrible practical consequences, are concealed in this position (Ibid.).

5. *Sollicitudo Rei Socialis,* 44.

6. "The Church respects *the legitimate autonomy of the democratic order* and is not entitled to express preferences for this or that institutional or constitutional solution. Her contribution to the political order is precisely her vision of the dignity of the person revealed in all its fullness in the mystery of the Incarnate Word" (*Centesimus Annus,* 47).

7. Adrian Karatnycky, "Democratic Church: Maligned as 'Autocratic,' the Catholic Church Has Become a Great Engine for Democratic Change," *National Review,* 4 May 1998, 38.

8. Ibid.
9. Ibid. Of course, the Pope's critics within the Church fault him for failing to democratize the Church itself. Indeed, they accuse him of exemplifying an "autocratic" management style and refusing to consider the views of Catholics who do not share his "conservative" doctrinal and moral views. There is room, I think, for legitimate debate about the respects in which certain aspects of the administration of the Church can and should be democratized. The Pope himself invites this debate in his encyclical letter *Ut Unum Sil* and elsewhere. The magisterium of the Church, however, was not constituted by Our Lord as a democracy; nor are the norms appropriate to political governance, including principles of democratic decision making, applicable to the resolution of disputed questions pertaining to matters of faith and morals. Moreover, the tone, circumstance, and content of much criticism of the pontificate of John Paul II makes abundantly clear that often the real objection of his critics is not to the nondemocratic nature of his decision making, but to the substance of the decisions he makes. It is ironic that liberal critics of the Pope's teaching on abortion, homosexuality, and other controversial moral questions demand the democratic resolution of these issues within the Church, while firmly resisting their democratic resolution in the political system. The last thing "pro-choice" Catholics and other friends of legalized abortion would support is the reversal of *Roe v. Wade* (1973) so that questions of public policy surrounding abortion could be settled by democratic decision making.
10. This is not to say that the Pope views democracy as a cure for all injustices and social ills. Much less is it to suggest that he believes that policies enacted by democratic procedures cannot themselves be seriously unjust. Even as he praises democratic political principles, he enters a warning:

> Democracy cannot be idolized to the point of making it a substitute for morality or a panacea for immorality. Fundamentally, democracy is a "system" and as such is a means and not an end. Its "moral" value is not automatic, but depends on conformity to the moral law to which it, like every other form of human behavior, must be subject: in other words, its morality depends on the morality of the ends which it pursues and of the means which it employs (*Evangelium Vitae*, 70).

11. "Religious freedom, which is still at times limited or restricted, remains the premise and guarantee of all the freedoms that ensure the common good of individuals and peoples" (John Paul II, *Redemptoris Missio*, 39).
12. "In the law of 1905 [in France]...the Church was arrogantly assigned a juridical status articulated in forty-four articles, whereby almost every aspect of her organization and action was minutely regulated. Moreover, this was done on principle—the principle of the primacy of the political, the principle of 'everything within the state, nothing above the state.' This was the cardinal thesis of sectarian Liberalism.... As the Syllabus and the explicatory documents [of Pius IX]—as well as the multitudinous writings of Leo XIII—make entirely clear, it was this thesis of the juridical omnipotence and omnicompetence of the state which was the central object of the Church's condemnation of the Jacobin development. It was because freedom of religion and separation of church and state were predicated on this thesis that the Church refused to accept them as

thesis" (John Courtney Murray, *We Hold These Truths: Catholic Reflections on the American Proposition* (New York: Sheed & Ward, 1960), 68).

13. "The Vatican Council declares that the human person has a right to religious freedom. Freedom of this kind means that all men should be immune from coercion on the part of individuals, social groups and every human power so that, within due limits, nobody is forced to act against his convictions nor is anyone to be restrained from acting in accordance with his convictions in religious matters in private or public, alone or in associations with others" (*Dignitatis Humanae*, 2).

14. See, e.g., *Dignitatis Humanae*, 6:

> The protection and promotion of the inviolable rights of man is an essential duty of every civil authority.... [T]he right of all citizens and religious communities to religious freedom must be recognized and respected as well.... [T]he civil authority must see to it that the equality of the citizens before the law...is never violated either openly or covertly for religious reasons and that there is no discrimination among citizens.

15. "[T]he Church in our time attaches great importance to all that is stated by the Second Vatican Council in its *Declaration on Religious Freedom*, both the first and the second part of the document" (John Paul II, *Redemptor Hominis*, 12).

16. "The Second Vatican Council considered especially necessary the preparation of a fairly long declaration on this subject. This is the document called *Dignitatis Humanae*.... Certainly the curtailment of the religious freedom of individuals and communities is not only a painful experience but it is above all an attack on man's very dignity, independently of the religion professed or of the concept of the world which these individuals and communities have. The curtailment and violation of religious freedom are in contrast with man's dignity and his objective rights.... In this case we are undoubtedly confronted with a radical injustice with regard to what is particularly deep within man, what is authentically human" (John Paul II, *Redemptor Hominis*, 17).

17. For some interesting reflections on this question, see generally Bork, *Slouching Towards Gomorrah.*.

18. Pius XI called *Rerum Novarum* "the Magna Carta on which all Christian activities in social matters are ultimately based" (Pius XI, *Quadragesimo Anno*, 1–3).

19. Catholic social teaching likewise emphasizes the social obligations of private property ownership and the rights of the worker. See, e.g., *Centesimus Annus*, 15: "[S]ociety and the State [are] both [to] assume responsibility...for protecting the worker from the nightmare of unemployment.... Furthermore, society and the State must ensure wage levels adequate for the maintenance of the worker and his family, including a certain amount for savings."

20. See, e.g., *Centesimus Annus*, 35: "[T]he market [must] be appropriately controlled by the forces of society and by the State, so as to guarantee that the basic needs of the whole society are satisfied." and Pius XI, *Quadragesimo Anno*, II-5: "Just as the unity of human society cannot be built upon class-warfare, so the proper ordering of economic affairs cannot be left to free competition alone."

21. "The Church has no models to present; models that are real and truly effective can only arise within the framework of different historical situations, through

the efforts of all those who responsibly confront concrete problems in all their social, economic, political and cultural aspects, as these interact with one another" (*Centesimus Annus,* 43).

22. "The Church, in fact, has something to say about specific human situations, both individual and communal, national and international. She formulates a genuine doctrine for these situations, a *corpus* which enables her to analyze social realities, to make judgments about them and to indicate directions to be taken for the just resolution of the problems involved.... In effect, to teach and to spread her social doctrine pertains to the Church's evangelizing mission and is an essential part of the Christian message, since this doctrine points out the direct consequences of that message in the life of society and situates daily work and struggles for justice in the context of bearing witness to Christ the Savior" (*Centesimus Annus,* 5).

23. See, e.g., *Centesimus Annus,* 49.

24. See, e.g., *Centesimus Annus,* 11 ("a specific form of primacy in the exercise of Christian charity").

25. E.g., *Centesimus Annus,* 15:

> The State must contribute to the achievement of these goals both directly and indirectly. Indirectly and *according to the principle of subsidiarity,* by creating favorable conditions for the free exercise of economic activity.... Directly and *according to the principle of solidarity,* by defending the weakest...

26. "Let it be regarded, therefore, as established that in seeking help for the masses this principle before all is to be considered as basic, namely, that private ownership must be preserved inviolate" (Leo XIII, *Rerum Novarum,* 23).

27. "*Rerum Novarum* is opposed to state control of the means of production, which would reduce every citizen to being a 'cog' in the state machine" (*Centesimus Annus,* 15).

28. "Is [capitalism] the model which ought to be proposed...? ...If by 'capitalism' is meant an economic system which recognizes the fundamental and positive role of business, the market, private property and the resulting responsibility for the means of production, as well as free human creativity in the economic sector, then the answer is certainly in the affirmative...." (*Centesimus Annus,* 42).

29. See, for instance, *Centesimus Annus,* 11, where John Paul II emphasizes the teaching of *Rerum Novarum* regarding the "necessary limits to the State's intervention [in the economy], and on its instrumental character, inasmuch as the individual, the family and society are prior to the State, and inasmuch as the State exists in order to protect their rights and not stifle them."

30. Excessive taxation is prohibited by Catholic social doctrine. See, e.g., *Quadragesimo Anno,* II-1.

31. Catholic social doctrine teaches that strengthening the health of the family is paramount—"The first and fundamental structure for 'human ecology' is *the family....* Here we mean the *family founded on marriage....* In the face of the so-called culture of death, the family is the heart of the culture of life" (*Centesimus Annus,* 39).

32. "Malfunctions and defects in the [Welfare] State are the result of an inadequate understanding of the tasks proper to the State. Here again *the principle of subsidiarity* must be respected: a community of a higher order should not

interfere in the internal life of a community of a lower order, depriving the latter of its functions, but rather should support it in case of need and help to coordinate its activity with the activities of the rest of society, always with a view to the common good.

"By intervening directly and depriving society of its responsibility, the [Welfare] State leads to a loss of human energies and an inordinate increase in public agencies, which are dominated more by bureaucratic ways of thinking than by concern for serving their clients, and which are accompanied by an enormous increase in spending. In fact, it would appear that needs are best understood and satisfied by people who are closest to them and who act as neighbors to those in need" (*Centesimus Annus,* 48).

33. E.g., "In situations strongly influenced by ideology, in which polarization obscured the awareness of a human dignity common to all, the Church affirmed clearly and forcefully that every individual—whatever his or her personal conviction—bears the image of God and therefore deserves respect" (*Centesimus Annus,* 22).

34. "[T]he root of modern totalitarianism is to be found in the denial of the transcendent dignity of the human person who, as the visible image of the invisible God, is therefore by his very nature the subject of rights which no one may violate—no individual, group, class, nation or State. Not even the majority of a social body may violate these rights..." (*Centesimus Annus,* 44).

35. Wilfred McClay, "Mr. Emerson's Tombstone," *First Things,* May 1998, 20.

36. For a vigorous attack on the use of "rights talk," see Joan Lockwood O'Donovan, "The Concept of Rights in Christian Moral Discourse," in Michael Cromartie, ed., *A Preserving Grace: Protestants, Catholics, and Natural Law* (Washington, D.C.: Eerdmans, 1997), 143–56. (I offer a critical response to Dr. O'Donovan's paper in the same volume, 157–61.) A more moderate (and, to my mind, more persuasive) critique of the (over)use of rights language can be found in Mary Ann Glendon, *Rights Talk* (New York: Free Press, 1991).

37. The Pope, for instance, speaks favorably of a document dismissed by many old fashioned conservatives—the Universal Declaration of Human Rights (passed by the United Nations General Assembly on December 10, 1948):

> The Declaration of Human Rights linked with the setting up of the United Nations Organization certainly had as its aim not only to depart from the horrible experiences of the last World War but also to create the basis for continual revision of programs, systems and regimes precisely from this single fundamental point of view, namely the welfare of man—or, let us say, of the person in the community—which must, as a fundamental factor in the common good, constitute the essential criterion for all programs, systems and regimes (*Redemptor Hominis,* 17).

For an analysis of the Universal Declaration which complements that of the Pope, see "On Human Rights: the Universal Declaration of Human Rights Fifty Years Later, a Statement by the Ramsey Colloquium," *First Things,* April 1998, 18–31.

38. "[W]e cannot fail to recall...the magnificent effort made to give life to the United Nations Organization, an effort conducive to the definition and establishment of man's objective and inviolable rights, with the member states

obliging each other to observe them rigorously. This commitment has been accepted and ratified by almost all present-day states, and this should constitute a guarantee that human rights will become throughout the world a fundamental principle of work for man's welfare" (*Redemptor Hominis,* 17).

39. "Yes, every man is his 'brother's keeper,' because God entrusts us to one another. And it is also in view of this entrusting that God gives everyone freedom, a freedom which possesses an *inherently relational dimension.* This is a great gift of the Creator, placed as it is at the service of the person and of his fulfillment through the gift of self and openness to others; but when freedom is made absolute in an individualistic way, it is emptied of its original content, and its very meaning and dignity are contradicted" (*Evangelium Vitae,* 19).

40. See, generally, *Redemptor Hominis,* III, 13–17, and *Evangelium Vitae,* 18–20, where these matters are thoroughly discussed.

41. "The process which once led to discovering the idea of 'human rights'—rights inherent in every person and prior to any Constitution and State legislation—is today marked by a *surprising contradiction.* Precisely in an age when the inviolable rights of the person are solemnly proclaimed and the value of life is publicly affirmed, the very right to life is being denied or trampled upon, especially at the more significant moments of existence: the moment of birth and the moment of death" (*Evangelium Vitae,* 18).

42. See Germain Grisez and Joseph M. Boyle, Jr., *Life and Death with Liberty and Justice: A Contribution to the Euthanasia Debate* (Notre Dame and London: University of Notre Dame Press, 1979), 19–99.

43. *Evangelium Vitae,* 56.

44. Ibid.

45. It is worth noting here that Pope John Paul II has not been content simply to condemn capital punishment in the abstract. He has repeatedly, in the course of his pontificate, intervened to plead on behalf of particular prisoners condemned to death by governments around the world. For example, sometime back he publicly pleaded for the commutation of the sentence of Karla Faye Tucker who, despite his intervention, was executed by the state of Texas.

46. Dodd's advocacy of "abortion rights" and his refusal to oppose even partial-birth abortion resulted in a highly publicized incident in which a parish priest returned his $5,000 contribution to a bankrupt Catholic elementary school. (Pro-life Americans donated more than $61,000 to the school in response.) ("'Blood Money' Rejection Rewarded," *Washington Times,* 16 December 1996.)

47. See *Congressional Record,* 20 May 1997, S-4715.

48. See chapter 14 for an extended discussion of the role Catholic politicians (and others) have played in frustrating the Catholic voice in the debate about bioethics.

49. See *Gaudium et Spes,* 51: "Abortus necnon infanticidium nefanda sunt crimina."

50. *Evangelium Vitae,* 62.

51. Ibid.

52. Cuomo, "Religious Belief."

53. As part of his argument, Cuomo invoked the "seamless garment" or "consistent ethic of life" idea that had been proposed a couple of years earlier by Joseph Cardinal Bernardin of Chicago. Cuomo argued that, because abortion "involves life and death," it "will always be a central concern for Catholics. But so will nuclear weapons, and hunger and homelessness and joblessness, all the

forces diminishing human life and threatening to destroy it" (ibid., 28–29). Critics of Cardinal Bernardin had feared that his "seamless garment" approach offered pro abortion Catholic politicians, such as Cuomo, a justification for claiming to be more closely in harmony with the great body of Catholic moral teaching than are their pro life conservative opponents. Several years after Cuomo spoke at Notre Dame, Cardinal Bernardin conceded in a newspaper interview that "some people on the Left" were using the "consistent ethic to give the impression that the abortion issue is not all that important anymore, that you should be against abortion in a general way but that there are more important issues, so don't hold anybody's feet to the fire just on abortion." Without mentioning Cuomo, or anyone else, the cardinal unequivocally condemned this "misuse" of the consistent ethic idea. "I deplore it," he declared. (Interview with Joseph Cardinal Bernardin, *National Catholic Register,* 12 June 1998.)

54. *Evangelium Vitae,* 71.
55. For further explanation, see Robert P. George, "Conscience and the Public Person," in *Catholic Conscience: Foundation and Formation,* ed. Russell E. Smith (Braintree, Mass.: The Pope John XXIII Medical-Moral Research and Education Center, 1991), ch. 18.
56. "By virtue of our sharing in Christ's royal mission, our support and promotion of human life must be accomplished through the *service of charity,* which finds expression in personal witness, various forms of volunteer work, social activity and political commitment.... In our service of charity, *we must be inspired and distinguished by a specific attitude:* we must care for the other as a person for whom God has made us responsible.... *Where life is involved, the service of charity must be profoundly consistent....* We need then to '*show care' for all life and for the life of everyone....* Newborn life is also served by *centres of assistance and...centres where new life receives a welcome.* Thanks to the work of such centres, many unmarried mothers and couples in difficulty discover new hope and find assistance and support in overcoming hardship and the fear of accepting a newly conceived life or life which has just come into the world" (*Evangelium Vitae,* 87 and 88).
57. For instance, through the Fund for the American Family, ex-Governor Robert P. Casey, well known for his opposition to abortion (as will be discussed *infra*), also worked hard to craft effective adoption and child welfare policies.
58. *Evangelium Vitae,* 73.
59. See George, "Conscience and the Public Person."
60. For an account, see Robert P. Casey, *Fighting for Life* (Dallas: Word Publishing, 1996), 184–92.
61. For an excellent analysis of the links among abortion, contraception, and sex education, see Kenneth D. Whitehead, "Do Sex Education and Access to Contraception Cut Down on Abortion?" *FCS Quarterly* (summer 1998): 22–42.
62. James Davison Hunter, *Culture Wars: The Struggle to Define America* (New York: Basic Books, 1991).
63. For a particularly lucid and thorough discussion of the teaching authority of the magisterium in matters of faith and morals, see Germain Grisez, *The Way of the Lord Jesus,* vol. 1: *Christian Moral Principles* (Chicago: Franciscan Herald Press, 1983), chs. 35 and 36.

64. *Lumen Gentium,* 25.

65. For an application of the political science analysis to a bishops' conference, see Thomas J. Reese, S.J., *A Flock of Shepherds: The National Conference of Catholic Bishops* (Kansas City, Mo.: Sheed & Ward, 1992). For a criticism of Reese's approach, see Richard John Neuhaus, "The Self-Constituted Church," *First Things,* October 1998, 85–87.

66. Such people will sometimes claim that their view is justified by Vatican II itself. That this is a complete misunderstanding of Vatican II, particularly *Dignitatis humanae,* see the statement of John Courtney Murray, S.J., the priest and scholar whose ideas were central to the shaping of that document in *The Documents of Vatican II,* ed. Walter Abbot, S.J. (New York: America Press, 1966), 679, n. 5:

> It is worth noting that the Declaration does not base the right to the free exercise of religion on "freedom of conscience." Nowhere does this phrase occur. And the Declaration nowhere lends its authority to the theory for which the phrase frequently stands, namely, that I have the right to do what my conscience tells me to do, simply because my conscience tells me to do it. This is perilous theory. Its particular peril is subjectivism—the notion, that, in the end, it is my conscience, not the objective truth, which determines what is right or wrong, true or false.

Vatican II, in fact, insisted that, in forming his conscience, a Catholic must "pay careful attention to the sacred and certain teaching of the Church" (*Dignitatis Humanae,* 14). In the *Pastoral Constitution on the Church in the Modern World,* the council noted that, while one's conscience might "go astray through ignorance...without...losing its dignity, [t]his cannot be said of the man who takes little trouble to find out what is true and good, or when conscience is by degrees almost blinded through the habit of committing sin" (*Gaudium et Spes,* 16).

67. Pope John Paul II has taught explicitly on the relationship of the authority of the Church to the consciences of Catholics:

> [T]he authority of the Church, when she pronounces on moral questions, in no way undermines the freedom of conscience of Christians. This is so not only because freedom of conscience is never freedom 'from' the truth but always and only freedom 'in' the truth, but also because the magisterium does not bring to the Christian conscience truths which are extraneous to it; rather it brings to light the truths which it ought already to possess, developing them from the starting point of the primordial act of faith. The Church puts herself always and only at the *service of conscience,* helping it to avoid being tossed to and fro by every wind of doctrine proposed by human deceit (cf. Eph 4:14), and helping it not to swerve from the truth about the good of man, but rather, especially in more difficult questions, to attain the truth with certainty and to abide in it (*Veritatis Splendor,* 64).

68. *Dignitatis Humanae,* 3.

69. See *Evangelium Vitae,* 71 (citing St. Thomas Aquinas, *Summa Theologiae* I-II, q. 96, a. 2).

Chapter 13

1. New York: Alfred A. Knopf, 1995.
2. See Sullivan's letter to the editor in *Commentary*, March 1997, responding to Norman Podhoretz's article, "How the Gay Rights Movement Won."
3. Daniel Mendelsohn demolishes many of the claims made by John Boswell in the latter's *Same-Sex Unions in Premodern Europe* (New York: Villard Books, 1994) in "The Man behind the Curtain," *Arion* III: 3 (1996): 241-73. See also Brent Shaw, "A Groom of One's Own," *The New Republic*, 18-25 July 1994, 33-41; and Robin Darling Young "Gay Marriage: Reimagining Church History," *First Things*, November 1994, 47.
4. On St. Paul's teaching regarding the "unnaturalness" of homosexual acts, see Jeffrey Satinover, *Homosexuality and the Politics of Truth* (Grand Rapids: Baker Books, 1996), 151-52.
5. "The Thoughts are to the Desires as Scouts and Spies to range abroad, and find the way to the things desired." Thomas Hobbes, *Leviathan*, pt. 1, ch. 8 (1651).
6. "Reason is, and ought only to be, the slave of the passions, and can never pretend to any office, other than to serve and obey them." David Hume, *A Treatise of Human Nature*, bk. 2, pt. 3, sec. III (1740).
7. At the same time, because the phrase "homosexual orientation" is used in ways that render its connotation uncertain, I think it generally preferable to speak of homosexual attraction, inclination, desires, tendencies or dispositions. On the "radically equivocal" character of the phrase as it is deployed in contemporary political debate, see John Finnis, "Law, Morality, and 'Sexual Orientation,'" *Notre Dame Law Review* 69 (1994): sec I., 1049-51.
8. Thus, Aquinas says that "the good of the human being is in accord with reason, and human evil is being outside the order of reasonableness." *Summa Theologiae*, I-II, q. 71, a. 2c, on which see John Finnis, *Natural Law and Natural Rights*, 36.
9. On basic human goods as reasons for action, see George, "Recent Criticism of Natural Law Theory," 1371-429. For my critique of the "naturalism" of Michael Perry—a prominent Catholic thinker who, I maintain, reduces human goods to matters of psychological satisfaction—see Robert P. George, "Human Flourishing as a Criterion of Morality: A Critique of Perry's Naturalism," *Tulane Law Review* 63 (1989), 1455-74.
10. See Finnis, "Law, Morality, and 'Sexual Orientation,'" sec. III, 1053-55.
11. See St. Augustine, *De bono coniugali* (9.9). For a critique of the Augustinian view, see George and Bradley, "Marriage and the Liberal Imagination," 301-20.
12. See, for example, Macedo "Homosexuality and the Conservative Mind," 261-300. For a critique of the liberal view, see George and Bradley, "Marriage and the Liberal Imagination."
13. Finnis, "Law, Morality, and 'Sexual Orientation,'" 1066.
14. See George and Bradley, "Marriage and the Liberal Imagination," 307-9, and the authorities cited therein.
15. For a further explanation and defense of this claim, see George and Bradley, "Marriage and the Liberal Imagination," ibid. Please note that a sexual act's being reproductive in type is a necessary, though not a sufficient, condition of

its being marital. Adulterous acts, for example, can be reproductive in type and even in effect, but (obviously and by definition) are non-marital.

16. Finnis, "Law, Morality, and 'Sexual Orientation,'" 1066–67. See also George and Bradley, "Marriage and the Liberal Imagination," 313–18. The argument is further developed in Lee and George, "What Sex Can Be."

17. On the reliance of liberal sex ethics on person-body dualism, see George and Bradley, "Marriage and the Liberal Imagination," 311, n. 32. For arguments that dualism of this sort is philosophically untenable, see the works cited therein.

18. See George and Bradley, "Marriage and the Liberal Imagination"; Lee and George, "What Sex Can Be"; and Finnis, "The Good of Marriage."

19. By the same token, many people who share this understanding find not just abstinence but also sexual *fidelity* to be pointless or even debilitating. It is a standing challenge (coming from both "liberationists" and "conservatives") to Sullivan and others who maintain that advocacy of same-sex "marriage" can be consistent with belief in the requirement of marital fidelity to identify a rational principle (or set of principles) consistent with this understanding which condemns "open" marriages and promiscuity in general as immoral. Of course, it is clear that some supporters of same-sex "marriage" do not, in fact, oppose promiscuity. After interviewing Sullivan, the editor of *The Harvard Gay and Lesbian Review* stated his own opinion on these matters:

> the attempt to sanitize same-sex marriage for tactical reasons has resulted in a kind of studied silence on the subject of sex.... We end up soft-pedaling sex in favor of "commitment." And while the discussion of sex within marriage has been avoided, the discussion of non-marital and extra-marital sex has also largely been missing.... And yet, in talking about an institution that most Americans define as fidelity to a single partner for a lifetime, how can we avoid discussing sexual promiscuity and serial monogamy and the myriad ways that long-term gay couples have defined their relationships. I for one know relatively few gay male couples whose relationship is not "open" to some extent. Gabriel Rotello and Andrew Sullivan...have regarded same-sex marriage as a possible antidote to gay male promiscuity and wildness—which it may well be, though I think it's just as likely that gay marriages would liven up the institution [of marriage] as submit to its traditional rules (which suits me fine). *Harvard Gay and Lesbian Review: A Quarterly Journal of Arts, Letters & Sciences* 4 (1997), 4.

Chapter 14

1. In saying that the American Catholic experience of contributing to public policy debates over bioethical issues has been marked by many disappointments and failures, I do not wish to obscure the fact that the lives of many unborn children and other vulnerable persons have been saved by the Church's witness to the core bioethical principle of respect for human life, nor to minimize the assistance the Church has provided through her concrete programs to pregnant women and others in need.

2. For analysis of the Supreme Court's decisions in the assisted suicide cases, see Robert P. George's contribution to the "Symposium on the Supreme Court's

1996–97 Term," *First Things,* October 1997.

3. Oregon, the one state—thus far—to have legalized physician-assisted suicide, did so by a very narrow margin (51 percent to 49 percent) in a referendum in 1994. In the autumn of 1997, however, Oregon voters, by a much larger margin, declined to reverse course and re-establish the legal prohibition of assisted suicide. It is worth observing that Oregon is the most highly secularized state in the union, having the nation's highest percentage of unbelievers and "unchurched" persons. (Its history, incidentally, is marked by notable instances of anti-religious and, particularly, anti-Catholic prejudice. Such prejudice has plainly been a feature of the campaign to establish and maintain legalized assisted suicide in Oregon.)

4. "At the heart of [constitutionally protected] liberty is the right to define one's own concept of existence, of meaning, of the universe, and of the mystery of human life" (*Planned Parenthood v. Casey,* 112 S. Ct. 2791, 2807 (1992)).

5. Clinton's original veto was denounced by the U.S. Catholic bishops as "shameful." Adding to the shame, Clinton arranged to veto the bill in the highly publicized presence of a group of women (and their families) who allegedly had undergone partial-birth abortions for health reasons. (It later became clear that the procedures performed on at least some of the women were not, in fact, partial-birth abortions.) Clinton went out of his way in public remarks to point out that some of these women were "personally pro-life" Roman Catholics; he did not mention the religious affiliations of the others.

6. To their shame, the following self-identified Catholic members of the United States Senate could not bring themselves to vote for a ban even on the graphically barbarous procedure known as partial-birth abortion: Christopher Dodd (Democrat, Conn.); Tom Harkin (Dem., Iowa); John Kerry (Dem., Mass.); Carol Moseley-Braun (Dem., Ill.); Jack Reed (Dem., R.I.); Richard Durbin (Dem., Ill.); Edward Kennedy (Dem., Mass.); Barbara Mikulski (Dem., Md.); Patty Murray (Dem., Wash.); and Susan Collins (Republican, Maine). At least four Catholic members of the Senate who usually support abortion drew the line at partial-birth abortion and supported the legislation prohibiting it: Joseph Biden (Dem., Del.); Tom Daschle (Dem., S. Dak.); Daniel Patrick Moynihan (Dem., N.Y.); and Mary Landrieu (Dem., La).

7. Drinan is an acknowledged leader in the field of international human rights. This renders his failure to work to protect the human rights of the unborn even more inexplicable and tragic.

8. If, as he said, Drinan believed there was a right to abortion under the Constitution (per *Roe v. Wade*), and if, as he also asserted, he subscribed to the Church's view on the grave injustice of abortion, it is impossible to understand why he consistently opposed efforts to amend the Constitution to protect the unborn.

9. Letter from Edward M. Kennedy, member of the United States Senate, to Thomas E. Dennelly of Great Neck, New York, 3 August 1971.

10. On Drinan's letters to constituents regarding abortion, see Mary Meehan, "Father Robert Drinan Under Siege," *Our Sunday Visitor,* 9 September 1996, 8, 9. Defenders of Drinan may assert that he was simply adding "nuances" to letters to different constituents as all politicians do. If, however, he were forced to stoop to such misleading actions by virtue of serving in elective office, that simply underscores the wisdom of the Holy See in requiring all priests to

withdraw from political office. In fact, Drinan's Jesuit superiors had discouraged him from being involved in elective office from the beginning. The sad story of the effort to evade their wishes is detailed in "The Strange Political Career of Father Drinan," *Catholic World Report,* July 1996, which is based on material from the archives of the New England Province of the Society of Jesus.

11. Support of the "pro-choice" position necessitates willing that only certain persons—the unborn—be denied the protection of the law and subjected to the risk of lethal violence, while all other persons continue to be protected by the law from this threat. See George, "Conscience and the Public Person," 217–31.

    Evangelium Vitae, following centuries of Catholic teaching, emphasizes that this position violates elementary principles of justice and the common good, which require the protection of the innocent:

    > The legal toleration of abortion...can in no way claim to be based on respect for the conscience of others, precisely because society has the right and the duty to protect itself against the abuses which can occur in the name of conscience and under the pretext of freedom. (para. 71)

    > In the case of an intrinsically unjust law, such as a law permitting abortion ...it is...never licit to...vote for it. (para. 73)

12. On Drinan's pro-abortion activities as a congressman and later as president of Americans for Democratic Action, see "The Strange Political Career of Father Drinan," *Catholic World Report,* July 1996, 38.

13. For an account of the episode, see "Father Drinan Retracts Controversial Remarks, Says He Was Wrong on Partial-Birth Abortion," *Catholic Standard,* 15 May 1997.

14. The idea that the Supreme Court's decision creating a right to abortion in *Roe v. Wade* was compelled by the Constitution itself, and was not a matter of the court imposing the independent moral and political preferences of a majority of its members, is hardly plausible.

15. See Nat Hentoff, "William Brennan: A Legacy of Liberty," *Washington Post,* 29 July 1997.

16. For a valuable historical account of the prevalence of anti-Catholicism among America's liberal elite, see John T. McGreevy, "Thinking on One's Own: Catholicism in the American Intellectual Imagination, 1928-1960," *The Journal of American History* 84/i (1997): 97–131.

17. Where a bishop has dared to act against, or even publicly to criticize, a Catholic politician for his or her pro-abortion record, the elite media has quickly depicted the politician in question as a martyr for freedom and the bishop as a modern day Torquemada. This is certainly true of the *New York Times'* coverage of Cardinal O'Connor's criticism of New York Congresswoman Geraldine Ferraro when she was the Democratic candidate for vice president of the United States in 1980. Of course, the *Times* sang a different tune a generation earlier when a Catholic bishop in New Orleans excommunicated a prominent politician who was taking a position contrary to the Church's moral teaching by actively opposing racial integration in Louisiana's parochial schools.

18. Remarks of Senator John F. Kennedy on Church and State, delivered to Greater Houston Ministerial Association, Houston, Texas, 12 September 1960.

19. Kennedy apparently endorsed the extreme version of church-state separation embraced by the Supreme Court in the 1947 case of *Everson v. Illinois*, and defended by American liberals ever since. Historical scholarship makes clear that this conception of the separation of church and state was alien to the thinking of those who framed and ratified the First Amendment to the U.S. Constitution which forbids Congress from making any law "respecting an establishment of religion or prohibiting the free exercise thereof." See Gerard V. Bradley, *Church-State Relationships in America* (New York: Greenwood Press, 1987). As I have already suggested, Kennedy's speech contributed massively to the tragic illusion that faith and politics are utterly separate spheres, hermetically sealed off from each other. For people in the grip of this illusion, any involvement of overtly religious people, and *a fortiori* of religious leaders, in politics is viewed with suspicion. A striking exception for American liberals is the involvement of clerics, particularly black Protestant ministers such as Martin Luther King and Jesse Jackson, in the political campaign for civil rights. It is interesting to note that even the prohibition on tax-exempt religious (and other) organizations (e.g., churches) from engaging in political activity is not a result of "the constitutional separation of church and state," but of a politically motivated change in the tax laws in 1954, reversing nearly 200 years of accepted practice. See "What If Churches Could Be More Politically Active?" *Our Sunday Visitor,* 17 August 1997 (discussing recent research).

20. These collections, published jointly by the National Conference of Catholic Bishops and United States Catholic Conference, under the title *Pastoral Letters of the United States Catholic Bishops,* are currently in five volumes. Volume 1 covers the years 1792–1940, volume II covers 1941–1961, volume III covers 1962–1974, volume IV covers 1975–1983, and volume V covers 1983–1988. [Hereinafter, individual volumes will be cited as "*Pastoral Letters,* vol. __."]

21. Following Vatican II, the bishops of the United States were organized into two bodies—the United States Catholic Conference (USCC) and the National Conference of Catholic Bishops (NCCB). The former replaced the National Catholic Welfare Conference as the body which dealt with public policy issues. As originally envisioned, the NCCB was formed to deal with internal church matters. Subsequently, this line of demarcation has blurred. For convenience we shall use "the United States Catholic Conference," "the Conference", and "the USCC" to refer to either or both.

22. *Pastoral Letters,* vol. III, 251.

23. See, generally, *Pastoral Letters,* vols. III and IV.

24. Letter of Edward M. Kennedy, to Thomas E. Dennelly.

25. Kennedy's current, permissive, views on abortion are, of course, well documented. One personal account—in which the author recounts that, following *Roe,* "Kennedy...stated to me publicly that he no longer knows when human life begins"—can be found in Letter from Joseph J. Reilly, Chairman, Massachusetts Citizens for Life, to the *Lawrence Eagle-Tribune,* 19 February 1980.

26. See *Pastoral Letters,* vol. III, 235, 236.

27. *Pastoral Letters,* vol. IV, 81.

28. See, e.g. "Statement on Abortion" and "Statement in Protest of U.S. Govern-

ment Programs against the Right to Life," in *Pastoral Letters,* vol. III.

29. *Pastoral Letters,* vol. IV, 129.
30. J. Brian Benestad, *The Pursuit of a Just Social Order: Policy Statements of the U.S. Catholic Bishops, 1966–80,* (Washington, D.C.: Ethics & Public Policy Center, 1982).
31. Quoted in *Pastoral Letters,* vol. IV, 302.
32. *Pastoral Letters,* vol. IV, 301.
33. The quotation appears in the pastoral, published by the NCCB as *The Challenge of Peace—God's Promise and Our Response,* iii.
34. This and subsequent speeches by Bernardin were collected as part of a symposium, drawing together scholarly commentators on the "seamless garment," at Loyola University of Chicago in November 1987, and published in Joseph Cardinal Bernardin et al. *Consistent Ethic of Life,* ed. Thomas G. Fuechtmann (Kansas City, Mo.: Sheed & Ward, 1988).
35. The Fordham speech appears in *Consistent Ethic,* 1.
36. See J. M. Finnis, "The Consistent Ethic—A Philosophical Critique," in *Consistent Ethic,* 140.
37. Bernardin spoke publicly against such an interpretation of the "seamless garment":

> I know that some people on the left, if I may use that term, have used the consistent ethic to give the impression that the abortion issue is not all that important any more, that you should be against abortion in a general way but that there are more important issues, so don't hold anybody's feet to the fire just on abortion. That is a misuse of the consistent ethic, and I deplore it. (Interviewed in *National Catholic Register,* 12 June 1988 [hereinafter, "Bernardin Interview"].)

38. Cuomo, "Religious Belief," 13.
39. Cuomo observed that the Church in antebellum America did not insist that slavery be abolished, nor does the Church insist that contraception and divorce be made illegal. He suggested that similarly the Church ought not to insist that abortion be legally prohibited. Of course, abortion is unlike contraception and divorce in a crucial respect: namely, its legal permission is incompatible with the moral right of its victims to the equal protection of the laws. In this same respect, it is like slavery, whose legal permission, the Church now plainly teaches, is never consistent with the requirements of justice. Surely Cuomo agrees that the Church's failure to teach this principle in the context of the debate over slavery in 19th century America was regrettable and certainly ought not to be emulated in the case of abortion.
40. For example, because abortion "involves life and death," Cuomo said, it "will always be a central concern of Catholics. But so will nuclear weapons, and hunger and homelessness and joblessness, all the forces diminishing human life and threatening to destroy it. The 'seamless garment' that Cardinal Bernardin has spoken of is a challenge to all Catholics in public office...." He then concluded: "We cannot justify our aspiration to goodness simply on the basis of the vigor of our demand for an elusive and questionable civil law declaring what we already know, that abortion is wrong" (Cuomo, "Religious Belief," 28–29).

41. *Evangelium Vitae* declares (para. 90):

> Although laws are not the only means of protecting human life, nevertheless, they do play a very important and sometimes decisive role in influencing patterns of thought and behaviour. I repeat once more that a law which violates an innocent person's natural right to life is unjust and, as such, is not valid as a law. For this reason I urgently appeal once more to all political leaders not to pass laws which, by disregarding the dignity of the person, undermine the very fabric of society.

42. The futility of the approach publicly advocated by Cuomo, Drinan, and others—allow abortion to be legal (and even pay for it with public funds) and "evangelize" against it—is shown by the fact that, as Professor Mary Ann Glendon of Harvard Law School has demonstrated, the United States now has the most radically permissive abortion laws in the democratic world and one of the highest rates of abortion. Indeed, despite the tireless efforts of pro-life counselors, abortion is among the most frequently performed surgical procedure in the United States.

43. Published as *Economic Justice for All: Pastoral Letter on Catholic Social Teaching and the U.S. Economy* by the National Conference of Catholic Bishops in November 1986. It was developed pursuant to the most extensive consultation process yet. Though it is clear that the bishops hoped that such wide consultation with nonclerics would give the document's conclusions greater persuasiveness, such consultation does not alleviate the basic problem of bishops—however well-informed—speaking on matters of prudential political judgment that should properly be left to the laity.

44. *Economic Justice,* ix.

45. Ibid., xii.

46. Ibid., xiii.

47. Although the bishops should certainly communicate the riches of Catholic social teaching to their flock, and while they should insist that Catholic laity who are grappling with difficult practical matters seek genuinely to advance the common good, the bishops should consider the benefits in social justice which society reaps through the proper catechesis of their flock. Much recent research demonstrates that religious practice (including regular church attendance) is one of the most important factors in reducing nearly every major social pathology in America, from drug abuse to out-of-wedlock births to crime to suicide. It is demonstrably beneficial in helping individuals to escape poverty. And it strengthens the family bond, greatly reducing the divorce and illegitimacy rates. Much of this research is summarized and discussed by Patrick Fagan in "Why Religion Matters: The Impact of Religious Practice on Social Stability" published by the Heritage Foundation in *Backgrounder,* no. 1064 (25 January 1996).

48. *Pastoral Letters,* vol. IV, 420.

49. See *Pastoral Letters,* vol. V.

50. See *Pastoral Letters,* vol. V, 1.

51. See *Pastoral Letters,* vol. V, 647.

52. *Pastoral Letters,* vol. V, 304.

53. "Everyone has an obligation to be at the service of life." (*Evangelium Vitae,* para.

79) Throughout chapter 4 of the encyclical, the Holy Father discusses the wide range of activities to which individuals are called in building the "culture of life."

54. See the Pastoral Statement of John J. Myers, Bishop of Peoria, "The Obligations of Catholics and the Rights of Unborn Children," *Origins* 20, no. 5 (1990): 65, 67–72. esp. sec. V.

55. *Cf. Evangelium Vitae,* para. 72:

> Disregard for the right to life, precisely because it leads to the killing of the person whom society exists to serve, is what most directly conflicts with the possibility of achieving the common good.

> Cardinal Bernardin, whose "consistent ethic" has often been misused to just such a purpose, said, "I don't see how you can subscribe to the consistent ethic and then vote for someone who feels that abortion is a 'basic right' of the individual" ("Bernardin Interview," 7).

56. *Pastoral Letters,* vol. IV, 40.

57. Quoted in "Bishops and Bishop-Bashers," *Catholic World Report,* June 1997, 36.

58. See *Pastoral Letters,* vols. III and IV.

59. In this regard, I am pleased to note that the teaching of *Evangelium Vitae*—particularly the need to resist the "culture of death" (especially abortion and euthanasia) and the centrality of the family in building the "culture of life"—is featured in the recent USCC statement "Faithful for Life: A Moral Reflection."

60. See *Evangelium Vitae:*

> [B]y the authority which Christ conferred upon Peter and his Successors, and in communion with the Bishops of the Catholic Church, I confirm that the direct and voluntary killing of an innocent human being is always gravely immoral. (para. 57)

> [B]y the authority which Christ conferred upon Peter and his Successors, in communion with the Bishops…I declare that direct abortion, that is, abortion willed as an end or as a means, always constitutes a grave moral disorder, since it is the deliberate killing of an innocent human being…. No circumstance, no purpose, no law whatsoever can ever make licit an act which is intrinsically illicit, since it is contrary to the law of God which is written in every human heart, knowable by reason itself, and proclaimed by the Church. (para. 62)

> [I]n harmony with the Magisterium of my Predecessors and in communion with the Bishops of the Catholic Church, I confirm that euthanasia is a grave violation of the law of God, since it is the deliberate and morally unacceptable killing of a human person. (para. 65)

61. "We [bishops] are also entrusted with the task of ensuring that the doctrine which is once again being set forth in this Encyclical is faithfully handed on in its integrity. We must use appropriate means to defend the faithful from all teaching which is contrary to it. We need to make sure that in theological faculties, seminaries and Catholic institutions sound doctrine is taught, explained and more fully investigated" (*Evangelium Vitae,* para. 82).

62. *Pastoral Letters,* vol. IV, 401.

INDEX